BOOKS ON COMPUTER SYSTEMS AND TELECOMMUNICATIONS

Video training courses are available on the subjects of these books in the James Martin ADVANCED TECHNOLOGY LIBRARY from Deltak Inc., East/West Technological Center, 1751 West Diehl Road, Naperville, Ill. 60566 (Tel: 312-369-3000).

VIDEOTEX	PRINCIPLES OF DISTRIBUTED PROCESSING	INTRODUCTION TO TELEPROCESSING	TELEMATIC SOCIETY
DESIGN OF MAN–COMPUTER DIALOGUES	COMPUTER NETWORKS AND DISTRIBUTED PROCESSING	INTRODUCTION TO COMPUTER NETWORKS	TELE-COMMUNICATIONS AND THE COMPUTER (second edition)
PROGRAMMING REAL-TIME COMPUTER SYSTEMS	DESIGN AND STRATEGY FOR DISTRIBUTED PROCESSING	TELEPROCESSING NETWORK ORGANIZATION	COMMUNICATIONS SATELLITE SYSTEMS
DESIGN OF REAL-TIME COMPUTER SYSTEMS	DISTRIBUTED FILE AND DATA-BASE DESIGN	SYSTEMS ANALYSIS FOR DATA TRANSMISSION	FUTURE DEVELOPMENTS IN TELE-COMMUNICATIONS (second edition)

Books On   Books On   Books On   Books On

**FOURTH-GENERATION
LANGUAGES**

A *James Martin* BOOK

FOURTH-

GENERATION LANGUAGES

Volume I
PRINCIPLES

JAMES MARTIN

PRENTICE-HALL, INC. Englewood Cliffs, New Jersey 07632

Library of Congress Cataloging in Publication Data

MARTIN, JAMES (date)
    Fourth-generation languages.

    Bibliography: p.
    Includes index.
    1. Programming languages (Electronic computers)
I. Title.
QA76.7.M35 1985   001.64′24   85–3692
ISBN 0–13–329673–3 (v. 1)

Editorial/production supervision: *Kathryn Gollin Marshak*
Jacket design: *Bruce Kenselaar*
Jacket art courtesy of *The National Gallery, London*
Manufacturing buyer: *Gordon Osbourne*

Fourth-Generation Languages, Volume I
James Martin

Printed in the United States of America

10 9 8 7 6 5 4 3 2

ISBN   0-13-329673-3   01

PRENTICE-HALL INTERNATIONAL (UK) LIMITED, *London*
PRENTICE-HALL OF AUSTRALIA PTY. LIMITED, *Sydney*
PRENTICE-HALL CANADA INC., *Toronto*
PRENTICE-HALL HISPANOAMERICANA, S.A., *Mexico*
PRENTICE-HALL OF INDIA PRIVATE LIMITED, *New Delhi*
PRENTICE-HALL OF JAPAN, INC., *Tokyo*
PRENTICE-HALL OF SOUTHEAST ASIA PTE. LTD., *Singapore*
EDITORA PRENTICE-HALL DO BRASIL, LTDA., *Rio de Janeiro*
WHITEHALL BOOKS LIMITED, *Wellington, New Zealand*

CONTENTS

8   Good and Bad Structuring in 4GLs   *173*

9   Human Factors   *193*

10   The Use of Natural English for Queries   *213*

11   Can We Use Human Language for More Complex Operations?   *227*

PREFACE

For a quarter of a century the languages for commercial computing have evolved only slowly. There have been syntax differences, but the basic constructs of FORTRAN, COBOL, PL/I, PASCAL, etc., are similar. Now we are seeing a flood of new languages and tools which are producing dramatic rises in DP productivity. Never before have the techniques of application development changed so dramatically.

New tools, referred to as "Fourth-generation languages" (FORTRAN, COBOL, etc., were third-generation), "High-productivity languages," "Non-procedural languages," and "Application generators," provide mankind with a leap forward in the ability to put the computer to use. Indeed, without this advance we would probably not be able to utilize the mass of VLSI machines that the newly automated computer factories will produce.

With fourth-generation languages computer power becomes accessible to any thinking person, without needing extensive training in DP. Their impact will shape data processing developments in the rest of the decade. These languages include boath procedural and nonprocedural languages, languages for DP professionals and languages for end-users, query languages and application generators. Some languages can be all of these; some are more limited.

The range of style of these languages is surprisingly broad. Some are powerful, concise and thereby cryptic at first sight. Some have excellent graphics. Some are suitable for end-users with little training; some are intended for professionals. Some are closely linked to their own data-base software; some will operate on many types of files.

However, this great variety and diverse scope of the products now in the market place naturally makes the prospective buyer very cautious. The salesmen's statements about their products have been misleading. The languages themselves are changing and improving fast. The relatively stable field of computer languages has suddenly become a boiling morass of originality and new ideas.

The dramatic effects on DP productivity are documented in many places and are often measured in thousands of percentage points for some types of systems. To achieve the most impressive productivity gains requires a change in both the design techniques and management techniques used. Some organizations have used fourth-generation languages badly and have gained little improvement. Many organizations are unaware of the enormous potential of the products or how to change their DP management methods to make full use of them. Tragically, some universities have ignored the field entirely.

This book seeks to set the field of fourth-generation languages into perspective, discussing the mechanisms, uses, and future evolution of the new tools. The book discusses principles rather than individual products. The more popular products are described and compared in depth in ''The James Martin Report on High-Productivity Languages,'' available as a subscription service from Technology Insight, Inc., 33 Washington St., Marblehead, MA 01945, (617)639-1958.

James Martin

1 WHAT ARE FOURTH-GENERATION LANGUAGES?

THE NEED FOR REVOLUTION A revolution is taking place in computer languages. The revolution is desperately needed. We need to be able to instruct computers much more easily and quickly than in the past. There are two reasons for this.

First, computers are increasing in quantity and speed at a rapid rate. Soon there will be many millions of personal computers, and some of these will be very powerful. Data processing computers will increase in speed by a factor of 40 to 50 in ten years, and minicomputers will continue to spread rapidly. The silicon factories of the world will be mass-producing ever-faster chips. The annual production of digital functions will increase by about 300 times in the next ten years, but most of these chips will operate at much higher speeds.

Suppose we assume that the number of machines that require programming increases by 25 percent per year (some will not require programming) and that they increase in speed by a factor of 40 over the next ten years. That would mean that in ten years, 372 times as much programming would have to be created per year as at present. The United States has 400,000 programmers today. If they continued to program in the same way, 148 million programmers would be needed. Everyone who worked would be employed as a programmer!

By any set of estimates of future computing power, the *productivity* of application development must increase by *two orders of magnitude over the next ten years*. This cannot happen if computers are programmed with COBOL, PL/I, PASCAL, or ADA.

Second, as computers spread, many people who are not DP professionals must be able to put them to work. Application development without professional programmers is becoming a vigorous trend in computing [1]. Applications will increasingly be created by end users, business consultants, and systems analysts. The business, or systems, analyst needs a powerful computer language with which he* can quickly build his own applications. His main concentration must be on the business or application, not on intricacies of coding. A great photographer spends his mental effort concentrating on the subject matter of the picture; the mechanics of operating the camera are second nature to him. A systems analyst should likewise concentrate on the subject matter and be able to put computers to work with powerful application building tools that, once learned, require little mental effort.

End users should also be able to build their own computer facilities. They need languages that are as easy to use as possible—user-friendly languages without the need to remember mnemonics, formats, sequences, and complex constructs.

The new generation of computer languages, then, needs to be much more powerful than the previous generation so that results can be obtained much faster, and it needs to be much more user-friendly.

NO CHAUFFEURS   In the early days of the U.S. car industry, production volumes were growing fast, and a well-known sociologist was asked to predict the total number of automobiles that would ever be manufactured. After a great deal of study, the sociologist reported that no more than 2 million would be manufactured in the life cycle of the car. If the car lasted ten years on average, the maximum annual production would never exceed 200,000. This conclusion was based on the much-researched figure that no more than 2 million people would be willing to serve as chauffeurs.

Today we might conclude that no more than 2 million people in the United States would be likely to become professional programmers—five times as many programmers as there are today. A few years from now, one computer will require far more than five times as much programming because of its increased speed. At that time, the sociologist might calculate that there could be no more computers than there are today because of lack of programmers.

Henry Ford not only created a mass-production line; he also simplified the controls of his Model T so that most people could drive it. The computer industry will have Model T–like computers mass-produced on production lines that differ from Henry Ford's in that almost no human being is in sight. Robot production lines already assemble one personal computer every 20 seconds or so. Computers will sell in the vast quantities possible only if they can be put to work *without* professional programmers. This is now beginning to happen. Application development without programmers is perhaps the most important revolution in computing since the invention of the transistor. It requires user-oriented languages.

*For simplicity of expression only, *his, him,* and *he* are used to mean "his or her," "him or her," and "he or she."

FOUR GENERATIONS OF LANGUAGES

The *first generation* of computer languages was machine language. There was no interpreter or compiler to translate the language into a different form. Early computers were programmed with a binary notation. For example

011011 000000 000000 000001 110101

might mean "clear the accumulator and add the contents of storage location 117 to it."

It was very difficult to program computers in this way without errors. The situation was improved slightly by using mnemonic codes to represent operations. Our sample instruction might then be

CLA 000000 000000 000001 110101

Later, numbers could be written for storage locations or registers. The instruction might become

CLA 0 0 117

Often a wired panel had to be plugged on the machine as part of the programming.

The *second generation* of language, which came into use in the mid-1950s, was *symbolic assembly language*. Symbolic addresses were used rather than physical machine addresses, for example, our sample instruction might become

CLA SALARY

where SALARY represents the location in memory where the variable **salary** is stored. Symbolic addressing was a great step forward because now when the physical locations of variables or instructions had to be changed (and they were constantly changed), the programmer did not have to reenter the new physical addresses. The early assembly languages would optimize the position of programmer instructions on a drum that stored the instructions.

Assembly languages had names like SAP (Symbolic Assembly Program, for the IBM 704), AUTOCODER, SPS, BAL, and EASYCODER.

The *third generation* came into use in the 1960s and was called *high-level languages*. Some of these were for scientific work, like ALGOL and FORTRAN; some were for commercial work, like COBOL. COBOL became by far the most commonly used computer language. Some languages, like PL/I and later ADA, encompassed both scientific and commercial computing.

With the third generation, the language became to a large extent independent of the hardware. A programmer could code programs without any knowledge of the machine instruction set and registers. He needed some knowledge of the machine if he wished to optimize execution efficiency. Because of this hardware independence, programs could be converted to run on different machines. Manufacturer-independent standards were created for third-generation languages, but nevertheless portability was still sometimes a problem.

One third-generation instruction usually compiled to several machine language instructions, whereas assembly language instructions usually matched machine language instructions. The amount of work needed to write programs was therefore reduced.

Third-generation languages moved a step toward the language of the user. They used English words and expressed formulas in mathematical notation. It is easier to write

$$X = (A + B) / (C + D)$$

than

```
CLA     C
ADD     D
STO     Y
CLA     A
ADD     B
DIV     Y
STO     X
```

Third-generation languages needed vast numbers of lines of codes for typical commercial systems and were designed for DP professionals rather than end users. It was time-consuming to debug them, and the modification of complex systems became very difficult. Many DP departments bogged down in complexities and became unable to respond to business needs as quickly as they should.

Fourth-generation languages (4GLs) were created in response to these problems to meet the following objectives:

- To speed up the application-building process
- To make applications easy and quick to change, thus reducing maintenance costs
- To minimize debugging problems
- To generate bug-free code from high-level expressions of requirement
- To make languages user-friendly so that end users could solve their own problems and put computers to work

Fourth-generation languages permit some applications to be generated with one order of magnitude fewer lines of code than would be needed with COBOL,

PL/I, ADA, or the like. They might be referred to as *high-productivity languages*. In addition to employing sequential statements like third-generation languages, they employ a diversity of other mechanisms, such as filling in forms or panels, screen interaction, and computer-aided graphics.

Many fourth-generation languages are dependent on a data base and its data dictionary or directory. The dictionary has in some cases evolved into a facility that can represent more than the data. It may contain screen formats, report formats, dialogue structures, associations among many data, validity checks, security controls, authorizations to read or modify data, calculations that are used to create derived fields, permissible ranges, and logical relationships among data values. The extension of the dictionary that contains business rules and logic is sometimes referred to as an *encyclopedia*. A major concern in the assessment or purchase of a fourth-generation language is the infrastructure needed to support it, which includes data bases, library, and dictionary or encyclopedia.

Third-generation languages use mainly von Neumann–like constructs; that is, they express a sequence of operations to be executed with branches and loops; their basic operations are broadly similar to the machine instruction set. Fourth-generation languages can differ substantially from von Neumann–like operations. Third-generation languages were varied in their syntax but offered a generally similar set of constructs; fourth-generation languages are surprisingly diverse in their constructs. We have entered an era of rich invention in computer languages.

FIFTH-GENERATION LANGUAGES

As I write this, the term *fifth-generation* usually refers to systems that use disciplines that originated in the field of artificial intelligence, especially:

- Knowledge-based systems
- Expert Systems
- Inference engines
- Processing of human languages

A fifth-generation system encodes complex knowledge so that a machine may draw inferences from it. In some cases, this inference processing is used to perform tasks that, although complex, seem trivial to humans, such as understanding speech, vision, and human language. In other cases, the fast processing of inferences that are not instinctive to humans makes the software appear to be highly intelligent. In highly specialized areas of knowledge, the machine can display an apparent expertise far greater than that of most humans.

Languages designed for these areas may be described as fifth-generation languages. In addition, fifth-generation computers are likely to employ highly parallel processors. It is economically desirable to have many mass-produced processors working on a problem simultaneously. Languages that are designed for highly parallel computing will emerge.

Languages that might be claimed to be fifth-generation are in an embryo state as yet. PROLOG is, perhaps, the best-known example. This language needs much enhancement and improvement. A variety of ''shells'' for constructing expert systems exist and provide a form of high-level language, often with LISP as an underlying base language. No more about such fifth-generation languages will be covered in this book.

Techniques for communicating with a computer in human language (usu-

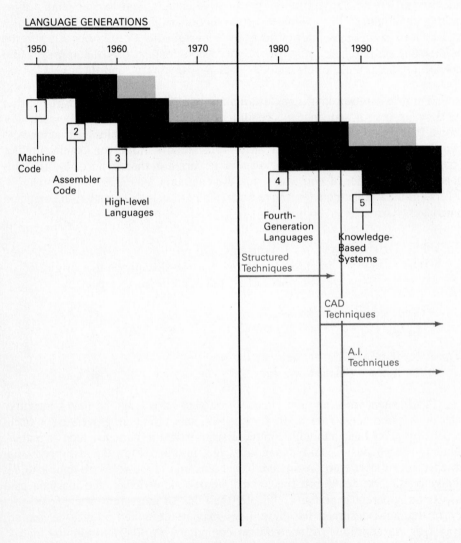

Figure 1.1   The generations of computer languages.

ally English) are sometimes described as "fifth-generation." These are currently used only for data-base queries and report generation (and hence may also be regarded as in an embryo state). Human language processing has much potential for improving fourth-generation techniques and is discussed in Chapters 10 and 11.

Figure 1.1 shows the time of evolution of the language generations. Computer-aided design with graphics and artificial intelligence techniques (red in Fig. 1.1) will greatly change the way computer applications are built.

PROCEDURAL VERSUS NONPROCEDURAL LANGUAGES   Some fourth-generation languages are referred to as "nonprocedural" languages. *Procedural* and *nonprocedural* are useful and much used language distinctions. A procedural language specifies *how* something is accomplished. A nonprocedural language specifies *what* is accomplished without describing *how*. Thus languages like COBOL and PL/I are procedural. Their programmers give precisely detailed instructions for how each action is accomplished. An application generator whose users fill in forms to tell it what to do is nonprocedural. The user merely says what is to be done and is not concerned with the detailed procedure for how it is done.

Most query languages, report generators, graphics packages, and application generators are nonprocedural. Some high-level *programming* languages are now acquiring nonprocedural capabilities. NOMAD, for example, is a high-level language with which some end users obtain fast results from a computer. Most professionals would call it a programming language because it has IF statements and DO loops. However, results can be obtained with brief nonprocedural statements such as

LIST BY CUSTOMER AVERAGE (INVOICE TOTAL)

This is a complete "program." It leaves the software to decide how the list should be formatted, when to skip pages, how to number pages, how to sort into CUSTOMER sequence, and how to compute an average.

Similarly,

PLOT REVENUE, EXPENSES, MARK-UP, EMPLOYEE BY MONTH

is a complete "program." It does not say what type of plot is needed. The software may be capable of many different types of plotting. It decides the best form of plot from the statement and nature of the variables. It may select colors, determine an appropriate scale, label the plot, and print a color key.

Some nonprocedural languages employ graphics. The user sees displays on a screen and can fill them in, point to them, and manipulate them. The result is a statement of requirements which the software can translate into executable code. A picture can be worth a thousand words, and graphics representations of requirements or logic can be made easy to use and manipulate.

Many nonprocedural languages can handle only limited classes of applications, such as query languages or report generators. A few, however, can handle general applications with highly complex logic.

While many languages are purely procedural or purely nonprocedural, others combine both of these types of statement. This is generally desirable because nonprocedural operation speeds up and simplifies the use of the language, whereas procedural code extends the range of applications that can be tackled, giving more flexibility of logical manipulation.

Powerful languages of the future will combine procedural code and nonprocedural code or screen interaction.

We can use the analogy of giving instructions to a taxi driver. With a *procedural* language, you have to tell him exactly *how* to proceed: "Drive 500 yards. Turn left. Drive 380 yards.Turn right. Drive to the traffic lights. If the lights are green, . . ." With a *nonprocedural* language, you tell him what you want: "Take me to the Criterion Cinema on Main Street."

We will see nonprocedural languages of greater power emerge. A more powerful semantics for instructing the taxi driver would be: "Take me to *Rocky VII*." The taxi driver has to solve the problem stated. He has to find out where *Rocky VII* is playing and take you there.

We would like to have the greatest power possible in computer languages. However, with more powerful semantics there is a danger that the computer might set out to do something more expensive or time-consuming than we want. It is possible that *Rocky VII* is not playing nearby. The nearest theater showing it is 1000 miles away. The taxi sets off on a long journey. When you eventually say that that was not what you wanted, he says, "I was only obeying orders." Computers obey orders, so we had better make sure the orders are correct. With powerful languages we need some feedback about the cost or consequences before we tell the machine to proceed.

Again, it is possible with certain forms of nonprocedural code to make statements that appear correct and give plausible results but are, in fact, incorrect, as are the results. The statements contain a semantic error (an error in meaning). The term *semantic disintegrity* is sometimes used to describe this situation. It is desirable that the software that interprets the user's statements check for semantic errors and warn the user as early as possible about any potential problems it detects. If possible, this should be done while the user is initially entering or building his procedure at the terminal. Some interpreters check for semantic problems (meaning); others only check syntax (correct formatting and spelling of commands). Semantics checking can be subtle and sometimes complex.

Nonprocedural languages or dialogues represent a higher level of automation of the application-creation process.

USER FRIENDLINESS

Third-generation languages were not user-friendly. It was assumed that the programmer would devote substantial professional effort to learning the syntax of the language. That syntax had no relation to human language syntax, although it allowed the use of English words.

When nonprocedural code is used, the situation changes. A vast diversity of techniques is possible for telling a computer *what* to do rather than *how* to do it. Many of these techniques can be made very user-friendly. *There is much greater scope for applying human-factoring methods.* Because of this, a major part of the quality judgment of a fourth-generation language should relate to its human factoring.

In some cases the software deserves a stronger term than user-friendly: We might describe it as *user-seductive.* User-seductive software captivates the timid, reluctant, or apprehensive user. It encourages him to take actions at the keyboard or screen and gives him impressive, fast, useful responses, often employing color and graphics effectively.

We have often made the mistake of assuming that certain classes of user would never operate a terminal or a computer. We said, ''The corporate president will never touch a boob tube.'' Now he is perhaps using videotex or LOTUS 1-2-3 and bringing the spreadsheets he generates with it to meetings. The difference may have occurred because of several factors. First, the language for obtaining results is user-seductive. Second, genuinely useful results are obtained quickly. Third, there may be an urgent problem that needs a computer solution.

BASIC was sold as being the easiest to use of the third-generation languages. Nevertheless, many end users and analysts will not learn and employ BASIC because it required too much work, yet they use and obtain results quickly with MAPPER, FOCUS, SQL, LOTUS, APPLICATION FACTORY, or some other such facility.

Glancing ahead, Box 7.1 and the end of Chapter 7 lists desirable human-factoring properties in a 4GL. It will be seen how completely this list separates our view of languages now from third-generation languages.

LIMITED FUNCTIONALITY

Fourth-generation languages vary greatly in their power and capabilities. Some are merely query languages; others are report generators or graphics generators; other can generate complete applications; some are very high level programming languages. Some languages may be employed by end users, or by systems analysts directly aiding the end users. Whereas third-generation languages could create all or most applications, some fourth-generation languages are designed only for a specific class or range of applications. Some are highly restricted in their range; others can handle a wide diversity of applications well.

In the fourth generation, much more than in the third, we have to select the language to fit the application.

A debate has ensued about whether query languages, report generators, and other languages of limited functionality should be called fourth-generation languages. Vendors of comprehensive products describe their more limited competition as "not true fourth-generation languages."

It is probably useful to describe all current nonprocedural languages as fourth-generation. Much of the computer industry refers to DEC's DATA-TRIEVE and IBM's SQL as "fourth-generation languages" although they are of limited functionality. It is also useful to employ the term *full-function fourth-generation language* to refer to languages that permit their users to build anything that could be built with COBOL. Of the languages mentioned in this book, MANTIS, IDEAL, NATURAL, and APPLICATION FACTORY are full-function fourth-generation languages; SQL, QBE, and ADRS are designed for more limited purposes.

It is often valuable to employ a language designed for a limited set of functions, because this language can be simpler than a full programming language and carefully targeted to a specific type of application. LOTUS 1-2-3, for example, gained a vast number of users quickly because it made it easy to manipulate spreadsheet data.

There is likely to be ongoing controversy about what is and what is not a fourth-generation language. Vendors of 4GLs often refer to competing products as "not a true fourth-generation language." Vendors of languages that are predominantly nonprocedural refer to languages with procedural code as "not true 4GLs." Vendors of languages with well-structured procedural code refer to products with nonprocedural code but poor structuring as "not true 4GLs." The term *nonprocedural language* is clearer in meaning, but many major 4GLs have procedural components. The term *high-productivity language* is perhaps better than *fourth-generation language,* but the publisher insisted that this book should be called *Fourth-Generation Languages.*

RESTRICTION OF OPTIONS   Higher-level languages often eliminate options that are available on lower-level languages. This can make them easier to learn and debug but causes protests from the lower-level-language programmers, who say that they need the *flexibility* of the lower language.

One of the differences between third- and second-generation languages was that most third-generation languages in the 1960s did not have the capability of modifying themselves at execution time, whereas assembly language did. Today, after years of structured programming, we react with horror to the idea of a program modifying itself in this way, but assembly language programmers of the early 1960s protested that they needed this facility.

A program would be far more difficult to debug if it could modify itself at execution time, so the restriction eliminated a certain class of dangerous bug. An objective of fourth-generation languages ought to be to eliminate as many bugs as possible when applications are being built. We want to verify the correctness of programs, as far as possible, when they are being created, before we have to test them. To achieve this we need language constructs that permit automatic verification where possible, and we want to avoid constructs that are likely to encourage errors. Some fourth-generation languages do not have a GO TO. All of them avoid the COBOL ALTER statement.

Taking this idea further, the AXES language used in the HOS software uses only constructs that are fully verifiable according to mathematically defined axioms.

Language restrictions, then, can prevent the user from making a mess. This applies not only to coding but also to systems aspects of program design—for example, calls to a data base or terminal dialogues. In one insurance company installation, the processing of a transaction in PL/I used many data-base calls. It was redeveloped with the fourth-generation language NATURAL, and then required only one data-base call. In processing a property and casualty policy, the PL/I system used many screen maps per policy. With NATURAL it needed 2 to 3 screen maps per policy and was much faster to use by terminal operators. The NATURAL expert stated that in NATURAL, "they could not do *that* much wrong!"

In a fourth-generation language, then, we would like to eliminate options that encourage misdesign, use constructs that are verifiable—before testing, where possible—and use constructs that are as powerful as possible in that much machine code is generated from a relatively quick and simple action by the developer. The code and system actions generated should use the best possible design principles. There is then less capability for bad design.

DEFAULT OPTIONS With most fourth-generation languages, a user does not have to specify everything. Instead, a compiler or interpreter makes intelligent assumptions about what it thinks the user needs. For example, it may automatically select a format for a report, put page numbers on it, select chart types for graphics display, put labels on the axes or on column headings, and ask the user in a friendly, understandable fashion when it needs more information.

The software may require many parameters to be specified for a certain operation. It gives the user a list of such parameters on the screen and fills them in with what appear to be appropriate values. For example, a user may move the cursor to a given field or cell on a screen and select the FORMAT option. The software may list the alignment options, types of format, number of decimals, and so on. It indicates the values it will select if the user does nothing. These are called *default options*. If the user wants something different from the default option, he types the first letter of his alternate choice or fills in a numeric value in the appropriate place on the screen.

This use of software-selected default options saves time and debugging. There is often much information that the software can use for making the defaults as comprehensive and as intelligent as possible. This capability often improves as the language evolves. The human factoring should make it as easy and natural as possible for the user to change the software-selected defaults.

MONOLOGUE AND DIALOGUE

Third-generation languages were designed so that a program would be written and then compiled by a computer. The programmer would not usually be present when the compilation occurred. Sometimes interpreters rather than compilers were used. With an interpreter, the programmer may be at a terminal while his source code is analyzed and converted to machine language. His errors may then be pointed out to him more rapidly, and he may execute the code as soon as it is interpreted. Nevertheless, the language is designed so that it can be a one-way set of instructions passed to a machine.

Some fourth-generation languages are designed so that a dialogue takes place between the user and the system as the user builds his application. The user may respond to menus, fill in panels presented to him on a screen, move a cursor or bar on a screen, manipulate data in screen windows, and so on. The software may ask the user questions, signal errors or inconsistencies as he builds his application, request that ambiguities or multiple-choice situations be resolved, and give him the capability to build and adjust reports, panels, and data layouts interactively.

Most third-generation languages were a monologue, with the user writing a program; many fourth-generation languages employ a dialogue, with the user and the computer interacting. Dialogues give much more scope for good human factoring and for catching most errors *while they are being made* so that later debugging is simplified.

ONE-DIMENSIONAL VERSUS TWO-DIMENSIONAL DIALOGUES

A dialogue can employ one-dimensional or two-dimensional interaction. With one-dimensional interaction, the computer and user exchange character streams. The user keys commands and operands into the computer. The computer may give the user lists of options from which he can select.

With two-dimensional interaction, the user responds to a screen. He may point to it, enter data into parts of it, or move items on the screen. He may scroll an imagined two-dimensional space of large size using the screen like a window, or be able to skip to view parts of a large data base spread out in two-dimensional tables. The software may provide tools for manipulating diagrams on the screen for building applications or representing logic structures.

There is generally much more capability for making a dialogue user-friendly if it employs screen interaction. Like an engineer doing computer-aided design, the application builder can manipulate diagrams in a fast and powerful way and can avoid creating many of the types of bugs found in third-generation coding.

SIMPLICITY

To a large extent, 4GLs represent a search for simplicity in computing. In the 1960s and 1970s we made computing too difficult. It was the province of highly specialized technicians who learned complex forms of encoding. Like ancient monks with hieroglyphics and Latin, they enjoyed their closed intellectual world, which the layman could not penetrate.

The developer of one of the leading 4GLs once commented, "Why did I develop it? Because I hate computing!" He hated JCL and the JCL mentality. He hated software professionals' conversations, which he could not understand. There seemed no need for the abstruse acronyms or the lengthy encoding of COBOL or PL/I. Why not say what you wanted the computer to do more directly? So he created the language NATURAL. At first, like other 4GLs, NATURAL could not do everything, but it slowly grew into a language that *could* do everything COBOL could do.

Removing unnecessary acronyms and complexity is very important because it allows the user to spend his mental effort on what really matters—the purpose of the application. Whitehead commented about mathematical notations: "By relieving the brain of all unnecessary work, a good notation sets it free to concentrate on more advanced problems, and in effect increases the mental power of the race" [2]. Before the introduction of Arabic notation for representing numbers, multiplication was difficult, and division was worse than JCL coding. Whitehead commented:

> Probably nothing in the modern world would have more astonished a Greek mathematician than to learn that . . . a large proportion of the population of Western Europe could perform the operation of division for the largest numbers. This fact would have seemed to him a sheer impossibility. [2]

Perhaps a 1970s expert on computer programming would be equally astonished to see what a major proportion of knowledge workers can create with computer software in the year 2000.

**MORE POWER
TO PROCESS
THE LANGUAGE**
4GLs often need substantial processing to translate from the application creator's language to the machine language or to carry out a screen dialogue with the application creator. This screen dialogue may be designed for the decisecond response time of a personal computer rather than the longer response of a terminal and phone line. The language may need access to a dictionary or encyclopedia via a network.

The change in languages, then was made practical by the lower cost of processing and later by the replacement of terminals with personal computers with substantial memory (or by other means of subsecond response time). The power of today's microelectronics must be employed to improve the usability of computers through better languages and dialogues.

**SOME BASIC
PRINCIPLES**
4GLs represent an effort to put the increased power of computers to work more effectively. Unlike third-generation languages, their design is concerned with people costs more than hardware costs. In devising the mechanisms of 4GLs, there are some important principles. These are listed in Box 1.1.

**AVOIDANCE OF
GOBBLEDYGOOK**
A particularly important principle is that of avoiding alien syntax and mnemonics. Imagine a busy, overworked, impatient executive. He wants to use computers, but there is no way that he is likely to find the time (or patience) to learn COBOL. We want to find a language, or technique, with which he can put computers to work. We know that we can create screen dialogues that require little training. However, if we try to make him learn mnemonics such as DIR, E:CTRL, and the like, he will resist learning them and, if he does learn them, will forget them only too quickly. Programmers and computer scientists greatly underestimate the rate at which busy people forget mnemonics. An alien syntax is worse than alien mnemonics. Most busy executives and professionals will not remember where to put commas and semicolons or whether periods, commas, or slashes are needed. But a language can avoid punctuation and mnemonics and still be alien and confusing. Languages like the following are advertised as "simple, easy to use, English language, and user-friendly":

```
TABLE FILE FORTUNE
SUM PCT. 81-SALES
BY INDUSTRY
END


TABLE FILE HOLD
PRINT INDUSTRY AND 81-SALES AND PCT.
BY HIGHEST 81-SALES
END
```

BOX 1.1   Some basic principles in the design of 4GLs

- **The principle of minimum work.** We want to put computers to work with the minimum effort.

- **The principle of minimum skill.** We should be able to put computers to work as easily as possible, without the need for esoteric training if it can be avoided. The maximum cross section of the public can then employ computers.

- **The principle of avoiding an alien syntax and mnemonics.** Language constructs should be devised to avoid making users learn syntax and mnemonics that are alien to them and that they are likely to forget or have difficulty with.

- **The principle of minimum time.** We want to make it possible to utilize computers without lengthy delays for application development.

- **The principle of minimum errors.** Techniques should be devised so that the probability of human error is minimized and that those that occur are caught automatically, if possible.

- **The principle of minimum maintenance.** The 4GL mechanisms should make applications easy to change. (Maintenance is horrifyingly expensive with third-generation languages.)

- **The principle of maximum results.** We want computer applications to be as powerful, useful, and interesting as possible. 4GLs should enable users to employ complex tools for decision support, command and control, automated design, and so on.

but to many executives this appears like a mysterious incantation. They do not take the time to remember the necessary constructs, and it infuriates them with error messages if they try.

The piece of code just shown is enormously easier and quicker to use than COBOL or ADA, but it is still gobbledygook to many busy people who ought to use such a language. The challenge of fourth-generation languages is *how to avoid gobbledygook.* Can we use a computer without an alien syntax? Can we build complex applications without an alien syntax?

The answer to these questions is definitely yes. We will see a variety of constructs for building applications, which avoid making the user learn mnemonics, special punctuation, or special entry sequences. But no fourth-generation language has gone far enough yet. *Every 4GL could be improved by incorporating ideas from some other 4GL.*

Computer scientists and creative programmers love to devise new language constructs. They almost always devise constructs that are appropriate for other computer scientists and programmers but are difficult for executives, accountants, and busy professionals. The systems analyst is a busy professional. He too would benefit from a language that he can use quickly, so that he can quickly show his users prototypes, refine the prototypes to make them fit the users' needs, and then adjust them so that they work efficiently.

Some 4GLs are like programming languages. Others have sought to escape from constructs similar to traditional programming. Many of the concepts of structured programming are very important but can be put to work in easier ways. This book describes a diversity of 4GL mechanisms. Be on the lookout for techniques that avoid mnemonics, unnatural punctuation, and alien word sequences. React with hostility to gobbledygook, which is avoidable.

SIMPLE TOOLS FOR SIMPLE TASKS

In keeping with the principles of minimum work and minimum skill, it is desirable to employ simple tools for simple tasks. Simple inquiries and report generation need simple nonprocedural languages. However, if simple nonprocedural languages are applied to more complex systems, they cannot do the job.

Suppose that the black line on Fig. 1.2 indicates the development effort in person-days for creating programs of varying complexity in COBOL. For simple query, report, and spreadsheet applications, results can be obtained much faster with a simple nonprocedural language, as shown. However, a simply query-update-and-report language cannot tackle complex applications. It may be used in conjunction with COBOL, but then the development effort rises fast.

A good procedural language can be used to program anything that can be programmed with COBOL. The development effort is substantially smaller than with COBOL; the number of instructions written is substantially smaller. On more complex projects, with more logic to be programmed, the Procedural 4GL curve in Fig. 1.2 moves closer to the COBOL curve. Query and report generation, simple data-base updating, business graphics generation, and spreadsheet manipulation are much easier to do with a nonprocedural 4GL.

What we really need is a 4GL that combines the best of the procedural and nonprocedural capabilities, as shown by the solid red line in Fig. 1.2. Even with complex systems, much of the work can be done nonprocedurally, including screen generation, report generation, dialogue generation, data-base generation, and access to data.

Some of the best of the 4GLs combine procedural and nonprocedural facilities. For simple tasks, a very easy to use query language, spreadsheet language, a report generator, or graphics generator is still the best choice.

NO STANDARDS

At the time of writing, there are no standards for fourth-generation languages. It is too early yet to cre-

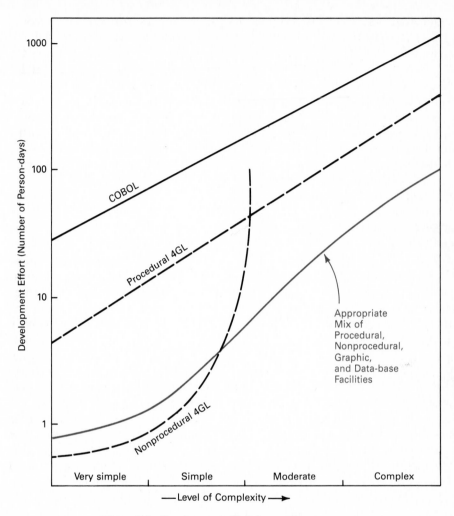

Figure 1.2   Development effort for creating programs.

ate standards because new ideas in language syntax, dialogue, and semantics are appearing at a furious rate. We are experiencing an explosion of creativity in the design of languages.

Standardization at too early a stage in the evolution of a technology can inhibit creativity. We have a few disastrous standards that are virtually impossible to change because of this.

DP executives sometimes worry about the lack of standards for the new languages. They worry about committing too much work to a language that might become obsolete or might not be supported on future machines. Some fourth-generation languages have already disappeared (including at least one from IBM). To make matters worse, most of the best languages come from small, relatively new vendors. There will certainly be mergers and takeovers among these vendors.

Appendix A gives a list of some of the languages. There are many others that are not on the list; new languages keep appearing every week. There are too many languages on the list for them all to survive.

It is generally forgotten how many third-generation languages disappeared. Jean Sammet's classic book on programming languages listed 120 third-generation languages in 1969 [3] (and it did not include ADA, PASCAL, or C). Box 1.2 lists some of these. Of the 120, fewer than ten are now in general use.

The ones that survived were not necessarily the best ones, but rather those supported by large organizations.

The death rate among 4GLs will probably be high. Some 4GLs from small corporations will survive because they are excellent and large organizations have adopted them.

An efficient DP operation cannot afford to ignore fourth-generation languages because of the huge increase in productivity they represent. The best course is to select software that gives fast results that are easy to maintain and that has a level of customer acceptance that seems likely to ensure its continued support. A few excellent packages do not yet have the support that is likely to ensure stability.

EXPERTS ON LANGUAGES

Many of the world's experts on computer languages are familiar with compiling or interpreting character streams but are not familiar with the more complex possibilities of screen interaction. Some do not even regard such a technique as a computer "language," although it is being used to build computer programs.

Indeed, at the time of writing there is something of a gulf between many of the world's language experts and the new languages. Many of the computer-science experts are working on ADA, PASCAL, C, and recent third-generation languages, whereas fourth-generation languages are being created in profusion by commercial enterprises, software houses, and maverick geniuses.

I have conducted an experiment on various language experts from universities. I write down a list of ten languages that I feel give systems analysts or users the best and fastest results in industry. The list might include FOCUS, RAMIS, NOMAD, SAS, NATURAL, IDEAL, MANTIS, USE. IT, LINC, CSP, ADS, UFO, QMF, APPLICATION FACTORY. Most computer-science language experts on whom I tried the experiment were unaware of the name of any one of the ten. This included a man who could lay claim to being the world's top authority on languages.

This lack of computer scientists' interest in, or knowledge of, fourth-generation languages is harmful. Most such languages have been built without theoretical foundation. Fourth-generation languages need theoretical underpin-

BOX 1.2 Third-generation languages

These are the third-generation languages listed in Sammet's *Programming Languages* in 1969 [3]. Fewer than ten of them are still in general use. Many of the fourth-generation languages in Appendix A will probably also disappear.

A-2 & A-3	GRAF
ADAM	ICES
AED	IPL-V
AESOP	IT
AIMACO	JOSS
ALGOL	JOVIAL
ALTRAN	KLERER-MAY
AMBIT	L6
AMTRAN	LANING AND ZIERLER
APL	LINCOLN RECKONER
APL/360	LISP 1.5
APT	LISP 2
BACAIC	MAD
BASEBALL	MADCAP
BASIC	MAGIC PAPER
C-10	MAP
CLIP	MATHLAB
CLP	MATH-MATIC
COBOL	META 5
COGENT	MILITRAN
COGO	MIRFAC
COLASL	NELIAC
COLINGO	OPS-3
COMIT	PL/I
COMMERCIAL TRANSLATOR	PRINT
CORAL	PROTOSYNTHEX
CPS	QUIKTRAN
DEACON	SHORT CODE
DYNAMO	SIMSCRIPT
473L QUERY	SIMULA
FACT	SNOBOL
FLAP	SOL
FLOW-MATIC	SPEEDCODING
FORMAC	STRESS
FORMULA ALGOL	SYMBOLIC MATH. LAB.
FORTRAN	TMG
FORTRANSIT	TRAC
FSL	TRANDIR
GAT	TREET
GPSS	UNICODE

nings just as do third-generation languages—perhaps more so because of the potentially more complex constructs and semantic dangers.

Most fourth-generation languages today are being created and improved by craftsman-programmers with no interest in the theory of languages. This is similar to previous technological history. Newcomen produced the first steam engine with a piston in 1712. For decades Newcomen's successors in this field were craftsmen-mechanics. The scientists of the era took no interest in the principles or theory of steam engines. Forty years after Newcomen's death, an engineer, John Smeaton, did meticulous research in the area, and this resulted in much better steam engines. Eventually computer scientists will direct their attention to high-productivity languages, and then we will probably see major improvements.

REFERENCES

1. J. Martin, *Application Development Without Programmers,* Englewood Cliffs, NJ: Prentice Hall, Inc., 1982.

2. A. N. Whitehead, *An Introduction to Mathematics,* Oxford: Oxford University Press, 1911.

3. J. E. Sammet, *Programming Languages,* Englewood Cliffs, NJ: Prentice-Hall, Inc., 1969.

2 CATEGORIES OF LANGUAGES

INTRODUCTION   Figure 2.1 categorizes software that creates applications without third-generation programming. Many of the languages or facilities available cover several parts of this diagram.

The categorization includes the following:

1. Simple-Query Facilities

These have existed since the earliest disk storage devices. They enable stored records to be printed or displayed in a suitable format.

2. Complex-Query-and-Update Languages

These are data-base user languages that permit the formulation of queries that may relate to several records. The queries sometimes invoke complex data-base searching or the joining of several records. For example, LIST ALL U.S. SHIPS WITHIN 500 MILES OF THE STRAITS OF HORMUZ CARRYING CREW MEMBERS WITH EXPERIENCE IN DESERT COMBAT. Because of the searching and joining, only certain data-base systems are appropriate for on-line use of such languages.

Many data-base user-languages now exist. They differ greatly in their syntax and structure. Some are marketed by the vendors of their host data-base management systems; others are marketed by independent software houses.

Many query languages permit users to enter and update data as well as query it. With some, users can create their own files.

	Suitable for End Users	Suitable for Systems Analysts	Suitable for Professional Programmers
Simple-Query Languages			
Complex-Query-and-Update Languages			
Report Generators			
Graphics Languages			
Decision-Support Languages			
Application Generators			
Specification Languages			
Very High Level Programming Languages			
Parameterized Application Packages			
Application Languages			

Figure 2.1   Categorization for comparing fourth-generation languages. Many languages include facilities in more than one category.

3. Report Generators

These are facilities for extracting data from a file or data base and formatting it into reports. Good report generators allow substantial arithmetic or logic to be performed on the data before they are displayed or printed.

Some report generators are independent of data-base or query facilities. Others are an extension of data-base query languages. Some are extremely easy and fast to use.

4. Graphics Languages

Graphics terminals are dropping in cost and provide a particularly attractive way for certain types of end users to display and manipulate data. Software for interactive graphics is steadily improving. It can enable users to ask for data and specify how they want it charted. They can search files or data bases and chart information according to different criteria. Like report generators, some graphics packages allow considerable arithmetical and logical manipulation of the data.

Some graphics facilities are designed primarily for graphics presentation purposes. Attractively laid out and labeled printouts or viewgraphs (for overhead projectors) can be created. Some elegant color plotting machines can be used for this purpose. Other graphics tools are designed primarily for revealing relationships and meaning in data and exploring what-if questions. Graphics techniques provide a powerful way to understand complex data.

5. Decision-Support Tools

A very valuable type of language is one designed to help in making decisions. Such languages make it easy for a user to build decision-support data bases and to perform calculations automatically on data when they are entered. Again, the user can explore what-if questions, enter formulas for manipulating data, and perform statistical, time-series, and trend analyses. Some decision-support languages are designed for financial or investment analysis or for business planning. They perform rate-of-return calculations, discounted cash flows, currency conversions, and the like. Some are linked to graphics tools.

Languages for ferreting truth from complex data have become a valuable resource in some enterprises. Occasionally the name of such a language is used as a verb. When data need investigating, you may hear people say, "Let's RAMIS it." Some languages allow complex models to be built.

Much business decision-making can be tackled with relatively simple tools designed for manipulating two-dimensional arrays of data, as with LOTUS 1-2-3 or MULTIPLAN. Some tools facilitate multidimensional computing on data. Some use a three-dimensional array showing for various what-if propositions a two-dimensional chart such as variables mapped against time periods, like this:

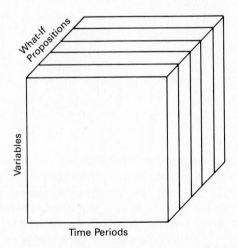

Some decision-support languages incorporate a diversity of decision-making or operations-research tools.

6. Application Generators

Languages for generating routine applications in data processing are often different from decision-support languages. They permit data-entry facilities to be generated with data validation. They permit the application creator to specify how files or data bases will be updated, what calculations and logic are performed, and what output is created. Generators can greatly speed up application development.

Machine performance is often a concern with routine data processing. Application generators need compilers that create optimized code modules and organize the data accesses as efficiently as possible. The accesses to data are, however, likely to be simpler than those used with decision-support systems or complex-query languages. A data base structured for decision support is usually inappropriate for routine heavy-duty computing, and vice versa.

Some can generate only part of an application. They need to be linked to programming languages or to be able to call routines written in a different language. Good generators, however, include a fourth-generation *procedural* language so that there is no requirement for third-generation programming.

7. Computable Specification Languages

We have traditionally written specifications for programs in English. This is generally imprecise, and much human interpretation by the programmer is needed to create the code. Formal ways of representing specifications with high precision now exist. These are called *specification languages*. A few specification languages are *computable,* and code can be generated directly from them. Chapter 8 discusses specification languages.

A computable specification language linked to a code generator is, in effect, an application generator. Most application-generator software, however, can generate applications only of a certain type. It might generate transaction-based data-base-update applications, for example. A specification language should be broader, with the ability to specify all types of applications. Some notations can specify highly complex logic. A particularly interesting specification language (USE.IT) has the ability to prove the correctness of the specification mathematically, permit its users to correct any faults easily, and generate bug-free code.

Most application generators are used only for commercial data processing. It is sometimes thought that fourth-generation languages are appropriate for commercial applications but not for scientific computing or computing with complex logic, such as programming telephone exchanges, missile detection, networking software, cryptanalysis, process control, and so on. The specification language USE.IT is employed for the latter types of computing; it can greatly speed up their development and make them easy to modify, thus lowering their formidable maintenance costs.

8. Very High Level Programming Languages

It is desirable to do as much application building as possible with *nonprocedural* languages because they are easy and quick to use and avoid common programming bugs. Some fourth-generation languages, however, are primarily *procedural*. In other words, they are programming languages. Cincom's MANTIS is an example of a programming language that can create programs often with one order of magnitude fewer instructions than are needed with COBOL. Part of the reason for its compactness and power is that it is a data-base language.

Many languages employ both procedural and nonprocedural code. Many employ high-level instructions that were not present in third-generation languages. With languages such as NOMAD the user can say LIST, PLOT, TITLE, INSERT, AVERAGE, SORT, SUM, and so on. He need not describe in code the format of a report. The software selects a reasonable format, and the user can adjust it if he wishes.

Most of these languages are relatively easy to use, a programmer writes a larger number of lines of code per day than he would with COBOL. Furthermore, a program can often be written in one-tenth the number of lines of code that COBOL requires. The code generally contains far fewer bugs and is easier to debug. All these factors make it possible to obtain results much faster than with traditional DP programming for many applications.

9. Parameterized Application Packages

Packages can be purchased for running certain applications. These preprogrammed packages are increasing in number, diversity, and quality. They often require a considerable amount of tailoring to fit the organization that installs them and are designed with parameters that can be chosen to modify their operation. This parameterization is the key to success in many cases. As the marketplace for packages grows, they tend to be built with a richer set of parameters so that they have wider applicability.

Some application packages are marketed directly to end users so that they can avoid involvement with their DP department.

A major problem with packages in the past has been the amount of modification they need and the difficulty of modifying them. This is being overcome in some cases by writing the package, at least in part, with fourth-generation languages, which are then made available for modifying the package. The user can generate his own reports, query the data base, extract data subsets for decision-support manipulation, and so on. The DP professional may be able to modify the data entry, change the data base, and add new features. The term *fourth-generation packages* is used for this.

A particularly comprehensive set of application packages is the Xerox Manufacturing System [1]. This provides a manufacturing corporation's key business applications and links them to fourth-generation languages for creating

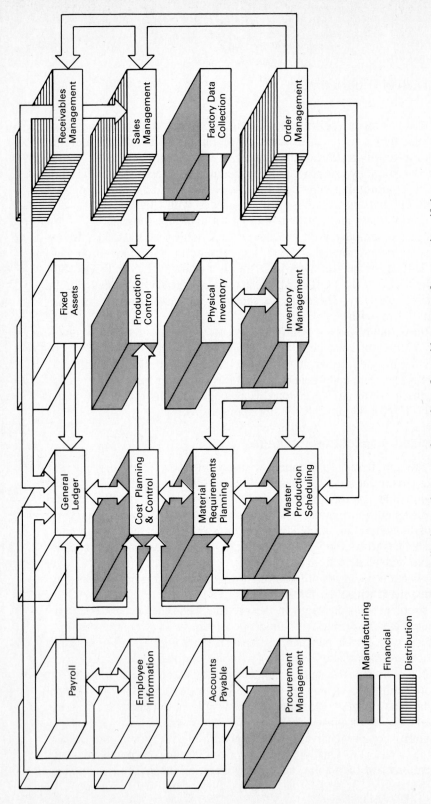

Figure 2.2 Application packages can be made to fit a wider range of corporations if they are programmed with or linked to fourth-generation languages. The Xerox Manufacturing System [1] provides an integrated set of on-line interactive data-base applications, shown here, designed to cover most business applications of a manufacturing company. End users can generate all types of reports from the data bases and use an extractor (like the report generator) to extract data into decision-support facilities or files from which user applications are run.

Manufacturing

Financial

Distribution

reports and graphs and performing decision-support functions. The report generator is designed for end users and is associated with an *extractor* using the same syntax; with this a user can extract specified data from the data bases and load them into files, which can be manipulated with fourth-generation languages. Often the user extracts the data into his personal computer for decision-support calculations. Figure 2.2 shows the main applications supported. These all have a unified architecture with comprehensive subject data bases. All transactions are processed interactively and often cause the real-time updating of many types of data record.

10. Application Languages

Many fourth-generation languages are general-purpose; others are designed for specific applications or application areas. They are development languages for a particular application rather than preprogrammed packages, and as such they give greater flexibility. Examples include languages for financial management, robot control, computer-aided design, numeric control of machine tools, surveying, and building design.

CATEGORIES OF USERS

The columns in Fig. 2.1 indicate a further categorization: Who is intended to use the language? Some languages are designed for end users; some are designed for DP professionals. It is useful to divide DP professionals into analysts and programmers. A programmer has little or no contact with the user; his job is to create code from specifications. An analyst works with the users and should devote his main attentions to communicating with them and understanding and solving their problems; he should not be a professional coder.

Many languages use techniques, which are largely nonprocedural, for allowing business or systems analysts to build applications or prototypes quickly. The analyst should become completely familiar with one or possibly more than one language with which he obtains results quickly.

Some languages remain more appropriate for the programmer because they require the memorization of mnemonics, formats, and sequences or because complex technical knowledge of the product is needed to obtain good machine performance. We might regard IBM's application generator ADF, for example, as belonging in the right-hand column of Fig. 2.1.

What makes the difference in the selection of the column in Fig. 2.1 is primarily the human factoring of the language. Application generators used predominantly by programmers could be made into tools for analysts by improving (usually substantially changing) the human factoring. Tools for DP professionals could similarly be brought into the realm of end users. There is much scope for criticism of the human factoring of many of the existing languages. Major improvements are desirable.

Almost all tools could be brought into the two left columns of Fig. 2.1 so that the use of professional programmers could be largely avoided except in specialized areas such as systems software development.

INTEGRATION OF FEATURES

Much software encompasses many of the categories in Fig. 2.1.

Application generators are not capable of generating all applications. Sometimes they lack the capability to generate particular logic or algorithms that are needed. An important feature of a generator is the capability to associate with it modules of logic written in programming languages. This is sometimes called an *escape* feature. Where possible, it is desirable that the user of the generator also be able to use the language to which the escape is made.

In some cases a programmer is required to handle the escape language, but if the programmer is part of the DP department, doing conventional coding, problems with programming backlog affect the use of the generator.

Ideally, then, the features in Fig. 2.1 should be integrated as much as possible. The query language should support the creation of reports and graphics and be the basis of an application generator. A high-level programming language should be available as part of the application generator. Many products in existence today do not yet have this degree of integration. Some computer manufacturers and software houses have created separate languages for database query, report generation, graphics, application generation, and high-level programming.

The features need to be integrated with a syntax that is compatible as far as possible, although the syntax of procedural code will always be different from that of a nonprocedural language.

An interactive language usually operates with an interpreter; a language for heavy-duty computing needs an optimizing compiler. These need not be incompatible. The interpreter may be used for building and prototyping the application a step at a time. When the application is satisfactory in prototype form, an optimizing compiler might then be used to generate efficient machine code.

DESIGNED FOR END USERS?

One of the most important characteristics of 4GLs is whether or not they are really end-user products.

Most vendors of such software claim that it is "designed for end users." In many cases this claim is questionable because the software requires more skill and training than most users will acquire. In many cases the software should be used by systems analysts who work with the end users.

Some of the software is excellent for end users. Some of the best database query-and-update facilities can be employed by users who have never touched a terminal before, for example, videotext sets [2], IBM's QUERY-BY-EXAMPLE, and Cullinet's ON-LINE ENGLISH. These languages, however, do not give the user much power. He needs more than query or query-and-update languages. Languages like LOTUS 1-2-3 and FRAMEWORK give him good decision-support tools. He can build spreadsheets and express the computation he requires in propagating calculation through the spreadsheets.

To build more complex procedures, the user needs to be able to think about them clearly. The software should be an aid to clear thinking. Clear thinking about complex procedures often relates to how we draw them. The user may draw them on a screen with computer assistance or draw them on paper in such a way that he can convert them directly to code. The more automation of clear thinking the software provides, the better.

With some software most end users learn to perform only the simpler functions. They might learn to query data and generate reports, but not to use the features of the language designed for the creation of programmed procedures. There is a barrier to the full use of the language caused by inadequate education and inadequate human factoring in the language.

A particularly critical factor with *important* end users is that they are very busy and short of time. They will only use facilities they can learn quickly and with which they can obtain valuable results without much expenditure of time. Important overworked users have neither the time nor the inclination to learn and write programs in BASIC, but a language like LOTUS 1-2-3 or SYSTEM W becomes second nature to them—like a pocket calculator but with enormously greater power.

The thought of end users doing nontrivial computing themselves is greeted with skepticism or astonishment by some old DP professionals. The chief scientist of one of America's giant electronics companies, in a book review, compared the idea of user's developing logically complex applications to *do-it-yourself brain surgery* [3]. At the time he wrote this, the end users at BankAmerica had already created 83,000 programs using NOMAD II and the Santa Fe Railroad had six of Univac's largest mainframes processing up to 100 transactions per second, in total, with applications developed entirely by end users using MAPPER.

Although users have employed NOMAD, MAPPER, and other such languages to develop data processing systems, they would not be likely to use an application generator like IBM's ADF. That and many others are designed for DP professionals, not end users.

TWO-DAY TEST

In the early days of computers, only programmers and computer operators had an active role in using the machines. When the spread of terminals began, it was thought that only users with detailed and lengthy training would use them. Ten years later, terminal dialogues had improved so that the person in the street could use terminals with no training or practice—for example, with videotext systems [2] or bank customer terminals. However, it was generally thought that end users could not *create* applications; only programmers could do that. Now it has become clear that end users can and should create certain types of applications. Only in this way can their unique knowledge be fully harnessed. We need to challenge knowledge workers everywhere to solve their own problems with computers.

The key to *user* creation of applications is the existence of terminal dialogues that are psychologically appropriate. Such software now exists and is rapidly improving. It is quite different from the software traditionally used by DP professionals. It needs to be sufficiently easy to use that the typical manager can employ it effortlessly to make more intelligent decisions. In a few organizations the use of such software has greatly improved the effectiveness of computers.

Unfortunately, almost every query language and report generator on the market is advertised as being "suitable for end users." Some are tried out and gain little acceptance. Some are used by systems analysts, not end users.

One language was advertised with the promise, "Learn to write computer programs in five minutes!" But in many organizations it did not prove to be suitable for or accepted by the end users.

We suggest that a test be applied to such products, the *two-day test*. This is described in Box 2.1.

If the users can learn to be *comfortable* with the product and carry out *useful work* with it in two days and need not necessarily return to classes on it later, then we can put it in the End User column of Fig. 2.1.

Some products are complex, and the two-day course may cover only part of their capability. It is a good idea to package products so that a useful subset can be taught and employed. When users are experienced in using this subset and find it valuable, they will be more receptive to learning advanced subsets.

An important aspect of the two-day test is that users should be able to leave the product for a week or more and concentrate on other matters, yet when they then confront the product again they should be able to use it. This is not likely to be the case if the product requires them to remember codes, mnemonics, formats, or fixed sequences of entry.

Having said this, it must be noted that *some* end users *do* make good use of products that would not pass this test. Some use programming languages, for example. But these end users are more dedicated than most. For the masses, the two-day test applies.

PRODUCTS DESIGNED FOR USER GROWTH

When end users are first confronted with a workstation on which they can obtain or manipulate data, the facility ought to be simple to use. Some data-base query languages are very easy to use—easy enough

BOX 2.1   The two-day test to determine whether products are suitable for end users

To pass the two-day test, a product should have the following properties:

- *Most* end users can learn to use it effectively in a two-day course. Some can learn it much faster.

- At the end of this course they are *comfortable* with it and can use it on their own.

- At the end of the course they can start getting *useful* work out of it. This emphasis on useful work is important. There is no point in learning gimmicks that have little relevance.

- After the course the end users can leave the product for a week and still be able to use it. (Most users would forget mnemonics or fixed entry sequences in this time.)

- The end users will not necessarily have to return to another class on the product.

- Users can expand or refresh their knowledge of the product at the terminal by using HELP features and computer-aided instruction.

(In some cases the two-day course may cover a useful subset of the products features, and more can be learned later, when the users have experience in using the product.)

to encourage the most fainthearted user. Some electronic mail and information retrieval systems are very easy to use.

The naive user tends to go through phases of fear, fascination when he begins to make something work, then euphoria. When he is confident and euphoric, he should be introduced to the next step up in system capability.

A good query language ought to lead to a data-base updating capability, report generation, and graphics generation, using the same style of dialogue and syntax. An electronic mail facility ought to lead to tools that enable a user to process an electronic in-basket or work queue. With these facilities a second level of sophistication is reached, as illustrated in Fig. 2.3.

A user might be left some weeks to master the techniques, or some of them, at this second level before he is introduced to further complications. Ideally, he should be able to grow to the fourth level in Fig. 2.3. Figure 2.4 shows a set of facilities for decision support rather than routine applications. Again,

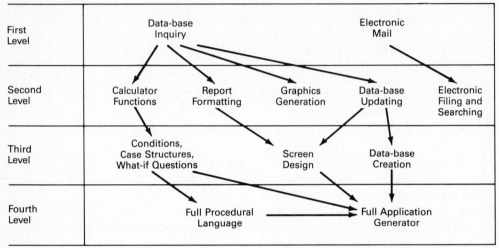

Figure 2.3 Users should learn simple facilities first—those in the first level. When comfortable with these, they can progress to the second level, then the third. Only certain users will progress to the fourth level.

Many products fall short of full HGL capability.

the user should be introduced a stage at a time until he learns the most sophisticated facilities appropriate for his job.

Again, ideally, the syntax and style of the dialogue ought to be the same in progressing from the second to the third level. Unfortunately, this is not true with much of the software listed in Appendix A. The vendors have not completely put their act together. A data-base query language is often no more than a query language. The same vendor may have an application generator, but one that has no relationship to the query language. IBM's QUERY-BY-EXAMPLE has no resemblance to its GIS (Generalized Information System), and that has no resemblance to DMS (Development Management System) or ADF (Application Development Facility). Cullinet's products for users of its IDMS data base are equally unrelated (at the time of writing). Ideally, everything in Fig. 2.3 ought to be provided by related products with similarly structured end-user dialogues. Some products on the market do encompass many of the facilities in Fig. 2.3.

Many good languages have grown in functionality at a rapid rate. The FOCUS manual used to be ¼ inch thick and now is 2 inches thick. This growth to richness of function is highly desirable. However, the user, confronted by a 2-inch-thick manual is likely to say, "I'll never be able to learn that!" He should be introduced first to a simple subset that makes it as easy as possible to

Levels of
Sophistication

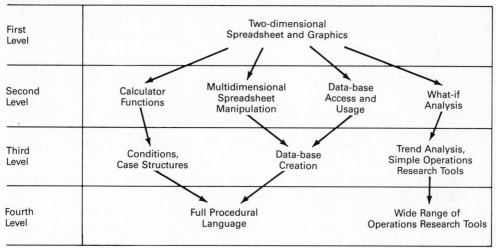

Figure 2.4   Levels of facilities appropriate to a decision-support environment.

begin, then a more comprehensive subset, and so on. Subsetting is very important in the introduction of functionally rich languages to nonprogrammers.

The type of subset the user begins with varies from situation to situation. Some learn a query language first; some start with word processing or electronic mail; some start with spreadsheet manipulation products like LOTUS 1-2-3.

Some products began their evolution as a query language and had features added that take them into other areas of Fig. 2.3. Sometimes these are well human-factored, with a major emphasis on use by naive users, but they do not have sophisticated application-generation capability.

Other products, such as APL or MANTIS, began their evolution as high-level programming languages. Nonprocedural features are added. Facilities are improved for querying data bases, generating reports and graphics, and handling electronic mail. This evolution gives sophisticated users much capability because of the power of the programming language, but it is sometimes not as easy for beginners or casual end users to employ.

The ideal language set ought to have all of the capabilities shown in Figs. 2.3 or 2.4. The first levels ought to be entirely nonprocedural, with elegant human factoring. The lower two levels ought to be extremely easy for the beginner to use. Commonality of syntax and dialogue style ought to make it natural for users to progress from one subset to another.

REACTIVE SYSTEMS

As microelectronics continues its downward plunge in cost, it becomes possible to put increasing amounts of computing power at the users' location. This may be in the form of minicomputers or intelligent terminals, but mostly it will be in the form of ever more powerful personal computers. It provides elaborate computing resources that interpret user input or create elegant color graphics displays on the user's screen.

It is no longer necessary to share a distant computer with many other users and access it by means of a low-bandwidth line. Each user can have substantial computing power *to himself*. The more microelectronics drops in cost, the more this will be true. Telecommunications will be used for accessing data rather than accessing computing power. If users can have substantial computing power at their fingertips at low cost, system design efforts should be directed to making the person's time on the computer as profitable as possible.

The term *reactive system* has been used by Alan Kay [4] to refer to systems in which a substantial processor has as its sole job the catering to a single user. It can afford to do relatively large amounts of processing when the user is doing the simplest of tasks. It can format data on the screen and add text so that it is easy to understand. It can check the user's spelling, make dictionary references, perform semantics checks, and flash any incorrect items. It may contain an interpreter or incremental compiler. It can assemble and maintain several forms of color graphics display and allow the user to interact with them. It may update many fields in a work area when the user takes a single action. It can afford to do extensive processing to figure out what the user wants to say or what information he is trying to obtain, and it can interact with him to deduce or refine his intended input.

As the price-to-performance ratio of microelectronics drops, a primary concern must be end-user efficiency rather than machine efficiency. End users will increasingly be given facilities that make it easy for them to obtain the information they need from distant data banks; manipulate the information; format it into meaningful graphics displays, reports, and intelligent spreadsheets; and create data-related applications.

**ON-LINE OR
OFF-LINE?**

A further categorization of the software in Fig. 2.1 can indicate whether it is on-line or off-line. Some query languages, report generators, and application generators operate interactively at a terminal; some operate off-line, with the users or systems analysts filling in forms or coding sheets. The use of forms gives the user time to think about what he needs. In some cases he may fill in the forms at home or away from his office.

Nevertheless, *on-line* operation can be much more satisfactory if it is well designed psychologically. It can lead the user a step at a time through what he is required to do. It can check the user's input as he creates it. It can make tutorial explanations available on-line and can assist if the user presses a HELP key. On-line operation can generally be made much more versatile than off-line operation. It can provide a wide diversity of fast-to-use mechanisms of great power.

ESCAPE FEATURE

Application generators are not capable of generating all applications. Sometimes they lack the capability to generate particular logic or algorithms that are needed. Too often a generator is rejected for this reason. An important feature of a generator is the capability to associate with it modules of logic written in programming languages. This can be done in several ways.

First, there may be an *escape feature,* which allows the user to branch into a conventional language such as COBOL or BASIC. IBM's generator DMS was used in local government for building a fairly complex medical assistance system. The system had 69 types of user panel for data entry and other operations. The builders had to escape into COBOL 68 times to perform small operations that DMS could not handle. A typical example was the editing of a data field so that it could be used for sorting. The month-day-year format was converted to year-month-day by a small COBOL program. The 68 escapes involved a total of 2100 lines of COBOL and took about 200 person-days to write. A COBOL programmer was kept busy for the duration of the system development time.

This type of escape is often not very satisfactory. It means that a nonprogrammer analyst (or team) is not capable of finishing the job. It may cause the backlog of work for COBOL programmers to slow down the 4GL application building. A much more satisfactory solution is to have the needed capability for editing and logic built into the 4GL. The 4GL may need to encompass a procedural language that gives it the necessary flexibility. The procedural language should have a compatible syntax.

Sometimes the 4GL needs to *call* subroutines from a library, and these may be written in a different language.

BASIC CHARACTERISTICS OF 4GLS

Here is a list of the basic selection criteria relating the different types of 4GL. Chapter 19 gives a more detailed list for comparison of the software packages.

- Is it intended for routine computing or ad hoc decision making?
- Is it intended for end users or DP professionals? (Many 4GLs are appropriate for both.)
- Does it require the skills of a programmer, or can an analyst who does not program in third-generation languages use it?
- Which of the following features does it provide?

1. Simple queries

2. Simple queries and updates

3. Complex queries

4. Complex queries and updates

5. The ability to create a data base quickly

6. Intelligent data-base operations, where the change of one value in the data base causes other operations to occur automatically, such as validity checks, cross references, and the updating of related values

7. Generation of data-entry screens for key-entry operators (with validation checks?)

8. Generation of data-update screens for key-entry operators (with validation checks?)

9. A procedural language giving full programming capability

10. Graphics techniques for application design

11. Spreadsheet manipulation

12. Multidimensional matrix manipulation

13. Report generation

14. Graphics generation

15. Graphics manipulation

16. Decision support for what-if questions

17. Mathematical analysis tools

18. Financial analysis tools

19. Other decision-support tools

20. Text manipulation

21. Electronic mailbox

- Is it on-line or off-line?

- Does it run on mainframes, minicomputers, or personal computers?

- Can it access mainframe or remote data bases?

- Is it genuinely easy to use?

- Can results be obtained with it very quickly?

PROPERTIES OF 4GLs

Now that we have the term *fourth-generation language,* it is likely that every new language will be called "fourth-generation" by its advertising copy-writers. Some new languages, however, have the characteristics more of third-generation languages. For a language to be worth calling "fourth-generation," it should have the following characteristics:

1. It is user-friendly.
2. A nonprofessional programmer can obtain results with it.
3. It employs a data-base management system directly.
4. Programs for most applications can be created with one order of magnitude fewer instructions than with COBOL.
5. Nonprocedural code is used, where possible.
6. It makes intelligent default assumptions about what the user wants, where possible.
7. It is designed for on-line operation.
8. It enforces or encourages structured code.
9. It makes it easy to understand and maintain another person's code.
10. Non-DP users can learn a subset of the language in a two-day training course.
11. It is designed for easy debugging.
12. Prototypes can be created and modified quickly.
13. Results can be obtained in one order of magnitude less time than with COBOL or PL/I for most applications.

Many new languages have these properties, but many also have the characteristic that they cannot create all types of applications. They are not general-purpose. That is a price we may have to pay for the great productivity improvements fourth-generation languages bring. In this case we have to *select the language to fit the application*. This is repugnant to some programmers and purists. But it is a vitally important fact that languages of limited scope are enabling users to obtain the results they need *fast,* whereas the traditional programming process in COBOL or PL/I was not.

Given the full costs of specification, coding, debugging, documenting, and maintenance in COBOL or PL/I, management ought to conduct an inquiry whenever a proposal is made to use these to see whether any higher-productivity alternative can be found. COBOL-level blow-by-blow coding should be avoided wherever possible.

COMPONENTS OF A 4GL

A good general-purpose 4GL has several nonprocedural components that may be linked to a procedural facility. This is illustrated in Fig. 2.5. At the top of the figure is an administrative aid for giving the procedure a name, cataloging it, stating which version this is and who is responsible for it, and so on. Next is a facility for creating a specification of the data used. In a file environment, the application designer may design his own files. In a data-base environment, he may employ data designed by the data administrator's section.

Next is a report generator. Reports may be specified and the specification stored in a dictionary. Similarly, a screen pointer may be used for designing

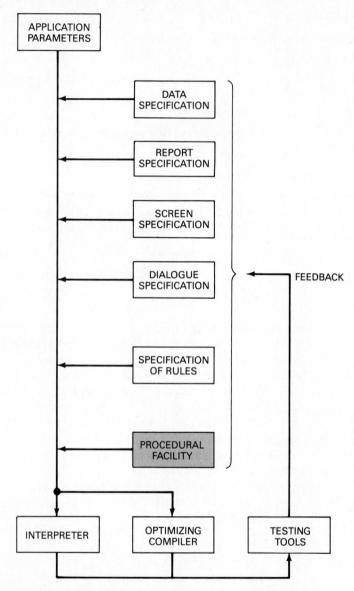

Figure 2.5 Components of a 4GL for building routine applications.

screens, which are also stored in the dictionary. A dialogue specifier may be used for giving the structure of person-computer interaction.

A means may be used for specifying complex decisions or conditions. This may employ a decision tree or table or a language for expressing rules. It is desirable that the specification of complex decisions or rules—for example, the determination of a complex discount—be separate from the body of the application, because then the rules or conditions can be changed neatly without changing the main application code.

In conjunction with the data specified, report generator, screen generator, dialogue generator, and rule specifier is a procedural facility (red in Fig. 2.5). This enables the structure of a program to be specified—loops, conditions, case structures, and nested routines. In most 4GLs, this is a simple programming language; however, it need not be. Procedural structures can be designed graphically without the need to remember program-structure commands. The user of a graphic approach often avoids the types of errors made by the user of a command language.

In many 4GLs, the specification of rules, shown separately in Fig. 2.5, is also done with the procedural programming-like language. It can be better for complex logic to use a separate decision tree, decision table, or rule-based facility.

A TIME OF CHANGE

The late 1980s is a period of great change in the tools and techniques for building computer systems. The powerful new techniques coming into use are illustrated in Fig. 2.6. These techniques strongly affect the language constructs that are the most productive.

TYPES OF PROGRAMMING LANGUAGES

Prior to 1980, the majority of programmers used procedural languages that, although different in syntax, were broadly similar in overall structure: COBOL, PL/I, FORTRAN, PASCAL, BASIC, ADA, and so on. These languages use the control constructs illustrated in Fig. 2.7.

There is a variety of other types of programming. The terms used to describe programming languages are summarized in Box 2.2. All of the types of language in Box 2.2 are found as components of 4GLs. Many 4GLs have more than one of these types of language. For example, they may use both procedural and nonprocedural code or both full-screen interaction and noninteractive entry of procedures.

Languages for commercial data processing rarely use functional programming, like LISP, in spite of the great enthusiasm of the artificial intelligence community for LISP. Rule-based programming ought to be an important component of commercial DP languages, but at the time of writing it is not a part of many 4GLs. The techniques used for building artificial intelligence systems, particularly expert systems, are often referred to as fifth-generation techniques. They need to be linked to the commercial data processing environment and ought to be employed as extensions of today's 4GLs.

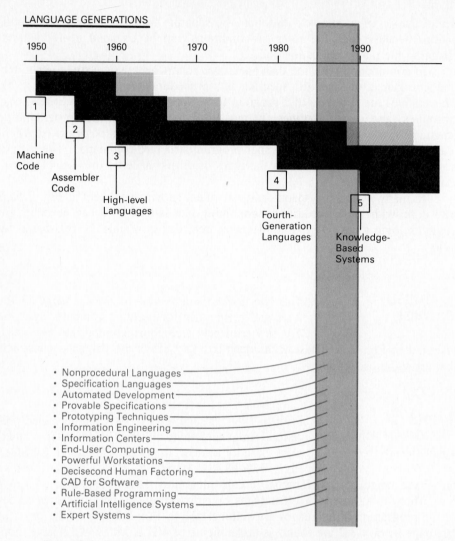

Figure 2.6 Important new techniques for application building. These techniques strongly affect the desirable choice of language constructs.

AVOIDANCE OF BEWILDERING SYNTAX

Perhaps the most important thrust in 4GL evolution is the avoidance of mnemonics and syntax that bewilder non-DP professionals. The early 4GLs did not go far enough in avoiding nonhuman syntax. As 4GLs have evolved, it has become clear that most computing can be done without bewildering mnemonics and an alien syntax.

Humans remember human language and the language of their profession.

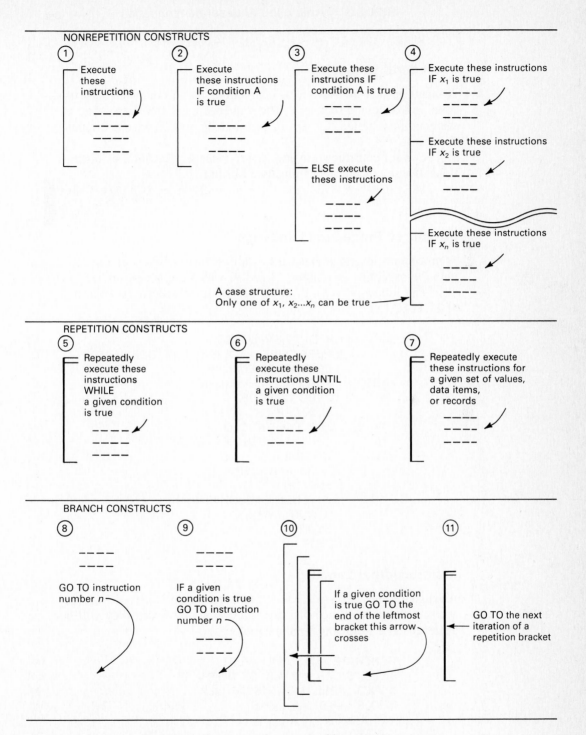

Figure 2.7 Constructs of a procedural language.

BOX 2.2   Terms used to describe languages

Procedural Language

A language that gives a set of instructions that a computer must execute in a specified sequence. The sequence may vary, depending on the conditions tested. Groups of instructions may be executed repetitively.

Control constructs govern the sequence of execution of instructions. These constructs are illustrated in Fig. 2.7.

Most first-, second-, and third-generation languages are of this type.

Structured Procedural Language

A procedural language that permits all of the constructs of Fig. 2.7, with the exception of numbers 8 and 9, which are not permitted.

The following is an example of structured procedural code in a 4GL, IDEAL:

```
<<EMP>> FOR EACH EMPLOYEE
          WHERE DEPT = 'D' AND JOB-CODE = 'J'
            DO NOTE-DJ-EMP
   <<DEP>> FOR EACH DEPENDENT
             DO NOTE-DEP
             IF DEP-AGE > 21
               DO TOO-OLD
               PROCESS NEXT DEP
             ENDIF
             DO ANAL-DEP
           ENDFOR
           IF FOUND-ENOUGH-EMP
             QUIT EMP
           ENDIF
         ENDFOR
```

Nonprocedural Language

A language that describes *what* results are to be achieved but does not specify the sequence of steps (procedure) by which they will be achieved. The following is an example:

```
GENERATE A MONTHLY PLOT
TITLE "SALES VOLUME BY DISTRICT"
X AXIS LABEL "MONTHS OF 1982"
Y AXIS LABEL "MILLIONS"
INPUT DATA
"WEST"
SELECT QUANTITY FROM SALES
```

BOX 2.2 *(Continued)*

```
WHERE DISTRICT = WEST AND YEAR = 1982
"EAST"
SELECT QUANTITY FROM SALES
WHERE DISTRICT = EAST AND YEAR = 1982
GO
```

Nonprocedural languages can have a great diversity of other forms of syntax.

Declarative Language

A language that declares a set of facts and permits the statement of queries or problems that use those facts. It does not completely specify the sequence of steps (procedure) for handling the query or problem. A declarative language is thus a form of nonprocedural language.

In a declarative language, one or more equations may be stated; for example,

$$\text{PRINCIPAL} = \text{INSTALLMENT} \times 100/\text{INTEREST\_RATE} (1 - (1$$

$$+ \text{INTEREST\_RATE}/100) ** -N)(1 + \text{INTEREST\_RATE}/100)$$

If *any* three of the four variables in this financial equation are entered, the fourth will be calculated. *The user does not give sequence of steps in doing the calculation.* Similarly, several simultaneous equations could be used.

Rule-based Language

A language with which a set of facts and rules can be described. These facts and rules can then be used to answer queries or solve problems. The behavior of a program can be changed by changing one or more facts or rules. (This term is sometimes used interchangeably with *declarative language*.)

PROLOG is an example of a rule-based language. Facts are expressed as follows:

```
female (mary)
male (john)
likes (john, mary)
book (future shock, toffler, random house)
```

Rules are expressed as follows:

```
sister (x,y): −female (x), parent (x,z), parent (y,z)
```

BOX 2.2 *(Continued)*

(This says that X is the sister of Y if X is female and if the parent of X is the same as the parent of Y.)

Queries are expressed as follows:

```
? - likes (mary, john)
? - route ("London", "Sydney", R) travel time (R, T)
? - sister (mary, fred)
```

The PROLOG system may have to process many rules to draw appropriate conclusions. The programmer does not explicitly state the sequence in which the rules are processed. The software selects the rule it needs at each stage in the processing.

Functional Programming Language

A language in which expressions composed of function calls, rather than statements, are the basic unit from which programs are constructed (also called *applicative language*).

Here is an example:

```
The function SUB 1 N returns (N−1)
The function FACTORIAL (SUB 1 N) returns (N−1)!
The function TIMES N (FACTORIAL (SUB 1 N) returns
    N(N−1)!
The function EQUAL N 1 returns T if N=1 and NIL if N≠1)!
The function COND (E1 X) (E2 Y) returns X if E1 is T,
    otherwise Y if E2 is T
The function COND ((EQUAL N 1) 1) (T(TIMES
    N(FACTORIAL(SUB 1 N)))) returns 1 if N = 1 otherwise
    N (N − 1)!
```

The following is a recursive program for calculating *N!*

```
FACTORIAL: (LAMBDA(N) (COND((EQUAL N 1)1)(T(TIMES
            N(FACTORIAL(SUB 1 N))))))
```

The code shown is an example of LISP, the predominant functional programming language. LISP is not normally regarded as a fourth-generation language, but it underlies many of the tool kits ("shells") for building "fifth-generation" expert systems.

BOX 2.2 *(Continued)*

Object-oriented Languages

Conventional programming specifies a sequence of *operations* carried out on a set of *operands*. Larger functions are built out of stored sequences. Still larger functions are built out of those. Instead of operations and operands, object-oriented languages use a different pair of primitives: *objects* and *messages*. An *object* is a packet of information and a description of how it is manipulated. It contains not only data but also the set of functions that are allowed to access those data. Each object communicates with other objects by sending *messages*. When an object receives a message, it decides what to do with it and usually sends messages to other objects. Thus instead of applying active functions to passive data, as in conventional programming, messages tell objects to do things, and the object, rather than calling code, decides how to implement the operation.

Objects are grouped in classes that *inherit* certain properties. Inheritance makes it possible to use new classes of objects by simply specializing an existing class rather than building it from scratch.

SMALLTALK and LOGO are well-known object-oriented languages. Both are strongly visually oriented. They are best suited to an exploratory style of programming. It is easy to create, test, and change prototypes. LOGO is used mainly as a teaching aid and has proved highly successful in enabling young children to create visually oriented programs and to think with the manipulation of symbols. SMALLTALK has been used for simulation in the broadest sense of the term. Objects and messages sent between them represent the simulation of ideas. SMALLTALK has been used with *icons* like those of Macintosh. People can absorb visual information much more rapidly than verbal information, so visual representation of ideas and objects in general is valuable. Object-oriented programming tools are valuable for writing software for graphics, modeling applications, simulation, and sophisticated user interfaces.

Dialogue Language or Interactive Language

A language in which a program is created as a result of an interactive dialogue between the user and the software. In the following example (EXPRESS), the computer prompts are in black, and the user responses are in red:

```
-> XREPORT
NAME FOR EXCEPTION LIST: > UNDERBUDGET
```

(Continued)

BOX 2.2 *(Continued)*

CRITERION FOR INCLUSION IN LIST: > DIST.SALES
LT.9*BUDGET
*EXCEPTIONS FOUND.
DATA NAMES TO INCLUDE IN REPORT: DIST.SALES BUDGET
PCT.DIF

A great variety of forms of dialogue are used in different 4GLs.

Full-Screen Interactive Language

A language in which the user interacts with a screen, filling in items, pointing to items, moving items, changing default values, and so on. Full-screen interaction is faster and more powerful than line-oriented interaction and can speed up the building of certain types of programs.

A great variety of forms of screen interaction are used. Some of them appear in various places in this book.

Graphic Programming Language

A language in which programs are built interactively with graphics techniques. Logic, control structures, decision trees, data-base navigation, rule processing, and so on, can be expressed clearly with diagrams. Diagrams can be built on a computer screen. One form of diagram can be converted into another. The diagrams can be linked to a data dictionary and used to generate code. In order to generate code from diagrams, the diagramming technique has to be suitably rigorous.

Graphic programming can be fast and powerful. Chapters 7 and 13 give some illustrations.

They remember clear graphic constructs. They can read most flowcharts, graphs, and New York subway maps. But they cannot remember computer mnemonics and syntax, which has to be precisely correct, unless they have spent much time learning and practicing. Most people who ought to be using computers have not spent this time, many have no intention of doing so because they are too busy.

Human language alone is not precise enough for most computing. It therefore needs to be combined with other clear, easy-to-remember constructs and machine interactions, especially interactive graphics. This can be done to produce languages that remove most of the difficulties of interacting with computers.

The computer world is full of programming masochists. They have learned to program machines the hard way and are highly resistant to the idea that it can be made easy. One of the most famous computer-science professors described graphics editors for making programming easier as "an idea which any serious computer scientist is only too anxious to ignore" [5].

In Russia, the early COBOL compilers were copied from the West. Because of this, DP programmers programmed in English-language COBOL for several years. Eventually, a Russian-language COBOL computer became available, but most professional COBOL programmers continued to use the English-language version. They made new entrants to their profession pay their dues by learning the English version, although English is a difficult language for most Russians. Somehow the foreign-language version seemed more professional, just as writing prescriptions in Latin seemed more professional to doctors until recently.

We cannot overemphasize the importance of avoiding alien syntax and avoiding computer responses that leave the user not knowing what to do next. Different components of different 4GLs indicate how far we can progress with this goal as new or improved 4GLs are created.

SOLVING THE WRONG PROBLEM

Much of today's research into the development process is oriented toward improving the existing methods. Improve programming with the move to structured programming. Improve systems analysis with the move to structured analysis. Formalize the conventional development life cycle and provide tools within it for documentation and review. Add yet more reserved words and instruction types to COBOL. Adapt languages and compilers for better-structured programming. Develop the ADA language. And so on.

In a sense, these activities (although valuable because much conventional programming will remain) are solving the wrong problem. The important problem is to migrate from conventional programming and the old development life cycle to development methodologies that are fast, flexible, and interactive and create provably correct code; methodologies in which interactive prototyping replaces formal, voluminous specifications that must be frozen; methodologies that are automated; methodologies with which end users, managers, specifiers, implementers, and maintainers can interact without mismatches.

If a hammer is not achieving much success in fixing screws, the solution is not to obtain a better hammer. The problem is that the wrong methodology is being used. More appropriate tools are now available for software development. In some cases, computer executives still want to use the old development life cycle, even with the new tools. This is rather like the old hammer enthusiasts driving in screws by hitting them hard with the handle of the screwdriver.

REFERENCES

1. Xerox Manufacturing System, Xerox Computer Services, 5310 Beethoven St., Los Angeles, CA 90066.

2. J. Martin, *Viewdata and the Information Society,* Englewood Cliffs, NJ: Prentice-Hall, Inc., 1981.

3. Private review of J. Martin, *Application Development Without Programmers,* Englewood Cliffs, NJ: Prentice-Hall, Inc., 1982, at the request of the publisher.

4. A. Kay, *Personal Computing,* ACM National Conference, August 1975.

5. Personal communication.

3 HOW ARE 4GLs USED?

Fourth-generation languages are changing DP management in some drastic ways. This chapter discusses their most effective types of use.

Fourth-generation languages are more commonly used in commercial data processing than in scientific and engineering applications; however, they can be found in use for almost all aspects of computing, and they have extended computing into vital new areas. They raise many management questions in DP.

4GLs are more commonly used in decision-support systems and management information systems than in routine data processing, but they can make massive improvements in the development of routine DP. If they are used for systems with high transaction volumes, careful attention must be paid to machine performance. A few 4GLs are designed for heavy-duty computing; most are not. Figure 3.1 shows the throughput of an IBM mainframe of routine transactions using the language NATURAL.

4GLs are used both for creating prototypes and for creating the final application. Prototypes can be extremely valuable in data processing. This use of 4GLs is discussed in Chapter 4.

Individual 4GLs differ greatly in their capabilities, so selecting the right 4GL for the job is very important. There are some horror stories about attempts to use a fourth-generation language on systems where its capabilities were not adequate for the task.

PROBLEMS WITH DATA PROCESSING

The power of today's computing technology is not being used as it should be in most enterprises. Data processing is bogged down in problems. Managers are not receiving the information they require from their systems. Many decisions that should be made with the aid of computers

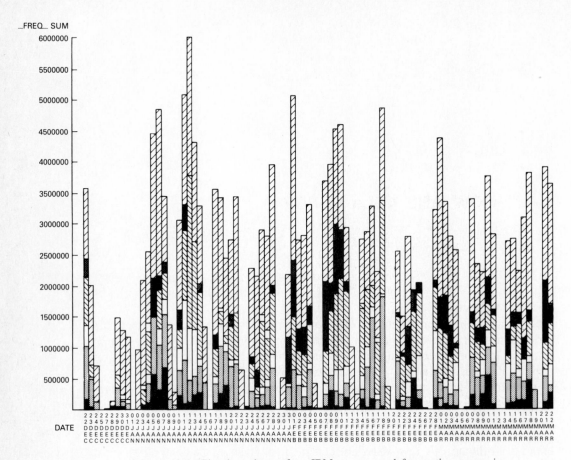

Figure 3.1 The throughput of an IBM system used for routine processing using the language NATURAL. The number of accesses per data base per day sometimes exceeds 5 million. (The chart was created with the language SAS/ GRAPH.)

are in fact being made with hand methods or inadequate information. Systems are so difficult to change that they often inhibit the implementation of new and important procedures that management requires. Computer users are increasingly hostile to DP but feel powerless to prevent the problems.

Among top managers there is often a sense of anger that they are spending so much on computing and yet seem unable to change procedures or obtain the information they need. In one corporation with an expensive and elegant worldwide computer network, the chief executive complained bitterly that for years he had been asking for daily or even weekly figures and cash balances but seemed no nearer to obtaining these or other information he needed.

Box 3.1 lists the problems of computing as seen by users and management.

BOX 3.1   Problems of computing as seen by users and management.

- Users cannot obtain applications when they want them. There is often a delay of years.
- It is difficult or impossible to obtain changes that management needs in a reasonable amount of time.
- The programs have errors in them or sometimes do not work.
- Systems delivered often do not match the true user requirements.
- It is difficult to understand DP and communicate precise requirements.
- Specifications, on which users have to sign off, are difficult to check.
- Systems cost much more to develop and to maintain than anticipated.
- Because of the long time required to obtain results, the most important decision-support systems are never implemented. The support is needed more quickly than the time needed to create the programs.

The computer is the most flexible machine invented, capable of a staggering diversity of applications. It is rapidly dropping in cost, and its power needs to be used as fully as possible for improving the efficiency of organizations. The problem lies not in the machine itself but in the methods we use for creating applications. The traditional "application-development life cycle" is slow and rigid. Its methods have been cast in concrete in many organizations with standards and procedures. But in many ways the procedures are not working.

This inability to use computers effectively should be regarded as a major organizational problem to which solutions *must* be found. The problem has reached crisis proportions. The 4GLs, application generators, specification languages, and decision-support languages described in this book provide the basis for solutions. It is because of the perception of DP's problems that so many software companies have perceived the creation of 4GLs as a major business opportunity.

Looking at the history of technology, we can observe certain times when a major break with past methods had to occur. In computing, a set of application-development methods has been accepted and slowly refined for more than two decades. We have now reached a point when these are inhibiting the most effective uses of computers. Fundamentally different methods are needed and are coming into use. Unfortunately, many DP organizations are not adopting the new methods rapidly enough.

Steam engines made earlier in this century were beautifully intricate machines. They had numerous polished brass sliding rods, levers, and cams. Engineers had invented elaborate mechanisms for extracting a fraction of a percent extra performance. They lovingly tuned the mechanisms and held technical symposiums on steam engines long after the electric motor was in use.

Comparing FOCUS, LOTUS, EXPRESS, SQL, ADS, MAPPER, and other such languages with third-generation languages is like comparing electric motors with steam engines. The architects and maintainers of the old software are making elaborate additions that provide only minor improvements when a switch to fundamentally better mechanisms is needed.

In Victorian factories with steam engines, there were overhead shafts 100 feet long with large pulleys and belts going down to each machine tool. With electric power, each machine tool could have its own motor. But the shafts remained in many factories long after their usefulness had ended. New tools often need fundamentally new methodologies. The procedures manuals in DP are often referred to as the "bible" of DP development, and it is heresy to disobey the bible, even when new software and techniques render it hopelessly obsolete. The old DP procedures, like the steam-driven shaft and pulleys, can prevent freedom to move flexibly with the new methods.

APPLICATION
BACKLOG

In most well-managed corporations, the demand for new applications is rising faster than DP can supply them. The imbalance between demand and supply is steadily becoming worse. Because of this, the backlog of needed applications is growing. Most corporations now have a backlog of two to four years. One bank executive stated that his bank's backlog was seven years. This situation is likely to become worse as machines drop in cost, unless better methods of creating applications are found.

The long backlog and the inability of computer departments to respond to end users' needs quickly are very frustrating for the users. In some cases the users have felt that they cannot wait and have obtained their own departmental minicomputer.

INVISIBLE
BACKLOG

Even though today's application backlogs are so long, they reveal only part of the story. When the documented backlog is several years (as it is in most installations), the end users do not even consider making requests for many of the applications they need. There is thus an *invisible* backlog.

The invisible backlog cannot easily be measured. Its size is indicated in installations where end users have acquired a capability to develop their own application quickly. Such examples indicate that the invisible backlog is often larger than the documented backlog.

The Sloan Business School set out to measure the invisible application backlog in typical FORTUNE 500 corporations [1]. It concluded that in the organizations it studied, the invisible backlog was about 168 percent of the formal measured backlog. In other words, many users need applications that would be valuable to them but do not ask for them because of the DP overload.

MAINTENANCE The problems of DP and software development are made worse by the maintenance problem. The term *maintenance* is used to refer to the rewriting of old programs to make them accommodate new requirements or make them work with changed system resources. Reprogramming is often needed because separately developed programs do not fit together or because interface problems exist when data are passed from one system to another. A needed change in one program sets off a whole chain reaction of changes that have to be made to other programs.

If not consciously minimized, maintenance tends to rise as the number of programs grows. The interactions among programs grow roughly as the square of the number of programs, unless deliberately controlled.

The growing maintenance burden greatly worsens the application backlog. In many organizations, often those moving fastest into on-line and interactive systems, the ratio of maintenance activity to new application development has reached 80 percent. Large corporations often have some systems or application areas where 100 percent of the programmer effort is spent on maintenance.

The U.S. Department of Defense spent $2 billion on maintenance of software in 1983 and has estimated that this will rise to $16 billion by the end of the 1980s. The United States as a whole is spending about $30 billion per year on maintenance. It would be catastrophic if this rose by the same ratio. There are tools and techniques with which much of the maintenance cost can be avoided [2].

It is often thought by systems analysts that existing programs that work well can be left alone. In reality, the data such programs create or use are needed by other applications and are almost always needed in a slightly different form, unless thorough logical data-base analysis has been performed.

The maintenance mess has become a nightmare in some large corporations. It is alarming to reflect what it would be like 20 years from now if more and more applications and systems were added with conventional methodologies.

**THE MAGNITUDE
OF THE COBOL
PROBLEM** The quantity of COBOL programs in existence is gigantic. At the time of writing, the world has about 75,000 mainframe computer installations, and about 80 percent of them use COBOL. An average mainframe installation has about 1.5 million lines of code.

It is estimated that mainframe installations, worldwide, have about 116 billion lines of code and that about 77 billion of these are COBOL. The cost of reprogramming this amount of COBOL would be over $1 trillion U.S. [3].

Horrifyingly, about 75 percent of these COBOL programs are unstructured code. The older programs have been maintained by many programmers with different styles and often by not very skilled programmers because good programmers hate working on maintenance. This makes it difficult to convert these programs to better languages.

The magnitude of these numbers makes it clear that COBOL (and PL/I) will not disappear quickly. Many new programmers are being trained in COBOL because of the vast commitment to it.

There is no question that program maintenance and backlog, particularly the vast quantities of spaghetti code in COBOL and PL/I, are damaging the capabilities of corporations to introduce new products and services quickly and to respond to changing business conditions. It should be a problem for top management because it affects the way they do business [4].

A few enlightened corporations have come to grips, aggressively, with this huge problem. Some have banned new development in COBOL or PL/I completely, or almost completely. Some have decreed that *only* the few very high volume applications can be written in COBOL, PL/I, or, on rare occasions, assembler language.

DEVELOPMENT THAT DOES NOT WORK

Today, because of the backlog with low-level application-development techniques, many DP managers perceive the pressure from end users for applications as being excessive. In reality, however, *most end users have barely begun to realize the potential of computing for improving the way they do their job*.

The growing demand for applications and the shortage of programmers would be powerful reasons for user-created computing. There is, however, another reason that is often more powerful: In many situations, the conventional development process *does not work*.

Time and time again one hears stories of a system being cut over after years of development effort and the end users saying it is not what they want or trying it for a while and then giving up. Frequently, after using a system, laboriously created, for a few weeks, the users say they want something different.

A common reaction to this unfortunate situation is to say that the requirements were not specified thoroughly enough. So more elaborate procedures have been devised for requirements specification, sometimes resulting in voluminous documentation. But still the system has been unsatisfactory.

The fact is that many of the most important potential users of DP do not know what they want until they experience using the system. When they first experience it, many changes are needed to make them comfortable with it and to meet their *basic* requirements. Once comfortable with it, their imaginations go to work, and they think of all sorts of different functions and variations that would be useful to them. And they want these changes *immediately*.

MORE RIGOROUS SPECIFICATIONS

Many DP organizations have realized that their application-creation process is not working to the satisfaction of the users and have taken steps to correct this. Unfortunately, the steps they take often make the situation worse.

Steps are often taken to enforce more formal procedures. Application creation, it is said, must be converted from a sloppy ad hoc operation to one that follows rules, like an engineering discipline.

This formal approach can work well *if and only if* the end users' requirements can be specified in fine detail before design and coding begin. With some systems they can and with others they cannot. The requirements for missile control can be specified completely beforehand. The requirements for management information systems cannot be specified beforehand, and almost every attempt to do so has failed. The requirements change as soon as an executive starts to use his terminal.

Most commercial organizations exist in an environment of constant, dynamic, unpredictable change. The requirements for computerized procedures cannot be predicted with accuracy. Predefined specifications for some systems are about as realistic as trying to call all the plays before a football game starts.

The classical development life cycle succeeds for certain types of systems. For other types of systems, it does not work, and the attempt to enforce it makes it impossible to attain the results that are needed. The types of systems for which it does not work are becoming more common and more important in running corporations.

A more ad hoc approach is replacing the classical life cycle for certain types of computer usage. It is characterized by quick and easy building of prototypes or applications, which can be quickly modified. This requires fourth-generation languages. It relies on interactive application building at a terminal screen and step-by-step refinement of the results.

Although these methods work well for most ordinary data processing, they are not appropriate for highly complex, technical systems such as those for refinery operation, satellite image processing, air traffic control, or rocket launches. With these, a very precise requirements specification and a formal development life cycle with tight controls are needed.

It is, then, necessary to distinguish between systems that need dynamic user-driven modification of requirements after the system is initially implemented and systems that need complete, formal requirements analysis and specification before implementation. We will call these *user-driven computing* and *prespecified computing,* respectively. All application development ought to be categorized as one or the other. Each requires entirely different techniques and management. Much commercial and administrative data processing and systems oriented to human needs fall into the former category. Their development requires a technique that facilitates trial and error. Step-by-step adjustment of a prototype is desirable.

Much computing that ought to be user-driven is being developed as prespecified computing today. When the power and efficiency of 4GLs increases substantially, it is likely that user-driven methods will be employable for most (but not all) commercial data processing, rather than the long life cycle of traditional DP. The data should be analyzed, modeled, and documented. After that, there is scope for argument about what ought to be prespecified.

Both user-driven and prespecified computing need changes in the classical development life cycle. The problem with prespecified computing is that the classical life cycle is *too slow and expensive,* and the specification techniques are *insufficiently rigorous*. The problem with user-driven computing is that the old methods are *insufficiently flexible*. With most user-driven computing, the classical life cycle is hopelessly slow. Results are often needed in a day, not a year, and changes must be made quickly.

A NEW TYPE OF DP IMPLEMENTATION   What is needed to deal with these problems can now be seen in operation in some installations. It represents a new type of DP implementation. At its best it is very impressive compared with the traditional DP development cycle. Its characteristics are as follows:

- It uses the types of software in Fig. 2.1.
- The creation of most applications is *fast*.
- Applications can be modified *quickly*.
- Where possible, users create their own applications. Often a systems analyst creates the application working at a terminal with the end user much of the time.
- Where possible, users modify their own applications; again, a systems analyst working with the end user may do this.
- Conventional programs are not written without prototyping. Prototypes largely replace lengthy written requirements documents. Where possible, the prototype is converted into the application directly.
- It takes longer to create a traditional written specification than to build the application with a 4GL. The prototype therefore *becomes* the specification.
- The process is incremental and interactive, as opposed to the single "great leap forward" associated with requirements documentation and a specification freeze.
- Prototypes created with 4GLs permit reality testing with users at the earliest possible stage.

• The process usually uses data-base facilities and needs tight data administration controls with computerized tools.

MANAGEMENT INFORMATION

Perhaps the most notorious class of systems that don't work has been management information systems. In spite of repeated failures, these are one of the most important classes of data processing.

Using the traditional development approach, the MIS designer would go to managers and ask them what information they would like to have. It took long and painful experience to discover that most managers do not really know. To know what information he needs, an executive must be aware of each type of decision he will (or should) make and how he will make it. Some executives play it safe and ask for everything. Some designers have tried to provide everything on bulky reports that tend to hide rather than reveal the few pieces of information that are pertinent.

In some cases an executive with a strong personality makes firm statements about the information he or his department wants. A systems analyst at last receives a clear directive, and an unambiguous statement of requirements is created. The project life cycle then rolls on, but by the time the programming and testing are finally done, the executive in question has moved on. His replacement does not like the system. Systems that are highly personalized almost never survive the departure of the user they were created for.

Excellent management information systems have been created with 4GLs. Some 4GLs provide the capability to extract data flexibly from data bases and quickly manipulate them in all sorts of different ways. Individuals or departments can create their own view of data, do calculations on them, and generate graphics and charts. They can create summary data and also drop down into detail when necessary. Bulky, unchangeable listings are often replaced with personal computer files that can be manipulated, scrolled, and modified and permit all manner of what-if calculations.

END-USER COMPUTING

Probably the most important effect of 4GLs is that they have given rise to computing by end users as opposed to computing by DP professionals. Historians in the twenty-first century, looking back at the extraordinary evolution of computing, a technology destined to change the entire future of mankind, may comment that a step in that evolution more important than the invention of the transistor was the coming of languages that enabled ordinary people to put computers to work. The users, expert at their own discipline or knowledgeable about their own problems, learned how to invent the computer applications that could help them best.

Even in the distant future, only a portion of computing will be performed by end users; certain types of application building will need DP professionals. However, the early experience of giving users the capability to build their own applications has revealed a huge pent-up demand for computer usage that is not being met by traditional DP. Some corporations have built departments called *information centers* to encourage and manage user computing, with the objective that this will lessen the DP backlog; in fact, the DP backlog has remained about the same because the users have put the new software to work on entirely different applications.

Users have much need for information and tools to help them make better decisions. Certain users need to do complex calculations; others need to do simple calculations on masses of data. Most have departmental or personal data that need to be better organized.

SPREADSHEET TOOLS

Perhaps no software product has had more effect on making users employ computers directly than VISI-CALC, LOTUS 1-2-3, and other spreadsheet tools. These are relatively simple decision-support tools. They enable a user to build his own files and manipulate the data in them. This activity takes place at a screen with a captivating, user-friendly dialogue. The data are perceived as being on large, two-dimensional work sheets, and the user can scroll the data past windows. He can use several windows, with the data scrolling linked or not linked so that parts of the work sheets can be aligned and compared. The user can enter calculations and formulas for manipulating the data. As one value is changed, the related values change automatically. Spreadsheet tools were originally created for business calculations but have found many uses among engineers, scientists, and architects and in many types of planning activities.

The user can employ the spreadsheets to represent future values of data. He can explore the effects of different assumptions and conditions. He can analyze data with ease in many different ways and plot or print the results. He can sort the data into columns or rows and can link different spreadsheets together.

Spreadsheet tools operate on personal computers, and for many business people they have become the predominant reason for employing personal computers.

These tools provide an excellent way of reporting complex information. Executives at all levels ought to ask for LOTUS-like reports rather than paper listings or terminal access to files. They can then explore the data, summarize and plot it as they want, ask what-if questions, and investigate the effect of different assumptions. They do not spend their time building and formatting the original report, but they can manipulate it quickly and powerfully. They can take the floppy disk home and explore it at their leisure. There is a world of difference between paper listings and spreadsheet disks.

Spreadsheet reports provide a tool for improving communication in business. Different users can have the same representations of complex data, can use the same windows, can modify the data or try what-if calculations, and can discuss their modifications. Large screen displays of the data can be manipulated in meetings. Such tools can improve the understanding of important data throughout an enterprise.

EXTRACTORS

The user with a personal or departmental decision-support facility often needs to extract data from central files or data bases into his own facility. The *extractor* is an important tool for this purpose.

Extractors work in various ways. Sometimes data are moved from a production system to the user system at night in a batch fashion. Sometimes the user can ask for data when he wants it, on-line, with an extractor language. The extractor language can be similar to a report-generator language. He asks for certain fields to be loaded into his own files or spreadsheet facility. Appropriate heading information from a dictionary may be loaded with them.

Sometimes extractors and decision-support tools with compatible syntax are provided as part of application packages that perform routine applications. Business application packages today *ought* to be linked to tools for user–decision makers.

PERSONAL VERSUS SHARED USER COMPUTING

It is important to divide user computing into that which is purely personal and that which is shared. In purely personal computing, the user develops his own tools or filing system for his own purposes. Nobody else uses them except perhaps close associates. There is no need to develop documentation for other uses or conform to the rules of data administrators or DP standards.

Shared computing relates to an environment in which the application is used by other people, is possibly modified or maintained by others, or creates data that are used elsewhere. In some corporations, shared applications are created by end users (as well as DP), and this has proved extremely valuable.

Figure 3.2 illustrates the distinction between personal and shared end-user computing. Much important computing is purely personal. The penetration of effective use of personal computing is only a minute fraction of what it ought to be.

Shared computing needs careful attention to documentation, usability, maintenance, testing, and integrity controls, as well as data administration controls. The software should be selected to facilitate these controls. Some 4GLs are largely self-documenting and encourage the application creator to add on-line comments and HELP displays. Some are designed to employ a data diction-ary or link into a major data-base management system with data administration controls. Some employ an *encyclopedia,* which both helps to speed up applica-tion creation and is designed to provide important controls.

Some 4GLs are good for maintenance and some are not. If a language is good for maintenance, it is possible to read somebody else's code and under-stand it readily so that it is easy to modify. When it is modified, all the *conse-quential* changes that ought to be made as a result of that modification should be clear and, where possible, made automatically. LOTUS and other spread-sheet software automatically propagates the effects of changing a cell or formula

Is more than one person involved in creating the application?		
Yes: Team project controls are needed.		**No**
Will other persons use the application?		
Yes: Documentation for use should be created		**No**
Will other persons modify the application?		
Yes: Documentation for maintenance should be created.		**No**
Does the application create data that are used elsewhere?		
Yes: The data administrator should examine the controls on data validity, accuracy, security, and auditability.		**No**
Has the answer to any of the above questions been yes?		
Yes External controls are needed.	**No** **Purely personal computing**	
	Does the application *use* data from elsewhere?	
	Yes The developer should employ the data administrator's model and dictionary if appropriate.	**No**

Figure 3.2   The important distinction between purely personal computing and shared end-user computing.

to other affected cells. When a logic or data change is made with USE.IT, the software highlights all the items that ought to be changed as a consequence. This highlighting of consequent changes is complex, and much 4GL software does not do it.

Many end users write complex personal programs that are neither documented nor designed for other people to maintain but are very valuable tools. If these users leave the organization, their programs leave with them; other staff cannot use them. Some such programs *ought* to be used by others. This raises the question of how to manage personal computing.

**OPERATIONS
SYSTEMS
BUILT BY
END USERS**

Although most user computing is designed to assist in personal or departmental decision making, filing, and calculations, some end users have built systems for routine operations to handle the basic data entry and processing of a business. One of the most spectacular examples of this took place at the Santa Fe Railroad.

The Santa Fe was a U.S. railroad with 12,000 route miles of track, nearly 2000 locomotives, 66,500 cars, and 34,000 employees. (It has since merged with Southern Pacific.) In the 1970s its ''piggyback'' operations were growing rapidly. This involves the loading of highway truck trailers on to railroad flatcars so that the trailers are sent by train. It saves fuel over highway cartage. To obtain this lucrative business, the railroad has to provide consistently excellent service; otherwise, the traffic will revert to highway transport.

Piggyback service generates blizzards of paperwork. The Corwith yard at Chicago is the world's largest piggyback facility, and the paperwork was becoming catastrophically out of control. Corwith is not much smaller than the world's giant container-shipping terminals like Rotterdam or San Francisco. Trains leave every 50 minutes at the peak period, and there is often as little as an hour between the arrival of the trailer at the checkpoint and the departure of the train. It was almost physically impossible to type 100 bills in that hour. Waybills had to be sent by teletype to a central computer at Topeka, Kansas. Waybills from Chicago often arrived at the computer center barely hours before the train arrived at Los Angeles or San Francisco.

The bills of lading had to be matched to the movement waybills after the train left. A clerk might be processing the bill of lading while a clerk at the next desk had the movement waybill, but the two clerks would not make the proper paperwork connection. The indexing and location process had become overwhelming. Because of paperwork delays the railroad was receiving large fines from the Interstate Commerce Commission for incorrectly assessing charges for storage of trailers.

The traffic was growing rapidly. It was clear that other yards would soon have problems as bad as those at Corwith. Adding more clerks worsened the difficulty of matching up the huge stacks of paper.

While Corwith was drowning in paperwork, DP was drowning in programming problems. A new ultramodern gravity-operated railroad yard was being built at Barstow in California to operate under full computer control. The huge cost of this dictated that the Santa Fe's information system department dedicated almost everybody to having its programs working on time. Traditional analysis and programming techniques were being used. The information system department, like many others, had its hands more than full.

Corwith formed a crisis committee, the OX ("operations expeditor") committee to deal with its problems. There were four staff members on the committee:

- An accountant
- A person in the freight train operations section with an operations research background but no DP experience
- A management trainee
- The head clerical supervisor at Corwith

The first two of this group had been looking at some new software from Univac called MAPPER, which at that time was in a very early stage of development. MAPPER is an on-line system that allows its users to create files, reports, and processing procedures at display terminals. MAPPER employs a relational data base, which can be thought of by the end users as a set of electronic filing cabinets. The users can design the files and data-entry screens; merge, sort, and search the data; do calculations; and generate reports and print-outs.

The Santa Fe used only IBM computers in those days, and the information system department could see no reason to take on a then unproven software system based on a revolutionary concept on a strange vendor's equipment. So the end-user group received opposition and no support. They obtained the cheapest possible computer that would run MAPPER, a used 1106. They were on their own!

The first application built by this user group was a billing system. It slowed the billing down too much during the critical peak period, so after five days it was abandoned, and the clerks reverted to the old manual system.

Univac made some software modifications. Disasters such as deadly embraces in core had to be avoided. The system designers worked on a better way to handle file updates. The clerks were given better training. And a second attempt at cutover was made five weeks after the first. This time it worked, and the manual billing typewriters were stored away in the basement for good!

That was the beginning of what was to become one of the world's spectacular DP success stories. Almost every clerical function in Corwith was computerized in 17 months by an end-user team of never more than four full-time people. None of these users had had any previous DP experience. Meanwhile, at the new yard at Barstow, 20 full-time professional programmers worked for two years to complete only one system of the many developed at Corwith, the yard system.

The Corwith applications were spread to many other railroad yards across the country. Other end users, observing the success, developed ways of solving their problems also with MAPPER. A variety of management reports was generated. Marketing staff had to produce a sourcebook each year for sales people in the field, showing Santa Fe's largest customers, what they ship, where the volume is growing or shrinking, and so on. This used to be a three-month project on word processors, running to several hundred pages. The users learned how to do it on MAPPER, and now the project takes about a week.

A few years after the start of this story, the system used about 2000 visual display terminals and 800 printers. It processes about 60 million inputs and outputs and 600 million report lines per day. Users initiate 420,000 runs per day. At the peak it handles about 100 transactions per second.

The error rate on waybill keying at Corwith dropped from 3 percent to 0.2 percent (one-fifteen the previous rate). The system had terminal microcomputers added so that vital functions stayed in operation when there was a mainframe or telecommunications failure.

The applications developed by end users (at the time of writing) consumed six of Univac's largest mainframes, the 1100/82, and many terminal microcomputers, whereas the applications created by the information systems department consumed one IBM 3033 and one Andahl V8.

The freight handled at Corwith doubled in the years after the applications there came on-line, and there were *no* increases in administrative staff. The railroads standard measure of productivity is revenue ton-miles employee-hour. For the five years before the system was implemented, this index rose by 13 percent; for the five years after the implementation, it rose by 28 percent. A large part of this improvement was due to the user-developed applications. A Wall Street analyst stated in his research report that the system had in effect added $1.50 to the value of each share.

CREATIVITY

There are many other examples of users solving their own problems with 4GLs. They differ greatly in their nature. Many are complex, interesting, and different from conventional DP.

Many of the major examples of user computing have been stories of rebellion. As in the Santa Fe case, such breakthroughs would not have occurred by following the DP guidelines, just as the electric motor would never have come from the steam-engine industry. More new, interesting uses of technology grow in environments where entrepreneurship is encouraged and the rebels are not suppressed. Rebels, entrepreneurs, and inventors often seem naive to the establishment. Large-company development staffs laughed at Jobs and Wasniac when they first built the Apple computer in their garage. Anderson and Sheppard, the originators of the Santa Fe project, say that it happened because they were too naive about DP to know that what they did was supposed to be impossible.

Creativity tends to happen, then, when we set free the rebels. However, the creative urge needs much help. Invention is 1 percent inspiration, 99 percent perspiration. End users who want to use computers to solve their own problems need training, help, budgets, and tools. When they create something large, as at Santa Fe, they need professional design of the hardware configuration, networks, data bases, and so on. End users can make all sorts of mistakes when they create systems—sometimes expensive mistakes. Much of what was built at the Santa Fe railroad needed to be rebuilt completely.

To deal with these concerns, a creative partnership is needed. Users should be encouraged to devise solutions to their problems, and DP professionals should help to engineer the solutions to be efficient and really work.

INFORMATION CENTERS

The primary vehicle for managing this creative partnership is commonly called the *information center*. (Some organizations have different names for it.) The growth of information centers is the most vigorous new trend in DP management.

An information center is a facility designed to encourage, train, and support end users who use computers directly, generating reports or creating applications. At the same time, the information center should manage user-driven computing to avoid its many potential problems.

Both the languages used and the types of applications differ greatly. Some users employ only data-base query languages; others do highly sophisticated computing, such as financial modeling, with languages like APL. Some users put computers to work entirely on their own; others need substantial help from the information center consultants.

The overriding objective of information center management is to speed up the creation of applications that end users require. The queue for conventional development, with its long application backlog, is *bypassed*. Users can extract data from data bases and manipulate them with a variety of decision-support tools.

One DP department was required to calculate the return on investment of all DP-developed applications. The average was 37 percent, with an average payback period of 30 months. This same DP department created an information center. This gave 100 percent return on investment [1]. A large firm in Chicago quoted a return on investment of 300 percent on its information center activities. The reason for these high figures is that the users are tackling problems that have a direct impact on cost or revenue—for example, making better financial decisions, making optimal purchases of bulk chemicals, or maximizing the goods that can be handled with given resources.

Most information centers employ terminals connected to mainframe computers. Increasingly, they are likely to employ personal computers. The information center seems to be the ideal vehicle for encouraging the spread of personal computers, making them as valuable as possible, and managing their selection and use. To be fully useful, most personal computers in corporations need to be linked to mainframe data bases with a good *data-extractor* language and need to employ 4GLs.

Some information centers adopt the strategy that the information center staff members help users but never develop applications themselves; only the users develop applications. Others encourage a do-it-yourself attitude but do build applications for important end users who do not have the time to do so themselves. The latter application building is usually fast and done hand in hand with users. The best information centers have a team of highly skilled professionals who can move very fast to create applications.

THE NEED FOR MANAGEMENT

When end users first start to create applications for themselves, and they need much training, handholding, encouragement, and comforting. Too often they give up because they were not helped appropriately or did not have access to the data and tools most useful to them.

In general, end-user computing needs management. Without help, training, and controls, all kinds of problems can develop. The information center is the management vehicle for user computing. The reasons we need such management are as follows:

- To assist and support the users through the start-up period
- To ensure that users have access to the data and tools most useful to them
- To help users develop applications as efficiently as possible
- To help avoid the numerous types of mistakes that users can make
- To spread the culture of user computing so that it reaches its full potential
- To ensure that data entered or maintained by the users are employed to their full potential rather than being in isolated personal electronic filing cabinets
- To ensure that adequate accuracy controls on data are used
- To avoid unnecessary redundancy in application creation
- To avoid integrity problems caused by repeated updating of data
- To ensure that the systems built are auditable and secure, where necessary
- To link the end-user activities into the data administration process

The information center concept should support a natural division of labor between the end users and the DP staff. Each group provides what it is best equipped for. The end users know what information, reports, and decision support they need to do their jobs well, and usually they need results quickly. The DP support group knows how these results can be obtained. The two groups work together in a close partnership, balancing their resources for maximum productivity.

Information center management is discussed in more detail elsewhere [4].

A WALL BETWEEN   The traditional techniques for application develop-
USER AND   ment tend to build a wall between the application
PROGRAMMER   *user* and the application *creator*. The programmer is
                       kept away from the end user.
The formal development life cycle requires written specifications to be created. This takes much time but is rarely adequate.

The specifications must be *frozen* at the start of the design and coding phase. Often they are frozen when the ideas about what the system ought to do are still fluid. The user often does not know what he wants until he sees it on a terminal and uses it. This is becoming increasingly so as we move to more complex applications. We have now done the simple, easily standardized applications—payroll, invoicing, and the like—and are faced with more subtle and valuable applications such as decision-support systems, operations control, and financial planning. With these applications, a rapid rate of adjustment is needed as the end users begin to change their methods of working. With many such applications, *prototypes* should be created quickly to see if the users like them. The prototypes should be rapidly changeable.

In this environment it is vital that the application creator work hand in hand with the application user. The systems analyst who learns to understand the user's needs should himself create the application and work with the user to adjust it interactively. For most applications this can be done with the new software for generating applications, graphics, reports, and data-base queries.

Programming in languages like COBOL or PL/I takes a long time. The programmer must document his code. In typical installations that are well controlled with a development standards manual, there are about ten pages of program documentation for each 1000 lines of code. In some installations, documentation never gets done. Often a production line is established for use of programmers. Jobs for coding wait in a queue until a programmer is free. This maximizes the use of programmers—the scarcest resource—but further adds to the overall elapsed time.

The user sees a multiyear delay before work starts on the application he needs. The time between specifying requirements and obtaining results is so long that during this time the requirements have changed. Many end users, now beginning to understand what computers could do for them, do not formally notify DP of their need because of overload on DP and the multiyear backlog.

The DP creation process is further slowed down by errors that have to be corrected. Most of the errors are in requirements analysis or interpretation, specification, and design.

Errors in analysis become less of a problem when the analysts can create the applications themselves, quickly, and show them to the end users. Relatively fast end-user feedback enables the analysts to make adjustments while they are still familiar with what they created. This fast cycle of application creation and feedback, using the new application-generation software, makes prototyping and adjustment a natural procedure.

Program bugs are reduced by the move to 4GLs. Errors are also reduced by removing, where possible, the traditional interaction between systems analyst and programmer. Too often the analyst's program specifications are misinterpreted. When the analyst creates the application directly, this cause of errors is removed.

To build this wall between application user and application creator is the worst thing we could do. It is becoming more serious as we evolve to more user-driven applications. New methods of application creation are vital to the future of the computer industry.

CHANGING THE DEVELOPMENT LIFE CYCLE

The uses of 4GLs change the traditional application development life cycle. The life cycle is illustrated in Fig. 3.3. Various organizations have their own version of it; Fig. 3.4 shows one of these.

Formal management of system development requires that certain documents be created and reviews be conducted at each stage. The phases of the life cycle are decomposed into subcycles and checklists. These components of the cycle are important for telling development staff members what to do, giving them guidelines, and ensuring that nothing important is forgotten.

Management standards associated with the traditional life cycle have acquired the force of law in many organizations. And yet there are obviously great problems associated with the traditional life cycle.

The historical life cycle grew up before the following tools and techniques existed:

- Nonprocedural languages
- Techniques that generate program code automatically
- Computable specification languages
- Rigorous verification techniques
- On-line graphics tools for design

- Formal data-modeling tools
- Strategic data planning techniques
- Information engineering
- Languages for rapid prototyping
- Languages for end users
- Distributed processing and microcomputers
- The information center concept

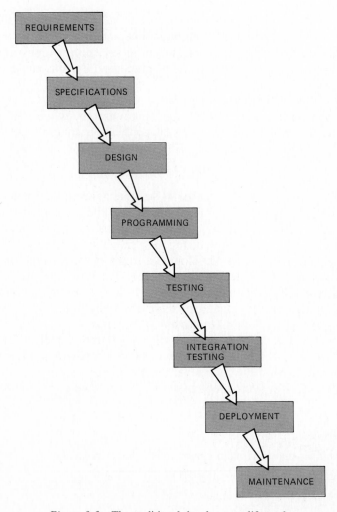

Figure 3.3　The traditional development life cycle.

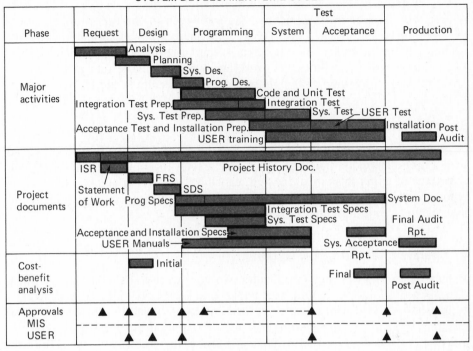

Figure 3.4 A system development life cycle in a commercial organization.

All of these tools and techniques have a major impact on the effectiveness of computer usage. Any one of them would change the historical life cycle. At each stage the life cycle needs to be reexamined to *maximize the degree of automation* of systems engineering; *build in thorough data modeling,* which is often independent of specific projects; ensure flexibility so that systems can be *easily changed* when necessary, employing prototyping to ensure that user needs are understood, and provide end users with facilities for *extracting* and themselves *manipulating* the information they need.

TYPES OF LIFE CYCLE

Several types of life cycle are found in use with 4GLs:

1. Ad Hoc System

Users or analysts extract data or create data and manipulate them, do calculations, build spreadsheets, and so on. There is no requirements analysis or written specifications. Such systems are maintained, if at all, by the creator. There is no formal life cycle. Much valuable user-driven computing is done this way.

2. Prototype Cycle

A prototype is built by systems analysts and given to the users to use. Users reactions to the prototype cause the systems analysts to modify it. Numerous versions of the prototype may be created until the users are satisfied with it. The prototype then becomes the working system, and the analysts may improve its documentation (preferably on-line documentation) and training aids.

3. Prototype-3GL Cycle

A prototype is created and refined as in case 2, but it then is reprogrammed with a third-generation language to achieve greater machine efficiency. The disadvantage of doing this is that the 4GL capability of making quick modifications is lost. We would prefer to have a 4GL with an optimizing compiler and a database or file system designed for machine efficiency.

4. Specification and 4GL Cycle

Requirements analysis and specification writing are done as with the traditional development life cycle, but the executable code is created with a code generator. This pattern is used with complex systems where very careful attention to specifications is required, as would be the case with a highly integrated manufacturing system, for example. For machine efficiency, the 4GL may be used for only part of the system, or two types of 4GL may be used, one that provides tight coding and one that provides flexibility of output. Two such 4GLs were used in creating the Xerox Manufacturing System illustrated in Fig. 2.2, for example.

5. Specification-Language Cycle

The disadvantage of case 4 is that manual specifications are usually inconsistent, ambiguous, incomplete, and prone to misinterpretation. A specification language that enforces rigor in the specifications may be used. The specification language should be computable and have a code generator. HOS software is an example of this [5].

To all of these patterns of life cycle we can add a further important consideration. Has data modeling been done before the cycle begins? In the fourth-generation environment, it is highly advantageous to have thorough data administration. The data administrator maintains a dictionary and data model describing the data used in the organization. Automated tools are used for building the data model. Subsets of the data are extracted for individual projects.

In an enterprise with good data administration, the developers of individual projects are relieved of the work of designing their data. This speeds up the project, gives precise communication about data between different developers, and ensures that data can be exchanged among different systems. Some enterprises have achieved excellent data administration. Others seem emotionally or organizationally incapable of achieving it, and this lack damages their overall usage of information systems.

It is clear that there is no longer one formal type of system development life cycle. There are different types of life cycle suitable for different types of development methodologies and tools. At the start of a major project, it is desirable to sketch out the life cycle appropriate to the methodologies and tools selected.

INFORMATION ENGINEERING

The term *information engineering* is used to describe the combination of data modeling and the use of 4GLs to build a computerized enterprise. Figure 3.5 illustrates the building blocks of information engineering—a set of integrated methodologies that need computerized tools and that ought to form the basis of fourth-generation standards and procedures for DP. A detailed description of this can be found elsewhere [6].

DIFFICULTIES OF UNLEARNING THE OLD METHODS

One factor about the powerful new languages and techniques is slightly alarming for the DP professional: New graduates often learn and become skilled with the new techniques faster than many established programmers. This phenomenon has been observed and measured with many application generators and 4GLs. IBM uses ADF extensively for its own internal DP development. It has measured the performance of many ADF users and discovered that new graduates do much better, on average, than experienced programmers. National CSS staff members sometimes refer to the NOMAD programs written by old COBOL programmers as "NOBOL" programs. The COBOL programmers, thinking in COBOL-like terms, fail to use the powerful but different constructs in the NOMAD language. Higher Order Software, Inc., has had certain non-DP persons achieve startlingly fast results in generating provably correct programs, while experienced programmers often describe the technique as user-unfriendly because their hard-learned experience of loops, branches, debugging techniques, and so forth does not apply to the new tool.

The new development software requires a new way of thinking about systems. The established programmer or analyst has to do much *unlearning* of his current thought patterns. Some 4GL vendors even comment that *arts* graduates learn to obtain results with their languages with less trouble than *computer science* graduates.

However, the established programmer or analyst does have much experience that is valuable, so he is challenged to put his knowledge to work with a methodology that will make him far more powerful. He needs to set aside his

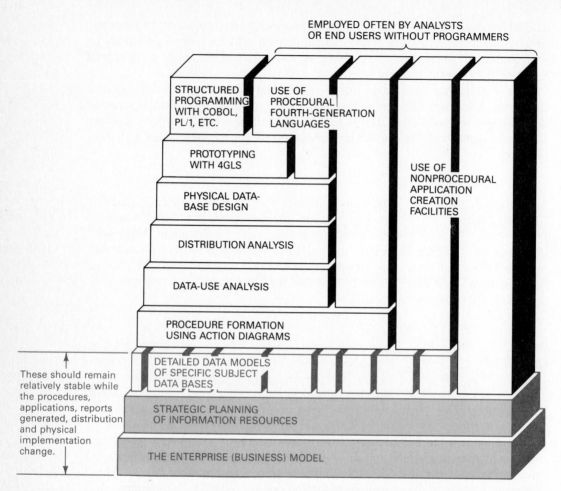

Figure 3.5 Information engineering [6]. Modern methodologies for DP management need information resource planning with sound modeling, data administration, and the full use of 4GLs.

hard-learned preconceptions about systems design and think about the future. The new techniques are easier than conventional programming once one is familiar with them.

Programmers should think about their career and determine to make themselves as powerful as possible with the new techniques. This needs a commitment to a substantial amount of learning. Some of the best programmers of new languages like RAMIS and FOCUS have been ex–COBOL coders who have thoroughly learned the new techniques. Their previous experience gives them a broader understanding than newcomers, which enables them to avoid mistakes.

When organizations first try out application generators or new types of application-development software, they should be aware of the culture-shock phenomenon and the difficulty that experienced programmers and analysts have in unlearning old techniques. For the new types of development, an organization should select employees who have the ingenuity to adapt to new techniques quickly and employ new graduates, perhaps from a business school, to work with them.

The change in DP culture, then, can be most quickly brought about by setting up separate channels of development employing many new graduates who are strongly motivated to learn the new techniques and obtain results with them as fast as possible. These new channels should be managed by highly innovative DP professionals who can understand the new methods, make them work, and be aware of their dangers. The information center is often managed as an entirely separate channel of DP development. Sometimes another separate group is set up to create non-user-driven computing. This has been given names like Advanced Technology Group and has built impressive expertise with ADF, USE.IT, MANTIS, and other tools that are designed for DP professionals rather than for an information center environment.

SUMMARY　　　　　　　　Box 3.2 summarizes the uses of 4GLs and indicates where more information can be obtained.

REFERENCES

1. R. B. Rosenberger, *The Information Center,* SHARE Proceedings No. 56, Session M372, SHARE, Inc., New York, March 1981.

2. J. Martin and C. McClure, *Software Maintenance: The Problem and Its Solutions,* Englewood Cliffs, NJ: Prentice-Hall, Inc., 1983.

3. Information from *EDP Industry Report,* International Data Corporation.

4. J. Martin, *An Information Systems Manifesto,* Englewood Cliffs, Prentice-Hall, Inc., 1984.

5. J. Martin, *System Design from Provably Correct Constructs,* Englewood Cliffs, NJ: Prentice-Hall, Inc., 1985.

6. J. Martin and C. Finkelstein, *Information Engineering* (Savant Technical Report No. 20, Carnforth, Lancs., England: Savant Institute, 1981.

7. J. Martin, *Application Development Without Programmers,* Englewood Cliffs, NJ: Prentice-Hall, Inc., 1982.

BOX 3.2   Uses of fourth-generation languages

- Prototyping routine applications [2]
- Building routine applications (software that gives good machine performance is needed) [7]
- Prototyping management information [2]
- Building management information systems more flexible than earlier types [4]
- Making application packages more flexible and hence more practicable
- Data extractors connected to application packages to facilitate use of their data
- Personal computing
- Personal filing and administration
- Information center support [4]
- Building decision-support systems [4]
- Improving business communication (with spreadsheet disks, business graphics, etc)
- Computer-aided design
- Prototyping complex logic (e.g., with USE.IT [5])
- Generating graphic presentation materials
- Reducing maintenance costs [2]
- Making systems easy to modify. Giving faster response to user and customer requests for changes [7]

4 THE EFFECTS OF 4GLs ON DP PRODUCTIVITY

INTRODUCTION   A major reason for moving to fourth-generation languages is to improve the productivity of application building. The experience in achieving this objective is extremely varied. It varies greatly with the type of system being built, with the individuals involved and with the project management techniques used. In some cases the move to using 4GLs has given little or no productivity improvement because inappropriate management techniques are applied or because the users of the 4GL have made a mess due to lack of a design methodology.

It is common to find a 4GL program for a moderately complex system having one-fifth or one-tenth the number of lines of code that the equivalent COBOL program would have. An average COBOL programmer writes about 20 lines of code per day (that is, the total number of lines of COBOL in the final system divided by the total number of programmer-days is typically about 20, including debugging and rewriting). A typical 4GL programmer does better than this, often achieving 40 and not uncommonly 100 lines of code when measured in the same way. It is often not practical to use the same measurement, however, because the 4GL may use techniques such as filling in panels on a screen.

COBOL-TO-4GL   The COBOL-to-4GL ratio varies greatly with the na-
RATIO   ture of the application. If the application program consists mainly of generating reports, using menu screens or data-entry screens, and accessing a data base, the 4GL will do much better than COBOL. If the application consists mainly of logic—nested routines, loops, case structures, and the like—with little report, screen, and database usage, the COBOL-to-4GL ratio will be small. Writing programs for chess-playing routines, 4GLs have little effect on productivity; using an action dia-

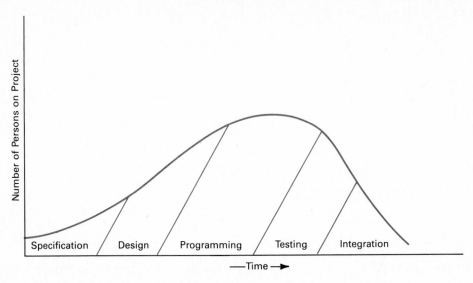

Figure 4.1   Usage of people during the typical 3GL development life cycle.

gram editor (Chapter 8) with a well-structured language such as C *does* improve productivity. Use of LISP by a person highly skilled with functional programming gives high productivity. Where very large programs are built, equivalent to about 200,000 lines of COBOL, it is extremely important to have a good design methodology and management control adapted to the 4GL use. Too often this has been missing. The design and management methodology for the 4GL may be completely different from that with traditional COBOL or PL/I development. It should include prototyping, iterative design, computerized data modeling, and computer-aided structuring.

The building of systems is traditionally done with a system development life cycle, illustrated in Fig. 3.3. The buildup of people in the traditional life cycle is as shown in Fig. 4.1.

The use of a different *programming* language affects only the programming part of the life cycle (including testing and maintenance). Its effect might be as illustrated in Fig. 4.2. This improvement is worth having, but something more than a *programming* language is needed. If the language generates reports, screens, dialogues, and data-base accesses, the improvement is greater, but much time is still needed for specification and design.

Some fourth-generation tools concentrate on the specification and design phases and generate code from the design. In order to generate code from the design, the design and specification must be precise, so more work is needed at the front end of the cycle. Figure 4.3 illustrates this. The main effort is focused on specification, prototyping, and design. The area under the curve is less than in Fig. 4.2, but there is another major advantage: The elapsed time for development is shortened substantially.

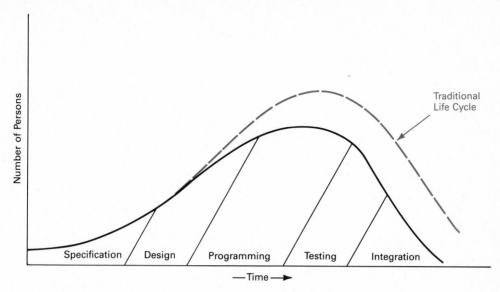

Figure 4.2 Usage of people with a 4GL that affects only the programming, testing (and maintenance) phases.

Table 4.1 Programs installed per person-month

Program Type	Using COBOL	Using ADF
Inventory locator	0.3675	20.44
Order billing	0.1365	35.11
Order processing	0.3220	11.11
Average	0.2753	22.22

In some cases an application happens to fit the techniques used in the 4GL particularly well. In this case, high production figures are likely.

Table 4.1 shows the numbers of programs installed per person-month at Playtex [1] using COBOL versus IBM's Application Development Facility (ADF), which employs an IMS data base. For the types of applications shown, this is an 80 to 1 improvement in productivity of application creation. However, there were other applications at Playtex for which ADF was not used because it did not fit the application well. ADF is less general-purpose in its capability than some other 4GLs.

While 80 to 1 improvements are found and in some cases documented, they are the exception rather than the rule. A 10 to 1 improvement over COBOL, however, is fairly typical with simple commercial DP applications.

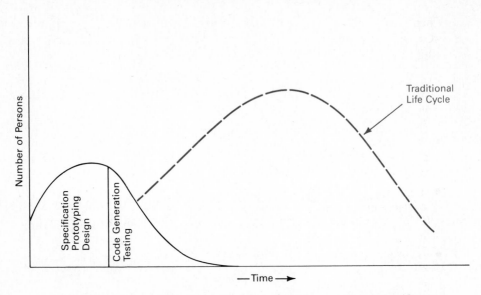

Figure 4.3   Usage of a fourth-generation tool that concentrates on specification and design, and generates code from the design.

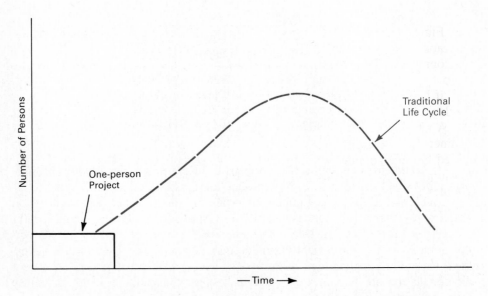

Figure 4.4   The effect of a tool that enables one person to build a system, where the system fits the design capabilities of the tool. Many relatively simple data processing applications are of this type. In many cases the one person is a bright end user working with the guidance of an information center.

There are some installations in which bad experiences have been reported with 4GLs, or few benefits in productivity. The reasons for this include the following:

- Much learning is needed to handle some 4GLs with skill. The organization has not invested the necessary money and time in building a team with sufficient skill and practice.

- Some application generators are limited in what they can generate. When applied to an inappropriate system, they can cause problems or fail to achieve the required results.

- To achieve a major reduction in development time, a major change in the management techniques and controls is needed. Sometimes controls appropriate for COBOL are used with an application generator, destroying much of its capability for fast development.

- A design methodology appropriate for the 4GL was not employed. For nontrivial systems computer-aided design is essential to achieve full productivity and maintenance benefits.

- The interactive prototyping features of the tool are not used; traditional specifications (which are usually inadequate) are insisted on, regardless of the tool.

- Some 4GLs are oversold and do not have the capabilities needed for complex systems.

Figure 4.5 shows one experience in developing systems with the fourth-generation language FOCUS in a large bank [2]. In this case, a formal system development methodology was insisted on, with formal handwritten documentation.

It is interesting to observe that in many examples of use of fourth-generation languages, the COBOL-to-4GL ratio is substantially higher than that in Fig. 4.5. A ratio of 10 to 1 is a reasonable target for most small- and medium-sized commercial DP systems. The relatively low ratio of Fig. 4.5 may have been caused by the insistence on using a methodology more appropriate for COBOL development. The bank in question had experienced problems before, when complex systems had been tackled in a casual manner with FOCUS. A formal methodology *is* needed, but one designed to condense the development life cycle in an appropriate manner.

Some persons build up a very high level of skill with a fourth-generation language and can obtain results with it very quickly. The better tools are of such a nature that a skilled person with sufficient practice can "speak the language" fluently and quickly. With an action diagram editor linked to the language, such a person can build complex program structures accurately and quickly. Some organizations have built up fast-moving teams of skilled 4GL programmer-analysts, challenging every individual to become fluent, fast, and accurate. Such organizations quote productivity ratios much better than that in Fig. 4.5.

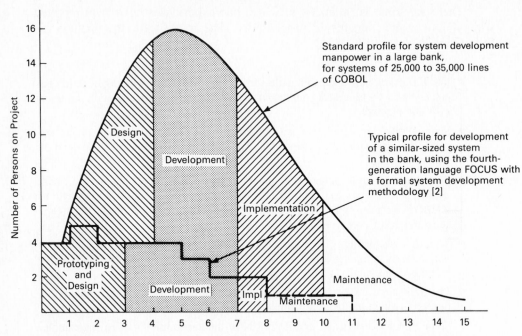

Figure 4.5   Comparison of COBOL and FOCUS development effort using a formal system development methodology.

ONE-PERSON PROJECTS

Many of the applications end users need can be generated by one person with appropriate 4GL tools. Figure 4.6 shows the person-time reduction in such a project of moderate complexity. It is usually with one-person projects that we see that largest productivity improvements from 4GLs.

Given appropriate query languages, report generators, and decision-support tools, many one-person projects can be done very quickly, compared with the 2½-month effort in Fig. 4.6. Decision-support computations are often done in a few hours. A skilled person using FOCUS, RAMIS, SAS, SYSTEM W, EXPRESS, or a similar language can generate in minutes reports and charts that would have required many days of effort with COBOL. Financial analysts build interactive applications with LOTUS 1-2-3 and other spreadsheet tools, where questions requesting data are put into some of the cells of the spreadsheet.

Many such one-person applications would not be tackled at all without the existence of fourth-generation tools. Often the one person in question is an end user, working with guidance from an information center. End users understand their own needs and, if they are skilled with appropriate tools, can create the reports and charts they need quickly and do far more elaborate business calculations than they would with pencil and calculator. One of the most important

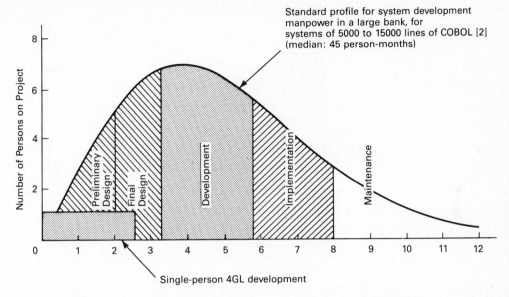

Figure 4.6 Comparison of COBOL and 4GL development effort for one-person 4GL projects of moderate size. Much one-person use of 4GLs is for much simpler report generation, queries, and decision-support functions.

effects of 4GLs is the rapid spread of computer literacy among end users. Management everywhere needs to encourage users to be creative with computers.

Systems analysts (as opposed to end users) also tackle one-person projects with fourth-generation languages, with results like those in Fig. 4.6. *DP management should seek out one-person projects wherever possible because of the productivity improvement that results.* In an environment of one-person projects, it is much more apparent which analysts are skilled and which are of limited use. The skilled ones should be trained in the use of the most powerful tools to use their capability to the fullest. The nonskilled ones are sometimes hostile to and critical of the spread of 4GL tools.

**GREAT
VARIATIONS IN
ONE-PERSON
PRODUCTIVITY**

In one-person projects, there is a great variation in 4GL productivity. This is because some individuals become much more skilled than others with their own particular 4GL.

Good programmers in any language can typically achieve ten times the results of poor programmers. Figure 4.7 shows a distribution of the productivity of programmers working with third-generation languages. A distribution with an even larger variance applies to fourth-generation languages. A brilliantly skilled implementor with a powerful 4GL and ap-

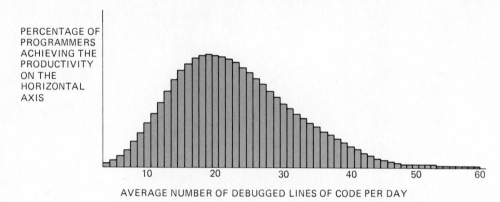

PERCENTAGE OF
PROGRAMMERS
ACHIEVING THE
PRODUCTIVITY
ON THE
HORIZONTAL
AXIS

AVERAGE NUMBER OF DEBUGGED LINES OF CODE PER DAY

Figure 4.7 Programmer productivity with traditional languages varies greatly
from one programmer to another. The best programmers are very good, but
difficult to find. Those on the left should be swung over to work with application generators rather than with programming languages. A small number
of brilliant programmers achieve results way beyond the right-hand end of this
scale. Most programmers achieve far more lines of code than this on small
stand-alone programs. The variance of productivity with powerful 4GLs is
greater than the variance with COBOL or PL/I.

propriate design tools can achieve one hundred times the productivity of an ill-
trained, casual, low-IQ implementor, who may have been reluctantly persuaded
to use the 4GL. The term *ADF acrobat* or *FOCUS acrobat* is often used to
describe persons who produce results with these languages exceptionally fast
and skillfully. Becoming fast and skilled requires thorough learning and constant
practice. It seems easier to become an acrobat with the best 4GLs and design
tools than with COBOL, so the 4GL world may have a higher acrobat ratio.

The brilliant developer often has less opportunity to display his talents or
to move in a fast, intensive fashion on large team projects. He tends to shine
on single-person or two-person projects. Single-person and two-person projects
are common with 4GLs, so outstanding performances by individuals are more
typical in the 4GL world. The good DP executive attempts to manage the 4GL
environment so as to draw out the talents of people capable of high performance.

A variety of factors affect the productivity of fast-moving 4GL developers
other than the language itself:

Subsecond Response Times

An intelligent person doing an interesting task can think and interact with a
computer screen very fast. He needs a response to his actions on the screen in
a small fraction of a second. Various studies have shown that longer response

times, such as 2 seconds, greatly slow down the rate with which the user interacts with the computer [3, 4, 5]. Subsecond response times can give double or triple the productivity of an application developer. To achieve such response times requires a personal computer workstation and/or a high-bandwidth local-area network.

In addition to the speeding up of human interaction that occurs with *subsecond* response times, the dialogue syntax can be completely changed with *decisecond* response times. This is observed on much of the software for personal computers. The improved dialogue syntax leads to faster and easier application building, as we will discuss later in the book.

Dedicated Machine

To achieve maximum productivity when building applications, the developer should have a machine to himself, or at least the appearance of a dedicated machine.

In some cases, much faster development is found in the PC environment than the mainframe environment. Some of the best developers are prone to work at their screen at any time of the day or night. It should be available when they need it. Major interruptions in machine availability can be very disruptive to the intense creative developer.

Graphics Editors

Fast interactive editors for diagrams that can be converted automatically into code structures help developers to think faster, conceptualize complex structures more clearly, make fewer errors, and be able to change structures quickly and accurately.

Data-Model Tools

Access to data dictionaries and data models designed with sound data administration removes from the developer the burden of designing data. Graphics tools can help the developer to visualize the data and navigate through it as required.

Freedom from Interference

The fast-working developer needs freedom from interruptions. In many corporate environments, his productivity is drastically reduced by telephone calls, visits from colleagues, numerous meetings, management requests, and trivia. There can be a vast difference between what a genius programmer accomplishes in this corporate environment and what he accomplishes when in an environment designed for intensive work on a dedicated machine, with freedom from telephone and managerial interruptions and with high motivation to complete interesting tasks.

TOTAL ELAPSED TIME   In some cases, the total elapsed time to create a system is more critical than the total number of person-days. An executive in charge of development centers at IBM commented that the average total elapsed time on projects with application generators was about one-third that on projects with traditional analysis and programming. This is much better than the bank experience shown in Fig. 4.5.

A RESEARCH STUDY OF 4GL EXPERIENCE   In a study at the University of Auckland, Dr. Eberhard Rudolph set out to compare the productivity of DP development in third-generation and fourth-generation languages [6]. He sought out a fourth-generation language with which there was measurable experience in building DP applications of typical complexity. The language he selected was Burroughs's LINC. He measured development experience using LINC in 11 systems in six corporations and compared this with COBOL and PL/I development of 21 systems in the same corporations. Both the third-generation and LINC systems had a complexity level ranging from about 10,000 lines of COBOL to 200,000 lines of COBOL. Figures 4.8 and 4.9 show the results. The 11 LINC applications are shown in Table 4.2.

It is difficult to find adequate measures of productivity in DP development. A common measure in the COBOL world is *number of lines of code per person-day*. With this measure, it is difficult to compare COBOL with a 4GL except by *estimating* the number of lines of COBOL code or person-days required with COBOL and comparing this with the 4GL experience. Attempts have been made to measure the size or complexity of applications independently of the language used. The most common technology-independent measure is to count the functions delivered by a program, rather than the volume or complexity of code. The *IBM Guide* user group has analyzed hundreds of programs to isolate the critical variables that determine programming productivity. Based on this research, Albrecht [7] introduced a technique called *function point evaluation*. This has been extensively used at IBM. This technique counts certain elements of a program and classifies them by three levels of complexity. A weighting factor is then applied to the total of each element. This technique measures the behavior of a program rather than its form.

Rudolph used *function points* for comparing 3GL and 4GL programs. In his study, one function point was equivalent to 114 lines of COBOL, on average, and 14 lines of LINC.

Table 4.2 shows the size of the applications, measured in function points. They range from an equivalent of 12,000 to 226,000 lines of COBOL.

Using LINC, the developers took about one hour, on average, per function point. With COBOL and PL/I, an average figure is about 20 hours per function points. Some of the most productive groups produce a function point in just

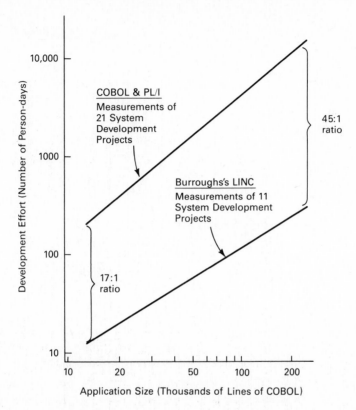

Figure 4.8 Measurements of development productivity, made by the University of Auckland, of data processing of substantial complexity, comparing COBOL development with development by DP professionals using the fourth-generation language LINC [6].

under 10 hours; some of the worst groups work for 70 hours per function point, or even more. The worst often avoid being measured.

Fosdick [8] described an application in which exceptional productivity was achieved with PL/I using sound management practices combined with modern software development tools and techniques to create an optimal IBM MVS, IMS environment. This group achieved 6 hours per function point, writing 84,000 lines of PL/I in 44 person-months (95 lines of code per person-day, on average). This exceptional PL/I effort is shown in the center of Fig. 4.9.

As shown in Fig. 4.8, the 3GL-to-4GL ratio ranged from about 17 to 1 to 45 to 1 in Rudolph's measurements. The effort per function point became greater with 3GL systems as the system size increased, because of increased interfaces between the work of separate developers. This is shown by the slope of the upper line in Fig. 4.9. The work per function point did not increase much

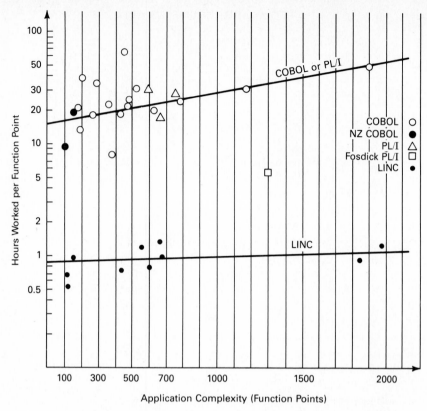

Figure 4.9 Measurements showing variation in productivity with application size for typical routine DP applications. COBOL and PL/I development is compared with that using the fourth-generation language LINC [6].

Table 4.2 The 11 LINC applications

Application	Work Needed to Develop the Application (person-hours)	Size of Application (function points)	Person-Hours per Function Point
Meat processing	495	601	0.82
Share purchase	148	149	1.0
Corporate accounting	2535	1986	1.28
Job costing	330	436	0.75
Rates	1650	1848	0.89
Work in process	660	549	1.2
Purchased material	75	110	0.68
Retail parts	660	675	0.97
Wholesale distribution	660	700	0.94
Message switching	62	117	0.53
Teller system	900	652	1.8

in LINC as the system size grew, shown by the slope of the lower line in Fig. 4.9. The most complex of the LINC systems was built by a team of two persons. The maximum LINC team size was three. Often one DP professional worked with one end user.

Unlike the environment of most information centers, the developers of the systems in Figs. 4.8 and 4.9 were mostly DP professionals. Systems analysts skilled with LINC built the system as they determined its requirements, and end users helped them. The experience described is DP-professional development rather than end-user development.

As with most 4GLs, the systems were very easy to change, compared with COBOL systems. Most modifications are made within a day.

Figure 4.10 sets into perspective some of the productivity measurements described. The upper curve shows typical COBOL productivity. With a purely procedural 4GL, the number of person-days may be reduced by a factor of 5 to 10, as shown by the second curve from the top in Fig. 4.10. The third curve shows the LINC experience described.

Good nonprocedural facilities enable users to produce reports, answer queries, and perform decision-support computations quickly, as shown by the bottom left curve in Fig. 4.10, but many such languages cannot tackle applications of typical DP complexity.

LINC is not a particularly elegant or fast language. Languages can be built with more power and much better human factoring. An appropriate mix of clean procedural code, powerful nonprocedural facilities, graphics for application design, full-screen interaction, good data-base facilities, and automatic generation of graphically oriented documentation should produce results like those indicated by the bottom right-hand curve in Fig. 4.10.

LARGE PROJECTS   Development productivity with large systems has traditionally been much lower than with small systems. Table 4.3 shows the number of lines of code per person-year for the development of systems with different size ranges [9]. These statistics relate to development in third-generation languages. The work done in these measurements includes analysis, design, coding, testing, and documentation.

The figures in Table 4.3 indicate that it is very important to subdivide large projects into relatively small autonomous modules. This is usually best accomplished by employing a centrally designed, fully normalized data model stored in a dictionary that is on-line to the developers' tools. Segments of the development activity can then proceed separately and autonomously, linked by the dictionary.

An objective of the use of fourth-generation methodologies should be to create subprojects, linked by a common dictionary or encyclopedia, and each with a relatively small number of lines of code. The subprojects should use common

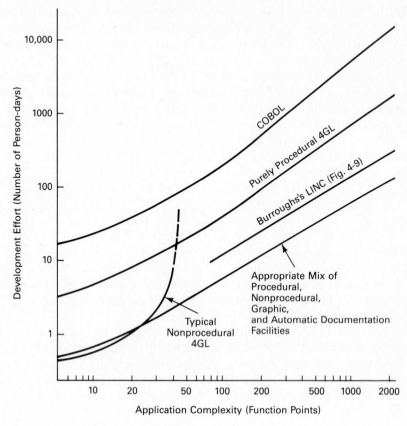

Figure 4.10

Table 4.3   Code written per person-year

Size of System	Number of Lines of Code in System	Median Number of Lines of Code Per Person-Year
Very large	Over 512,000	800
Large	64,000 to 512,000	1300
Medium	16,000 to 64,000	2000
Low to Medium	2000 to 16,000	4000
Small	500 to 2000	8000
Very small	Below 500	15,000

screen design aids, report generators, database facilities, and on-line design tools to result in commonality among the work of different developers. The subprojects should use a common action diagram editor which employs the commands of a 4GL. Where possible each subproject should be the work of one person.

A machine-efficient 4GL with an on-line dictionary and powerful design tools makes it possible to apply ''divide and conquer'' principles to large projects.

PRODUCTIVITY TOOLS AND TECHNIQUES To achieve the best results in improving productivity, more than merely a fourth-generation programming language is needed. Design tools are important, and the life cycle management must be adapted to the best uses of prototyping and information engineering techniques. Box 4.1 lists factors important for high-productivity development.

BOX 4.1   Characteristics of high-productivity development

The use of 4GLs without the adoption of the listed design and management techniques may not achieve the highest productivity possible.

- A 4GL that enforces fully structured code with the maximum use of defaults and nonprocedural functions
- Graphics tools for design automation
- An action diagram editor for specifications and procedural code
- An on-line dictionary
- A fully normalized data model
- Dedicated workstations for developers, linked to a central dictionary or encyclopedia
- Fast prototyping
- An iterative development life cycle
- Computer-aided conversion of prototypes into final code, if necessary
- Automated documentation
- A library of reusable modules

(Continued)

BOX 4.1 *(Continued)*

- One-person projects where possible
- Thorough training and practice with the tools
- Division of large programs into smaller autonomous modules linked via a data model (and possibly an encyclopedia)
- Use of preprogrammed functions or packages where possible
- Management techniques adapted to the above

CAUTION   Although the success stories with 4GLs are spectacular, there have also been many serious problems. Reports have been generated with incorrect data. Excessive machine use has occurred. Thirty-hour runs have been written without checkpoints. Chaos has grown up in the representation of data. Systems that are unauditable have been built. New types of structured techniques are important in the use of 4GLs. One information center executive in New York lamented, "I can list 200 types of mistakes that end users have made."

In some cases there have been outright failures. The attempt to develop a system with a 4GL has been abandoned and a new start made with traditional techniques.

The failures have had many causes: lack of training, lack of commitment, lack of controls, unsuitability of the new language for the application, lack of understanding of how to achieve adequate machine performance.

It requires considerable skill to select 4GLs, ensure that they are suited to a complex application, and ensure that they are used so as to give adequate machine performance. In general, a high level of professionalism is needed in guiding the use of the languages. The developers may have a low level of skill in employing a user-friendly language, but a high level of skill is needed in controlling the operation.

We need professionalism in the control and management of user computing. A vital function of the information center is to put the professionalism into place. The end users need much training and handholding in adapting to new systems. The information center consultant can work closely with the users, showing them how to employ the facilities. In some cases substantial use is made of computer-based training and videotapes [10].

It is necessary to prevent the spread of chaos in uncataloged routines and incompatible data. Given time, user-developed computing can become widespread and pervade a whole organization. Reflect on BankAmerica's 83,000 applications developed by users or the Santa Fe Railroad's use of nearly 2000 screen terminals and 800 printers handling 60 million inputs and outputs per day and you will understand that management controls on such computing are needed.

Given the need for professionalism and good management, the results shown in this chapter are a very important step forward in DP. Opposition to or ignorance of 4GLs on the part of some DP staff members and executives schooled in third-generation techniques seems grossly irresponsible.

REFERENCES

1. *IMS/VS Users Talk About Productivity and Control* (Publication No. G520-3511-0), White Plains, NY: IBM Corporation, 1980.

2. K. McGilloway, *Bankers Trust Company's Experiences and Approaches to Using Focus,* FUSE Conference, Orlando, FL, 1984.

3. *The Economic Value of Rapid Response Time,* (Form No. GE20-0752), White Plains, NY: IBM Corporation.

4. "Subsecond response time: A Way to Improve Interactive User Productivity," *IBM Systems Management Controls Newsletter (spec. ed.),* 82, no. 19 (November 1982).

5. G. N. Lambert, "A Comparative Study of System Response Time on Program Developer Productivity," *IBM Systems Journal,* 23, no.1 (1984).

6. E. E. Rudolph, *Productivity in Computer Application Development,* Auckland, New Zealand: University of Auckland, 1984.

7. A. J. Albrecht, "Measuring Application Development Productivity," Proceedings of the Joint SHARE/GUIDE/IBM Application Development Symposium, October 1979.

8. H. Fosdick, "Productivity in a Database Environment" *Datamation,* August 1982.

9. Statistics collected by T. Capers Jones, from his lectures in James Martin Seminars.

10. Videotapes and computer-based courses created by the author are available through Deltak, Inc., East/West Technological Center, 1751 West Diehl Road, Naperville, IL 60566 (Tel. 312-369-3000).

5 DIALOGUE USE IN 4GLs

INTRODUCTION Fourth-generation languages are designed mostly for interactive use. The user employs a terminal or personal computer dialogue. Some of the dialogue mechanisms are so different from traditional languages that a few language experts do not want to refer to them as languages. If you fill in a specification table on a screen, is this really a language? We find the word *language* useful for this but will avoid calling it a "programming language."

PHYSICAL APPROACH Not only have the languages changed with different stages of computer evolution, but the physical approach to the machine has changed also. The earliest computers were given instructions with binary switches in a laboratory-like environment. Later, the programmer punched his own paper tape. Many first-generation computers needed a wired panel to be plugged with colored wires, to supplement the coded program. When testing, the programmer might spend hours adjusting his program at the console. On at least one computer the programmer, testing and adjusting his program, needed a chair with wheels so that he could move at high speed from the console to the plug-wired panel and back.

With the second generation, the programmer still confronted the machine face to face when he tested his program, but now he was usually not allowed to adjust his program at the console. He might have a 15-minute debugging slot once a day. Third-generation programmers rarely saw the machine. They submitted programs to an operating staff and often received the results the next day. In the languages there was no concept of interacting with the computer. That, it was thought, would be much too expensive and inefficient.

Later, terminals began to spread, and the programmer could be on-line to the computer. Some third-generation languages were adjusted for this environment. FORTRAN, for example, was adapted to form QUIKTRAN by adding terminal control and on-line debugging facilities. The programmer could then adjust his program at a terminal as he tested it. BASIC was designed as a terminal-oriented language, intended to be simple to use and debug. APL is a more powerful interactive language.

An assumption of the APL designers was that programmers would key instructions into the terminal; hence the language was designed so that they key in a minimum number of characters. COBOL was designed with no thought of interactive programming; it is a very wordy language, in complete contrast to the conciseness of APL.

The first terminal-oriented languages were designed on the assumption that terminals would be like typewriters, capable of typing at about 15 characters per second. If the terminal is assumed to be a screen device operating on a 1200-baud (bits per second) telephone line, the language can operate differently. It can present the user screens to fill in. Languages like FOCUS and RAMIS made this assumption.

The first screen terminals were still fairly slow. At 1200 baud it often takes eight seconds to paint a screen. To this must be added the response time of the computer, which may be several seconds. If, instead, the system reacted in a tenth of a second, one would design very different dialogue techniques. The machine and person could interact with one another fast.

When personal computers came on the scene, a new generation of users became used to fast interaction. This was particularly so with young people who became hooked on video games, which often tested the user's ability to react at very high speed.

Fast-reaction mechanisms began to appear in languages for personal computers. The user could tap a key several times a second to move a bar down a menu, scroll across a large matrix, or zoom into successively more detailed panels. The machine could give him a table with many default options filled in, and he could quickly alter the choice of options where he wished. As he worked fast, perhaps looking at the keyboard, the machine might beep audibly to interrupt him. It might then signal INVALID CHOICE or KEY IN A NUMERIC VALUE or RIGHT PARENTHESIS OMITTED. The machine could display and manipulate diagrams for representing logic, program structures, or new ways of conceptualizing the design. The user could have what is, in effect, a *diagram typewriter,* where one key causes a box to appear, another displays a connector, and lines can be drawn and moved on the screen. Various icons (pictures) that have different symbolic meanings are used. Just as a word processor can manipulate text, graphics software can manipulate pictures. Names of variables, functions, control structures, and objects can be keyed into the diagram.

The early personal computers were not too fast and had little memory and limited graphics. Later ones were much faster and had fairly large main memories, substantial Winchester disks, and excellent graphics. They could store many graphic images, data dictionaries, encyclopedias, and the like and could be on-line to mainframes and data bases. To persons who learned their computing knowledge with personal computer languages like VISICALC, LOGO, and LOTUS 1-2-3, programming in COBOL seems as clumsy as doing arithmetic in Roman numerals.

The third-generation languages were mostly designed for professional programmers sitting at coding sheets. The new generation can be designed for interaction with a graphics screen with subsecond response times. There is all the difference in the world between these environments. We are entering a period of chaotic creativity in the languages for putting computers to work.

The programs created with personal computers can be compiled to run on mainframes where appropriate. Personal computers in the future will often be linked to mainframes with local area networks that give transmission speeds many times faster than telephone circuits. This will often be the application-development environment of the future.

The environment of the personal computer is itself changing. To persons who learned computing with Macintosh or Lisa, the difficult-to-remember commands of MS. DOS or UNIX seem atrocious. Such persons are used to graphics screens on which images can be moved and changed fast. Pop-on menus and easy-to-learn graphics are largely obvious in meaning and replace mnemonics and difficult syntax.

DIFFERENT MEDIA   Not all 4GLs have used screen interaction, and none of the early ones used personal computers. With some, the user filled in a form off-line; with others, he used a typewriter-like terminal.

The early versions of IBM's DMS (Development Management System, an application generator) used off-line form filling. Figure 5.1 shows an example of one of the DMS forms. The application creator fills in the form to show the image that should appear on a user's terminal screen (4 in Fig. 5.1). He shows the permissible user responses and the action the program should take to different responses (5). He shows the DL/I data-base records that are to be accessed in conjunction with this panel (2) and any display fields and files (7).

Form filling is a useful technique. Information can be conveyed to the compiler much more quickly and accurately than with a typical COBOL program. Languages of the future, however, are likely to have on-line form filling rather than off-line. With on-line operations, the computer can lead the developer through the process a step at a time, give him brief explanations, and—if he selects the HELP function (or enters "?")—give him detailed explanations. Particularly important, the computer can check the validity of each entry as it is made. It may do range and type checks, cross-reference checks, and may be able to do semantics checks, checking the logic of what is being asked for. The developer builds the panel, which the user will employ on the same type of

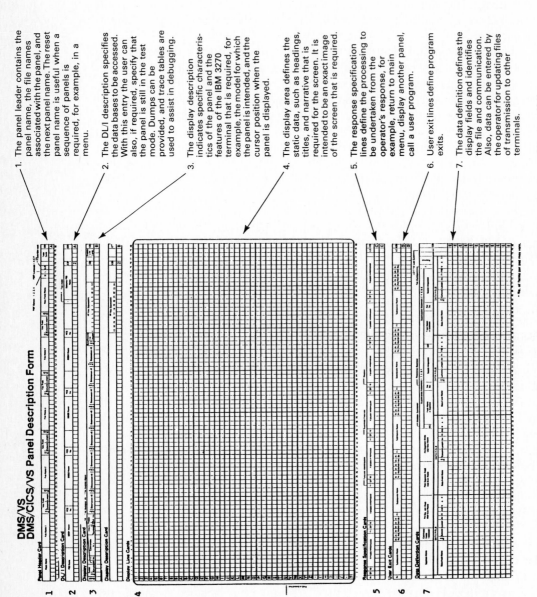

1. The panel leader contains the panel name, the file names associated with the panel, and the next panel name. The reset panel name is useful when a sequence of panels is required, for example, in a menu.

2. The DL/I description specifies the data bases to be accessed. With this entry the user can also, if required, specify that the panel is still in the test mode. Dumps can be provided, and trace tables are used to assist in debugging.

3. The display description indicates specific characteristics of the panel and the features of the IBM 3270 terminal that is required, for example, the model for which the panel is intended, and the cursor position when the panel is displayed.

4. The display area defines the static data, such as headings, titles, and narrative that is required for the screen. It is intended to be an exact image of the screen that is required.

5. The response specification lines define the processing to be undertaken from the operator's response, for example, return to main menu, display another panel, call a user program.

6. User exit lines define program exits.

7. The data definition defines the display fields and identifies the file and communication. Also, data can be entered by the operator for updating files of transmission to other terminals.

Figure 5.1 Using IBM's application generator, DMS, the application developer fills in off-line forms like this one.

screen. He can see what it looks like and adjust it. He may build tables or areas that the user scrolls up, down, left, or right with the arrow keys on the terminal:

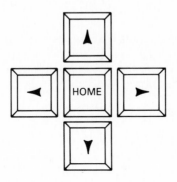

DIALOGUE ORIGINATION

When a person communicates with a computer terminal, the interaction is built from pairs of messages, each pair being a statement or question followed by a response to it. In some cases the person originates the pair; he says something and the computer responds. In other cases the computer originates the pair and the person responds. We can contrast *computer-originated* interchanges and *person-originated* interchanges. Some dialogues consist of entirely one or the other; some contain a mixture of both.

The advantage of *person-originated* interchanges is that the person can enter *anything* that the software can interpret at any time. There is a high level of flexibility. The disadvantage is that the person has to know what the software can accept and must know precisely how to format it.

The advantage of *computer-originated* interchanges is that the software can indicate to the user what he should do. It can lead the user through a sequence of steps. The user's responses are often straightforward and brief. The disadvantage may be a loss of flexibility. The user cannot enter any command at any time. The sequence of steps that constitute a computer-originated dialogue may take longer than those of a person-originated dialogue [1].

A computer-originated dialogue works far better with inexperienced users who have not learned a command language. It is normally much easier to build a user-friendly interface to the machine with a computer-initiated dialogue than with a person-initiated dialogue. The computer can prompt and guide the user in an easy-to-follow fashion.

The following is an example of careful prompting by ADT (Application Design Tool), an optional feature of DEC's language DATATRIEVE.

Software: ARE THERE ANY MORE FIELDS IN PAYROLL? (YES or NO)

User: Y

Software: WHAT DO YOU WANT TO NAME THE NEXT FIELD IN PAYROLL?

User: REVIEW-DATE

Software: WHAT IS THE QUERY ABBREVIATION FOR REVIEW-DATE?

User: REVIEW

Software: WHAT'S IN REVIEW-DATE?
              A DATE
              A PERCENT
              MONEY
              NUMBERS USED IN ARITHMETIC
              or ANYTHING ELSE (CHARACTERS)?

              ENTER ONE OF THE ABOVE

User: D

Software: FOUR DATE FORMATS ARE AVAILABLE

1	MM/DD/YY	6/29/84
2	DD-MMM-YY	29-JUN-84
3	DD-MMM-YYYY	29-JUN-1984
4	DD,MM,YY	29.06.84

              ENTER FORMAT NUMBER 1,2,3 or 4

User: 1

   This prompting dialogue is slow. An experienced person would want more abbreviated prompting or would want to enter the information directly with commands—a person-initiated dialogue.

   Much faster prompting can take place on a screen than with a typewriter-like terminal. On a screen the user may be given a table or form to fill in with many entries.

DIALOGUE DIMENSIONS

We can distinguish between one-dimensional and two-dimensional dialogues. In a one-dimensional dialogue, the participants exchange messages as they would with a typewriter-like terminal. In a two-dimensional dialogue, the user reacts to or builds a two-dimensional image on a screen. He may point to something on the screen, move a cursor or highlight bar, scroll the image, fill in parts of the image, manipulate diagrams, or in some cases zoom into an image so that a portion of it is expanded to fill the screen, and more detail is added as that happens.

It is natural and easy for humans to react to two-dimensional spaces. We are used to working with pieces of paper and diagrams. The retina of our eye is two-dimensional. It is natural to point at a two-dimensional space or fill it in, and the mechanisms for moving items on the screen are fascinating and enjoyable to use. The response time, however, must be sufficiently fast. Interaction with a screen with long response times is frustrating, like talking to a person would be if he always paused for several seconds before each conversational interaction.

With screen data entry, our sample dialogue might appear like this:

Enter the fields in the record: PAYROLL

Field name	Abbreviated name	Type of field	Length of field
		Numeric Characters Money Date Percent	

The user fills in the name and abbreviated name of a field. If the field is numeric (the most likely situation), he takes no action in the **Type of field** column. If it is a date, he would move the highlight box (edit cursor) from **Numeric** to **Date** by pressing the TAB key three times. When he selects **Date,** the following instruction appears:

Enter date format: 6/29/84   29-JUN-84   29-JUN-1984   29.06.84

If the date format is like 6/29/84 (the most likely situation), he presses the RETURN key. If not, he tabs the highlight box to the format he requires. The **Length of field** entry in this case is filled in automatically.

TWO-DIMENSIONAL QUERY AND UPDATE
Using a two-dimensional display, a table or matrix can be quickly built, filled in, recalled, and manipulated. This can provide an easy way to query, update, and manipulate data in a data base.

Consider the following situation. A report is required that lists patients in a group of hospitals who are in quarantine wards and who have had a previous stay at the hospital within one year of their present admittance. The report should look something like Fig. 5.2.

To generate the report, three records are used; HOSPITAL, WARD, and PATIENT, containing the following fields (and perhaps other fields not shown):

HOSPITAL:	HOSPNAME	ADDRESS	PHONE

WARD:	WARDNO	HOSPNAME	TOTROOMS	TOTBEDS	BEDAVAIL	WARDTYPE

PATIENT:	PATNAME	HOSPNAME	WARDNO	BED	ADMITDAT	PREVDATE	PREVHOSP	REASON

With a two-dimensional dialogue, pictures of the records can be displayed on a screen as follows:

HOSPITAL	HOSPNAME	ADDRESS	PHONE	

WARD	WARDNO	HOSPNAME	TOTROOMS	TOTBEDS	BEDAVAIL	WARDTYPE	

PATIENT	PATNAME	HOSPNAME	WARDNO	BED	ADMITDAT	PREVDATE	PREVHOSP	REASON	

The user who wants to examine data from the data base can fill in certain fields to indicate what he wants. He might fill in PATNAME to obtain details about a given patient, for example.

In this case he needs to link the three records together (in technical terms, "perform a relational join"). Using IBM's QUERY-BY-EXAMPLE, he can do this simply by putting the same underlined mark in fields that must become the same. He might join the records on hospital name by putting x in the HOSP-NAME column and join PATIENT and WARD on ward number by putting y in the WARDNO column:

HOSPITAL	HOSPNAME	ADDRESS	PHONE	
	_x			

WARD	WARDNO	HOSPNAME	TOTROOMS	TOTBEDS	BEDAVAIL	WARDTYPE	
	_y	_x					

PATIENT	PATNAME	HOSPNAME	WARDNO	BED	ADMITDAT	PREVDATE	PREVHOSP	REASON
		_x	_y					

Any entry could have been used instead of _**x** and _**y** to accomplish the join.

The user indicates that he is interested in quarantine wards by putting QUARANTINE in WARDTYPE. He indicates that he is interested in patients whose admittance date is within 365 days of their previous admittance date by putting _**d** (or any underlined value) in PREVDATE and ≤ _**d** + 365 in ADMITDAT.

HOSPITAL	HOSPNAME	ADDRESS	PHONE	
	_x			

WARD	WARDNO	HOSPNAME	TOTROOMS	TOTBEDS	BEDAVAIL	WARDTYPE	
	_y	_x				QUARANTINE	

PATIENT	PATNAME	HOSPNAME	WARDNO	BED	ADMITDAT	PREVDATE	PREVHOSP	REASON
		_x	_y		≤_d + 365	_d		

The user may now put a print indication, P., in every field that he wants printed and press the RETURN key.

The visual approach to data usage is appealing to users, easy to use, and relatively error-free. A one-dimensional dialogue for accomplishing the same result can be written with IBM's SQL, as follows:

```
SELECT HOSPNAME, ADDRESS, PHONE
FROM HOSPITAL
AND SELECT WARDNO, TOTROOMS, TOTBEDS, BEDAVAIL,
```

PREVIOUS STAY REPORT

PAGE 1

HOSPITAL NAME	HOSPITAL ADDRESS	HOSP PHONE
MAC NEAL	1234 MAIN STREET, CHICAGO IL	3125554376

WARD NO	TOT ROOMS	TOT BEDS	BEDS AVAIL	WARD TYPE
01	34	112	018	QUARANTINE

PATIENT NAME	BED	ADMIT DATE	PREV DATE	PREVIOUS HOSPITAL	PREVIOUS REASON
O'HARA	0050	062377	1176	MAC NEAL	BUBONIC PLAGUE
OZIER	0051	052177	1176	ST JOSEPH	BUBONIC PLAGUE
PARELLA	0056	052777	1076	MAC NEAL	BUBONIC PLAGUE
WRIGHT	0057	052677	1176	MAC NEAL	BUBONIC PLAGUE
YANCEY	0058	052977	0976	RIVEREDGE	BUBONIC PLAGUE
ERIN	0059	051277	1176	MAC NEAL	BUBONIC PLAGUE
KAPP	0060	061777	1076	MAC NEAL	BUBONIC PLAGUE
CLAPPER	0070	071877	1176	MAC NEAL	BUBONIC PLAGUE
LEBEN	0071	080177	1076	ST JOSEPH	BUBONIC PLAGUE
CAROL	0072	080177	1176	MAC NEAL	BUBONIC PLAGUE
JOE	0074	071777	1076	RIVEREDGE	BUBONIC PLAGUE
KATIE	0077	080177	1176	MAC NEAL	BUBONIC PLAGUE
PAT	0078	072677	1076	ST JOSEPH	BUBONIC PLAGUE
LANOU	0079	072677	1076	MAC NEAL	BUBONIC PLAGUE
ELLGLASS	0080	072277	1176	MAC NEAL	BUBONIC PLAGUE
CARLSON	0082	072177	1176	MAC NEAL	BUBONIC PLAGUE
BUHL	0090	072477	1076	MAC NEAL	BUBONIC PLAGUE

Figure 5.2 Sample page of the Previous Stay Report.

```
        WARDTYPE
        FROM WARD
        AND SELECT
        NAME, BED, ADMITDAT, PREVDATE, PREVHOSP, REASON
        FROM PATIENT
        WHERE ADMITDAT LE (PREVDATE + 365)
        AND WARD.WARDTYPE = "QUARANTINE"
        AND PATIENT.HOSPNAME = WARD.HOSPNAME
        AND PATIENT.HOSPNAME = HOSPITAL.HOSPNAME
        AND PATIENT.WARDNO = WARD.WARDNO
```

Many end users employ SQL with success, but it is used mainly for simple queries and reports. It is difficult to express convoluted queries for a complex data base with SQL, but it is much easier when graphic screen interaction is used. Psychologists Greenblatt and Waxman compared QUERY-BY-EXAM-PLE with SQL and another one-dimensional language by conducting tests on how efficiently undergraduate students used them [1]. The mean time per query was 0.9 minutes with QUERY-BY-EXAMPLE and 2.5 and 3.0 minutes with the one-dimensional languages. The accuracy of query expression was slightly better with QUERY-BY-EXAMPLE than with SQL, and the training time was somewhat shorter. Many end users do not bother to learn command languages but are highly successful in employing languages that have them react to screen images.

INTELLIGENT GRID

It is attractive to develop a dialogue on the same terminal with which it will be employed because the developer can use, test, and adjust it. Testing, using, and adjusting must go hand in hand. It greatly slows down creativity if testing and adjusting occur at separate times.

To develop a user screen, the developer may start with an empty grid. Its rows and columns are numbered. The developer may refer to a row or column with its number; for example, R17 is row 17, and C3 is column 3. A cell is the intersection of a row and a column, for example, R17C3. An area is a rectangular area of cells described by defining the top left and bottom right cell, thus, R17C3:R23C9.

The developer can designate areas of the screen and give them different properties. An area might be a literal, like a title or a dotted line. A cell might have a variable that the user can enter. It might be a derived variable that is automatically computed from other variables on the screen. As soon as the input variables are entered, the derived variable is computed and appears on the screen. This might be a simple computation like adding up a total, or it might be a complex computation involving IF clauses or references to a data base.

As the developer selects a cell, row, column, or area, he may be given a set of functions he can use for formatting it and defining its properties. He may select word processing functions for editing text. In this way he can create an invoice, a purchase order, an accountant's spreadsheet, a form letter with variables to fill in, or any other document.

He may build big arrays much larger than the screen so that both he and the user have to scroll. He may design so that when the user selects a given cell he receives a new screen, or a split screen, with a menu or formatted requests for input. The selection of a cell may trigger data-base actions.

The developer may thus create a dialogue for the users to enter their expense accounts. As they do so, the totals are automatically added and displayed. Range checks are done on the variables. If a financial value is too high, an explanation is demanded and an exception file may be created. A data base is interactively updated. The developer may be able to create this application in an hour, whereas it would have taken a month to create and debug the 600 lines of COBOL needed to do the same.

Almost all commercial data processing can be created in this interactive fashion.

FUNCTIONS

The application developer may have a choice of functions available to him. He may have this choice of functions appearing on the screen when he needs it:

FUNCTIONS: Blank Case Copy Database Delete Dialogue Edit Enter Format Help Insert Load Lock Logic Mail Math Move Name Print Quit Save Sort Text Transfer Value Window

The box or highlight is set to DIALOGUE. By pressing the SPACE BAR or the BACKSPACE key, the developer can zip it forward or backward rapidly to any function he chooses. He then presses the RETURN key. For many of the functions he may then receive a second list like the above, showing more detailed options.

SOFT KEYS

Functions that can be invoked at any time might employ the program function (PF) keys on the keyboard. These are sometimes called "soft" keys. Most keys are "hard" keys with an unchangeable label. "Soft" keys can assume different meanings at different times. Some terminals and software are designed so the PF keys are at the bottom of the screen and the labels they assume are displayed next to them on the screen. This is a flexible and easy-to-use device. Again, we see the hardware design affecting the language dialogue.

DEFAULT OPTIONS   An important principle in the design of 4GLs should be to use *default options* wherever possible. If a user has a choice of options and does not exercise this choice, the software makes the selection for him. The software's choice is called a *default option,* or simply a *default.* The term does not imply that the user has done anything wrong, merely that he is trusting the software to make a good selection.

The use of default options is important because it can enable results to be obtained quickly. The application builder does not have to spell out every detail, as he would with COBOL or PL/I. The more the software makes its own choices, the less the effort required to obtain results. We therefore want the software to exercise intelligent choices wherever it can.

At one extreme, the software may select formats, screen layouts, access mechanisms, and so on, without giving the user a choice. This is fast but inflexible. At the other extreme, the user has to tell the software everything, as in a typical COBOL program. This is flexible but slow. We can achieve both speed and flexibility if the software makes choices but allows the user to override them. There is a range of possibilities with selectable options, illustrated in Fig. 5.3.

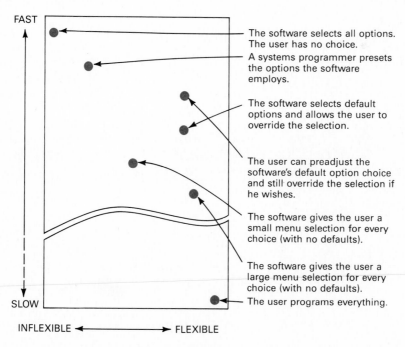

Figure 5.3 Selectable options and default options.

REPORT FORMATTING

A common example of the use of default options is in report generation. The software may format the report its own way without the user's being involved in the choice. Much of the time this is perfectly satisfactory. The user is concerned with the information on the report, and as long as it is clearly intelligible, he does not mind whether it is double-spaced, left-justified, or has dashes separating columns. In NOMAD, for example he might simply say:

```
LIST BY DEPARTMENT EMPLOYEE#
EMPLOYEE-NAME SALARY POSITION
```

The software chooses a satisfactory format for this report. The user could adjust the format, but to do so he has to know more NOMAD commands.

Figure 5.4 gives another illustration of NOMAD report generation.

In the report generator of the IDEAL language, on the other hand, the user is given a display relating to report format parameters (see Fig. 5.5). He must fill in the REPORT NAME at the top of this display. He may fill in the HEADING line near the bottom. He may fill in the TITLE for the final summary in the middle of the display. All the rest is done for him as default options, but he can change any option if he wishes. If he wants the report to have 40 lines per page, he would change 60 to 40 in the row labeled **Lines per page on printout.**

The user types:

LIST BY PRODNAME ACROSS MONTH SUM (SALES) ROWTOT TOTAL

This requests a total for each row.

This requests a total for the entire report.

The computer responds:

PROD NAME	JAN SUM $SALES PER MONTH	FEB SUM $SALES PER MONTH	MAR SUM $SALES PER MONTH	APR SUM $SALES PER MONTH	MAY SUM $SALES PER MONTH	JUN SUM $SALES PER MONTH	TOTAL SUM $SALES PER MONTH
BLIVETS	$ 651.38	$ 556.91	$ 470.10	$ 497.56	$ 576.14	$ 316.16	$ 3,068.25
JARVERS	400.68	208.59	442.18	161.11	282.21	444.48	1,939.25
LINKERS	168.23	204.12	278.08	253.55	193.95	243.36	1,341.29
WIDGETS	534.90	473.40	581.20	1,327.45	688.53	885.77	4,491.25
	$ 1,755.19	$ 1,443.02	$ 1,771.56	$ 2,239.67	$ 1,740.83	$ 1,889.77	$ 10,840.04

Figure 5.4 An example of the NOMAD LIST command using defaults. The software makes its own decision to format the report as shown and put page numbers on it.

He can then fill in a display giving details of the report, as shown in Fig. 5.6. On the left he fills in the field names that are to appear on the report as columns. If there is to be a column heading, he puts Y under COLUMN HDG. The system looks up the heading to be used in its dictionary. He may indicate a column width or tab spacing. Usually he does not do this, and a default option is selected.

He may indicate a field on which the report is to be sorted. He enters A or D in the SORT A/D column to indicate whether the sorting is in ascending or descending sequence.

If several sort fields are used, he indicates which is the primary sort field, which is secondary, and so on, as follows:

	SORT	
FIELD NAME	L A V / L D	
YEAR	1 A	
MODEL NUMBER	2 A	
CUSTOMER	3 A	

Here the software will sort on CUSTOMER within MODEL NUMBER within YEAR.

Similarly, he can indicate leveling, skipping, and indentations with the BREAK column and can state whether a total, maximum, minimum, or average is required in the FUNCTION column.

On the left he can enter literals, as well as functions or arithmetic to be performed on the data and listed.

A separate panel enables him to enter documentation about the report, and another enables him to create a heading page, with variables, if desired.

With these mechanisms a report with many possible options can be specified in minutes. The developer can then immediately examine it on the screen and adjust it to reflect his desires.

FIELD FORMATTING

A similar use of choices and default options can be used for field formatting. Using MULTIPLAN, the user may select FORMAT from a menu of commands. He is then given a second-level menu, as follows:

CELLS, DEFAULT, OPTIONS, WIDTH

CELLS has been selected by default, but he may want to specify the width

```
= >
= >
= >
```

IDEAL: RPT PARAMETERS   SYS: DOC   FILL-IN

Lines per page on printout	60	(1 thru 99)
Report width	132	(40 thru 132)
Spacing between lines	1	(1 thru 3)
Spacing between columns	2	(0 thru 66 OR A = Automatic)
Summaries only	N	(Y = Yes,N = No)
Column headings desired	Y	(Y = Yes,N = No)
Column headings indication	D	(U = Underscore, N = None,D = Dashes)
Control break heading	N	(Y = Yes,N = No)
Control break footing	Y	(Y = Yes,N = No)
Group continuation at top of page	Y	(Y = Yes,N = No)
Annotated count in control footings	N	(Y = Yes,N = No)
Report final summary title	Y	(Y = Yes,N = No)
Spacing before summary	2	(1 thru 9 = Lines,P = New Page)
Title		

Date
  Position   NO   (NO = None, BR = Bot.Right, BL = Bot.Left, BC = Bot.Ctr., TR = Top Right, TL = Top Left, TC = Top Center)
  Format   MM/DD/YY

Page Numbers
  Position   BC
  Format   H   (D = Digits only, H = with hyphens, P = PAGE   nnn)

Page Heading
  Heading
  Position   C   (C = Center, L = Left justify, R = Right justify)

Figure 5.5   A panel for filling in parameters of a report specified with the language IDEAL, from ADR. This is followed by the panel giving field names, shown in Fig 5.6.

```
=>
=>
=>
------------------------------------------------------------------------------------------------------------
IDEAL: RPT DETAIL DEFN.                                                          SYS: DOC     FILL-IN

FIELD NAME,              SORT    BREAK     FUNCTION       COLUMN
LITERAL FUNCTION,        L  A    L  S  I   T  M  M  A     H  W
OR ARITHMETIC            V  /    V  K  N   O  A  I  V     D  ID   TAB   EDIT PATTERN    COMMAND
EXPRESSION               L  D    L  P  D   T  X  N  G     G  TH
------------------------ --- --- --- --- --- --- --- --- --- --- ---- ------ ---------------- ------------
________________________ _  _    _  _  _   _  _  _  _     _  __   ___   ______________  __________
________________________ _  _    _  _  _   _  _  _  _     _  __   ___   ______________  __________
________________________ _  _    _  _  _   _  _  _  _     _  __   ___   ______________  __________
________________________ _  _    _  _  _   _  _  _  _     _  __   ___   ______________  __________
________________________ _  _    _  _  _   _  _  _  _     _  __   ___   ______________  __________
________________________ _  _    _  _  _   _  _  _  _     _  __   ___   ______________  __________
________________________ _  _    _  _  _   _  _  _  _     _  __   ___   ______________  __________
________________________ _  _    _  _  _   _  _  _  _     _  __   ___   ______________  __________
________________________ _  _    _  _  _   _  _  _  _     _  __   ___   ______________  __________
________________________ _  _    _  _  _   _  _  _  _     _  __   ___   ______________  __________
________________________ _  _    _  _  _   _  _  _  _     _  __   ___   ______________  __________
________________________ _  _    _  _  _   _  _  _  _     _  __   ___   ______________  __________
________________________ _  _    _  _  _   _  _  _  _     _  __   ___   ______________  __________
________________________ _  _    _  _  _   _  _  _  _     _  __   ___   ______________  __________
________________________ _  _    _  _  _   _  _  _  _     _  __   ___   ______________  __________
________________________ _  _    _  _  _   _  _  _  _     _  __   ___   ______________  __________
________________________ _  _    _  _  _   _  _  _  _     _  __   ___   ______________  __________
________________________ _  _    _  _  _   _  _  _  _     _  __   ___   ______________  __________
________________________ _  _    _  _  _   _  _  _  _     _  __   ___   ______________  __________
________________________ _  _    _  _  _   _  _  _  _     _  __   ___   ______________  __________
________________________ _  _    _  _  _   _  _  _  _     _  __   ___   ______________  __________
________________________ _  _    _  _  _   _  _  _  _     _  __   ___   ______________  __________
________________________ _  _    _  _  _   _  _  _  _     _  __   ___   ______________  __________
________________________ _  _    _  _  _   _  _  _  _     _  __   ___   ______________  __________
________________________ _  _    _  _  _   _  _  _  _     _  __   ___   ______________  __________
________________________ _  _    _  _  _   _  _  _  _     _  __   ___   ______________  __________
```

Figure 5.6 The second panel of the IDEAL report generator. The user names the fields to be displayed on the report and gives details of sort order, breaks, functions, etc.

of a field. He tabs the box to WIDTH and presses the return key. He then sees:

FORMAT WIDTH IN CHARS OR DEFAULT: 10 COLUMN: 16 THROUGH: 16

If he presses the RETURN key, he obtains the default width of 10 characters in column 16 (which is where the cursor was set). He may enter new digits as follows:

FORMAT WIDTH IN CHARS OR DEFAULT:7 COLUMN:16 THROUGH:20

He has now made columns 16 through 20 of width 7.

He may return to his formatting menu:

CELLS, DEFAULT, OPTIONS, WIDTH

He selects cells by pressing the RETURN key and is given the following display:

ALIGNMENT : DEF, CTR, GEN, LEFT, RIGHT, —
FORMAT CODE : DEF, CONT, EXP, FIX, GEN, INT, $, *, %, —
OF DECIMALS : 0

He may tab to ALIGNMENT and then use the SPACE BAR to move the choice box to RIGHT. He tabs to FORMAT CODE and moves the choice box to FIX. He tabs to # OF DECIMALS and changes the digit to 3:

ALIGNMENT : DEF, CTR, GEN, LEFT, RIGHT, —
FORMAT CODE : DEF, CONT, EXP, FIX, GEN, INT, $, *, %, —
OF DECIMALS : 3

The field now has a width of 7 and contains a right-justified, fixed-point number with three decimal places.

Again, the use of option choices and defaults is easy to use, gives quick results, and is free from the bugs found in traditional coding.

HIGH-LEVEL DEFAULTS

The defaults we have illustrated relate to fairly basic functions such as report formatting and field formatting. More elaborate defaults are desirable and should be used as fully as possible. The software may select file organizations and optimize the storage layout and accesses. It should make its own decisions in the use of graphics (giving impressive color charts where appropriate). It should assist in program structuring. If the analyst writes an IF, LOOP, or FOR instruction on the screen, it may automatically insert an ENDIF, ENDLOOP, or END-FOR lower on the screen. The analyst may fill in a generated program skeleton. It should automatically indent the user's code. If an analyst is creating a dialogue for the users of his application, the software may create a standard dialogue, allowing the analyst to fill it in or adjust it.

Many valuable defaults are application-oriented. A decision-support system may help the user look at data in the most appropriate way. It may automatically give a well-thought-out graphic analysis of investments, for example. The software may offer a standard format for purchase orders, invoices, and other documents. It might use preprogrammed routines for inventory control, reordering, regression analysis, and the like. It may offer standard forms of financial analysis.

Defaults such as these enable analysts and users to obtain powerful results quickly.

EFFECT OF SUBSECOND RESPONSE TIMES

The early 4GLs were almost all designed for use with simple terminals. Later 4GLs were designed for use with personal computers replacing terminals, and in some cases stand-alone personal computers. The personal computer responds in a tenth of a second when performing simple operations like menu selection, moving a window, or scrolling. A terminal on a telephone line may take two or three seconds before the response begins and then several seconds to paint the screen.

The decisecond (tenth of a second) response time of personal computers and workstations has a major effect on the choice of dialogue structures that are valuable in a 4GL.

Menus are commonly used as a basis for user-friendly dialogues. The user is presented with a list on a screen and selects an item from it. Sometimes he must choose from among thousands of possibilities, so the list is divided hierarchically. The user may look at the top block in the hierarchy first, which might have ten items on it. He selects one and sees a block of ten from the second level down. He selects one of these and sees a block from the third level down, and so on.

If the response time is measured in seconds and the screen painting is at telephone speeds, the use of hierarchies of menus can be frustratingly slow. It was common for 4GL designers to recognize this and replace the use of menus with an input where the user types a *command*. The problem with this is that the user has to know what the command is. It is sometimes a complex command with many options.

In some cases the user is given a choice. He can use menu selection when he first begins and use command entries when he becomes more expert. He might, for example, format a field by moving the cursor to it and tabbing the box on the following display to FORMAT:

FUNCTION: Copy Database Delete Edit Enter Format Help Insert
                 Load Move Print Quit Save Sort Text Transfer Value

He then receives:

FORMAT: Cells Default Options Width

He presses the enter key and receives:

ALIGNMENT: Def Ctr Left Right −
FORMAT CODE: Def Cont Exp Fix Gen Int $ * % −
OF DECIMALS: 0

Stepping through these displays would be slow with a dumb terminal, so the alternative might be to key in a command such as one of these:

FORMAT R25C16 PICTURE @#ZZZ,ZZ9.99 −
FOR R25C16 PIC @#ZZZ,ZZ9.99 −

The latter has the disadvantage that the user needs much more education and would be more likely to make mistakes. Most end users would never bother to learn the elaborate command structures. It is therefore common to distinguish between a language "designed for end users" and one "designed for DP professionals."

With decisecond response times, however, the end-user version of the dialogue can be made about as speedy as the DP-professional version. The user can skip through menus very fast.

Moving the highlight (edit cursor) to FORMAT on the following display takes about a second. The TAB key or SPACE BAR is pressed hard, and the edit cursor zips along the list.

FUNCTION: Copy Database Delete Edit Enter Format Help Insert
                 Load Move Print Quit Save Sort Text Transfer Value

He presses the RETURN key as soon as he receives the next display.

FORMAT: Cells Default Options Width

He may press the RETURN key again to select the default choices of the next display.

The entire format selection might take an experienced user two or three seconds. If the same user had to enter a command such as

FOR R25C16 PIC @#ZZZ,ZZ9.99 –

he would be likely to take many seconds, would often make mistakes, and might have to look up the command in the manual.

The ability to zip through menus or hierarchic structures at a decisecond per item makes user-friendly techniques good for the fast-moving professional as well as for the end user. In this environment the software should not force anyone to employ complex-syntax commands. The fullest use should be made of menus, command lists, high-speed scrolling, windows, a mouse, and fast, interactive graphics.

ADJUSTABLE MENUS

There are several ways in which the process of responding to menus or command lists can be speeded up. One is to use increased finger pressure on a TAB, SPACE, or arrow key so that the edit cursor zips across the menu to the required position. Another is to provide a means of skipping long lists in big jumps. The list might be arranged like a matrix, and the arrow keys permit movement up and down, left and right. Another method is to use a mouse.

When a list appears on the screen, the most likely selection may be highlighted so that often the user does not have to change the selection. He merely accepts it by pressing the RETURN key. The user may have indicated to the software what the preselected options should be.

The user may employ only a few of the many items on a menu. In this case he may tell the software to display only the ones he is interested in, greatly shortening the menus he sees and hence speeding up his menu-selection process. If he wants a menu item not displayed, he can ask for the full menu.

Menus and command lists, then, can be tailored to the user's needs with the intention of simplifying and speeding up the user's choice.

STANDARD DEFAULTS

The analysts who work with the end users may select the defaults to be used and select the menu items displayed. The choice of defaults should be made with the principle of least surprise. The user sees what he most expects to see.

The default options selected may form the basis of corporate standards. They can provide unified, hence familiar, reporting. They can provide standards for purchase orders or other documents. The choice of defaults or the tailoring of menus might, like data administration, be a central function designed to help and unify user-driven computing.

USE OF A MOUSE   Many personal computers now employ a mouse. A mouse can be added to computers that were originally designed without one. Users of IBM personal computers, for example, have added a mouse from Microsoft or elsewhere.

Using the mouse, pointers and cursor bars can be moved around a screen very rapidly. Clicking the mouse button on one menu item can instantly produce a more detailed menu. Clicking on an item from that menu can produce a still more detailed level of menu, if needed, and so on. With a little practice, a mouse user can navigate through menus and diagrams very quickly, scroll over large display spaces and so on.

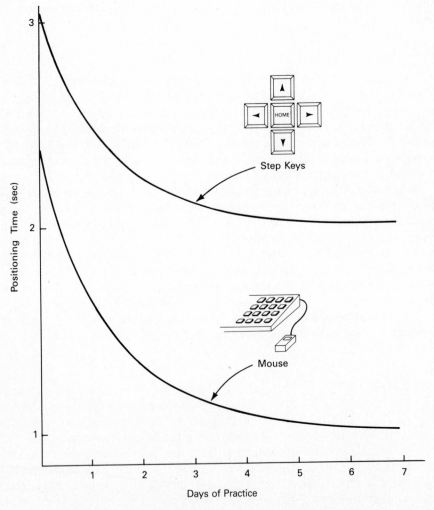

Figure 5.7   Positioning time for the movement of screen cursors [2].

A mouse is even more valuable where graphics are used. Graphics can represent logic or structure that is to be built into a 4GL program or data base. With a mouse, the user may point at part of a diagram and then display a pop-on menu or instruction panel.

Psychologists at Stanford University conducted experiments to measure users' speed in pointing at screen text with various pointing devices [2]. Figures 5.7 to 5.9 show some results from the experiments. Figure 5.7 shows performance improving with practice. The users did two to three hours of operations with the device per day. The pointing time with the mouse was substantially lower than using the keys to move the cursor.

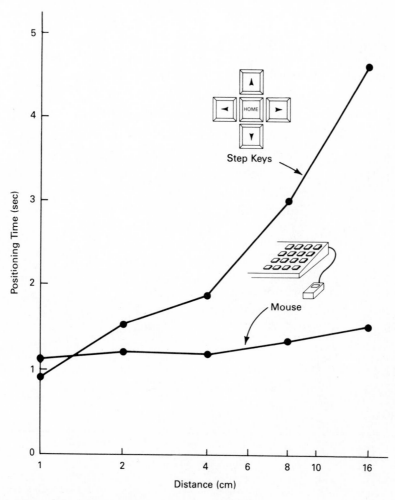

Figure 5.8   Effect of target distance on positioning time, using step keys and using a mouse [2].

The effect of distance of cursor movement on positioning time is shown in Fig. 5.8. The greater the cursor movement, the greater the advantage of using the mouse.

The error rates in positioning are shown in Fig. 5.9. The error rates are less when the target size is large. For small targets, the mouse is much better than the keyboard.

In summary, a mouse is much faster than a keyboard for manipulating large menus or diagrams, but the users do need some practice at becoming fast with a mouse. Like riding a bicycle, once users have become skilled at mouse movement, it is a skill they do not forget.

WAVES OF 4GLS

Relating to the issues we have discussed with terminals, work stations and response times, we can see several waves of 4GL development.

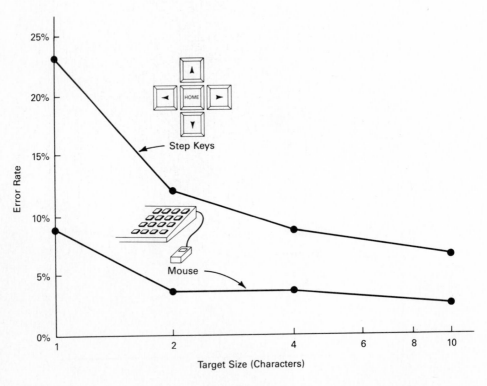

Figure 5.9 Effect of target size on error rate, using step keys and using a mouse [2].

1. *Off-line languages with which the user fills in forms*. These are generally poor compared with on-line terminal-oriented languages. Examples are MARK IV and DMS.

2. *Languages that can operate on a typewriter-like terminal* and process a character stream. Examples are NOMAD, SQL, and DATATRIEVE.

3. *Languages designed for dumb visual display units,* in which the user interacts with a two-dimensional display. This interaction permits more user-friendly dialogues than the one-dimensional dialogues that can operate on typewriter-like terminals. Examples are MAPPER, FOCUS, RAMIS, and QUERY-BY-EXAMPLE.

4. *Languages designed for the decisecond response times of personal computers or local area networks*. The subsecond response times permit the avoidance of command inputs that may be error-prone, user-threatening, or difficult to remember. Constructs such as fast windowing, fast menu skipping, and fast graphics manipulation can be used. Examples are MULTIPLAN, LOTUS, SYMPHONIE, and FRAMEWORK. This wave of 4GL development is far more effective than the earlier three in terms of making the language friendly and fast to use by a large cross section of users.

5. *Languages using graphics for program design*. The use of good diagrams can be very valuable in helping to visualize and design complex structures. Today we have graphic editors with which elaborate diagrams can be built, manipulated, and edited. These editors can run effectively on personal computers with a graphics screen and a mouse. With a graphics editor, a system designer can design the logic of his application with a computer giving him various types of help. If the diagramming technique is suitably rigorous and incorporates tools such as a screen design aid, report design aid, and data dictionary, code can be generated from the diagrams.

There are many possible variations on this theme. The technique can facilitate the building of complex systems without a complex and difficult-to-remember language syntax. It is a tool for the systems analyst equivalent to CAD/CAM tools for designer engineers.

A picture is worth a thousand words of COBOL.

USES OF ARTIFICIAL INTELLIGENCE TECHNIQUES

Work originally classed as artificial intelligence has led to software that can parse the complex grammar of English. This is used today in query languages such as INTELLECT and RAMIS ENGLISH, described in Chapter 10. To achieve more complex applications with natural English, English-language processing needs to be combined with other constructs. It is particularly appealing to combine human language processing with graphics (Chapter 11).

Artificial intelligence work has also led to rule-based systems in which rules are stored along with facts in a "knowledge base." Complex applications can be built using such rules for inference processing. Natural-language interpretation employs such a technique, the rules for interpreting grammar being stored in the knowledge base along with the vocabulary. Rule processing is a desirable enhancement to the current capability of 4GLs. It is likely that fourth-generation languages will evolve into fifth-generation tools in which inference processing, rule-based processing, knowledge bases, and natural human language play a vital role. Figure 5.10 illustrates the evolution of high-productivity languages.

SUMMARY   Both the DP analyst and the end user need a wide range of tools with a compatible syntax—tools for filing, electronic mail, office management, a calendar, intelligent spreadsheets,

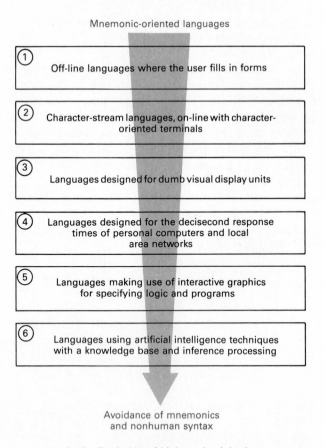

Mnemonic-oriented languages

① Off-line languages where the user fills in forms

② Character-stream languages, on-line with character-oriented terminals

③ Languages designed for dumb visual display units

④ Languages designed for the decisecond response times of personal computers and local area networks

⑤ Languages making use of interactive graphics for specifying logic and programs

⑥ Languages using artificial intelligence techniques with a knowledge base and inference processing

Avoidance of mnemonics and nonhuman syntax

Figure 5.10   Evolution of high-productivity languages.

decision support, graphics, and application creation. Some software vendors seem trapped with an earlier wave of 4GL syntax. They have languages that are mnemonic-based or more programming-like than the fast, efficient subsecond-response languages. In the future most knowledge workers will have workstations rather than dumb terminals. The workstations will give decisecond response times to noncomplex *local* operations either because they are a personal computer or because they are connected to a local computer. They will give multisecond response times to operations involving a distant computer. 4GLs, from now on, ought to be designed to reap the major advantages of decisecond screen responses, interactive graphics, and, eventually, rule-based systems and human-language processing.

REFERENCES

1. D. Greenblatt and J. Waxman, "A Study of Three Database Query Languages," in B. Shneiderman, *Databases: Improving Usability and Responsiveness,* New York: Academic Press, 1978.

2. S. K. Card, T. P. Moran, and A. J. Newall, *The Psychology of Human-Computer Interaction,* Hillsdale, NJ: Lawrence Erlbaum Associates, 1983. An excellent text giving many numeric results that can be used for design purposes.

6 EXAMPLES OF 4GL MECHANISMS

The dialogue structures illustrated in Chapter 5 make 4GLs fundamentally different from COBOL, PL/I, and traditional languages. This chapter illustrates other mechanisms that characterize 4GLs.

THE PRINCIPLE OF MINIMUM WORK Perhaps the most important of the 4GL principles listed in Chapter 1 is the principle of minimum work.
We want to get computers into action with the minimum effort. We want to avoid using complex techniques to achieve simple results.

In Chapter 5 we illustrated the use of QUERY-BY-EXAMPLE for producing a hospital report. The following screen can be created for this in less than five minutes by a typical QBE user:

HOSPITAL	HOSPNAME	ADDRESS	PHONE	
	_x			

WARD	WARDNO	HOSPNAME	TOTROOMS	TOTBEDS	BEDAVAIL	WARDTYPE	
	_y	_x				QUARANTINE	

PATIENT	PATNAME	HOSPNAME	WARDNO	BED	ADMITDAT	PREVDATE	PREVHOSP	REASON	
		_x	_y		≤_d + 365	_d			

We commented that experiments have shown that users of one-dimensional dialogues, including SQL, take more time to obtain results than QBE users. Nevertheless, using SQL is fast compared with many other approaches.

Some 4GLs are better than others in meeting the objective of minimum work. The following is an example of the Swedish language MIMER/PG generating the hospital report created above by QBE and in Chapter 5 by SQL. It uses a data base called HOSPDB and specifies HOSPSTAY to be a function of various fields in this data base:

```
INCLUDE HOSPDB;
SPECIFY HOSPSTAY (HOSPNAME, ADDRESS, PHONE, WARDNO,
    TOTROOMS, TOTBEDS, BEDAVAIL, WARDTYPE, PATNAME,
    BED, ADMITDAT, PREVDATE, PREVHOSP, PREVREAS) = . . .
```

To abbreviate the coding, the HOSPITAL record is referred to as H, the WARD record as W, and the PATIENT record as P. This is done with the following ALIAS statements:

```
ALIAS HOSPITAL (H);
ALIAS WARD (W);
ALIAS PATIENT (P);
```

The three relational joins are then expressed as follows:

```
WHERE    W.HOSPNAME EQ H.HOSPNAME AND
         P.HOSPNAME EQ W.HOSPNAME AND
         P.WARDNO EQ W.WARDNO;
```

The entire program is as follows:

```
INCLUDE HOSPDB;

SPECIFY HOSPSTAY(HOSPNAME,ADDRESS,PHONE,WARDNO,TOTROOMS,TOTBEDS,BEDAVAIL,
                 WARDTYPE,PATNAME,BED,ADMITDAT,PREVDATE,PREVHOSP,PREVREAS)=

(INIT(30;"PREVIOUS STAY REPORT";
     30;"===================";/;/);

CHANGE HOSPNAME;
("HOSPITAL NAME";17;"HOSPITAL ADDRESS";59;"HOSP. PHONE";/;
 HOSPNAME;        17; ADDRESS;            59; PHONE;/;/;

 "WARD NO";10;"TOT ROOMS";20;"TOT BEDS";30;"BEDS AVAIL";42;"WARD TYPE";/;
 WARDNO;  10; TOTROOMS;  20; TOTBEDS;  30; BEDAVAIL;   42; WARDTYPE;/;/;

 "PATIENT NAME";17;"BED";25;"ADMIT DATE";36;"PREV DATE";
 46;"PREV. HOSPITAL";61;"PREVIOUS REASON";/;/);

(TEMPDATE:=PREVDATE + 10000;
```

```
IF ADMITDAT LE TEMPDATE THEN
   PATNAME;        17; BED; 25; ADMITDAT;    36;PREVDATE;
   46; PREVHOSP;        61; PREVREAS;/));
```

```
ALIAS HOSPITAL (H);
ALIAS WARD (W);
ALIAS PATIENT (P);
```

```
PROGRAM GOHOSP=HOSPSTAY GET H.HOSPNAME, H.ADDRESS, H.PHONE,
                            W.WARDNO, W.TOTROOMS, W.TOTBEDS, W.BEDAVAIL,
                            W.WARDTYPE, P.PATNAME, P.BED, P.ADMITDAT,
                            P.PREVDATE, P PREVHOSP, P.PREVREAS
                        WHERE
                            W.HOSPNAME EQ H.HOSPNAME      AND
                            W.WARDTYPE EQ "QUARANTINE"    AND
                            P.HOSPNAME EQ W.HOSPNAME      AND
                            P.WARDNO   EQ W.WARDNO;
```

Much of the coding in this example is used to specify the format of the report. It specifies the positions of the fields on a line in statements such as PATNAME; 17; BED; 25; ADMITDAT; 36; PREVDATE; 46; PREVHOSP; 61; PREVREAS;. The principle of minimum work indicates that the software, not the user, should allocate space for the fields on a line. The software knows the length of each field and can allocate space appropriately.

The coding puts column headings or labels on the fields, which are printed with statements such as

```
"HOSPITAL NAME"; 17; "HOSPITAL ADDRESS"; 59; "HOSP.PHONE";/;
HOSPNAME; 17; ADDRESS; 59; PHONE;/;/;
"WARD NO"; 10; "TOT ROOMS"; 20; "TOTBEDS"; 30; "BEDS AVAIL";
42; "WARD TYPE";/;
WARDNO; 10; TOTROOMS; 20; TOTBEDS; 30; BEDAVAIL; 42;
WARDTYPE;/;/;
```

This coding can be avoided if the software already knows the full names of fields as well as their abbreviated names. It should automatically associate "HOSPITAL NAME" with HOSPNAME and allocate the necessary space for it. This information should be in the dictionary of the data base used.

In third-generation languages, much coding was needed to describe in detail the format of a report. In 4GLs, the software should make its own assumptions about the report format unless the user overrides it. Everything possible should be handled with default options. Sometimes the software may execute considerable logic to determine what is the best default.

In general, the final formatting and dressing up of a report is best done interactively at a screen where the user can see the result. Fast, easy-to-use interactive mechanisms exist for this. Sometimes the user needs word processing facilities associated with his report creation tools.

COMPARISON
WITH COBOL

The MIMER solution may be unnecessarily lengthy, but it is a dream compared with COBOL. Figure 6.1 shows the COBOL version. Using industry average figures, the COBOL version would require 18 days to code and debug. (It took a programmer almost a week to create Fig. 6.1). The QUERY-BY-EXAMPLE version took less than five minutes and the MIMER version a few hours.

GENERATION OF
COBOL

Some 4GL interpreters and compilers generate COBOL, FORTRAN, or other third-generation code, which then has to be separately compiled. Others generate machine code directly.

It is clearly more efficient to generate machine code directly than go through two translation stages. In some cases 4GLs employ precoded blocks of machine code that have been tightly optimized. These blocks can be more machine-efficient than code from a COBOL compiler (though the linkage between blocks introduces other inefficiencies).

```
000100 ID DIVISION.
000200 PROGRAM-ID. CHAP5C.
000300 AUTHOR. DKAPP.
000400 DATE-WRITTEN.  APRIL 26 1977.
000500 DATE-COMPILED.
000600
000610 REMARKS.
000700         THE OUTPUT OF THIS PROGRAM IS A LIST OF PATIENTS WHO
000800         ARE IN QUARANTINE WARDS PRESENTLY BUT ALSO HAVE
000900         BEEN IN A HOSPITAL WITHIN THE PAST YEAR.
001000
001100
001200 ENVIRONMENT DIVISION.
001300
001400 CONFIGURATION SECTION.
001500
001600 SOURCE-COMPUTER.    IBM-370-158.
001700 OBJECT-COMPUTER.    IBM-370-158.
001800
001900 INPUT-OUTPUT SECTION.
002000 FILE-CONTROL.
002100
002200     SELECT  PARMETER   ASSIGN TO UT-S-INPUT.
002300     SELECT  PRNTER     ASSIGN TO UT-S-OUTPUT.
002400
002500     EJECT
002600 DATA DIVISION.
002700
002800 FILE SECTION.
002900
003000 FD  PARMETER
003100
003200     BLOCK CONTAINS 0 RECORDS
003300     RECORDING MODE IS F
```

Figure 6.1   COBOL program of 368 lines of code that produces the report in Fig. 5.2   (continued on following pages).

```
003400        LABEL RECORDS ARE OMITTED
003500        DATA RECORD IS PARM-CARD.
003600
003700 01  PARM-CARD.
003800        05  HOSPCONST  PIC XX.
003900        05  IHOSPNAM   PIC X(20).
004000        05  FILLER     PIC X(58).
004100
004200
004300 FD  PRNTER
004400
004500        BLOCK CONTAINS 0 RECORDS
004600        RECORDING MODE IS F
004700        LABEL RECORDS  ARE OMITTED
004800        DATA RECORD IS A-LINE.
004900
005000 01  A-LINE.
005100        05  PRINT-CTL   PIC X.
005200        05  PRINT-AREA  PIC X(132).
005400 WORKING-STORAGE SECTION.
005500
005600 77  NO-HOSPITAL     PIC X       VALUE '0'.
005700 77  NO-WARDS        PIC X       VALUE '0'.
005800 77  NO-PATIENTS     PIC X       VALUE '0'.
005900 77  TOP-PAGE        PIC X       VALUE '1'.
006000 77  DOUBLE-SPACE    PIC X       VALUE '0'.
006100 77  SINGLE-SPACE    PIC X       VALUE ' '.
006200 77  TRIPLE-SPACE    PIC X       VALUE '-'.
006300 77  END-DATABASE    PIC XX      VALUE 'GB'.
006400 77  SEG-NOT-FOUND   PIC XX      VALUE 'GE'.
006500 77  GET-UNIQUE      PIC XXXX    VALUE 'GU  '.
006600 77  GET-NEXT        PIC XXXX    VALUE 'GN  '.
006700 77  GET-NEXT-P      PIC XXXX    VALUE 'GNP '.
006800 77  LINE-CNT        PIC 99      VALUE 52.
006900 77  PAGE-CNT        PIC 9(4)    VALUE ZERO.
007000 77  CALL-SUCCESSFUL PIC XX      VALUE '  '.
007100 77  END-HOSP-DATA   PIC X       VALUE SPACE.
007200 77  HOSP-NOT-FOUND  PIC X(20)   VALUE SPACE.
007300 77  NEW-MONTH       PIC S99.
007400 77  NEW-YEAR        PIC S99.
007500 77  WRDTYPE         PIC X(20)   VALUE SPACE.
007600
007700 01  CURR-DATE.
007800        05  CURRMO      PIC S99.
007900        05  FILLER      PIC X       VALUE  '/'.
008000        05  CURRDAY     PIC S99.
008100        05  FILLER      PIC X       VALUE  '/'.
008200        05  CURRYR      PIC S99.
008300
008400 01  WS-PREV-DATE.
008500        05  PREVMO          PIC S99.
008600        05  PREVYR          PIC S99.
008700        EJECT
009800 01  HOSP-I-O-AREA COPY HOSPITAL.
008900
009000 01  WARD-I-O-AREA COPY WARD.
009100
009200 01  PAT-I-O-AREA COPY PATIENT.
009300
009400 01  SSA-HOSP.
```

Figure 6.1   (Continued)

```
009500     05   HOSPSEG           PIC X(8)    VALUE 'HOSPITAL'.
009600     05   FILLER            PIC X       VALUE '('.
009700     05   SEG-SEARCH-NAM    PIC X(8)    VALUE 'HOSPNAME'.
009800     05   HOSP-REL-OP       PIC XX      VALUE 'EQ'.
009900     05   HOSP-NAME         PIC X(20).
010000     05   FILLER            PIC X       VALUE ')'.
010100
010200 01  SSA-WARD.
010300
010400     05   WARDSEG           PIC X(8)    VALUE 'WARD
010500     05   FILLER            PIC X       VALUE '('.
010600     05   SEG-SEARCH-NAME   PIC X(8)    VALUE 'WARDTYPE'.
010700     05   WARD-REL-OP       PIC XX      VALUE 'EQ'.
010800     05   WARD-TYPE         PIC X(20)   VALUE 'QUARANTINE
010900     05   FILLER            PIC X       VALUE ')
010905
010910 01  SSA-PATIENT           PIC X(9)    VALUE 'PATIENT
011100 01  HEAD-1.
011200
011300     05   FILLER            PIC X(26) VALUE SPACES.
011400     05   TITLE             PIC X(106) VALUE
011500               'P R E V I O U S   S T A Y   R E P O R T'.
011700
011800 01  HEAD-2.
011900
012100     05   FILLER            PIC X(5)    VALUE 'PAGE'.
012200     05   HPAGE-CTR         PIC ZZZ9.
012300     05   FILLER            PIC X(123) VALUE SPACES.
012400
012500 01  HEAD-3.
012600
012800     05   HHOSPNAM          PIC X(25) VALUE 'HOSPITAL NAME'.
013000     05   HHOSPADR          PIC X(35) VALUE 'HOSPITAL ADDRESS'.
013200     05   HHOSPHON          PIC X(10) VALUE 'HOSP PHONE'.
013300     05   FILLER            PIC X(62) VALUE SPACE.
013400
013500 01  HEAD-4.
013600
013800     05   HWARDNO           PIC X(12) VALUE 'WARD NO'.
013900     05   HTOTRMS           PIC X(14) VALUE 'TOT ROOMS'.
014000     05   HTOTBDS           PIC X(13) VALUE 'TOT BEDS'.
014100     05   HBDSAVAI          PIC X(15) VALUE 'BEDS AVAIL'.
014200     03   HBDAVAIL          PIC X(20) VALUE 'WARD TYPE'.
014300     05   FILLER            PIC X(58) VALUE SPACE.
014400
014500 01  HEAD-5.
014600
014800     05   HPATNAM           PIC X(21) VALUE 'PATIENT NAME'.
014900     05   HBDID             PIC X(6)  VALUE 'BED'.
015000     05   HDATADMIT         PIC X(12) VALUE 'ADMIT DATE'.
015100     05   HPREVDAT          PIC X(11) VALUE 'PREV DATE'.
015200     05   HPREVHOS          PIC X(21) VALUE 'PREVIOUS HOSPITAL'.
015400     05   HPREV-REASON      PIC X(30) VALUE 'PREVIOUS REASON'.
015500     05   FILLER            PIC X(31) VALUE SPACE.
015700 01  DETAIL-1.
015800
016000     05   DHOSPNAM          PIC X(20).
016100     05   FILLER            PIC X(5)  VALUE SPACE.
016200     05   DHOSP-ADDRESS     PIC X(30).
016300     05   FILLER            PIC X(5)  VALUE SPACE.
```

Figure 6.1   (Continued)

126

```
016400      05  DHOSPHON        PIC X(10).
016500      05  FILLER          PIC X(62) VALUE SPACE.
016600
016700 01  DETAIL-2.
016800
016900      05  FILLER          PIC X(3)  VALUE SPACE.
017000      05  DWARDNO         PIC 99.
017100      05  FILLER          PIC X(10) VALUE SPACE.
017200      05  DTOTRMS         PIC 999.
017300      05  FILLER          PIC X(11) VALUE SPACE.
017400      05  DTOT-BEDS       PIC 999.
017500      05  FILLER          PIC X(10) VALUE SPACE.
017600      05  DBDSAVAIL       PIC 999.
017700      05  FILLER          PIC X(9)  VALUE SPACE.
017800      05  DWARDTYPE       PIC X(20).
017900      05  FILLER          PIC X(58) VALUE SPACE.
018000
018100 01  DETAIL-3.
018200
018400      05  DPATNAM         PIC X(20).
018500      05  FILLER          PIC X     VALUE SPACE.
018600      05  DBEDID          PIC 9999.
018700      05  FILLER          PIC X(4)  VALUE SPACE.
018800      05  DDATADMIT       PIC X(6).
018900      05  FILLER          PIC X(6)  VALUE SPACE.
019000      05  DPREV-DATE      PIC X(4).
019100      05  FILLER          PIC X(5)  VALUE SPACE.
019200      05  DPREV-HOSP      PIC X(20).
019300      05  FILLER          PIC X     VALUE SPACE.
019400      05  DPREV-REASONN   PIC X(30).
019500      05  FILLER          PIC X(31) VALUE SPACE.
019600
019700 01  NO-HOSP-LINE.
019800
020100      05  ERR-HOSPNAM PIC X(20).
020110      05  FILLER      PIC X(5)    VALUE SPACE.
020200      05  FILLER      PIC X(107)   VALUE
020300                  '****  HOSPITAL NOT FOUND  ****'.
020310
020311 01  NO-WARD-LINE    PIC X(132)   VALUE
020312                  '****  NO QUARANTINE WARDS ****'.
020313
020314 01  NO-PAT-LINE     PIC X(132)   VALUE
020315                  '****  NO PATIENTS WITH PREVIOUS STAY  ****'.
020500 LINKAGE SECTION.
020600 01  DB-PCB-HOSP COPY MASKC.
020800 PROCEDURE DIVISION.
021000 ENTRY-POINT.
021200          ENTRY 'DLITCBL' USING DB-PCB-HOSP.
021300          OPEN INPUT PARMETER  OUTPUT PRNTER.
021500          MOVE CURRENT-DATE TO CURR-DATE.
021600
021700 READ-CARD.
021900      READ PARMETER AT END GO TO END-JOB.
022000      MOVE IHOSPNAM TO HOSP-NAME.
022100      MOVE 45 TO LINE-CNT.
022200
022300      CALL 'CBLTDLI' USING GET-UNIQUE
022400                          DB-PCB-HOSP
022500                          HOSP-I-O-AREA
```

Figure 6.1 (Continued)

```
022600                        SSA-HOSP.
022700
022900      IF STATUS-CODE NOT EQUAL '  '
022900
023000          PERFORM HOSPITAL-NOT-FOUND
023100          GO TO READ-CARD.
023200
023300      MOVE HOSPNAME      TO  DHOSPNAM.
023400      MOVE HOSP-ADDRESS  TO  DHOSP-ADDRESS.
023500      MOVE HOSP-PHONE    TO  DHOSPHON.
023600
023700      CALL 'CBLTDLI' USING GET-UNIQUE
023800                           DB-PCB-HOSP
023900                           WARD-I-O-AREA
024000                           SSA-HOSP
024100                           SSA-WARD
024200
024300      IF STATUS-CODE NOT EQUAL '  '
024400
024500          PERFORM WARD-NOT-FOUND
024600          GO TO READ-CARD.
024700
024710      MOVE WARDNO        TO  DWARDNO.
024800      MOVE TOT-ROOMS     TO  DTOTRMS.
024900      MOVE TOT-BEDS      TO  DTOT-BEDS.
025000      MOVE BEDAVAIL      TO  DBDSAVAIL.
025100      MOVE WARDTYPE      TO  DWARDTYPE.
025200      MOVE '0' TO NO-PATIENTS.
025300
025400      PERFORM  CALL-PATIENT THRU CALL-PATIENT-EXIT
025600                           UNTIL STATUS-CODE = 'GE'.
025610
025700      IF NO-PATIENTS EQUAL '0'
025800
025900          MOVE NO-PAT-LINE  TO DETAIL-3
026000          PERFORM WRITE-RTN THRU WRITE-RTN-EXIT
026100          MOVE SPACE TO DETAIL-3.
026200
026300      MOVE '0' TO NO-PATIENTS.
026400      GO TO READ-CARD.
026600 CALL-PATIENT.
026700
026800      CALL 'CBLTDLI' USING GET-NEXT-P
026900                           DB-PCB-HOSP
027000                           PAT-I-O-AREA
027010                           SSA-PATIENT.
027100
027200      IF STATUS-CODE EQUAL 'GE' GO TO CALL-PATIENT-EXIT.
027300      IF STATUS-CODE NOT EQUAL '  '
027400
027500          MOVE DB-PCB-HOSP TO DETAIL-3
027600          PERFORM WRITE-RTN THRU WRITE-RTN-EXIT
027700          MOVE SPACE TO DETAIL-3
027800          GO TO READ-CARD.
027900
029000      IF   PREV-STAY-FLAG NOT EQUAL '1' GO TO CALL-PATIENT-EXIT.
029100
029200          MOVE PREV-DATE TO WS-PREV-DATE.
029300          SUBTRACT PREVMO FROM CURRMO GIVING NEW-MONTH.
029500          SUBTRACT PREVYR FROM CURRYR GIVING NEW-YEAR.
```

Figure 6.1   (Continued)

```
028700
029000      IF    NEW-YEAR GREATER THAN 1 GO TO CALL-PATIENT-EXIT.
029100      IF    NEW-YEAR EQUAL 0
029200
029300                PERFORM WRITE-PAT-DATA
029400                MOVE '1' TO NO-PATIENTS
029500                GO TO CALL-PATIENT-EXIT.
029600
029700      IF    NEW-YEAR  EQUAL     1
029800      AND   NEW-MONTH LESS THAN 1
029900
030000                PERFORM WRITE-PAT-DATA
030100                MOVE '1' TO NO-PATIENTS.
030110
030200 CALL-PATIENT-EXIT.
030300      EXIT.
030500 WRITE-RTN.
030600      IF LINE-CNT LESS THAN 44 GO TO WRITE-PAT-LINE.
030700
030800          MOVE 1 TO LINE-CNT.
030900          MOVE HEAD-1 TO PRINT-AREA.
031000          WRITE A-LINE AFTER POSITIONING TOP-PAGE.
031010
031100          ADD 1 TO PAGE-CNT.
031200          MOVE PAGE-CNT TO HPAGE-CTR.
031300          MOVE HEAD-2 TO PRINT-AREA.
031400          WRITE A-LINE AFTER POSITIONING DOUBLE-SPACE.
031410
031500          MOVE HEAD-3  TO PRINT-AREA.
031600          WRITE A-LINE AFTER POSITIONING DOUBLE-SPACE.
031610
031700          MOVE DETAIL-1    TO PRINT-AREA.
031800          WRITE A-LINE AFTER POSITIONING DOUBLE-SPACE.
031900
032000      IF NO-HOSPITAL EQUAL '1' GO TO WRITE-RTN-EXIT.
032010
032200              MOVE HEAD-4 TO PRINT-AREA.
032300              WRITE A-LINE AFTER POSITIONING DOUBLE-SPACE.
032310
032400              MOVE DETAIL-2 TO PRINT-AREA.
032500              WRITE A-LINE AFTER POSITIONING DOUBLE-SPACE.
032600
032700      IF NO-WARDS EQUAL '1' GO TO WRITE-RTN-EXIT.
032710
032900              MOVE HEAD-5 TO PRINT-AREA.
033000              WRITE A-LINE AFTER POSITIONING DOUBLE-SPACE.
033010
033100              MOVE SPACE TO PRINT-AREA.
033200              WRITE A-LINE AFTER POSITIONING SINGLE-SPACE.
033210
033220 WRITE-PAT-LINE.
033230
033300
033400      MOVE DETAIL-3 TO PRINT-AREA.
033500      WRITE A-LINE AFTER POSITIONING SINGLE-SPACE.
033600      ADD 1 TO LINE-CNT.
033700
033800 WRITE-RTN-EXIT.
033900      EXIT.
034100 WRITE-PAT-DATA.
```

Figure 6.1   (Continued)

```
034200
034300        MOVE PATNAME TO DPATNAM.
034400        MOVE BEDIDENT TO DBEDID.
034500        MOVE DATEADMT TO DDATADMIT.
034600        MOVE PREV-HOSP TO DPREV-HOSP.
034700        MOVE PREV-DATE TO DPREV-DATE.
034800        MOVE PREV-REASON TO DPREV-REASONN.
034900        PERFORM   WRITE-RTN THRU WRITE-RTN-EXIT.
035000
035100 HOSPITAL-NOT-FOUND.
035200
035300        MOVE '1' TO NO-HOSPITAL.
035310        MOVE IHOSPNAM TO ERR-HOSPNAM.
035400        MOVE NO-HOSP-LINE TO  DETAIL-1.
035500        PERFORM   WRITE-RTN THRU WRITE-RTN-EXIT.
035510        MOVE SPACE TO DETAIL-1.
035600        MOVE '0' TO NO-HOSPITAL.
035700
035800 WARD-NOT-FOUND.
035900
036000        MOVE '1' TO NO-WARDS.
036100        MOVE NO-WARD-LINE TO DETAIL-2.
036200        PERFORM WRITE-RTN THRU WRITE-RTN-EXIT.
036210        MOVE SPACE TO DETAIL-2.
036300        MOVE '0' TO NO-WARDS.
036400
036500 END-JOB.
036600
036700        CLOSE PARMETER PRNTER.
036800             GOBACK.
```

Figure 6.1   (Continued)

Some systems analysts and DP executives have insisted on using 4GLs that generate COBOL (or other third-generation language) because COBOL is familiar. To some people, generating COBOL (or PL/I, PASCAL, or another) improves their feeling of comfort. They cling to this link to familiarity. Such insistence is generally irrational. The COBOL code generated by the 4GL should *never* normally be modified. To modify it would incur the danger of introducing errors and preventing low-cost maintenance.

Figure 6.2 shows COBOL code generated by MIMER/PG for the same example.

THE DATA-BASE CONNECTION

Many 4GLs employ a data base. Some cannot function without a data base. When you buy SQL, NOMAD, or MAPPER, you buy a data-base management system with the flexibility to support the power of these languages.

A key to efficient application generation is that the data structures for an application *already exist;* they are represented in a dictionary that the software can use. The creator of the application does not need to design the data or their structuring. The data-base dictionary is the foundation of many report generators, query languages, and application generators. The term *integrated data dic-*

```
  IDENTIFICATION DIVISION.
*
* THIS IS A PROGRAM GENERATED BY MIMER/PG
* DATE OF CREATION IS 1983-09-15 11:16
* GENERATED ON VAX COMPUTER
* FOR VAX-11 COMPUTER
*
  PROGRAM-ID. COBPGM.
  ENVIRONMENT DIVISION.
  CONFIGURATION SECTION.
  OBJECT-COMPUTER. VAX-11.
*
  DATA DIVISION.
  WORKING-STORAGE SECTION.
  77   BLANKA PICTURE X(130) VALUE SPACES.
  77   NOCHANGE PICTURE S9(8) COMPUTATIONAL.
  77   REFQ PICTURE X(9) VALUE "LISTING?!".
  77   REFRES PICTURE S9(8) COMPUTATIONAL.
  77   ISIZE PICTURE S9(8) COMPUTATIONAL VALUE 16.
  77   UTFIL PICTURE S9(8) COMPUTATIONAL VALUE 1.
  77   I PICTURE S9(8) COMPUTATIONAL.
  77   MAXPOS PICTURE S9(8) COMPUTATIONAL VALUE 130.
  77   IPOS PICTURE S9(8) COMPUTATIONAL VALUE 0.
  77   ILENGTH PICTURE S9(8) COMPUTATIONAL.
  77   TABPOS PICTURE S9(8) COMPUTATIONAL VALUE 0.
  77   LINENR PICTURE S9(8) COMPUTATIONAL VALUE 1.
  77   HEIGHT PICTURE S9(8) COMPUTATIONAL VALUE 0.
  77   EJECTFLG PICTURE S9(8) COMPUTATIONAL VALUE 0.
  77   EJECTNR PICTURE S9(8) COMPUTATIONAL VALUE 0.
  77   ITOCLEN20 PICTURE S9(8) COMPUTATIONAL VALUE 20.
  77   R-WACCESS PICTURE S9(8) COMPUTATIONAL VALUE 3.
  77   WACCESS PICTURE S9(8) COMPUTATIONAL VALUE 2.
  77   SEQLEN PICTURE S9(8) COMPUTATIONAL VALUE 130.
  77   CNTLEN PICTURE S9(8) COMPUTATIONAL VALUE 6.
  77   CNTCOND PICTURE S9(8) COMPUTATIONAL.
  77   CNTLEN1 PICTURE S9(8) COMPUTATIONAL VALUE 20.
  77   FILENAME PICTURE X(40).
  77   SEQNAME PICTURE X(40) VALUE "T".
  77   XZERO PICTURE S9(8) COMPUTATIONAL VALUE 0.
  77   EIGHTY PICTURE S9(8) COMPUTATIONAL VALUE 79.
  01   MESSLINE PICTURE X(80).
  01   RESRAD PICTURE X(130).
  01   SEQFID.
       02 SEQFID1 PICTURE S9(8) COMPUTATIONAL.
       02 SEQFID2 PICTURE S9(8) COMPUTATIONAL.
       02 SEQFID3 PICTURE S9(8) COMPUTATIONAL.
  01   CNTREF.
       02 CNTREFC PICTURE X(6).
       02 CNTREFT PICTURE X(14) VALUE " REFERENCES ".
  01   STRBUFF.
       02 STRBUFARR PICTURE X OCCURS 256.
  01   RAD.
       02 RADARR PICTURE X OCCURS 130.
  01   V-34 PICTURE X(1) VALUE "X".
  01   V-33 PICTURE X(1) VALUE "*".
  01   V-32 PICTURE X(8) VALUE "WORK    ".
  01   V-31 PICTURE X(8) VALUE "DEMO    ".
  01   V-30 PICTURE X(8) VALUE "PHONE   ".
  01   V-29 PICTURE S9(8) COMPUTATIONAL VALUE 40.
  01   V-28 PICTURE X(8) VALUE "ADDRESS ".
  01   V-27 PICTURE X(8) VALUE "BEDAVAIL".
  01   V-26 PICTURE X(8) VALUE "TOTBEDS ".
  01   V-25 PICTURE X(8) VALUE "TOTROOMS".
  01   V-24 PICTURE S9(8) COMPUTATIONAL VALUE 10.
  01   V-23 PICTURE X(8) VALUE "WARDTYPE".
```

Figure 6.2   COBOL code automatically generated by MIMER/PG.

(Continued)

```
01  V-22 PICTURE X(8) VALUE "PATNAME ".
01  V-21 PICTURE X(8) VALUE "BED     ".
01  V-20 PICTURE X(8) VALUE "ADMITDAT".
01  V-19 PICTURE X(1) VALUE "I".
01  V-18 PICTURE X(8) VALUE "PREVDATE".
01  V-17 PICTURE X(8) VALUE "PREVHOSP".
01  V-16 PICTURE S9(8) COMPUTATIONAL VALUE 20.
01  V-15 PICTURE X(2) VALUE "RW".
01  V-14 PICTURE X(8) VALUE "PREVPEAS".
01  V-13 PICTURE S9(8) COMPUTATIONAL VALUE 15.
01  V-12 PICTURE X(8) VALUE "HOSPNAME".
01  V-11 PICTURE X(1) VALUE "A".
01  V-10 PICTURE S9(8) COMPUTATIONAL VALUE 4.
01  V-9 PICTURE X(1) VALUE "C".
01  V-8 PICTURE X(2) VALUE "EQ".
01  V-7 PICTURE X(8) VALUE "WARDNO  ".
01  V-6 PICTURE X(1) VALUE "F".
01  V-5 PICTURE X(8) VALUE "HOSPITAL".
01  V-4 PICTURE X(8) VALUE "WARD    ".
01  V-3 PICTURE X(1) VALUE "R".
01  V-2 PICTURE X(8) VALUE "PATIENT ".
01  V-1 PICTURE X(8) VALUE "HOSPDB  ".
01  A19 PICTURE S9(8) COMPUTATIONAL.
01  A18 PICTURE X(15).
01  A17 PICTURE S9(8) COMPUTATIONAL.
01  CNT1 PICTURE S9(8) COMPUTATIONAL.
01  A16 PICTURE X(20).
01  A15 PICTURE X(15).
01  A14 PICTURE S9(8) COMPUTATIONAL.
01  A13 PICTURE S9(8) COMPUTATIONAL.
01  A12 PICTURE X(4).
01  A11 PICTURE X(15).
01  A10 PICTURE X(15).
01  A9 PICTURE S9(8) COMPUTATIONAL.
01  A8 PICTURE S9(8) COMPUTATIONAL.
01  A7 PICTURE S9(8) COMPUTATIONAL.
01  A6 PICTURE X(15).
01  A5 PICTURE X(40).
01  A4 PICTURE X(4).
01  A3 PICTURE X(15).
01  A2 PICTURE X(10) VALUE "QUARANTINE".
01  A1 PICTURE X(15).
* FILTAB
 01  CUR1.
       02 RETCODE PICTURE S9(8) COMPUTATIONAL.
       02 FILLER OCCURS 4.
          03 FILLER PICTURE S9(8) COMPUTATIONAL.
 01  CUR4.
       02 RETCODE PICTURE S9(8) COMPUTATIONAL.
       02 FILLER OCCURS 4.
          03 FILLER PICTURE S9(8) COMPUTATIONAL.
 01  CUR3.
       02 RETCODE PICTURE S9(8) COMPUTATIONAL.
       02 FILLER OCCURS 4.
          03 FILLER PICTURE S9(8) COMPUTATIONAL.
 01  CUR2.
       02 RETCODE PICTURE S9(8) COMPUTATIONAL.
       02 FILLER OCCURS 4.
          03 FILLER PICTURE S9(8) COMPUTATIONAL.
* END FILTAB
 PROCEDURE DIVISION.
 MAINPROC SECTION.
 MAINPROCX.
     MOVE BLANKA TO RAD.
     CALL "BEGIN4".
```

Figure 6.2   (Continued)

```
        CALL "OPEN2" USING CUR4 V-1 V-2 V-3.
        CALL "OPEN2" USING CUR3 V-1 V-4 V-3.
        CALL "OPEN2" USING CUR2 V-1 V-5 V-3.
* PROJECT SELECT CURSOR CUR4 ALIAS (HOSPDB PATIENT)
        CALL "SELEC2" USING CUR4 V-6 V-7 V-8 BLANKA A4 V-9 V-10.
        CALL "SELEC2" USING CUR4 V-11 V-12 V-8 BLANKA A3 V-9 V-13.
        CALL "PROJE2" USING CUR4 V-6 V-14 V-15 BLANKA A16 V-9 V-16.
        CALL "PROJE2" USING CUR4 V-11 V-17 V-15 BLANKA A15 V-9 V-13.
        CALL "PROJE2" USING CUR4 V-11 V-18 V-15 BLANKA A14 V-19 V-10.
        CALL "PROJE2" USING CUR4 V-11 V-20 V-15 BLANKA A13 V-19 V-10.
        CALL "PROJE2" USING CUR4 V-11 V-21 V-15 BLANKA A12 V-9 V-10.
        CALL "PROJE2" USING CUR4 V-11 V-22 V-15 BLANKA A11 V-9 V-13.
* PROJECT SELECT CURSOR CUR3 ALIAS (HOSPDB WARD)
        CALL "SELEC2" USING CUR3 V-6 V-12 V-8 BLANKA A1 V-9 V-13.
        CALL "SELEC2" USING CUR3 V-11 V-23 V-8 BLANKA A2 V-9 V-24.
        CALL "PROJE2" USING CUR3 V-6 V-25 V-15 BLANKA A7 V-19 V-10.
        CALL "PROJE2" USING CUR3 V-11 V-26 V-15 BLANKA A8 V-19 V-10.
        CALL "PROJE2" USING CUR3 V-11 V-27 V-15 BLANKA A9 V-19 V-10.
        CALL "PROJE2" USING CUR3 V-11 V-23 V-15 BLANKA A10 V-9 V-13.
        CALL "PROJE2" USING CUR3 V-11 V-7 V-15 BLANKA A4 V-9 V-10.
        CALL "PROJE2" USING CUR3 V-11 V-12 V-15 BLANKA A3 V-9 V-13.
* PROJECT SELECT CURSOR CUR2 ALIAS (HOSPDB HOSPITAL)
        CALL "PROJE2" USING CUR2 V-6 V-28 V-15 BLANKA A5 V-9 V-29.
        CALL "PROJE2" USING CUR2 V-11 V-30 V-15 BLANKA A6 V-9 V-13.
        CALL "PROJE2" USING CUR2 V-11 V-12 V-15 BLANKA A1 V-9 V-13.
* END OPEN
* NEWMIMFILE DEMO      WORK
        CALL "DROPP2" USING V-31 V-32.
        CALL "DEFTAB" USING CUR1 V-19 V-31 V-32 V-12 V-33 V-9 V-13.
        CALL "DEFTAB" USING CUR1 V-19 V-31 V-32 V-28 V-33 V-9 V-29.
        CALL "DEFTAB" USING CUR1 V-19 V-31 V-32 V-30 V-33 V-9 V-13.
        CALL "DEFTAB" USING CUR1 V-19 V-31 V-32 V-7 V-33 V-9 V-10.
        CALL "DEFTAB" USING CUR1 V-19 V-31 V-32 V-25 V-33 V-19 V-10.
        CALL "DEFTAB" USING CUR1 V-19 V-31 V-32 V-26 V-33 V-19 V-10.
        CALL "DEFTAB" USING CUR1 V-19 V-31 V-32 V-27 V-33 V-19 V-10.
        CALL "DEFTAB" USING CUR1 V-19 V-31 V-32 V-23 V-33 V-9 V-13.
        CALL "DEFTAB" USING CUR1 V-19 V-31 V-32 V-22 V-33 V-9 V-13.
        CALL "DEFTAB" USING CUR1 V-19 V-31 V-32 V-21 V-33 V-9 V-10.
        CALL "DEFTAB" USING CUR1 V-19 V-31 V-32 V-20 V-33 V-19 V-10.
        CALL "DEFTAB" USING CUR1 V-19 V-31 V-32 V-18 V-33 V-19 V-10.
        CALL "DEFTAB" USING CUR1 V-19 V-31 V-32 V-17 V-33 V-9 V-13.
        CALL "DEFTAB" USING CUR1 V-19 V-31 V-32 V-14 V-33 V-9 V-16.
        CALL "OPEN2" USING CUR1 V-31 V-32 V-34.
* END NEWMIMFILE
        CALL "PROJE2" USING CUR1 V-6 V-12 V-15 BLANKA A1 V-9 V-13.
        CALL "PROJE2" USING CUR1 V-11 V-28 V-15 BLANKA A5 V-9 V-29.
        CALL "PROJE2" USING CUR1 V-11 V-30 V-15 BLANKA A6 V-9 V-13.
        CALL "PROJE2" USING CUR1 V-11 V-7 V-15 BLANKA A4 V-9 V-10.
        CALL "PROJE2" USING CUR1 V-11 V-25 V-15 BLANKA A7 V-19 V-10.
        CALL "PROJE2" USING CUR1 V-11 V-26 V-15 BLANKA A8 V-19 V-10.
        CALL "PROJE2" USING CUR1 V-11 V-27 V-15 BLANKA A9 V-19 V-10.
        CALL "PROJE2" USING CUR1 V-11 V-23 V-15 BLANKA A10 V-9 V-13.
        CALL "PROJE2" USING CUR1 V-11 V-22 V-15 BLANKA A11 V-9 V-13.
        CALL "PROJE2" USING CUR1 V-11 V-21 V-15 BLANKA A12 V-9 V-10.
        CALL "PROJE2" USING CUR1 V-11 V-20 V-15 BLANKA A13 V-19 V-10.
        CALL "PROJE2" USING CUR1 V-11 V-18 V-15 BLANKA A14 V-19 V-10.
        CALL "PROJE2" USING CUR1 V-11 V-17 V-15 BLANKA A15 V-9 V-13.
        CALL "PROJE2" USING CUR1 V-11 V-14 V-15 BLANKA A16 V-9 V-16.
        MOVE 0 TO CNT1.
        MOVE 0 TO HEIGHT MOVE 80 TO MAXPOS.
        MOVE 0 TO LINENR.
* READLOOP (HOSPDB HOSPITAL)
        CALL "SET2" USING CUR2 BLANKA.
  LABEL1.
        CALL "GET2" USING CUR2, BLANKA.
```

Figure 6.2   (Continued)

```
        IF RETCODE OF CUR2 > 0 GO TO LABEL2.
* READLOOP (HOSPDB WARD)
        CALL "SET2" USING CUR3 BLANKA.
 LABEL3.
        CALL "GET2" USING CUR3, BLANKA.
        IF RETCODE OF CUR3 > 0 GO TO LABEL4.
* READLOOP (HOSPDB PATIENT)
        CALL "SET2" USING CUR4 BLANKA.
 LABEL5.
        CALL "GET2" USING CUR4, BLANKA.
        IF RETCODE OF CUR4 > 0 GO TO LABEL6.
        CALL "LOAD2" USING CUR1 BLANKA.
        GO TO LABEL5.
 LABEL6.
* END READLOOP CUR4 (HOSPDB PATIENT)
        GO TO LABEL3.
 LABEL4.
* END READLOOP CUR3 (HOSPDB WARD)
        GO TO LABEL1.
 LABEL2.
* END READLOOP CUR2 (HOSPDB HOSPITAL)
        CALL "SET2" USING CUR1 BLANKA.
* READLOOP (DEMO WORK)
        CALL "SET2" USING CUR1 BLANKA.
 LABEL7.
        CALL "GET2" USING CUR1, BLANKA.
        IF RETCODE OF CUR1 > 0 GO TO LABEL8.
* TEST IF TUPLE DIFFERENT FROM PREVIOUS ONE
        MOVE CNT1 TO NOCHANGE.
        IF NOCHANGE = 0 MOVE 1 TO A17 ELSE IF A1 = A18 MOVE 0 TO A17 ELSE
         MOVE 0 TO NOCHANGE MOVE 1 TO A17.
* END OF TEST
        IF CNT1 NOT. = 0 GO TO LABEL9.
        MOVE 30 TO I.
        PERFORM TAB.
        MOVE "PREVIOUS STAY REPORT" TO STRBUFF MOVE 20 TO ILENGTH.
        PERFORM PRIN3.
        MOVE 30 TO I.
        PERFORM TAB.
        MOVE "====================" TO STRBUFF MOVE 20 TO ILENGTH.
        PERFORM PRIN3.
        PERFORM TERPRI.
        PERFORM TERPRI.
 LABEL9.
        ADD 1 TO CNT1.
        IF A17 NOT = 1 GO TO LABEL10.
        MOVE "HOSPITAL NAME" TO STRBUFF MOVE 13 TO ILENGTH.
        PERFORM PRIN3.
        MOVE 17 TO I.
        PERFORM TAB.
        MOVE "HOSPITAL ADDRESS" TO STRBUFF MOVE 16 TO ILENGTH.
        PERFORM PRIN3.
        MOVE 59 TO I.
        PERFORM TAB.
        MOVE "HOSP. PHONE" TO STRBUFF MOVE 11 TO ILENGTH.
        PERFORM PRIN3.
        PERFORM TERPRI.
        MOVE A1 TO STRBUFF MOVE 15 TO ILENGTH.
        PERFORM PRIN1.
        MOVE 17 TO I.
        PERFORM TAB.
        MOVE A5 TO STRBUFF MOVE 40 TO ILENGTH.
        PERFORM PRIN1.
        MOVE 59 TO I.
        PERFORM TAB.
```

Figure 6.2   (Continued)

```
MOVE A6 TO STRBUFF MOVE 15 TO ILENGTH.
PERFORM PRIN1.
PERFORM TERPRI.
PERFORM TERPRI.
MOVE "WARD NO" TO STRBUFF MOVE 7 TO ILENGTH.
PERFORM PRIN3.
MOVE 10 TO I.
PERFORM TAB.
MOVE "TOT ROOMS" TO STRBUFF MOVE 9 TO ILENGTH.
PERFORM PRIN3.
MOVE 20 TO I.
PERFORM TAB.
MOVE "TOT BEDS" TO STRBUFF MOVE 8 TO ILENGTH.
PERFORM PRIN3.
MOVE 30 TO I.
PERFORM TAB.
MOVE "BEDS AVAIL" TO STRBUFF MOVE 10 TO ILENGTH.
PERFORM PRIN3.
MOVE 42 TO I.
PERFORM TAB.
MOVE "WARD TYPE" TO STRBUFF MOVE 9 TO ILENGTH.
PERFORM PRIN3.
PERFORM TERPRI.
MOVE A4 TO STRBUFF MOVE 4 TO ILENGTH.
PERFORM PRIN1.
MOVE 10 TO I.
PERFORM TAB.
MOVE A7 TO I.
PERFORM PRINI1.
PERFORM PRIN1.
MOVE 20 TO I.
PERFORM TAB.
MOVE A8 TO I.
PERFORM PRINI1.
PERFORM PRIN1.
MOVE 30 TO I.
PERFORM TAB.
MOVE A9 TO I.
PERFORM PRINI1.
PERFORM PRIN1.
MOVE 42 TO I.
PERFORM TAB.
MOVE A10 TO STRBUFF MOVE 15 TO ILENGTH.
PERFORM PRIN1.
PERFORM TERPRI.
PERFORM TERPRI.
MOVE "PATIENT NAME" TO STRBUFF MOVE 12 TO ILENGTH.
PERFORM PRIN3.
MOVE 17 TO I.
PERFORM TAB.
MOVE "BED" TO STRBUFF MOVE 3 TO ILENGTH.
PERFORM PRIN3.
MOVE 25 TO I.
PERFORM TAB.
MOVE "ADMIT DATE" TO STRBUFF MOVE 10 TO ILENGTH.
PERFORM PRIN3.
MOVE 36 TO I.
PERFORM TAB.
MOVE "PREV DATE" TO STRBUFF MOVE 9 TO ILENGTH.
PERFORM PRIN3.
MOVE 46 TO I.
PERFORM TAB.
MOVE "PREV. HOSPITAL" TO STRBUFF MOVE 14 TO ILENGTH.
PERFORM PRIN3.
MOVE 61 TO I.
```

Figure 6.2   (Continued)

```
        PERFORM TAB.
        MOVE "PREVIOUS REASON" TO STRBUFF MOVE 15 TO ILENGTH.
        PERFORM PRIN3.
        PERFORM TERPRI.
        PERFORM TERPRI.
    LABEL10.
        COMPUTE A19 = A14 + 10000.
        IF A13 ) A19 GO TO LABEL11.
        MOVE A11 TO STRBUFF MOVE 15 TO ILENGTH.
        PERFORM PRIN1.
    LABEL11.
        MOVE 17 TO I.
        PERFORM TAB.
        MOVE A12 TO STRBUFF MOVE 4 TO ILENGTH.
        PERFORM PRIN1.
        MOVE 25 TO I.
        PERFORM TAB.
        MOVE A13 TO I.
        PERFORM PRINI1.
        PERFORM PRIN1.
        MOVE 36 TO I.
        PERFORM TAB.
        MOVE A14 TO I.
        PERFORM PRINI1.
        PERFORM PRIN1.
        MOVE 46 TO I.
        PERFORM TAB.
        MOVE A15 TO STRBUFF MOVE 15 TO ILENGTH.
        PERFORM PRIN1.
        MOVE 61 TO I.
        PERFORM TAB.
        MOVE A16 TO STRBUFF MOVE 20 TO ILENGTH.
        PERFORM PRIN1.
        PERFORM TERPRI.
        IF IPOS ) 0 PERFORM TERPRI.
        IF A17 = 1 MOVE A1 TO A18.
        GO TO LABEL7.
     LABEL8.
   * END READLOOP CUR1 (DEMO WORK)
        CALL "CLOSE2" USING CUR1.
   * BEGIN CLOSE
        CALL "CLOSE2" USING CUR4.
        CALL "CLOSE2" USING CUR3.
        CALL "CLOSE2" USING CUR2.
     FINITO.
        CALL "END2".
        IF UTFIL NOT = 1 CALL "MDRCSF" USING SEQFID ELSE CALL "MDRCTF".
        MOVE "BYE" TO MESSLINE CALL "MDRWTT" USING XZERO MESSLINE EIGHTY.
        STOP RUN.
    TERPRI SECTION.
    TERPRIX.
        PERFORM TERPRII.
        MOVE 0 TO IPOS TABPOS.
    TERPRII SECTION.
    TERPRIIX.
        PERFORM CTERPRII.
        MOVE 0 TO IPOS.
        IF HEIGHT ) 0 AND LINENR NOT ( HEIGHT PERFORM EJECTP.
    CTERPRII SECTION.
    CTERPRIIX.
        IF UTFIL = 2 MOVE IPOS TO SEQFID3 CALL "MDRWRR" USING SEQFID RAD
          ELSE CALL "MDRWTT" USING XZERO RAD IPOS.
        MOVE BLANKA TO RAD.
        MOVE 0 TO IPOS.
        IF HEIGHT ) 0 ADD 1 TO LINENR.
```

Figure 6.2   (Continued)

```
        EJECTIT SECTION.
        EJECTITX.
            IF UTFIL = 2 MOVE "***EJECT" TO RESRAD CALL "MDRWRR" USING SEQFID
              RESRAD ELSE CALL "EJECT".
            MOVE O TO LINENR.
        PRIN1 SECTION.
        PRIN1X.
            IF ILENGTH > O IF STRBUFARR (ILENGTH) = SPACE SUBTRACT 1 FROM
              ILENGTH GO TO PRIN1X.
            PERFORM PRIN2 VARYING I FROM 1 BY 1 UNTIL I > ILENGTH.
        PRIN2 SECTION.
        PRIN2X.
            IF IPOS NOT < MAXPOS PERFORM TERPRII MOVE TABPOS TO IPOS.
            ADD 1 TO IPOS.
            MOVE STRBUFARR (I) TO RADARR (IPOS).
        TAB SECTION.
        TABX.
            IF I > MAXPOS SUBTRACT MAXPOS FROM I GO TO TABX.
            IF IPOS > O AND I NOT > IPOS PERFORM TERPRI.
            MOVE I TO IPOS TABPOS.
        PRIN3 SECTION.
        PRIN3X.
            PERFORM PRIN2 VARYING I FROM 1 BY 1 UNTIL I > ILENGTH.
        EJECTP SECTION.
        EJECTPX.
            MOVE O TO LINENR.
            PERFORM EJECTIT.
        PRINI1 SECTION.
        PRINI1X.
            CALL "ITOC" USING I STRBUFF ILENGTH ITOCLEN20.
        NEWOUTFILE SECTION.
        NEWOUTFILEX.
      * UTFIL = 2 WHEN RESULT IS PRIMARY OUTPUT
            IF UTFIL NOT = 1 CALL "MDRCSF" USING SEQFID ELSE MOVE SEQLEN TO
              SEQFID3 MOVE WACCESS TO SEQFID1.
            MOVE FILENAME TO SEQNAME.
            IF FILENAME = "T" MOVE 1 TO UTFIL ELSE MOVE 2 TO UTFIL.
            IF UTFIL = 2 CALL "MDROSF" USING SEQFID SEQNAME.
```

Figure 6.2   (Continued)

tionary is used by some software vendors to describe this role. In addition to describing the data, such dictionaries may contain report headings, alternate names for data (aliases), report formats, screen layouts, titles for fields that can be placed in column headings, and so on. If a user asks that two fields be added when one is binary and the other is decimal, that does not matter. The dictionary indicates their formats, and they are converted to a compatible format before adding.

Use of an existing data dictionary saves work. The person designing the application does not have to worry about formatting fields and laying out records. They already exist. But there is a more important reason for sound data administration. User-friendly languages encourage users to design their own data. The same type of data field may be created many times by different groups. Multiple versions of similar records that are incompatible come into existence. Data that ought to be coordinated will not be. Data that ought to be passed from the factory floor or the warehouse to other information systems will not be. Data cannot be pulled together from separate systems for overall management reporting. Coordination is needed of most data. Often the same collection of data should be shared by several users, who may employ it for different purposes.

Information centers and 4GL developers need a dictionary used with sound data administration.

INTELLIGENT DATA BASE

We can distinguish between an intelligent data base and a dumb data base, just as we can distinguish between intelligent and dumb terminals. A dumb data base does not perform logic operations on the data; it merely stores the data and makes different views of the data available to different users. The logic is all in the application programs. An intelligent data base automatically performs specified logic operations or calculations on the data. Data and logic associated with the data are stored in an application-independent fashion.

An intelligent data base may automatically apply range and integrity checks to the data as they are entered. These checks can be defined in the data dictionary. It may execute security checks, apply cryptography, ask for passwords, and so on. Audit trails may be created automatically. Actions that change the data base may automatically *trigger* specified procedures. The nature of the trigger and the resulting action may be defined in software associated with the data base rather than with its users.

We can distinguish between *active* and *passive* data bases. A *passive* data base merely stores the data and allows users to modify them. It does not *initiate* application procedures. An *active* data base may automatically initiate a procedure when specified data values exceed a given range or hit a trigger value. With a passive data base, the users have to tell it everything; with an active data base, it may inform the users when it wants them to know something. A red light might be flashing on your office workstation because the data base wants to notify you of a condition.

An intelligent data base may employ derived data items. A given data item is always derived from other data items using a specified formula. An invoice total, for example, might be stored in a data base. This data item is defined as being derived from the line item totals on the invoice, and these may be derived from prices, quantities, and discounts.

VISICALC, MULTIPLAN, and LOTUS 1-2-3 (among others) are intelligent file systems (as opposed to data-base systems). The user defines the data in certain cells, columns, or rows as being derived from other data. The value in *column C row R*, for example, might be defined as being that in *column $(C-1)$ row R* plus that in *column C row $(R-1)$*. *Column C* becomes a cumulative total of the values in *column $(C-1)$*. When a value is entered at the bottom of *column $(C-1)$*, a corresponding cumulative total value appears at the bottom of *column C*. If a value is changed in the middle of *column $(C-1)$*, values will be automatically changed in *column C* as a consequence. If a user tries to change a value in *column C*, he might be prevented from doing so because it is locked and can only be changed by derivation from other changes. Far more elaborate computations are built by users into such spreadsheets.

Derived data may be computed immediately when a change is made in its constituent data, or the computations and changes may be deferred to a later time when they can be performed as a group.

ENCYCLOPEDIA　　　Data dictionaries range from the simple storing of data definitions to the storing of as much information as possible to help in the application-development process. The term *dictionary* is sometimes used for tools that store only data definitions; the term *directory* is sometimes used for tools that store screen layouts, report formats, and other such information about data structures; the term *encyclopedia* is used for tools that store *logic* as well as data—the logic of an intelligent data base, the logic of business rules, or logic represented in design diagrams.

The dictionary, directory, or encyclopedia should be employed on-line by a compiler or an interpreter. The person who creates the application ought to interact via the 4GL software with the dictionary, directory, or encyclopedia. This interaction should give him the maximum help in speeding up his work and ensuring that the resulting system is bug-free as far as possible.

Some data-base systems still, unfortunately, do not have on-line dictionaries usable directly by a 4GL.

AUTOMATIC　　　Using a programming language such as COBOL or
NAVIGATION　　　PL/I, a programmer *navigates* through a data base.
　　　　　　　　　　He accesses one record at a time and follows pointer links between the records one at a time. To do so he must have detailed knowledge of the data-base structure. A good 4GL has *automatic* navigation in its data base. It protects the user from having to know the detailed structure of the data base.

Figure 6.3 shows a simple data model. Figures 6.4 to 6.6 show it represented as hierarchical, CODASYL, and relational data bases.

Suppose that we wanted to produce from these data structures a report that lists part number, quantity on hand, quantity ordered, and delivery date. Using a conventional programming language, this would mean navigating among the PART record, LINE ITEM record, and ORDER record. The whole report might take 50 or so lines of code in COBOL. With the NOMAD language, which employs a relational data base, the report can be generated with one line of code:

LIST PART# QUANTITY-ON-HAND QUANTITY-ORDERED DELIVERY-DATE

The software uses a dictionary to locate which record contains each of these data items. It then executes a relational join to produce the required combination of data items.

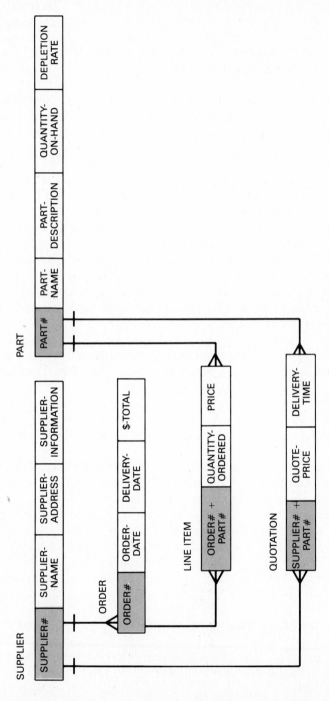

Figure 6.3 Plex structure of associations among records. This can be represented with a hierarchical approach (Fig. 6.4), a network approach (Fig. 6.5), or a relational approach (Fig. 6.6).

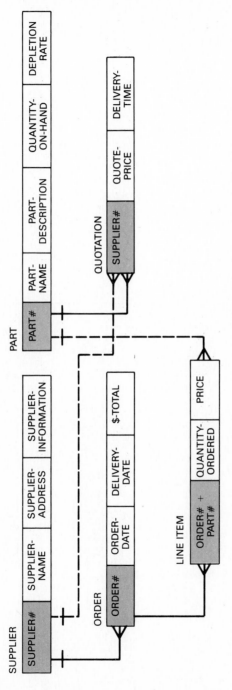

Figure 6.4 Hierarchical (tree-structure) version of the data structure in Fig. 6.3.

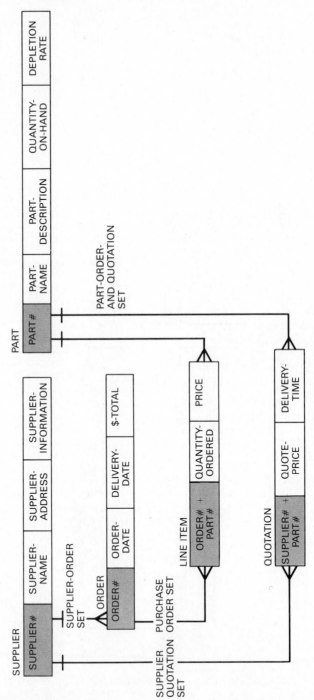

Figure 6.5   Network (CODASYL) version of the data structure in Fig. 6.3.

SUPPLIER

SUPPLIER#	SUPPLIER-NAME	SUPPLIER-ADDRESS	SUPPLIER-INFORMATION

PART

PART#	PART-NAME	PART-DESCRIPTION	QUANTITY-ON-HAND	DEPLETION RATE

QUOTATION

SUPPLIER#	PART#	QUOTE-PRICE	DELIVERY-TIME

ORDER

ORDER#	SUPPLIER#	ORDER-DATE	DELIVERY-DATE	$-TOTAL

LINE-ITEM

ORDER#	PART#	QUANTITY-ORDERED	PRICE

Figure 6.6   Relational version of the data structure in Fig. 6.3.

The result could be sorted to put at the top of the report the parts with the greatest risk of running out. Items with lower values of QUANTITY-ON-HAND/DEPLETION-RATE should be higher on the report. The user adds another line of code:

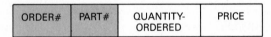

ORDER BY (QUANTITY-ON-HAND/DEPLETION-RATE)

These operations would require much navigation if done with a conventional program, which tackles them one record at a time. Using higher-level data-base commands, the navigation is automatic. A wide variety of data-base languages employ automatic navigation. Fairly complex software is needed in the DBMS to handle automatic navigation efficiently. Some DBMSs do not have this capability.

The QUERY-BY-EXAMPLE illustration at the start of this chapter uses automatic navigation. The user knows nothing about the record structures other than the view that the language has displayed on the screen. In this example the user specifies the joins that must occur. He similarly specifies joins in the last three statements of this SQL version of the same operation:

```
SELECT HOSPNAME, ADDRESS, PHONE
FROM HOSPITAL
AND SELECT WARDNO, TOTROOMS, TOTBEDS, BEDAVAIL, WARDTYPE
FROM WARD
AND SELECT*
FROM PATIENT
WHERE ADMITDAT LE (PREVDATE + 365)
AND WARD.WARDTYPE = "QUARANTINE"
AND PATIENT.HOSPNAME = WARD.HOSPNAME
AND PATIENT.HOSPNAME = HOSPITAL.HOSPNAME
AND PATIENT.WARDNO = WARD.WARDNO
```

In some languages, as with the NOMAD example, the user does not need to state explicitly what joins are needed. Provided that the software can correctly recognize the fields that are referred to, it can determine what joins to execute. In the English-input language INTELLECT, for example, the user might say:

```
GIVE ME QUANTITY-ON-HAND FOR EACH PART NUMBER AND
SHOW QUANTITIES ORDERED WITH DELIVERY DATE.
```

After some interaction with the user to clarify this query, the software performs the necessary joins and navigation.

Automatic navigation is in keeping with our principle of minimum work. It saves much programming. It can also save much maintenance work because it gives statements that are easy to change. It has certain dangers and may give incorrect results if the software does not understand and handle the data structures correctly. Chapter 18 discusses this.

With certain data-base systems, high-level statements that provide automatic navigation can be included in conventional programs. Statements of DEC's DATATRIEVE language or IBM's SQL, for example, can be inserted into COBOL or PL/I programs. The compiler translates the SQL statements into compact routines in machine language. These precompiled routines may access many records in an optimized sequence. They are called whenever the COBOL or PL/I program is executed.

It is more efficient to use precompiled, optimized routines for automatic navigation, but more often the high-level statements are entered interactively by end users and are interpreted rather than compiled.

Automatic navigation is most commonly associated with relational data bases. It should not be thought of as a property of relational DBMSs only. Some pointer-linked or CODASYL DBMSs also have automatic navigation. Automatic navigation leads to high flexibility of data-base use, so the flexibility that a relational DBMS provides of creating new access paths is important.

SYSTEM   Complex design processes begin with *sketches* and
SKETCHES   progress into representations that have greater detail.
Eventually a level of detail is reached from which a system is implemented. A house architect, for example, begins with sketches of what a home may look like. He converts these a stage at a time into detailed drawings from which the builders work. A computer application designer starts with sketches of the application, and these are broken down into more detail until programs are created.

An extremely important property of the sketch is that it can be readily understood by the end users. Would-be homeowners want to think about the architect's first sketches before he goes into too much detail. We need to have ways of representing what a system will do that the would-be users can readily understand and think about. The more they think and argue about the sketches, the more likely they are to be pleased with the final result.

We have a variety of ways of sketching what a system will do. Different forms of sketches may be needed to represent different aspects of a systems behavior. Some of them are necessarily more abstract than an architect's sketch of a house. The user must learn how to read them, and the form of sketch must be designed so that this is easy for him.

Action diagrams with brackets are a type of sketch [1]. With a graphics tool, they can be drawn on a screen, edited, and successively converted into 4GL with some automation of the coding.

Among types of sketches used are the following:

- Prototyping
- Data-flow diagrams
- HIPO diagrams
- Action diagrams [1]
- Data-base action diagrams
- Warnier diagrams
- Nassi-Shneiderman charts
- HOS notation

Prototyping is by far the most effective for giving the user a clear, realistic representation of the system to be built. Various users employ the prototype and determine whether it deals with their problems effectively. They usually discover omissions, inconsistencies, and misunderstandings. Often the need for improved human factoring is revealed. The analysts successively refine the prototype until it meets the users' needs as effectively as possible.

A prototype is tangible and real, and it enables the users to make contributions to the design that would otherwise never be made. Prototyping is often the only way to be *sure* that the would-be users will like the system. It may not, however, reveal all the logic of the system or complex interactions between subsystems. Other forms of the sketch are needed showing these.

Action diagrams show structure and logic [1]. Data-base action diagrams show logic and its relation to data-base structures. Data-flow diagrams show the interactions among separate processes. HOS diagrams show formal decomposition of functions. Any of these can be manipulated on a graphics screen.

Some of the types of sketch that systems analysts have employed are difficult for end users to learn and argue about. A major emphasis is needed on finding the most user-friendly form of a sketch. The sketch needs one other property: It should be translatable into a system design *as directly as possible*. Figure 6.7 shows these two properties of the form of sketch.

COMPUTABLE DESIGNS

The system design that fills in detail from the sketch has one very important property. It should be *computable,* convertible directly into executable code. It must be unambiguous and rigorous. If the design technique has this property, a program generator that creates the code automatically can be written. This saves much time and also produces code that is free from the types of errors made by human coders. The program testing time is therefore greatly reduced, and applications are created much faster.

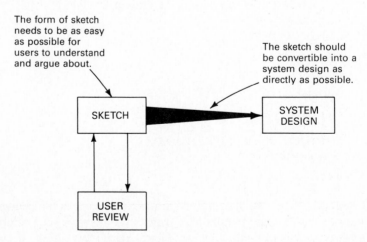

Figure 6.7   Properties of system sketches.

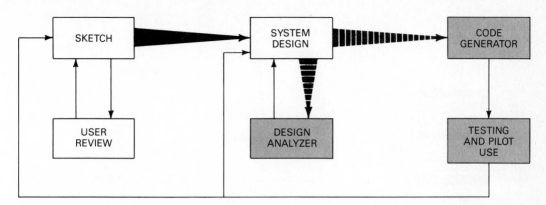

Figure 6.8 The system design should (ideally) be done in a form that is computable, that is, a form that can be automatically analyzed and converted into program code. The striped arrows show linkages that should be automated.

Figure 6.8 shows what is needed for coding automation. The design is checked by a design *analyzer*. This checks for syntax errors and as far as possible for semantics errors. It reveals any inconsistencies or incompleteness that would prevent code generation. When the analyzer indicates that the design is correct and complete enough to generate code, the design is passed to a program generator. The striped arrows of Fig. 6.8 show that the linkage between the design representation and the analyzer and code generator are automatic.

When the code is generated, it is tested to ensure that it does what was intended. The testing may cause modifications to be made to the system design or possibly to the sketch. With the best software of this type, the testing process is brief because most errors have already been detected by the analyzer. Human program-coding errors do not exist.

The code generator may produce a portion of a system rather than the complete system. This portion may be tested in a simulation mode with the parts of the system not yet coded being manually simulated or bridged.

Where possible, the link between the sketch and the system design should also be automatic. The sketch is an approximate overview design that needs to be refined into more detail until it is computable. The sketch may be representable on a computer screen in such a way that the designer can decompose it into the greater levels of detail needed for code generation.

It is usually the case that system sketches are changed many times as refinements are made and modifications explored. A neat drawing of each modification by hand is very time-consuming. Computer-aided editing of the sketch and computer graphics for drawing it (even if crudely) increase the productivity of the design process and encourage the developers to explore the alternatives more comprehensively.

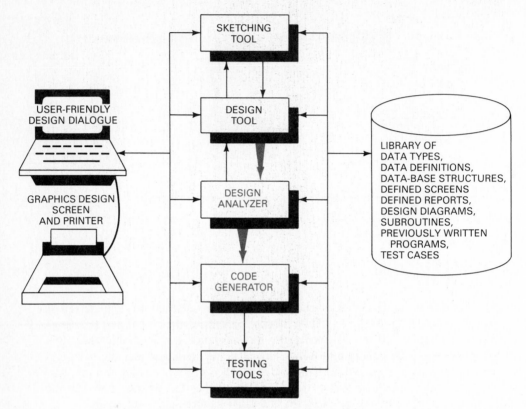

Figure 6.9   A designer's workbench is needed for automating the design process as fully as possible.

A design workbench is needed, as illustrated in Fig. 6.9, for automating the design process and the generation of code as fully as possible.

A certain stage in the evolution of the specification sketch may be regarded as detailed design, which may be handed over to a different team. This team can add refinements to the chart; these are then checked by the original specifiers.

There is often argument about what should be in the requirements statement, what should be in the specification, and what should be in the design documents. This is an artificial distinction. Requirements, specification, and design are all the same process carried to greater levels of detail. It is possible to have one diagramming technique and language that handles all of these.

Different languages and techniques have been developed for different aspects of the development life cycle. Sometimes one language is used for the requirements statement (often English); a different language or technique is used for the specification—for example, data-flow diagrams—and yet a different one for detailed program design; then a programming language is used for coding.

The specification writers commonly misinterpret the requirements. The program designers commonly misinterpret the specifications. The coders make errors in coding from the design diagrams. There are many opportunities to introduce manual processes during and between the phases of the life cycle. At each of these, new errors arise. Using a computable specification technique that can be extended from a high-level overview to specifications detailed enough for code generation avoids these problems.

THE STRUCTURED REVOLUTION

Much has been written about the "revolution" in application design represented by structured techniques. Most of the structured techniques that have been much advertised and sold, however, do not produce *computable* designs. They are insufficiently rigorous to be a basis for automatic generation of code.

I believe that the *real* revolution is not the refinement of hand methods used with hand coding but rather the use of design techniques that automate the process.

I have commented that the human brain is good at some tasks and bad at others. Fortunately, the computer is good at certain tasks that the brain does badly. Our brain cannot do long, meticulous logic operations without making errors. It needs automated tools to help it.

System design, then, needs to start with ways that make it easy for users to conceptualize what computers will do for them, to modify and refine these statements of requirements easily, and then to translate them automatically into bug-free code. It is important for all persons involved with computing to understand that this is possible and that software that does this exists for even the most complex of systems. There is, however, much scope for improving the sketching and conceptualization techniques and the code generation and machine-efficient execution.

INTERPRETERS AND COMPILERS

The languages we use for creating applications are very different from machine language. Fourth-generation languages are much farther from machine language than third-generation languages are. It is necessary to translate from the language of application creation into executable machine code. Fourth-generation languages' developers assume that machine cycles are cheap and that far more of them can be used for translation than with third-generation languages.

The code written in a third-generation language is called the *source code.* This is translated with a compiler to form *object code,* which executes on the target computer aided by its operating system. We distinguish between a compiler and an interpreter. A *compiler* operates off-line. It scans the entire program, usually several times, creating tables of variables to enable it to make the translation to object code. An *interpreter* operates on-line. It translates on a unit-by-unit basis, translating and executing what are usually the smallest meaningful units of source code. A compiler produces an *object program,* which will be executed at a later time. An interpreter produces *results.* It executes the source code as it translates it, on-line.

An interpreter is usually much less efficient in machine usage than a compiler. Parts of the translation are done repetitively. Each time the interpreter encounters a statement, it has to translate it, even if it has already encountered it many times. This contrasts with a compiler, which scans the whole program many times, building its tables. A compiler can be designed to optimize the code it produces. An interpreter cannot optimize code in the same way and has to retranslate each time the program is rerun.

Distinctions between compilers and interpreters become more blurred with 4GLs. Most 4GLs are designed for on-line operation, and a dialogue takes place between the language software and the person building the application. Before there is any attempt at complete interpretation or compilation, the *dialogue* helps the user to build his program and checks it for errors. The initial checks are usually done like an interpreter. One input at a time is checked and possibly modified, then the smallest executable unit may be checked. Before translation, the software may perform a lengthier set of checks, possibly scanning the whole program looking for errors or checking the correctness of linkages to other programs or subroutines. A compiler-like check may be done while the application creator is at the terminal.

SUCCESSIVE LEVELS OF VERIFICATION

The AXES language of HOS enables the user to express high-level functions and decompose these into successively lower-level functions until functions are reached for which code can be generated. The software goes through several phases of verification. The user builds his system on a terminal screen, and the dialogue interrupts the user if he uses the commands incorrectly. It then enters its first phase of verification of what the designer has created. This is a syntax check, which checks one statement at a time. It produces error messages such as these:

UNKNOWN SYNTAX
ILLEGAL FUNCTION FORM
NAME(S) MISSING
DUPLICATE INPUT (A function has duplicate input variables.)
INCOMPLETE TREE (A parent exists without two offspring.)

The second pass checks larger logical units. It ensures that when a function is decomposed by the designer into components, this decomposition is correct. The decomposition has to obey rigorously defined rules. This pass produces error messages such as these:

```
INPUT NOT PASSED RIGHT
OUTPUT NOT PASSED LEFT
DATA NOT PASSED ACROSS
OUTPUT NOT SHARED
INPUT NOT PARTITIONED
BAD VARIABLE ORDERING
UNUSED OUTPUT RIGHT
NON-UNIQUE FUNCTION
```

The third pass checks the overall design. It ensures that the lowest-level nodes can be compiled and that there are no references to nodes or programs that do not exist. It ensures that linkages to other structures are correct and that there are no inconsistent uses of data types or problems with looping (recursion). It produces error messages such as these:

```
SUBTREE LABEL NOT FOUND
NO SUCH FUNCTION
TOP OF SUBTREE DIFFERS FROM REFERENCE
NO PLUG-IN
EMPTY REFERENCE
INFINITE RECURSION
NO NEW DATA IN RECURSION
MULTIPLE RECURSION
```

When the user has adjusted his design so that it passes this third level of verification, he can then request that his design be translated into program code, which is compiled. He often executes portions of his program with simulated data before the whole application is completed.

We thus see a mixture of interpreter-like and compiler-like operations in an ongoing dialogue with the application designer.

BOTH INTERPRETER AND COMPILER

Many 4GLs use an interpreter and because of this have acquired the reputation of being inappropriate for heavy-duty computing with high transaction volumes. Some 4GLs use an optimizing compiler and are designed for heavy-duty computing. In the future it will make sense for certain classes of 4GL to have *both* an interpreter and a compiler. The compiler helps to achieve machine efficiency; the interpreter helps the designer to do on-line verification and testing. The designer may build his application using an interpreter, try out prototypes with the end users, and then, when he is satisfied, feed the source code into an optimizing compiler.

The interpreter should enable the user to see results as fast as possible; the compiler should produce code that is as machine-efficient as possible.

The compiler may compile the source code so that it can run on a different target machine. The portability problem may be overcome, in part, by being able to recompile programs to run on different, incompatible machines.

APPLICATION FACTORY, from Cortex [2], is software that enables a systems analyst to build applications by filling in panels on a screen. The analyst tests application as he builds them and can leave them with end users to try out as prototypes. This uses an interpreter. The designer can take the code created once the users are happy with it and compile it with a separate product called ACCELERATOR (Fig. 6.10). ACCELERATOR is a multipass optimizing compiler that can create code that runs efficiently on a target computer. The APPLICATION FACTORY code can be ''accelerated'' for different computers. It can also produce COBOL, if required, which can be used in COBOL environments.

A particularly attractive aspect of the use of separate compilers is that a prototype can be built on a personal computer and then compiled to run efficiently on a mainframe.

CATCHING
ERRORS
AS EARLY AS
POSSIBLE

An important principle of software for application development ought to be to catch errors as early as possible. The earlier the error is caught, the less expensive it is. If an error is detected during the initial conceptualization of a system, it causes no problems. If it finds its way into the written specifications, it becomes much more expensive. Statistics from various organizations show that the errors detected during program testing are ten or more times as expensive to correct as errors detected at the specification stage. Correcting errors at the maintenance stage is another order of magnitude more costly. Figure 6.11 illustrates this.

On one avionics system, the cost per line of code, including debugging and documentation, was reported to be $70. Its cost per line of code of maintenance, however, was $4000 [3]. These figures were unusually high because of the complexity of the system, but they would clearly have been much lower if techniques could have been used for thoroughly debugging the specifications and design.

Traditionally, most errors are caught in the program testing or maintenance phases. Many of these are specification errors, which by then are very expensive to correct. An objective of 4GLs ought to be to find every problem as early in the development cycle as possible.

With on-line development, it is easy to catch syntax errors when they are made. Much more troublesome are errors of logic and meaning.

INFRASTRUCTURE   Good 4GLs require a substantial infrastructure to support them. Like third-generation languages, they

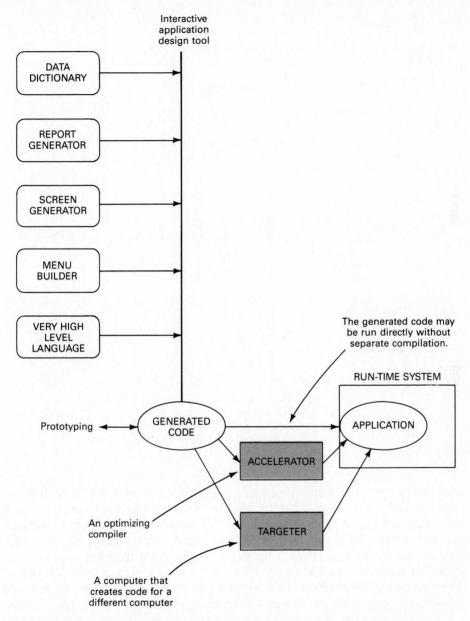

Figure 6.10 APPLICATION FACTORY from Cortex [2], gives its users the choice of using a separate compiler or software that compiles code for a different computer.

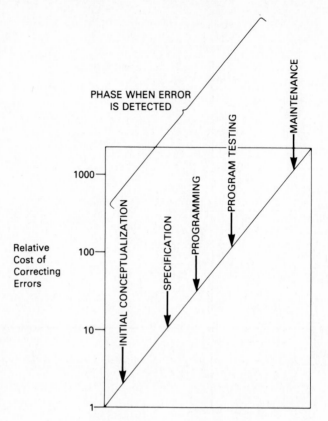

Figure 6.11 It is much less expensive to catch errors early. An objective of 4GL design ought to be to catch as many errors as possible before they become expensive and troublesome.

need interpreters and compilers, but in addition many of them need dialogue facilities such as those described in Chapter 5. Some of these require personal computers connected to mainframes, or fast communication links to achieve subsecond response times. Good 4GLs are highly dependent on the data base they are linked to. This requires tight coupling between the interpreter or compiler and the data-base dictionary. The user dialogue employs the dictionary. The data base often requires other properties that earlier data bases did not (and still do not) have, such as automatic navigation, relational concurrency controls, and knowledge of the data model with rules that can prevent semantic disintegrity. (This, described in Chapter 9, is still missing in many 4GL products.) The language may employ an encyclopedia that is tightly linked to the data base.

Often the 4GL users need to extract data from a separate data base or file system. The *extractor* ought to be an important feature of the language. It can have essentially the same syntax as the report generator so that a user can specify data which he wants extracted from a separate data base. This extraction may then occur on-line or off-line.

In some cases the user needs to employ data stored at several distributed computer sites. Distributed data-base access needs a good data network with an appropriate dictionary or directory and integrity and security controls. It requires a highly complex infrastructure.

Unlike third-generation languages, then, the most valuable 4GLs cannot be bought in isolation from their infrastructure, which involves a data base, a dictionary, and possibly an encyclopedia, a data network, extractor tools, and distributed data-base controls. The 4GL may be linked to and (at least partially) compatible with office automation products that provide functions from the same work station such as text processing, electronic mail, electronic filing, graphics editing and printing, and possibly an electronic "desk," which enables the user to switch his attention quickly among several work areas or documents he is currently employing.

Toward the end of his life, Isaac Newton wrote that insofar as he had achieved anything worthwhile, he had done so by standing on the shoulders of giants. Richard Hamming comments that programmers do not tend to stand on each others' shoulders; they stand on each others' feet!

It is desirable that the tools we use should build ever growing, ever more powerful libraries of subroutines and callable programs. It is desirable to be able to find out what exists in the library and be able to understand it and use it. Most large computing installations reinvent the same routines over and over again because this capability is missing. We need to be able to link these routines into new programs without interface errors. Rigorous techniques for checking for interface errors are vital.

A well-organized library is an essential part of the infrastructure. A directory or thesaurus of callable modules is needed to make the modules easy to find.

REFERENCES

1. J. Martin and C. McClure, *Action Diagrams: Clearly Structured Program Design,* Englewood Cliffs, N.J., Prentice-Hall Inc., 1985.

2. APPLICATION FACTORY manuals are available from Cortex Corporation, 55 William Street, Wellesley, MA 02181.

3. W. L. Trainer, "Software: From Satan to Savior," *Proceedings of the NAECON Conference,* May 1973.

7 PROCEDURAL CODE AND ACTION DIAGRAMS

Although many of the more basic operations of commercial data processing can be expressed with nonprocedural techniques, many 4GLs also employ procedural coding for loops, conditions, and nested procedures. It is desirable that the 4GL enforce *structural design* of procedures and make the structure as clear as possible. Some of the existing 4GLs make the structuring of complex programs clear and simple. With other 4GLs, it is a mess.

In the design and understanding of complex code, it helps greatly to be able to draw simple diagrams of its structure. The most effective form of diagram for doing this is the action diagram [1]. Action diagrams and the code that fits them can be quickly edited on the screen of a personal computer [2]. With some 4GLs, the code for control structures can be fitted *automatically* onto the action diagrams.

Action diagrams are a basic tool in using 4GLs. They are also a useful tool for judging how well structured a 4GL is. If the control statements of a 4GL do not fit well onto the brackets of action diagrams, the language has structural deficiencies.

If I were teaching users to employ 4GLs with procedural statements, I would begin by teaching them action diagrams.

ACTION DIAGRAM BRACKETS

Using action diagrams, loops, conditions, and nested procedures are sketched with brackets:

Inside the bracket is a sequence of actions such as data-base accesses and calculations. A simple control rule applies to the bracket. You enter it at the top, do the things in it in a top-to-bottom order, and exit at the bottom.

Sometimes the bracket is conditional: The items in the bracket may be executed only if a certain condition applies. In this case, the condition is written at the head of the bracket:

```
┌─ IF CUSTOMER# IS VALID
│    ─ ─ ─ ─ ─ ─
│    ─ ─ ─ ─ ─ ─
└─   ─ ─ ─ ─ ─ ─
```

To clarify what is the end of the IF routine, some 4GLs use an ENDIF statement:

```
┌─ IF CUSTOMER# IS VALID
│    ─ ─ ─ ─ ─ ─
│    ─ ─ ─ ─ ─ ─
│    ─ ─ ─ ─ ─ ─
└─ ENDIF
```

To draw mutually exclusive conditions, more than one division is shown in the same bracket:

```
┌─ IF CUSTOMER# IS VALID
│    ─ ─ ─ ─ ─ ─
│    ─ ─ ─ ─ ─ ─
├─ ELSE
│    ─ ─ ─ ─ ─ ─
└─ ENDIF
```

This has only two mutually exclusive conditions, an IF and an ELSE. Sometimes there are many mutually exclusive conditions. These are drawn with a multistep bracket:

```
┌─ WHEN KEY = "1"
│    ─ ─ ─ ─ ─ ─
│    ─ ─ ─ ─ ─ ─
├─ WHEN KEY = "2"
│    ─ ─ ─ ─ ─ ─
│    ─ ─ ─ ─ ─ ─
├─ WHEN KEY = "3"
│    ─ ─ ─ ─ ─ ─
│    ─ ─ ─ ─ ─ ─
├─ WHEN KEY = "4"
│    ─ ─ ─ ─ ─ ─
│    ─ ─ ─ ─ ─ ─
└─ END
```

To make it clear what the END relates to, some 4GLs call this a CASE or SELECT structure and use an ENDCASE or ENDSELECT statement to terminate it:

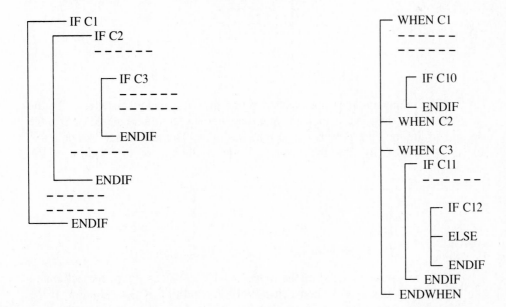

```
┌─ SELECT
│  WHEN KEY = "1"
│  ─ ─ ─ ─ ─ ─
│  ─ ─ ─ ─ ─ ─
├─ WHEN KEY = "2"
│  ─ ─ ─ ─ ─ ─
│  ─ ─ ─ ─ ─ ─
├─ WHEN KEY = "3"
│  ─ ─ ─ ─ ─ ─
│  ─ ─ ─ ─ ─ ─
├─ WHEN KEY = "4"
│  ─ ─ ─ ─ ─ ─
│  ─ ─ ─ ─ ─ ─
├─ WHEN OTHER
│  ─ ─ ─ ─ ─ ─
└─ ENDSELECT
```

Brackets are often nested, showing how multiple conditions are handled:

```
┌── IF C1
│  ┌── IF C2
│  │    ─ ─ ─ ─ ─ ─
│  │  ┌─ IF C3
│  │  │   ─ ─ ─ ─ ─ ─
│  │  │   ─ ─ ─ ─ ─ ─
│  │  └─ ENDIF
│  │    ─ ─ ─ ─ ─ ─
│  └─── ENDIF
│    ─ ─ ─ ─ ─ ─
│    ─ ─ ─ ─ ─ ─
└─── ENDIF
```

```
┌─ WHEN C1
│   ─ ─ ─ ─ ─ ─
│   ─ ─ ─ ─ ─ ─
│  ┌─ IF C10
│  └─ ENDIF
├─ WHEN C2
│
├─ WHEN C3
│  ┌─ IF C11
│  │   ─ ─ ─ ─ ─ ─
│  │  ┌─ IF C12
│  │  ├─ ELSE
│  │  └─ ENDIF
│  └─ ENDIF
└─ ENDWHEN
```

REPEATED ACTIONS

Some actions are executed repetitively in computer procedures. This is controlled by a loop in a program. Actions that are repeated are indicated by a thick bracket drawn with a double line at the top:

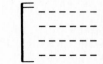

Repetition brackets are just like other brackets except that the condition that controls the execution of the bracket is tested repeatedly to determine whether the activities in the bracket are executed.

When repetition is indicated in any type of language, it is necessary to show clearly what terminates the repetition. Music also uses a double line in the score to indicate repetition. However, one unfortunate pianist at a London Promenade Concert a few years ago got into a closed loop during the slow movement of Rachmaninoff's Second Piano Concerto and could not find her way out.

Some 4GLs use statements like LOOP and ENDLOOP to begin and terminate loops:

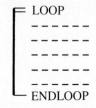

When many people first start to program, they make mistakes with the point at which they test a loop. Sometimes the test should be made *before* the actions of the loop are performed, sometimes *after*. This difference can be made clear on brackets by drawing the test either at the top or the bottom of the bracket:

If the test is at the head of the loop, as with a WHILE loop, the actions in the loop may never be executed if the WHILE condition is not satisfied. If the test is at the bottom of the loop, as with an UNTIL loop, the actions in the loop are executed at least once. They will be executed more than once if the condition is fulfilled.

SETS OF DATA

Sometimes a procedure needs to be executed on all of the items in a set of items. It might be applied to all transactions or all records in a file; for example:

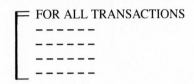

FOR ALL TRANSACTIONS

This operation is described with a FOR and ENDFOR statement in some languages:

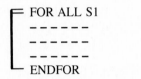

FOR ALL S1

ENDFOR

Here *all* the items in set S1 will be processed. In some cases the items in the set will be processed only where they meet some condition. Instead of a FOR ALL statement, a FOR EACH–WHERE statement might be used:

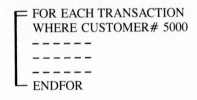

FOR EACH TRANSACTION
WHERE CUSTOMER# 5000

ENDFOR

TERMINATIONS

Certain conditions may cause a procedure to be terminated. They may cause the termination of the bracket in which the condition occurs, or they may cause the termination of several nested brackets.

Terminations can be drawn by showing an arrow going to the left from the statement of the termination condition and through the bracket:

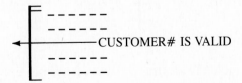

CUSTOMER# IS VALID

The following shows the simultaneous termination of several brackets:

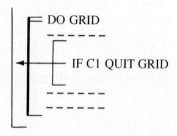

The next instruction to be executed is the one after the bottom of the leftmost bracket that is terminated.

The term QUIT (or one like it) is used in some 4GLs to indicate the termination of a procedure. QUIT may be followed by a procedure name to indicate the brackets being terminated:

```
  ┌── DO GRID
  │   ┌─ ─ ─ ─ ─ ─
  │   ┌─
◄─┼───┼─ IF C1 QUIT GRID
  │   └
  │   └─ ─ ─ ─ ─ ─
  │   ─ ─ ─ ─ ─ ─
  └
```

NEXT ITERATION

In a repetition bracket (loop), there can be two types of terminations:

1. Exit the entire loop.
2. Terminate the current cycle through the loop and commence the next cycle.

We will refer to these with the words ESCAPE and NEXT. ESCAPE leaves a bracket completely and is drawn with the arrow passing through the bracket:

```
      ┌
◄─────┼─ESCAPE
      └
```

NEXT is like an END in that it causes a further execution of the loop code. It is drawn with an arrow that does not penetrate the bracket.

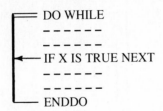

A termination of a bracket must be an *orderly* termination. It resets everything that would be reset if a normal END occurred.

WORDING ON THE BRACKETS

When fourth-generation languages are used, the wording on the action diagram may be the wording that is used on coding programs with the language. Some examples of this follow.

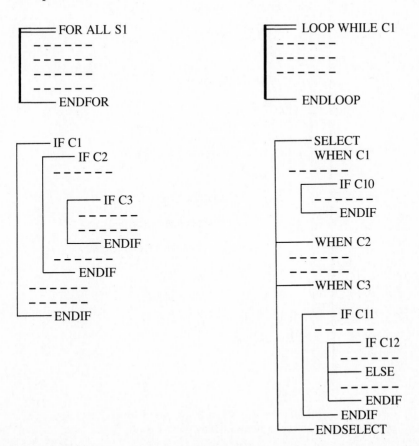

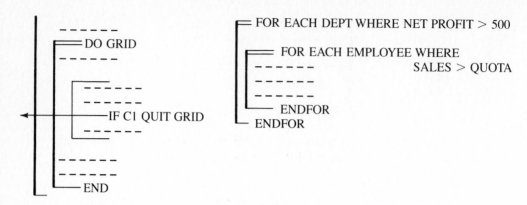

Figure 7.1 shows an action diagram for a procedure using control statements from the language IDEAL, from ADR [3].

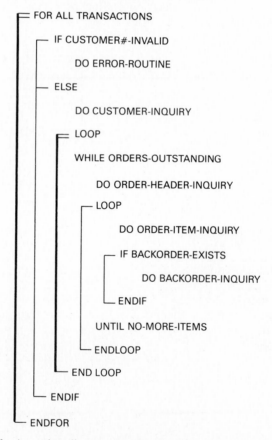

Figure 7.1 An action diagram showing the procedure for customer order entry using the control statements from the language IDEAL [3].

MANTIS, a fourth-generation language from Cincom Systems [4], automatically indents a user's code to show its structure. For example, the user might write:

```
ENTRY ROUTINE-1
DO SET-UP
CLEAR
UNTIL KEY = "CANCEL"
INDEX = 1
UNTIL INDEX = 22
A = INT (RND(10)+1)
SHOW FUNC(A)
INDEX = INDEX+1
END
END
SHOW "------------"
EXIT
```

MANTIS prints this program indented with dots as follows:

```
ENTRY ROUTINE__1
. DO SET__UP
. CLEAR
. UNTIL KEY = "CANCEL"
. . INDEX = 1
. . UNTIL INDEX = 22
. . . A = INT (RND(10)+1)
. . . SHOW FUNC(A)
. . . INDEX = INDEX + 1
. . END
. END
. SHOW "------"
EXIT
```

When there is a statement beginning with IF, ELSE, WHILE, UNTIL, or ENTRY, the following statement is automatically indented. The IF, ELSE, WHILE, and UNTIL statements must have a corresponding END statement; the ENTRY must have a corresponding EXIT. The indenting stops at the END or EXIT statement. This automatic indenting helps the programmer to check for missing END or EXIT statements or incorrect structuring.

The WHEN statement may occur many times before an END statement so that multiple tests and associated actions are in one block of code:

```
. . WHEN KEY = "1"
. . . SHOW FIRST (A)
. . WHEN KEY = "2"
. . . SHOW SECOND (A)
. . WHEN KEY = "3"
```

```
        . . . SHOW THIRD (A)
        . . WHEN KEY = "4"
        . . . SHOW FOURTH (A)
        . . WHEN KEY = "5"
        . . . SHOW FIFTH (A)
        . . END
```

Figure 7.2 shows a program written in MANTIS.

```
 10  ENTRY BUZZ_PHRASE_GENERATOR
 20  . DO SET_UP_VOCABULARY
 30  . HEAD "BUZZ PHRASE GENERATOR"
 40  . CLEAR
 50  . SHOW "I WILL GENERATE A SCREEN FULL OF 'BUZZ
      PHRASES' EVERY "
 60  . ' "TIME YOU HIT 'ENTER'. WHEN YOU WANT TO STOP, HIT
      'PA2'."
 70  . UNTIL KEY = "CANCEL"
 80  . . INDEX = 1
 90  . . UNTIL INDEX = 22
100  . . . A = INT(RND(10) + 1)
110  . . . B = INT(RND(10) + 1)
120  . . . C = INT(RND(10) + 1)
130  . . . SHOW FIRST(A) + " " + SECOND(B) + " " + NOUN(C)
140  . . . INDEX = INDEX + 1
150  . . END
160  . . WAIT
170  . END
180  . CHAIN "GAMES_MENU"
190  EXIT
200
210  ENTRY SET_UP_VOCABULARY
220  . TEXT FIRST(10,16),SECOND(10,16),NOUN(10,16)
230  . FIRST(1) = "INTEGRATED","TOTAL","SYSTEMATIZED","PARALLEL",
240  . ' "FUNCTIONAL","RESPONSIVE","OPTIONAL","SYNCHRONIZED",
250  . ' "COMPATIBLE","BALANCED"
260  . SECOND(1) = "MANAGEMENT","ORGANIZATIONAL","MONITORED",
270  . ' "RECIPROCAL","DIGITAL","LOGISTICAL","TRANSITIONAL",
280  . ' "INCREMENTAL","THIRD GENERATION","POLICY"
290  . NOUN(1) = "OPTION","FLEXIBILITY","CAPABILITY","MOBILITY",
300  . ' "PROGRAMMING","CONCEPT","TIME PHASE","PROJECTION",
310  . ' "HARDWARE","CONTINGENCY"
320  . SEED
330  EXIT
```

Figure 7.2 MANTIS, a procedural 4GL, automatically inserts the dots following the line numbers to show the leveling in the code. Reprinted with permission [4].

The automatic indentation of MANTIS helps, but in a sense the procedure is backward. Instead of typing difficult-to-remember control words and having the software fit indentation to these, we should first create a control structure, represented graphically, and have the software fit the control words to the structure.

ACTION DIAGRAM EDITORS

Simple action diagram editors on personal computers speed up the production and modification of programs and help eliminate bugs in control structures [2]. Action diagram editors may be used *independently* of any particular language for designing a system. They may be used *with* a particular language for creating and editing the programs. Where code is fitted automatically to the action diagram, it is impossible to have hanging or missing END statements, incorrect case structures, or other such errors.

APPLICATION FACTORY, from Cortex [5], incorporates action diagrams into its basic design tool. The user creates the control structures he needs, visually, and the tool fills in the words of the language, as shown in Fig. 7.3. Employing this, the program structure can be easily and rapidly modified. It is easy to follow another person's code, so the tool makes maintenance easy and fast.

The procedural component of APPLICATION FACTORY, from Cortex, builds its code with action diagrams on the screen as follows:

The user may type EACH and press the ENTER key. The following appears on the screen (in these diagrams, the square is the cursor):

```
┌═══ EACH
│     □
└─── ENDEACH
```

The user then types ON CHANGE IN THIS CUST. NO: #IZ. The following appears on the screen:

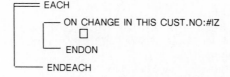

```
┌═══ EACH
│   ┌── ON CHANGE IN THIS CUST.NO:#IZ
│   │     □
│   └── ENDON
└──── ENDEACH
```

Figure 7.3 Procedural code being built with an action diagram editor, which is part of the 4GL software. This eliminates many common types of programming mistakes and makes the procedural code easy to change. (Diagrams courtesy Cortex Corporation, Wellesley, MA.)

(Continued)

The user enters a process, and the editor draws it as follows:

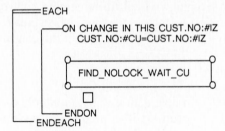

The user enters an IF bracket, another process, and an EXIT:

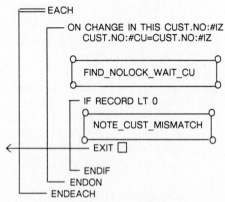

The user can move the cursor at any time to fill in other parts of the diagram:

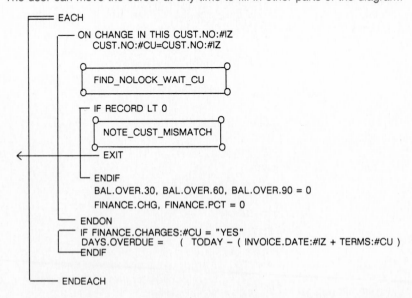

Figure 7.3   (Continued)

Here there is a syntax error. The cursor jumps to the place where the error is detected, and a flashing message appears on the screen:

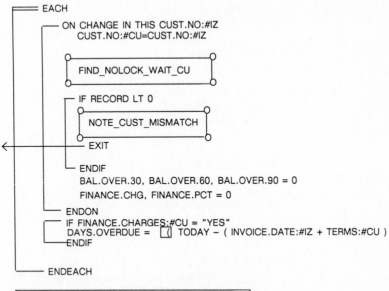

ERROR AT CURSOR – UNBALANCED PARENTHESIS

The user removes the incorrect parenthesis and enters a case (conditional) structure:

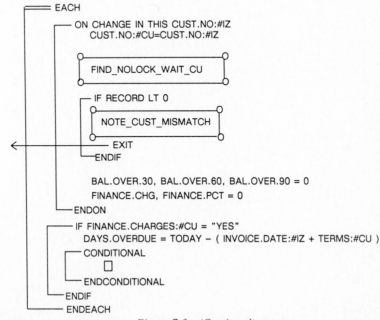

Figure 7.3   (Continued)

The user can enter numerous cases into this case structure:

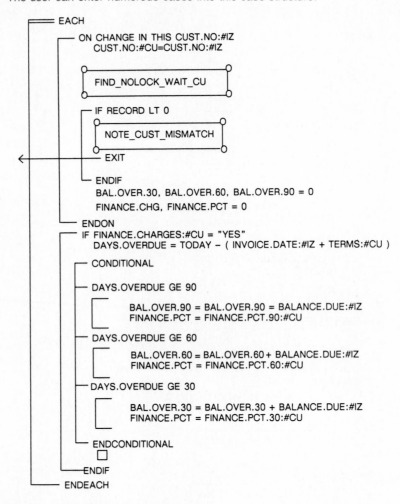

```
EACH
    ON CHANGE IN THIS CUST.NO:#IZ
        CUST.NO:#CU=CUST.NO:#IZ

        FIND_NOLOCK_WAIT_CU

        IF RECORD LT 0
            NOTE_CUST_MISMATCH
            EXIT
        ENDIF
        BAL.OVER.30, BAL.OVER.60, BAL.OVER.90 = 0
        FINANCE.CHG, FINANCE.PCT = 0
    ENDON
    IF FINANCE.CHARGES:#CU = "YES"
        DAYS.OVERDUE = TODAY – ( INVOICE.DATE:#IZ + TERMS:#CU )

        CONDITIONAL

        DAYS.OVERDUE GE 90
            BAL.OVER.90 = BAL.OVER.90 = BALANCE.DUE:#IZ
            FINANCE.PCT = FINANCE.PCT.90:#CU

        DAYS.OVERDUE GE 60
            BAL.OVER.60 = BAL.OVER.60 + BALANCE.DUE:#IZ
            FINANCE.PCT = FINANCE.PCT.60:#CU

        DAYS.OVERDUE GE 30
            BAL.OVER.30 = BAL.OVER.30 + BALANCE.DUE:#IZ
            FINANCE.PCT = FINANCE.PCT.30:#CU

        ENDCONDITIONAL

    ENDIF
ENDEACH
```

The following is the completed program:

Figure 7.3   (Continued)

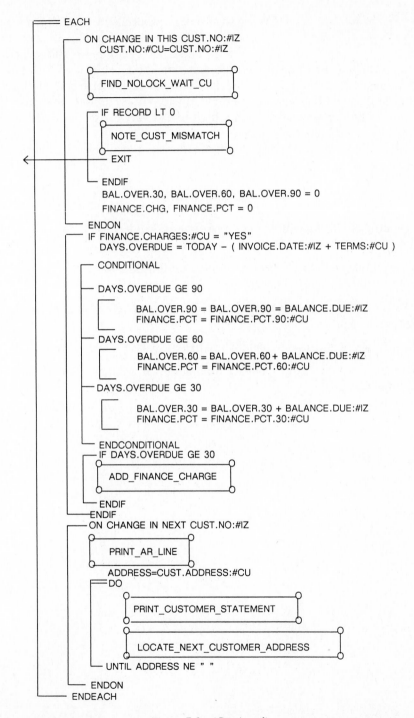

EACH
  ON CHANGE IN THIS CUST.NO:#IZ
    CUST.NO:#CU=CUST.NO:#IZ

```
FIND_NOLOCK_WAIT_CU
```

  IF RECORD LT 0

```
NOTE_CUST_MISMATCH
```

    EXIT

  ENDIF
    BAL.OVER.30, BAL.OVER.60, BAL.OVER.90 = 0
    FINANCE.CHG, FINANCE.PCT = 0
  ENDON
  IF FINANCE.CHARGES:#CU = "YES"
    DAYS.OVERDUE = TODAY − (INVOICE.DATE:#IZ + TERMS:#CU)

    CONDITIONAL

    DAYS.OVERDUE GE 90

        BAL.OVER.90 = BAL.OVER.90 = BALANCE.DUE:#IZ
        FINANCE.PCT = FINANCE.PCT.90:#CU

    DAYS.OVERDUE GE 60

        BAL.OVER.60 = BAL.OVER.60 + BALANCE.DUE:#IZ
        FINANCE.PCT = FINANCE.PCT.60:#CU

    DAYS.OVERDUE GE 30

        BAL.OVER.30 = BAL.OVER.30 + BALANCE.DUE:#IZ
        FINANCE.PCT = FINANCE.PCT.30:#CU

    ENDCONDITIONAL
    IF DAYS.OVERDUE GE 30

```
ADD_FINANCE_CHARGE
```

    ENDIF
  ENDIF
  ON CHANGE IN NEXT CUST.NO:#IZ

```
PRINT_AR_LINE
```

    ADDRESS=CUST.ADDRESS:#CU
    DO

```
PRINT_CUSTOMER_STATEMENT
```

```
LOCATE_NEXT_CUSTOMER_ADDRESS
```

    UNTIL ADDRESS NE " "
  ENDON
ENDEACH

Figure 7.3   (Continued)

FUNCTIONAL DECOMPOSITION Much system design proceeds in a top-down fashion. The designer initially has a high-level overview of what he is to build. He decomposes this overview a step at a time into more detail. Action diagrams are a useful tool for representing this functional decomposition. Unlike some of the other forms of structured design, they enable the designer to draw repetition, conditions, and case structures and to progress steadily from a high-level overview to the detailed levels that become executable code.

More details on the use of action diagrams are available elsewhere [1].

REFERENCES

1. J. Martin and C. McClure, *Action Diagrams,* Englewood Cliffs, NJ: Prentice Hall, Inc., 1985.

2. For example, *Action Diagrammer* software for IBM and other personal computers, from Database Design, Inc., Ann Arbor, MI.

3. IDEAL manuals are available from ADR, Applied Data Research, Inc., Princeton, NJ.

4. *MANTIS User's Guide,* Cincinnati: Cincom Systems, Inc., 1983.

5. Manuals available from Cortex Corporation, 55 William Street, Wellesley, MA 02181.

8 GOOD AND BAD STRUCTURING IN 4GLs

INTRODUCTION   Where procedural code is written with 4GLs, it is desirable that the principles of structured programming be fully adhered to. As commented earlier, some 4GLs have been designed with a good understanding of structured programming; others are a mess.

We can draw the structures of structured programming with action diagram brackets. Figure 8.1 does this. Language-independent labels are used on the brackets of Fig. 8.1. We can replace these labels with the commands of specific languages.

A 4GL should be designed to give as much help in creating structural code as possible. A useful way to judge the quality of the procedural part of a language is to fill in the brackets of Fig. 8.1 with the language commands. When a prospective buyer does this, he will find that some languages are ill-structured and incomplete. Some are confusing in their command structures. Some make extensive use of GO TO commands, which encourage ''spaghetti code'' that is difficult to understand and maintain. Others are well structured, with clear commands and no GO TOs.

If the commands of a prospective 4GL are such that Fig. 8.1 cannot be filled in with them, the language cannot create many of the program constructs needed in clean, well-structured program design. Ill-structured languages are best avoided.

Almost all 4GLs for building complex systems need procedural code (in addition to as much as possible being done nonprocedurally). It is desirable that the language have a set of clear control words equivalent to those in Fig. 8.1. It would help if standard words for this existed in the computer industry.

MAKING BRACKET STARTS AND ENDS CLEAR   A good 4GL ought to make it obvious and clear where the brackets start and end. IDEAL offers an excellent illustration of this.

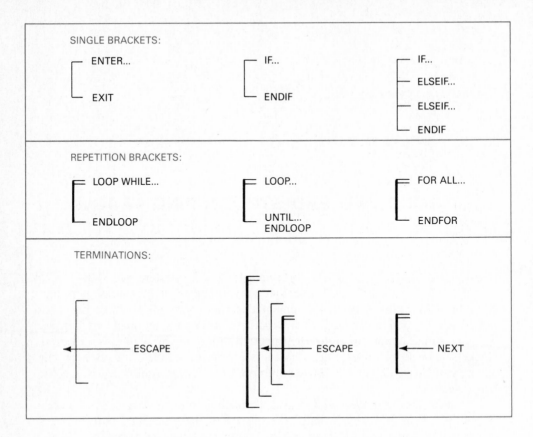

Figure 8.1   Control constructs with language-independent labels.

- An IF bracket terminates with ENDIF.
- A SELECT bracket terminates with ENDSELECT.
- A LOOP bracket terminates with ENDLOOP.
- A FOR bracket terminates with ENDFOR.
- A PROC (or PROCEDURE) bracket terminates with ENDPROC (or ENDPRO-CEDURE).

These types of control structures are needed in most full-capability 4GLs. It ought to be immediately clear which start of bracket each END statement is associated with. It is generally a bad practice to have no END statement for a bracket. It is a bad practice to have one END statement for more than one bracket. Such practices make programs more difficult to debug and increase the probability of errors. A person familiar with structured design might be surprised that I even mention such obvious deficiencies, but some major 4GLs do indeed have conditions, blocks, or loops that violate these guidelines and lack the requisite clarity.

If you are unfamiliar with NATURAL, examine the following segment of code and ask, first, does it appear to be correct? Second, where do you think the brackets open and close?

```
FIND EMPLOYEE_FILE WITH JOB_CODE = 3
FIND PROJECT_FILE WITH EMPLOYEE # = EMPLOYEE #
END DATA
MOVE AVER (RATING) TO X(N2)
MOVE MAX (RATING) TO M(N2)
LOOP
IF X > 6 DO
ADD 1000 TO SALARY
MOVE M TO MAXRAT
UPDATE SAME RECORD
END TRANSACTION
DOEND
LOOP
END
```

Most people who are not familiar with NATURAL and examine this code are confused by it, cannot add correct brackets to it, and assume that it is incorrect.

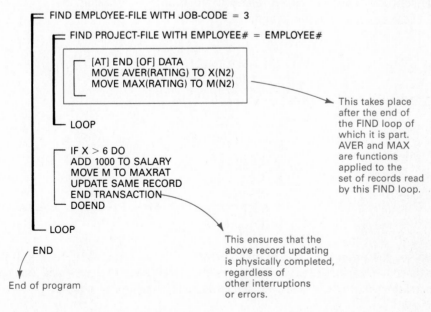

Figure 8.2   An action diagram for the above NATURAL example.

In fact it *is* correct, and is a fairly typical illustration of the use of NAT-URAL. Figure 8.2 shows the same code drawn with an action diagram. (Users well trained with NATURAL become used to such anomalies and find it a valuable and powerful language.)

ENFORCING CLEANLY STRUCTURED PROGRAMS

The older third-generation languages were created before there was an understanding of structured programming. They allowed convoluted code in which it was easy to make errors. Consider, for example, the following PL/I code:

```
IF A = B THEN IF P = Q THEN IF W < S THEN B = 1;
    ELSE Q = W;
    ELSE;
ELSE A = 4;
```

Each ELSE clause is associated with the innermost preceding IF clause that does not yet have an ELSE clause. The second ELSE here has no statement with it, merely a semicolon. It is used to balance the second IF so that the statement after the third ELSE relates to the first IF. Confusing!

Drawn with an action diagram, it is clearer:

```
┌─ IF A = B THEN
│     ┌─ IF P = Q THEN
│     │     ┌─ IF W<5 THEN
│     │     │      B = 1;
│     │     │  ELSE
│     │     └      Q = W;
│     │
│     ├─ ELSE;
│     └
├─ ELSE
└   A = 4;
```

Even so, the programmer may make errors with the semicolons. A good 4GL avoids this confusion and so decreases the probability of errors and incorrect punctuation. With MANTIS, the same example is clean and simple:

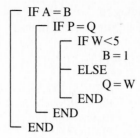

```
┌─ IF A = B
│   ┌─ IF P = Q
│   │   ┌─ IF W<5
│   │   │       B = 1
│   │   ├─ ELSE
│   │   │       Q = W
│   │   └─ END
│   └─ END
└─ END
```

IF WITHOUT END   With some 4GLs, an IF does not have an associated
                      END or ENDIF statement. In this case, a DO-END
clause may follow the IF. This is less simple than the above IF-END structure.

The following is a piece of code with a coding error that took several days
to detect:

```
IF GRID_SWITCH = 'Y'
    IF ROW_COUNT = 01
        IF TYPE_CODE = 'A'
             PERFORM TITLE_PRINT
        ELSE
             PERFORM SCALE_PROCESS
ELSE SET LINE_NO TO +1
```

As shown by the indentation, the programmer intended to perform SET
LINE_NO TO +1 when the condition GRID_SWITCH = 'Y' is false. When
scanning the code, would-be debuggers assumed that the indentation correctly
represented how the code worked. However, this is not the correct interpretation. MANTIS would have made this clear by printing its own indentation with
dots:

```
IF GRID_SWITCH = 'Y'
. IF ROW_COUNT = 01
. . IF TYPE_CODE = 'A'
. . . PERFORM TITLE_PRINT
. . ELSE
. . . PERFORM SCALE_PROCESS
. . END
. ELSE
. . SET LINE_NO TO +1
. END
.
.
.
```

Better still, if action diagrams had been used, SET LINE_NO TO +1 would have been positioned on the correct bracket:

```
┌─ IF GRID-SWITCH = 'Y'
│    ┌─ IF ROW-COUNT = 01
│    │    ┌─ IF TYPE-CODE = 'A'
│    │    │  PERFORM TITLE-PRINT
│    │    ├─ ELSE
│    │    │  PERFORM SCALE-PROCESS
│    │    └─ END
│    ├─ ELSE
│    │  ?????
│    └─ END
├─ ELSE
│  SET LINE-NO TO +1
└─ END
```

In the design of *new* languages, it is desirable that the control structures fit onto action diagram brackets and that designers be able to build their control structures graphically. The graphic, easy-to-visualize designs should be automatically converted to code structures.

AVOIDANCE OF GO TO INSTRUCTIONS

A program that has many GO TO instructions can be difficult to debug. Some GO TO instructions are more harmful than others. Some GO TOs merely cause the program reader to trail after spaghetti-like branches. More harmful GO TOs can cause coupling between code modules that cause subtle problems. The term *pathological coupling* is used to describe a situation in which a branch causes one module of code to refer to or change the internals of another module. One module may be modified without anyone's realizing that the modification has a dramatic effect on the connected module.

Dijkstra complained that GO TO statements widen the "gap between static representation of the program and its dynamic process" [1]—in other words, between how it appears on paper and what it does in dynamic execution. Shneiderman showed experimentally that the more GO TO statements in a program, the more errors the program is likely to have [2].

In a well-structured 4GL, GO TO statements can be avoided completely. To make such a language easy to use in practice, it should be possible to *escape* from one or more brackets—that is, transfer control to the end of those brackets. Languages such as IDEAL and NATURAL had no GO TO statement. This improves (rather than worsens) ease of programming and makes the programs much easier to maintain.

Some 4GLs do have GO TO statements, and it is not hard to find users' programs that are full of GO TOs and are extremely difficult to maintain. The following is a typical specimen of such code (written in FOCUS):

```
CASE BROWSE2
IF NEWYEAR EQ 'CHG' THEN GOTO CHANGE;
IF NEWYEAR EQ 'ADD' THEN GOTO NEW;
IF NEWYEAR EQ 'END' THEN GOTO STARTUP;
IF NEWYEAR EQ 'DEL' THEN GOTO DELETE;
IF NEWYEAR EQ 'QUIT' THEN GOTO EXIT;
COMPUTE
      XDATE = NEWMO/NEW DAY/NEW YEAR;
      XYEAR = NEWYEAR;
      RETURN = 'BRW';
      ZGROUP/A4 = XGROUP;
GO TO GETKEY
ENDCASE
MATCH DIVISION
ON NOMATCH GOTO BROWSE3
ON MATCH COMPUTE
      PRODUCT = ' ';
      VAR = ' ';
ON MATCH GOTO BROWSE3A
ENDCASE
```

ESCAPE CONSTRUCT

A key to avoiding GO TOs is to have good bracket-termination commands. A bracket may be exited at any point with an ESCAPE structure.

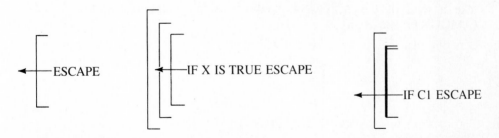

An ESCAPE must be an *orderly* termination of a bracket. It resets everything that would be reset if a normal END occurred. In this way it is different from a GO TO instruction, which merely branches without an orderly close-down of the bracket.

In repetition (loop) brackets, as discussed previously, there can be two types of termination, which we called ESCAPE and NEXT:

The ESCAPE leaves the loop completely. The NEXT behaves like an END; it terminates the current cycle through the loop so that the next cycle can begin.

Many 4GLs have an ESCAPE but not a NEXT construct. If there is no NEXT construct, a simple IF bracket can perform the same task:

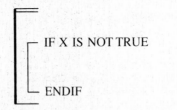

This is so simple (especially with an action diagram editor) that there is no need for the NEXT construct in a language. It is one additional construct for the user to learn.

LOOP-CONTROLLED It is often necessary to carry out operations on a set
VARIABLES of field values that are encountered in a loop or during the processing of a file. It may be necessary to take a total of the AMOUNT filed by using a function such as TOTAL (AMOUNT), for example:

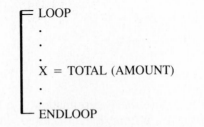

Each time through, the loop TOTAL (AMOUNT) is added to.

This type of operation is particularly useful when processing files, where it is often necessary to take the sum or average of a field.

```
 ┌─ FOR ALL TRANSACTIONS
 │   •
 │   •
 │   •
 │   X = TOTAL (AMOUNT)
 │   •
 │   •
 └─ ENDFOR

 ┌─ READ PERSONNEL WITH STATE = 'VT'
 │   •
 │   •
 │   •
 │   AVSAL = AVERAGE (SALARY)
 │   •
 │   •
 └─ END

    PRINT AVSAL
```

NATURAL allows the following operations to be carried out:

AVER (field)	The average of all values of the field.
NAVER (field)	The average of all values of the field excluding null values
COUNT (field)	A count of the number of values of the field
NCOUNT (field)	A count of the numbers of values of the field excluding null values
MAX (field)	The maximum value of the field
MIN (field)	The minimum value of the field
NMIN (field)	The minimum value of the field excluding null values

Other languages allow standard deviations or variances to be expressed.

These are sometimes called *loop-controlled variables*. Their value is successively changed each time through a loop. It is necessary to be clear *when* the successive changes start and end. The simple rule is that they are changed only by the bracket that contains them, not by brackets to the left of it (that is, not by loops that contain the loop they are in).

Thus, in the following example, A becomes the total amount of all order items on one order. B becomes the total amount of all orders of one customer. C becomes the total amount ordered by all customers. D becomes the average order amount of one customer's orders.

```
┌ FOR EACH CUSTOMER
│  ┌ FOR EACH ORDER
│  │  ┌ FOR EACH ORDER-ITEM
│  │  │  .
│  │  │  .
│  │  │  .
│  │  │  A = TOTAL (AMOUNT)
│  │  │  .
│  │  │  .
│  │  └ ENDFOR
│  │  .
│  │  .
│  │  D = AVERAGE (A)
│  │  B = TOTAL (A)
│  │  .
│  │  .
│  └ ENDFOR
│  .
│  .
│  .
│  C = TOTAL (B)
│  .
│  .
└ ENDFOR
```

Clear bracket demarcation is necessary when employing these loop-controlled variables.

END-OF-LOOP AND START-OF-LOOP SUBROUTINES

Sometimes it is desirable to have a group of statements that is executed once at the start or end of the loop and is executed *only* if there is at least one pass through the loop:

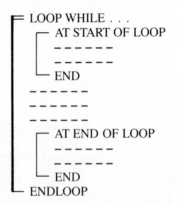

```
┌ LOOP WHILE . . .
│  ┌ AT START OF LOOP
│  │  ─ ─ ─ ─ ─
│  │  ─ ─ ─ ─ ─
│  └ END
│  ─ ─ ─ ─ ─
│  ─ ─ ─ ─ ─
│  ─ ─ ─ ─ ─
│  ┌ AT END OF LOOP
│  │  ─ ─ ─ ─ ─
│  │  ─ ─ ─ ─ ─
│  └ END
└ ENDLOOP
```

The AT START OF LOOP and AT END OF LOOP statements are rather like IF statements that are executed only if it is the start or end of the loop (and only if there is at least one pass through the loop).

Sometimes these loop-initialization and loop-termination brackets contain loop-controlled variables, as in the following example written in NATURAL:

```
┌─ READ EMPLOYEE FILE WHERE CITY = PARIS
│  ─ ─ ─ ─ ─ ─
│  ─ ─ ─ ─ ─ ─
│  ─ ─ ─ ─ ─ ─
│     ┌─ AT END OF DATA DO
│     │  SKIP 2
│     │  PRINT 'MAXIMUM SALARY:' MAX(SALARY)
│     │  PRINT 'MINIMUM SALARY:' MIN(SALARY)
│     │  PRINT 'AVERAGE SALARY:' AVER(SALARY)
│     └─ DOEND
└─ END
```

End-of-loop or start-of-loop subroutines with loop-controlled variables are potentially confusing. If they are employed, the bracket control statements need to be made very clear. If they are clear, start-of-loop and end-of-loop subroutines can be very useful. They are employed to good effect in NATURAL.

END-USER COMPUTING   Perhaps the best way to program is to use an efficient fourth-generation language and to design the programs with an interactive action diagram editor that automatically puts the language control commands on the brackets.

The existence of fourth-generation languages that are easy to learn is encouraging many end users to build their own systems. With languages such as NOMAD, FOCUS, RAMIS, SAS, NATURAL, and APPLICATION FACTORY, they sometimes build complex applications. At BankAmerica, more than 100,000 systems have been built by end users, mostly using NOMAD 2. Many such programs are short, but some are long and complex. (Some are equivalent to over 100,000 lines of COBOL code.)

I have examined a variety of programs written by end users. They are often ill-structured. They are often difficult to understand and very difficult to maintain. Users often make mistakes with incorrect END commands, case structures, GO TOs, and the like. With complex programs, users can make a mess. When users are taught to draw action diagram brackets and fit the code to them, incorrect structures are infrequent. The code is easy to read, understand, and maintain. Better, they should create programs with an action diagram editor.

The first thing taught in any basic training course on programming ought to be action diagrams. The commands that fit the action diagrams should be taught only after the learner is familiar with drawing the control structures [3].

Box 8.1 gives a checklist for evaluating how well structured the procedural component of a 4GL is. Some items on the checklist are more important than others. An ideal 4GL ought to have all of them. At the time of writing, no 4GL does. However, 4GLs

**BOX 8.1   Checklist for evaluating how well structured
a 4GL is**

An ideal 4GL should have all the features in this table. Three languages are evaluated with the checklist. (Note that the evaluation may become out-of-date as new features are added to these languages.)		IDEAL (from ADR)	NATURAL (from Software AG)	MANTIS (from Cincom)
Avoidance of GO TOs		√	√	
REFORM (named subroutine)		√	√	√
Single-execution brackets	DO	√	√	√
	IF	√	√	√
	IF-ELSE	√		√
	CASE	√		√
Repetition brackets	DO WHILE	√		√
	DO UNTIL	√	√	√
	FOR (relating to variables)	√		√
	FOR (relating to files or data bases)	√	√	√
ESCAPE (one bracket)		√	√	
ESCAPE (more than one bracket)		√		
Clear END statements for all brackets		√		√
LOOP-INITIALIZATION and LOOP-TERMINATION brackets			√	
Loop-controlled variables			√	

are improving rapidly. A new version of NATURAL will shortly be available, for example, with more complete structuring.

EXAMPLES OF 4GL CONTROL STRUCTURES

Figures 8.3 through 8.11 show the control structure commands of various languages.

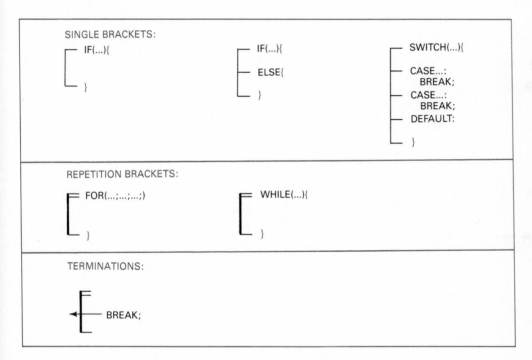

Figure 8.3   Control constructs used by the language "C".

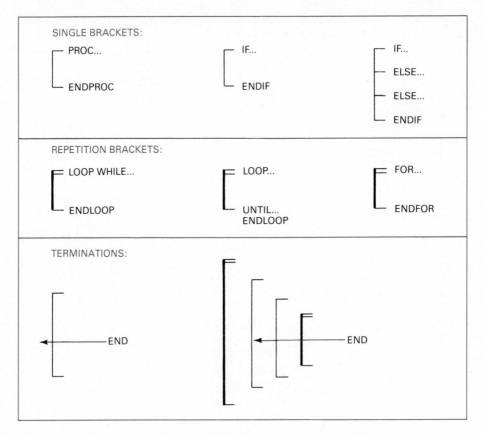

Figure 8.4   Control constructs used by the language IDEAL.

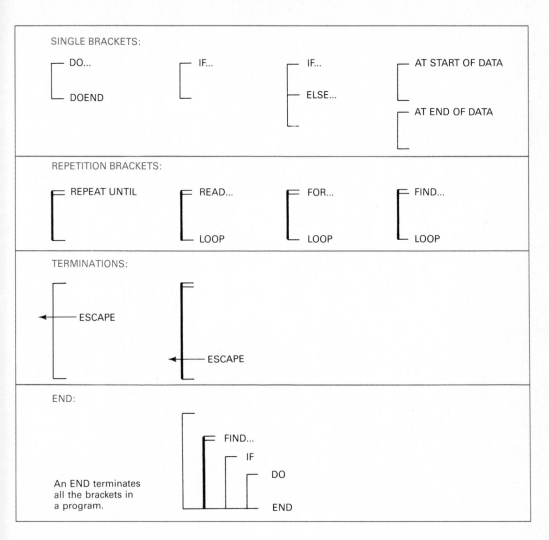

SINGLE BRACKETS:

DO...
DOEND

IF...

IF...
ELSE...

AT START OF DATA

AT END OF DATA

REPETITION BRACKETS:

REPEAT UNTIL

READ...
LOOP

FOR...
LOOP

FIND...
LOOP

TERMINATIONS:

ESCAPE

ESCAPE

END:

An END terminates
all the brackets in
a program.

FIND...
IF
DO
END

Figure 8.5   Control constructs used by the language NATURAL.

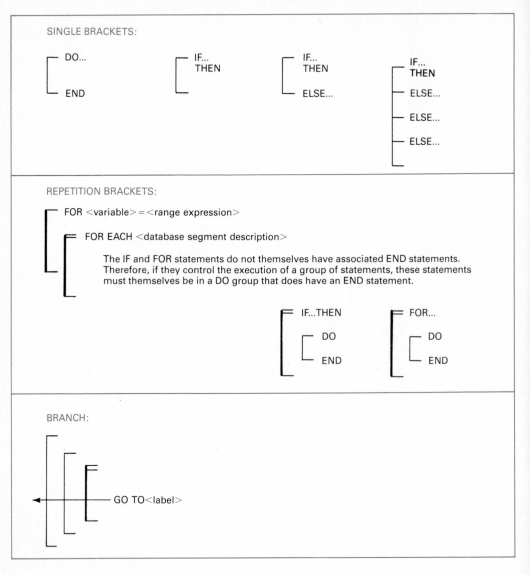

Figure 8.6 Control constructs used by the language NOMAD 2.

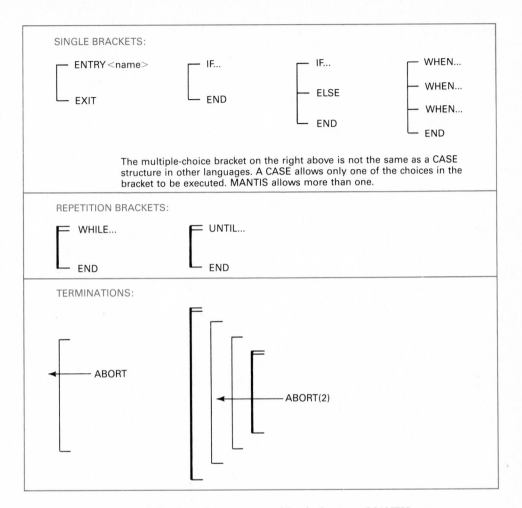

The multiple-choice bracket on the right above is not the same as a CASE structure in other languages. A CASE allows only one of the choices in the bracket to be executed. MANTIS allows more than one.

Figure 8.7 Control constructs used by the language MANTIS.

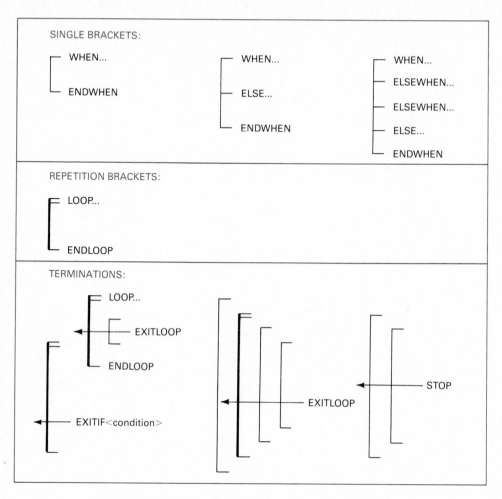

Figure 8.8 Control constructs used by the language SYSTEM W.

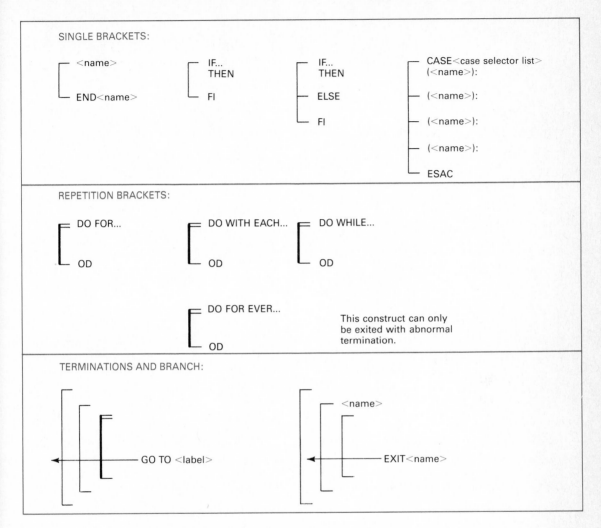

Figure 8.9 Control constructs used by the language CHILL.

REFERENCES

1. E. Dijkstra, *GO TO Statement Considered Harmful, CACM* 11, no. 3 (March 1965), 147–148.

2. B. Shneiderman, *Software Psychology,* MA: Winthrop, Cambridge, 1980, pp. 66–90.

3. J. Martin and C. McClure, *Action Diagrams: Clearly Structured Program Design,* Englewood Cliffs, NJ: Prentice-Hall Inc., 1985.

9 HUMAN FACTORS

INTRODUCTION In the design of 4GLs, the vital importance of human factoring cannot be underestimated. Many of the 4GLs on the market are still poorly human-factored. Some of the best human factoring seems to have been done by newcomers to computing, including college students, entrepreneurs with personal computers, advertising agencies with videotext, and video-game builders. Some of the worst human factoring has appeared from big organizations, which, curiously enough, have spent the most money on human factors research.

Good human factoring has various effects. First, it makes the languages easy to use so that they encourage a more diverse set of people to use them. We want analysts rather than programmers to create applications. End-user computing is particularly valuable, and we want important users who are short of time and patience to employ computers directly. 4GLs need to be user-friendly, nonthreatening, easy to learn, and easy to remember.

As mentioned earlier, the term *user-seductive* might be more appropriate for certain classes of situation. We want potential users to find their computers fascinating, captivating, and an important way to achieve results. A certain amount of pizzazz—good use of a mouse or color graphics, for example—can help to make software user-seductive even though it does not directly change the functions. But particularly important is the ability to obtain valuable results quickly or to achieve a better way to organize or represent data. The best spreadsheet tools are user-seductive because they produce valuable results that would take far too long to calculate by hand.

Good human factoring can make it quicker to achieve results. The application creator interacts with the machine faster and does not have to stop and scratch his head, experiment, or read the manual.

Good human factoring has a major effect on minimizing errors. The developer makes fewer mistakes, spends less time debugging, is less often confused, and can spend his mental effort on thinking about the problem and how to use computers creatively. Good design of the tools should minimize not only mistakes in syntax but also mistakes in meaning and logic.

One of the most important effects of human factoring, and one least often discussed, is that it can change the way people think about problems; it can encourage analysts and users to adopt different types of solutions and use computers more creatively. Some of the most interesting 4GLs provide a way to think about systems or problems. They can change their users' capability to handle complexities and increase their problem-solving power.

LOTUS 1-2-3 and SUPERCALC give their users a way to manipulate large spreadsheets and do what-if computations with them. Graphics languages give users a way to explore complex data and see them in perspective. Regression analysis and time-series analysis give analysts tools for understanding patterns and making forecasts. Financial languages can teach users to think in appropriate ways about complex financial data. USE.IT gives analysts a new way to think about complex logic and to handle greater levels of complexity in specifications. Personal relational data bases encourage users to file their information in better-organized ways. Good reporting and report-manipulation tools linked to data networks encourage clearer and more consistent communication among people about data.

We want people who work with information and logistics to understand better how computers could help them and to invent creative and better ways to tackle problems and manage their enterprises.

DIALOGUE STRUCTURE

Some computer vendors' human factors experts are concerned most of the time with such factors as the feel of the keyboard, the positions of the switches, and the glare on the screen. Much more important is the structure of the dialogue. What does the machine say to the user? Can he understand it? Is he confused by any part of it? Does he know how to respond or how to initiate an interchange?

Psychological structuring of the dialogue is a complex subject. Guidelines can be established [1, 2], but it cannot be reduced to an exact science. It is more akin to style in writing than to the layout of instruments in an airplane cockpit, although it has elements of both.

Many of the early terminal dialogues required the operators to remember mnemonics and fixed sequences of input. Sometimes this was done to create a dialogue with a small number of characters, because every character has to be transmitted over the communications links. Often it was done because the dialogues were created by programmers, who spend their lives using mnemonics and assumed that terminal users could use them also.

It is important to understand that most potential end users do not think like programmers and are remarkably poor at remembering mnemonics, fixed sequences, and formats. If they are full-time terminal operators, spending their entire working day using the terminal, they can be expected to remember such things, but most future end users are doing some other job and use terminals only occasionally. The rate at which they forget mnemonics, fixed sequences, and so on, is much greater than most programmers realize.

Today, on some systems, we are seeing much better end-user dialogues. It is important to understand that the principles of good dialogues should be applied to the application-development process also.

MNEMONICS AND FIXED SEQUENCES
In the dialogues used on airline reservation systems, NN2 means "two seats are required," HS2 means "two seats are available," ORD means "Chicago." In one factory shop-floor system, the foreman has to type PX748K123 to check the status of job 123. In the new standard for access to public data networks (CCITT Recommendation X.28), DER means "out of order," NP means "unobtainable," OCC means "number busy." It is unnatural and difficult for the average potential end user to learn and retain such mnemonics.

Even worse, in many dialogues for dumb terminals, the user has to remember a fixed input format. He must key in a string of fields that must be the right length and in the right sequence. In a typical airline reservation system, the operator who wants to inquire about seat availability on a flight has to key in

021Y06MARLAXJFKNN1

0 is the segment entry; 21 is the flight number; Y means tourist class; 06MAR is the date (it is amazing how many different ways of entering dates there are); LAX is Los Angeles, and JFK is Kennedy Airport, New York; NN1 means that one seat is required. If the user omits any field, changes the sequence, or uses a wrong-length field (e.g., 6MAR), the message will be in error. The error may be detected by the computer, or the message may be processed erroneously.

AVOIDANCE OF MNEMONICS
In most dialogues it is possible to avoid completely the use of mnemonics and formats that the user has to memorize.

The sample request for seat availability on a flight could be handled as follows. The operator indicates that he is interested in seats, either by pressing a key labeled SEATS on the terminal or by selecting SEATS from an application menu on the screen. The following display then appears:

```
SEAT AVAILABILITY REQUEST
PLEASE ENTER THE FOLLOWING INFORMATION:
FLIGHT NUMBER (if known):
CLASS OF SEAT:
NUMBER OF SEATS REQUESTED:
DATE OF DEPARTURE:
DEPARTURE CITY:
DESTINATION CITY:
```

The cursor jumps rapidly to the successive entry positions.

If the user enters the flight number, he may omit the departure city and destination city. The computer (possibly a small distributed processor close to the user) displays the cities at which that flight stops and asks the user which he requires.

```
PLEASE TYPE 1 AFTER THE
DEPARTURE AND DESTINATION CITIES:
NEW YORK:
LONDON:
ATHENS:
TEHERAN:
NEW DELHI:
```

Most languages for application development force the user to remember mnemonics, formats, and sequences of entry. Just as in other interactive dialogues, this is unnecessary. Much better human factoring is needed to make the tools user-friendly.

Some powerful 4GLs are well human-factored, and others are very poor. The following is a section of coding for IBM's application generator, ADF (Application Development Facility).

```
SYSTEM     SYSID = SAMP,DBID = PA,
           SOMTX = OR,
           SIGNON = YES,
```

```
               POMENU = (A,B,C,D,E,F,H,I),
               PCBNO = 1,
               SDBNAME = 'ASSEMBLY PARTS',
               SHEADING = 'S A M P  L E  P R O B L E M',
               SFORMAT = DASH,
               PGROUP = ZZ,
               ASMLIST = NOLIST
SEGMENT        LEVEL = 1,ID = PA,NAME = PARTROOT,LENGTH = 50,
               SNAME = 'PARTSEGMENT',SKSEG = 18
FIELD          ID = KEY,LENGTH = 17,POS = 1,KEY = YES,NAME = PARTKEY,
               SNAME = 'PART NUMBER',DISP = YES,REL = YES
FIELD          ID = DESC,LENGTH = 20,POS = 27,SNAME = 'DESCRIPTION',
               DISP = YES,REL = YES
SEGMENT        ID = IV,PARENT = PA,NAME = STOKSTAT,KEYNAME =
               STOCKEY,LENGTH = 160,
               SNAME = 'INVENTORY',
               SKLEFT = 'INVENTORY       UNIT        CURRENT',
               SKLEFT = 'LOCATION        PRICE       REQMNTS',
               SKRIGHT = '  ON     TOTAL      DISBURSEMENTS',
               SKRIGHT = '  ORDER  STOCK     PLANNED  UNPLANNED',
FIELD          ID = W,LENGTH = 2,POS = 1,KEY = YES,TYPE = DEC,SNAME =
               'OO',DISP = NO,COL = 1,SLENGTH = 2
FIELD          ID = AREA,LENGTH = 1,KEY = YES,SNAME = 'AREA',DISP =
               YES,COL = 3
FIELD          ID = INVD,LENGTH = 2,KEY = YES,SNAME = 'INV
               DEPT',DISP = YES,COL = 4
FIELD          ID = PROJ,LENGTH = 3,KEY = YES,SNAME = 'PROJECT',
               DISP = YES,COL = 6
FIELD          ID = DIV,LENGTH = 2,KEY = YES,SNAME = 'DIVISION',DISP =
               YES,COL = 9
FIELD          ID = FILL,LENGTH = 6,KEY = YES,SNAME = 'FILLER',DISP =
               NO,COL = 11
FIELD          ID = PRIC,LENGTH = 9,POS = 21,TYPE = DEC,DEC =
               2,SLENGTH = 9,SNAME = 'UNITPRICE',DISP = YES
```

The developer has to remember the mnemonics and formats. The same generator mechanisms could be used with fast option-selection screens. This would make the tool easier and faster to use and would greatly lessen the number of syntax errors made.

VISUALLY ORIENTED EXPRESSIONS

With some visually oriented software, calculations can be expressed visually. Suppose that an array of data contains five columns:

QUANTITY-A	QUANTITY-B	PRICE-A	PRICE-B	REVENUE

In a conventional computer language, we might use the following statement:

REVENUE = QUANTITY_A*PRICE A + QUANTITY_B*PRICE_B

In MULTIPLAN, a visual approach is used. The cursor is placed in the revenue column as shown by the box in that column in the diagram. MULTIPLAN asks the user to express a calculation. The user moves the cursor left to the QUANTITY_A column. The screen shows a relative address, RC(-4). R means the row where the cursor started. C(-4) means the cell four cells to the left of where the cursor started. The user presses the $*$ key, and the cursor jumps back to its original position. The user then moves it left to the PRICE_A column. The screen shows:

VALUE: RC(-4)*RC(-2)

The user presses + and the cursor again jumps back to its original position. The user moves it left to the QUANTITY_B column. The screen then shows:

VALUE: *RC(-4)*RC(-2) + RC(-3)

Then the user presses $*$. The cursor jumps back again. The user moves it one place to the left and then presses the RETURN key. The screen shows the value of the cell:

RC(-4)*RC(-2) + RC(-3)*RC(-1)

The user can then duplicate this expression into any other cells in that column.

This visual representation of an expression can be used for more complex expressions, including those containing functions such as AVERAGE, SUM, MIN, SIN, COS, TAN, NPV (net present value), and LOG10. To a programmer this visual representation of expressions may seem strange and perhaps pointless. However, nonprogramming users building intelligent spreadsheets learn it fast and use it quickly, usually without making syntax errors. It works effectively for such users.

ARGUMENTS AGAINST USER FRIENDLINESS

Although it is acknowledged that end users need dialogues that are friendly, it is often thought that DP professionals can learn mnemonics and sequences and write code like that in the ADF example. However, the use of difficult coding makes the DP professional concentrate on the wrong thing. We want him to spend his mental efforts as powerfully as possible on the problems that computing can solve. Let us repeat Alfred North Whitehead's quote: "By relieving the brain of all unnecessary work [difficult encoding], a good notation [language] sets it free to concentrate on more advanced problems, and in effect increases the mental power of the race" [3].

An argument in the past against good human factoring has been that it is too expensive in machine cycles. Today, however, a powerful personal computer has the machine cycles and memory needed to process all of the user-friendly interactions we describe in this book. The personal computer may possibly pass the checked code to a mainframe for compilation because they may take far more machine cycles. As personal computers drop in cost and increase in power, we cannot use this argument against user friendliness.

Some dialogue structures that are easy to use have been time-consuming because of multiple response times. The menu-selection technique of *videotext* may cause a user to display several menus, each with a response time of two seconds, say, plus a screen-painting time of several seconds. This becomes frustratingly slow, so the argument has it that the professional should enter a mnemonic instead. However, if the menus are stored in a fast personal computer, a decisecond response time can be achieved for most responses. Selecting from three levels of option list (like three successive menus) on a personal computer often takes less time than entering the equivalent commands mnemonically, and the user is much less likely to make mistakes. Part of the reason for the speed with option lists is that the software often guesses correctly which option the user will select, so the user merely flicks the RETURN key and the subsequent list appears immediately.

Personal computers, or in general, decisecond response times, change our choice of human-factoring technique.

Where a user-friendly technique *does* take more time, the user can be given a choice of either doing it the user-friendly way or speeding it up with the input of mnemonics.

MEASURING HUMAN FACTORING

Executives in the computer industry tend to want hard scientific measurements of what is produced. Human factoring has sometimes eluded their ability to achieve measurements. Human factoring is to some extent an art rather than something that can be reduced to algorithms. It is more akin to good writing than to good computation. Art forms are difficult to measure. How would you measure if Shakespeare's writing is better than that of a modern playwright? This argument does not sit well with traditional computer executives. They say, "If I can't measure it, I can't manage it." This has been used in large corporations as an argument against trying to achieve the best human factoring.

One good measure of the human factoring of software is to determine how long it takes a given type of user to become competent in using it. We should ask, "What is the elapsed time between the customer's taking the cellophane wrapping off the software and achieving valuable results from it?" With some powerful software, this time is less than an hour. With other software, it is days or weeks for a new user. Software management should set an objective for this measure. For much software, the objective for this elapsed time should be no greater than one hour. Imagine the difference if this was an objective of the mainframe vendors.

Other measures (which could be captured automatically) should relate to how often the user uses the HELP function, how often he receives INVALID OPERATION messages, and so on.

BACKTRACKING AFTER MISTAKES

Another major failing with some dialogues is that the user can reach a point where he does not know what to do next. The terminal may have done something that surprises him. He may have pressed a wrong key. Now what does he do? There is no obvious means of recovery. Guessing, he makes another entry, but that only puts him in worse trouble.

A senior civil servant once took me into his office to demonstrate, proudly, his new terminal. I asked him if he could obtain a slightly different result, and he said yes. However, the device produced an unexpected response. He tried repeatedly to get the dialogue back onto the correct track, but it eluded him. Eventually, the only way he could continue the demonstration was to put down the telephone handset, redial the computer, reload the program, and enter the dialogue from the beginning. A month later the terminal sat in his office largely unused.

All terminal users will do things wrong and get surprises at the terminal. The dialogue should be structured so that when that happens, the user has an obvious and natural way to recover. The simplest way is a key or an option labeled BACK that can be selected. The dialogue should be designed so that the user can backtrack to an earlier point in the dialogue whenever he needs to. If he makes a mistake or takes a wrong path, he can say BACK, BACK, BACK until he arrives at where he was before the mistake or surprise occurred. The backtracking should happen in the peripheral machine, usually without any transmission to or involvement of the higher-level computer.

In addition to BACK, there should be a key or selectable option labeled ESCAPE. This terminates the current operation and returns the user to a main menu of options.

Sometimes the user enters data to be filed or to update records in a distant machine. These data may be entered erroneously. Any accuracy checks that can be applied in the local machine should be applied before the data are transmitted to the higher-level computer.

NON-THOUGHT-DISRUPTIVENESS

An important aspect of user friendliness is that the user can use the computer without serious interruption to his train of thought about the problem at hand. We might say that a dialogue should be non-thought-disruptive. We could measure the degree to which different dialogues disrupt a train of thought.

If a LOTUS or SUPERCALC user is manipulating an intelligent spreadsheet and wants to add another column, he can do this almost immediately without substantially interrupting his work on his problem. He tabs the cursor bar to INSERT. The system asks whether he wants to insert a column or a row. He tabs to COLUMN. The software inserts a new column where the cursor is positioned and renumbers the other columns accordingly. To have done the same with COBOL or PL/I would have required hours of work, then testing.

A user working on a problem needs the requisite tools and services to be available without thought disruption. If a surgeon is operating on a patient and needs a certain implement, he holds out his hand and asks for it, possibly without taking his eyes off the patient's intestines. A nurse puts the tool into his hand, and he uses it immediately. If he had to stop and key in JCL commands to obtain the tool, this would disrupt his train of thought, and he might join the wrong arteries.

LAW OF CONSERVATION OF HUMAN MISTAKES

Humans make mistakes when handling complex logic or intricate detail. The computer is infuriating to some users because it mercilessly reveals their mistakes, and it is fascinating to others because it obeys elaborate sequences of instructions with meticulous accuracy.

There are many statistics on human error rates with conventional programming. The early experience with fourth-generation languages indicates that the human typically creates one order of magnitude fewer bugs in building a given application. It appears that if the human writes one-tenth of the lines of code to create an application, he makes one-tenth of the mistakes. In other words, he makes about the same number of mistakes per line of code.

However, if he obtains results ten times as fast, he can accomplish ten times as much work. In so doing, he makes about the same total number of mistakes per day. It is suggested that there is an approximate law of conservation of human mistakes saying that a person creating programs will make mistakes at about the same rate regardless of the power of the programming language [4].

The way to break this law is to have the person create applications at a computer screen with a language and interpreter designed so that as many mistakes as possible are caught when the user makes them. Some software makes a beeping noise when an error is made. The user makes an entry or gives an instruction, confidently, perhaps without looking at the screen, and the beep stops him in his tracks.

FAST FEEDBACK

This fast feedback to the user has two effects. First, he can correct the error quickly; the subject matter is still in his short-term memory. Second, fast feedback is important in teaching. Experiments show that correct behavior is reinforced much more strongly if there is immediate feedback to deviations from correct behavior. This is an important learning principle.

Fast feedback has enabled users, particularly with personal computers, to teach themselves to use fairly complex software, such as spreadsheet tools, quickly and so create remarkably few bugs compared with traditional programming. A principle of future languages ought to be to use constructs that enable users to catch as many errors as possible immediately after they are made and give fast feedback and help to the user.

HELPFUL ERROR MESSAGES

The form of error message is important. The software should not just say INVALID OPERATION or SORRY, I CANNOT HANDLE 37562.417; it should explain why the operation is invalid or why it cannot handle the input. If 37562.417 is too large or has too many decimal places, the software should say so. When the user is stopped in his tracks by an error message, he wants to know what to do next. After any error message, the user should be able to press HELP or ? and receive an explanation.

An unforgivably bad form of error message is one that is simply a number or code, such as PXT1759. The recipient of such a message is supposed to look up its meaning in a manual. It is easy to display an explanatory sentence on the screen, with further text available if the user presses HELP. One vendor (who had spent a fortune on human factors research) was demonstrating a new tool, and it produced an error message like Q3.498.ZLW.5781 and refused to go any further. The demonstrator spent 40 minutes on the telephone trying to find out what to do next. This is a sadly common occurrence. In one case the *creators* of a software product could not proceed with a demonstration to the author of their own product because they could not understand their own error message.

To be nonthreatening to new users, harsh or abrupt error messages such as ILLEGAL FUNCTION should be replaced with polite explanatory sentences such as SORRY, THERE IS NO COMMAND ''C.'' PLEASE PRESS ''ESCAPE'' TO RETURN TO THE COMMAND LIST.

Some examples of helpful and user-friendly error messages are as follows:

> I CANNOT FIND AN OPENING LEFT PARENTHESIS.
> I CANNOT FIND A ";" SO I DISCONTINUED SCANNING THE LINE.
> SORRY, I CAN'T SUBTOTAL MORE THAN 16 LEVELS.
> I WAS SCANNING FOR A "FRAME" FUNCTION WITH NO LUCK.
> I WAS LOOKING FOR A CONTINUATION OF A "DO.WHEN."

One 4GL produced the following message:

> I GOT CONFUSED SCANNING THIS LINE AND GAVE UP.

This is less user-threatening than saying INVALID STATEMENT.

SYNTAX AND SEMANTICS

We can distinguish between syntax and semantics in languages. *Syntax* refers to *how* something is being said. *Semantics* refers to *what* is being said. The Oxford Dictionary defines *syntax* as ''sentence construction; the grammatical arrangement of words (in language); set of rules governing this.'' It defines *semantic* as ''relating to meaning in language.''

Most compilers and interpreters check for *syntax* errors—misspelled words, commands without the required variables, missing END statements, and so on. They cannot check the *meaning* of the language. Languages of higher level than programming languages can make some checks on *what* is being said, not just how. We are not likely to have specification languages soon that can make *complete* semantic checks. This would take us into the realms of artificial intelligence, which is increasingly concerned with computer representation of meaning.

Because a nonprocedural language is concerned with what is said rather than how it is said, this type of language should make whatever checks are possible on what is being said and provide as much fast feedback to the user as possible about any detectable errors in this. A powerful query language that uses relational operations ought to do some checks on what is being asked for, to warn about semantic disintegrity. Spreadsheet tools propagate the effect of entering a formula throughout the spreadsheet to see whether there are any detectable incorrect consequences. The specification language USE.IT from HOS checks the validity of functions, data types, and control mechanisms based on mathematical axioms that control their behavior. This approach enables internal inconsistencies in meaning to be detected. It ensures that the specifications a user creates are internally correct and computable so that code can be generated from them automatically. This type of semantic checking is a major step forward in automated design verification.

INTERNAL AND EXTERNAL SEMANTICS

We should distinguish between *internal semantics* and *external semantics*. Internal semantics relates to whether what is being said obeys the rules established in the basic axioms. External semantics relates to whether the system is solving the right problem. Verification techniques can deal with internal semantics, not external semantics.

We might say to a science-fiction robot, "Get me a dry blartini with a twist." It will tell us there is a *syntax error* and ask whether the word *blartini* should be *martini*.

If we tell it to get a dry martini made with 7-Up, it will tell us we have an *internal semantics error*. Our instruction violates a basic axiom of martini-making.

If we want a vodka martini and only say, "Get me a dry martini with a twist," it might bring a gin martini. Now we have an *external semantics error* that the software has not caught.

You might say that the robot should have detected that our specifications were incomplete. It should have known that there are two types of martini and asked, "Vodka or gin?" There are other options. It should say, "With ice or straight up?" But where does it stop? It might say "Gordons, Juniper, Beefeater, Boodles, Tanqueray, Bombay, Schenley, Skol, London, Mr. Boston, Burnett's, Crystal Palace, Seagram's, Calvert, Booth's, Fleischmann's, S. S. Pierce, Five O'Clock, Gilbey's . . .," and we lose patience and say, "Fetch the damned thing!"

To be computable, specifications have to have much detail, or else default options. Default options are important in nonprocedural languages to lessen the amount of work needed and consequently the number of possible errors.

DEFAULT OPTIONS

Using a screen, the martini-ordering dialogue might go something like this:

COCKTAILS.

SELECT ONE OF THE FOLLOWING:

- BLOODY MARY, BRANDY ALEXANDER, GIN AND TONIC, MANHATTAN, MARTINI, PINA COLADA, TOM COLLINS, WHISKEY SOUR

The user moves the cursor to the item in question.

MARTINI.

ADJUST THE SELECTION OF OPTIONS IF DESIRED:

- GIN, VODKA
- STRAIGHT UP, WITH ICE
- WITH AN OLIVE, WITH A TWIST
- BEEFEATER, BOODLES, BOOTHS, GILBEYS,
  GORDONS, TANQUERAY

The user may press RETURN to select the choices shown or may tab to one or more of the option lines and use the SPACE BAR to move the indicator to a different option.

The computer, here, provided a default option for MARTINI consisting of Tanqueray gin, straight up, with a twist. The user could change this if he wished. Similar defaults are used in nonprocedural languages for field formats, report formats, dialogue structures, MOVE commands, EDIT commands, and so on. The computer selects the most likely default options, to minimize the probability of the user's needing to change them.

THE CONCEPTUAL MAPPING PROBLEM

An end user such as a business professional thinks about problems in a conceptual way that is different from the way a computer approaches problems. Somehow the terminology must be translated from one world to the other. In the past, a systems analyst has done this translation. Now, in many cases, we would like an important user with little computer training to make the translation with the aid of software.

We will refer to this as *the conceptual mapping problem*.

Suppose, for example, that an executive wants to know "for each market, how do the actual sales of copiers last quarter compare to the estimates?"

This is a simple question. We would like to make it as simple to answer as possible. To answer it with COBOL might take a week, as in Fig. 6.1. In order to answer it, several things need to be known:

What files must be accessed?
   Are the data all in one file? No, we need the file for actual sales and the file for estimated sales. How are they to be linked together?

What field names must be used?
   The words *actual, sales, last quarter,* and *estimates* need to be translated into field names such as 1985_Q3_ACT_SALES, 1985_Q3_EST_SALES, or worse, ACT_SALES (53), EST_SALES (53).

What records must be selected?
> Does "copiers" refer to one product type or to several different products? If several products, the records for these must be identified and their sales added.

Are sales stored by quarter?
> If they are stored by month, the sales for the months in question must be added.

What subtotals must be calculated for comparison?
> Are subtotals already on the files? If not, what code must be generated for calculating the subtotals?

What formula is used to compare the subtotals?
> Is the difference between the absolute numbers computed? Is the percentage of actual to estimate computed? Or both?

How should the report be formatted?

We would like as many of these questions as possible to be answered *automatically* by the software. It is interesting to note that at least one software package answers them *all* automatically. With INTELLECT, discussed in Chapter 10, the user simply keys in the original question. INTELLECT displays its interpretation of the question and produces a report.

Most 4GLs do not go as far as INTELLECT in aiding the conceptual mapping. On the other hand, INTELLECT can handle only query processing. A user who wants to do more complex processing has to move closer to understanding the computer's view of problem solving.

Most business professionals are not comfortable with the alien syntax and mnemonics of computer languages. They sit at a screen not knowing what to do next when the machine says BAD COMMAND and refuses to accept their input. The challenge of 4GLs is to go as far as possible in allowing the user to instruct the machine without alien syntax and mnemonics. As much of the conceptual mapping as possible should be done by the software.

IMPROVING AN ORGANIZATION'S PROCEDURES

The best uses of computers completely change the procedures in an organization. When everyone has access to a screen workstation linked to shared data bases, the procedures for factory control or office paperwork should be entirely different from those that existed before. The most important effect of good human factoring is to encourage employees everywhere to change their procedures in order to use computers and information as effectively as possible. Third-generation languages and the traditional development life cycle entirely inhibit this.

When the traditional system analyst and potential end users first come face to face, they come from widely different cultures. It is rather like a Victorian missionary first entering an African village. Unlike the missionary, they have to produce a very precise document—the specification of requirements.

The missionary is steeped in computer terminology and analysis methods. The villagers' culture is accounting, plans and budgets, or production control—this is a culture with a complex folklore. The villagers and the missionary use different languages, yet somehow they are supposed to communicate with no ambiguities or misunderstandings. If the missionary is skillful at communicating and can offer the villagers a promise of better things, they can begin to learn each other's conceptual framework. However, there is no way that either can understand the nuances and subtleties of the other's way of thinking.

In an attempt to clarify and formalize the process, specifications are written for the applications that must be programmed. This can take person-years to complete and results in a set of documents that are inches or even feet thick. For his own protection, the missionary needs the villagers to sign this document.

The specification document is extremely important in the traditional DP life cycle. It is the document from which the third-generation coders work. However, there are serious problems with the typical specification process. It takes much too long. It usually prevents ongoing creativity. It usually does not represent the true end users' needs very well.

The specification document is usually so long that key managers do not read it all. They read the summary because the rest is incredibly boring, and this causes it to be skip-read by many people who should read it fully. It contains technical terms, systems analysis charts, and various forms of professional shorthand, all of which the end users do not fully understand. It contains words that have very precise meanings in the user areas but that programmers do not understand, and most systems analysts do not appreciate their nuances.

The end users fail to comprehend things that are obvious to the computer staff, and vice versa. A user may have signed off on a data field in *month-day-year* format and cannot be expected to realize that records cannot be sorted into time sequence with this field. A programmer cannot be expected to know that "benefit effective date" is different from "benefit posted date," although this is obvious to the end user. A DP professional may not realize that an oil well has many different definitions or that the oil it accesses spreads underground to areas with different ownership. A user may have signed off on a document referring to "rating basis" without understanding that the systems analyst meant something entirely different by that. The DP professional might read phrases like the following over and over again without knowing what they mean: "indicates the date on which a given qualification was verified in the context of the structure within which it existed." (This is a real example! Its meaning is obvious to the end users in question.) Such examples are endless.

Much of the vital specification document is misinterpreted on both sides. Often its readers think they understand it but in fact do not.

Sometimes much trivia or "motherhood" is added to the document. Both sides understand this. It increases the comfort level but has zero value. Specification documents are bad enough with batch processing; with interactive systems they tend to be worse because they cannot capture the dynamic quality of the user interaction.

Not surprisingly, specifications in practice contain many errors. Statistics about the bugs in systems delivered to users indicate that there are often more errors in the original specification than in the programmers' coding from the specification [5]. We clearly have to have specifications for certain types of complex computing. But there are other types of computing for which a much more dynamic approach is needed.

Often the business needs change substantially while the lengthy process of third-generation coding from specifications is under way. Worse, in many cases when users employ the delivered system, they start to change their minds about what they really need. This mind change often evolves rapidly into fundamentally different notions.

THE UNCERTAINTY PRINCIPLE

The uncertainty principle in physics says that the act of *observing* subatomic events *changes* those events.

There is an uncertainty principle with data processing. The act of providing what an end user says he needs changes his perception of those needs.

The mere act of implementing a user-driven system changes the requirements for that system. The solution to a problem changes the problem.

As the system becomes live, it will affect the rest of the department in a variety of unforeseen ways. It suddenly becomes possible to move work from one person's screen to another. Salesmen can suddenly provide a service that was previously so difficult that they ignored it, and demands for that service boom. A manager suddenly sees information that was previously hidden from him, and he makes changes in the department. Some users do not like the system and insist on using their previous methods. Others want new types of reports or want the computer to do calculations not in the system requirements.

The system has many unforeseen psychological effects. It may make some employees feel unwanted and resentful. Some become prima donnas with the new terminals. The system changes the organizational interaction and power patterns.

End users have a long learning curve to climb in assessing how they should use today's data processing. They cannot climb far on this curve as long as it remains at the talking stage. It is only when they have a workstation and use it for their own work that they begin to understand the reality of the computer's challenge and limitations. Their imagination slowly begins to realize what they *could* do with that screen. After implementation, the users have a common basis for discussion of the system. They argue at lunch about what it does well and badly, what it ought to do better, and how it could benefit them in different ways from what it is doing now. They would like to modify its behavior *quickly*.

In many cases the functions of a user-driven system when first installed are less than a tenth of those they feel they need a few months after installation. These new functions are more valuable because they are based on experience. For example, the system makes it possible to have more finely structured inventory reorder points. The reordering rules can now be changed easily to adapt better to seasonal peaks. It becomes possible to deal with problems on the shop floor that were quietly ignored before, but to do so needs additions to the data base or different patterns of data entry.

It is often the case that the end user does not know what he wants until he gets it. When he gets it, he wants something different.

The human-factoring challenge of today's computer languages, then, is to enable users, often helped by DP professionals, to invent and build the facilities they need and to adjust them continuously so that the use of computers in an organization rapidly evolves to provide more efficient controls and procedures.

In the best examples of 4GL use, this can be found. The challenge of computer users everywhere is to make this the rule rather than the exception.

AVOIDANCE OF GOBBLEDYGOOK IN COMPUTING

Computer professionals have thrived on creating mnemonics, punctuation, and difficult-to-remember sequences of characters. They constantly invent difficulties where there is no need for difficulties. There is often a subconscious feeling that a language needs complex-looking mnemonics in order to appear professional. As a doctor wants to have Latin prescriptions, the computer professional wants to have commands the layman cannot read.

In the world of fourth-generation computing it is desirable to involve the end-user as fully as possible. To do so it is necessary to remove the gobbledygook in computing. There are many techniques for avoiding an alien syntax, for avoiding the need to remember mnemonics, strange punctuation, and difficult-to-remember sequences. A number of these are listed in Box 9.1. The decisecond response time of the personal-computer workstation makes practical the avoidance of most alien syntax in computing.

The greater the need to have high-level, busy, impatient staff or executives using computers, the greater the need to avoid gobbledygook in computing. This is especially true with decision-support languages. It is important for DP professionals themselves, however, to avoid command languages. A good systems analyst should be able to use a dozen languages or tools. There is no way to learn these if each has a different, alien syntax. Some computer science professors—the worst offenders in creating gobbledygook in computing—are completely unable to use the tools they should when confronted with a computer.

In many cases the replacement of a command language with a fast, command-free, mouse-driven screen dialogue *speeds up* the process of instructing the computer and greatly reduces the number of errors that can be made.

BOX 9.1   Avoidance of gobbledygook in computing

Use of techniques such as the following avoids the need to use an alien syntax or command language. It is desirable to avoid difficult-to-remember constructs in computing.

- Menus
- Pull-down menus (as on the Macintosh)
- Multilevel menus (as on videotext)
- Use of natural English (or other human language)
- Action diagrams (to show a structured specification or program structure)
- An action diagram editor in which the computer adds program commands to the action diagrams
- Action diagrams combined with English that can be interpreted by the software (see Chapter 11)
- Other types of diagrams for expressing logic or operations
- Use of icons (as on the Macintosh)
- Computer-initiated dialogues (in which the computer asks the operator to enter items of information)
- Fill-in-the-blanks dialogue
- Touch screens
- Use of a mouse to speed up positioning, multilevel menu navigation, filling in instruction panels, etc.
- Use of decisecond response times (on a PC) to make navigation through multilevel menus or selection panels fast.
- Pop-on window panels (which appear on the screen to aid the operator). The following items list types of panels.
  Guidance panel (for telling the user what to do next)
  Selection panel (for building a sentence or command by selecting permissible items which the computer checks
  Instruction panel (giving the operator items to fill in or choose)

BOX 9.2 Desirable human-factoring properties of 4GLs

- The means of establishing contact with the computer and signing on should be simple, natural, and *obvious* (with appropriate security routines).

- The user should be required to know as little as possible to get started.

- The dialogue should completely avoid forcing the user to remember mnemonics or an alien syntax (see Box 9.1).

- The dialogue should completely avoid forcing the user to remember formats or entry sequences.

- The dialogue should never put the user in a situation where he does not know what to do next.

- The dialogue should provide a simple, natural, and *obvious* means for the user to recover from any mistakes or surprises. The user should be able to backtrack easily to the point before the surprise occurred.

- All error messages should be fully self-explanatory.

- Techniques should be selected that enable the user to obtain results *as fast as possible*.

- The fullest possible use should be made of default options.

- If a technique for achieving user friendliness is slow or oversimplified, the user should be given an alternate technique, fast and comprehensive, to use when he becomes expert.

- Graphics techniques should be used, where possible, as an aid to clear thinking.

- Full use should be made of a data dictionary, directory, or encyclopedia.

- The techniques used should maximize the use of semantics checking and integrity checking as well as syntax checking.

- Tools for on-line testing should be comprehensive.

- Full use should be made of the decisecond response-time capabilities of personal computers, which may, instead of terminals, be connected to a mainframe.

- The language should be designed to maximize the benefits of interaction with a two-dimensional space, with scrolling, windows, split screens, and fast movement of pointers, highlight bars, windows, and so on.

- The software should be designed so that the user's main focus of concentration is on his problem; the syntax and mechanisms of the computer language should be as non-thought-disruptive as possible.

- The software should be self-teaching, with good-quality computer-aided instruction that can be invoked at any point during the building of a program.

Each of these properties can be found in practice in some 4GLs. However, most of today's 4GLs fall short of the full range of human-factoring qualities now practicable.

SUMMARY   Box 9.2 summarizes human-factoring properties that
                           are desirable in 4GLs. Any one of these properties
can be demonstrated in many languages; however, few, if any, languages have
all of the desirable properties yet. Most 4GLs at the time of writing need substantial improvements in human factoring.

REFERENCES

1. J. Martin, *Design of Man-Computer Dialogues,* Englewood Cliffs, NJ: Prentice-Hall, Inc., 1973.

2. Guidelines for dialogue structuring are explored in the series of courses on the terminal-user interface in the James Martin Advanced Technology Library of Deltak, Oak Brook, IL.

3. A. N. Whitehead, *An Introduction to Mathematics,* Oxford: Oxford University Press, 1911.

4. Suggested in a private book review by Richard Hamming.

5. Tom De Marco, *Structured Analysis and System Specification,* New York: Yourdon Press, 1979.

10 THE USE OF NATURAL ENGLISH FOR QUERIES

INTRODUCTION   It might seem that the easiest way for humans to communicate with computers is to talk to them in *natural* human language. We will use English to illustrate this.

When we say *natural* human language, we mean language like that which we normally write or speak, not constrained English like COBOL, FOCUS, or other "English-like" 4GLs. The objective would be to enable ordinary people to communicate with computers without learning an unnatural syntax.

INTELLECT   The first software product with large sales that made English input to computers practical was INTELLECT, a language for querying data bases and generating reports [1, 2]. INTELLECT allows end users to enter queries or commands in freely worded English such as the following:

> HOW MANY EMPLOYEES IN THE WASHINGTON OFFICE ARE MALE ADMINISTRATORS WHO MAKE OVER $45,000?
> GIVE ME A PLOT COMPARING THE QUARTERLY REVENUE FOR EACH COURSE FOR THE FIRST FIVE YEARS WITH THE AVERAGE REVENUE.

Having a computer process inputs like these is more complex than it might appear. Our own language is extremely ambiguous. The same word has subtly different meanings in different contexts. We can use words in an almost infinite number of combinations. When you read or listen to someone talk, you are doing much complex subconscious processing to extract meaning from what is said and to interpret the ambiguities. Most of the early attempts to make computers accept free English input failed because the complexities and ambiguities of our language had been underestimated.

Because of the alternate meanings of words, some sentences are very difficult to parse by programming. For example, in the sentence "Time flies like an arrow," it is possible that either *time, flies,* or *like* could be the verb. ("Fruit flies like a banana"!)

To understand free-form English, a computer must parse it and resolve these ambiguities. Many grammatical rules are needed to achieve this. A major area of the discipline of artificial intelligence is concerned with processing rules and deducing inferences from rules. The term *knowledge base* is used in conjunction with this. A knowledge base stores facts and rules in such a way that these can be used for inference processing. INTELLECT contains a knowledge base relating to English grammar and the processing of data-base queries. The logical complexities of this are surprisingly great. For this reason, INTELLECT is expensive compared with other query languages and for some years had little competition of a similar nature. Today it does have competition. RAMIS ENGLISH is a similar product using the 4GL RAMIS II data base. RAMIS ENGLISH took 32 person-years to build. Now such a product could be created with substantially *less* effort. So the use of human language input to computers has become economically practical.

The use of natural language makes it much easier to communicate with computers without having to spend time learning precise syntax. It encourages untrained users to start. It lessens the frustration, bewilderment, and anger caused by BAD COMMAND responses.

The following is a specimen of a query in a typical 4GL query language described in vendor literature as an easy-to-use, user-friendly, English-language query:

```
LIST BY REGION (83_ACT_SEP_SALES),
SUM (83_EST_SEP_SALES), (SUM (83_ACT_SEP_SALES)
- SUM (83_EST_SEP_SALES)), (SUM (83_ACT_SEP_SALES)
- SUM (83_EST_SEP_SALES))/SUM (83_ACT_SEP_SALES)
IF REGION = 'EAST' OR REGION = 'WEST'
```

Most overworked, impatient executives are unlikely to learn to communicate with a machine with such statements. They suffer the frustration of the machine's abrupt error messages. The same query in INTELLECT can be phrased in many natural ways, for example:

```
FOR THE EASTERN AND WESTERN REGIONS, HOW DID ACTUAL
SALES FOR LAST MONTH COMPARE TO FORECASTS?
```

INTELLECT responds:

REGION	MAY 1983 ACTUAL SALES	MAY 1983 FORECAST SALES	CHANGE	% CHANGE
EAST	2820	2000	820	41.00
WEST	3180	2800	380	13.57

Here is another specimen from a popular 4GL:

```
TABLE FILE FORTUNE
SUM PCT. 81_SALES
BY INDUSTRY
END
TABLE FILE HOLD
PRINT INDUSTRY AND 81_SALES AND PCT.
BY HIGHEST 81_SALES
END
```

Many end users would not have the patience to get this correct. An INTEL-
LECT version of the same query is:

SHOW ME A RANKED PERCENT OF TOTAL SALES BY INDUSTRY.

INTELLECT responds:

INDUSTRY	1981 SALES (000'S)	PERCENT
PETROLEUM REFINING	$561,096,647	31.64
MOTOR VEHICLES	$156,021,144	8.80
ELECTRONICS	$137,082,745	7.73
FOOD	$123,872,646	6.98
CHEMICAL	$106,943,043	6.03

These examples illustrate the need for human-language products. In using
INTELLECT and RAMIS ENGLISH, with a well-developed lexicon, we find
that these products do respond in a reasonable fashion to almost all reasonable
inputs.

ECHOBACK

When INTELLECT translates the human input into
something it can process against the data base, it displays its interpretation of the query to the user:

User: HOW MANY ANALYSTS DO WE HAVE?

INTELLECT: COUNT EMPLOYEES WITH JOB = SYSTEMS ANALYST
           ANSWER: 25

This *echoback* ables the user to check that the software has understood what he meant or that the query relates appropriately to the data base.

UNRECOGNIZABLE WORDS

If INTELLECT cannot recognize a word in the user's request, it asks for clarification:

User: LIST ALL ELECTRONICS COMPANIES WITH SALES > $ BILLION

INTELLECT: I'M NOT FAMILIAR WITH THE WORD "ELECTRONICS."
           IF IT'S A WORD YOU EXPECT TO FIND IN THE DATABASE, HIT THE RETURN KEY.
           OTHERWISE EITHER FIX ITS SPELLING OR ENTER A SYNONYM FOR IT.

User: ELECTRONICS

INTELLECT: PRINT NAME OF ALL CORPORATIONS WITH
           INDUSTRY = ELECTRONICS
           ANNUAL SALES > $1,000,000,000.
           THE NUMBER OF RECORDS TO RETRIEVE IS 12.

NAME	ANNUAL SALES ($ MILLION)
BURROUGHS	4,128
CONTROL DATA	3,094
.	
.	
.	

User: WHAT ARE THE CUSTOMERS IN POUGHKEEPSIE?

INTELLECT: I'M NOT FAMILIAR WITH THE WORD "POUGHKEEPSIE."
           IF IT'S A WORD YOU EXPECT TO FIND IN THE
           DATABASE, HIT THE RETURN KEY.
           OTHERWISE EITHER FIX ITS SPELLING OR ENTER A
           SYNONYM FOR IT.

User: (presses the ENTER key)

INTELLECT: WHAT FIELD SHOULD IT APPEAR IN?

User: CITY

INTELLECT: PRINT THE NAMES OF ALL CUSTOMERS WITH
           CITY = POUGHKEEPSIE.
           THE NUMBER TO RETRIEVE IS 38.

CHAINED QUERIES   One query often follows on from the previous one. For example, after the response about customers in Poughkeepsie, the user might say:

WHO IS THEIR SALESMAN AND HOW MUCH HAS BEEN SOLD?

Or the user might simply say:

DETAILS

WHAT'S IN THE DATA BASE?   The user may approach a data base knowing nothing about it. He can say:

WHAT'S IN THE DATA BASE?

The software tells him the files that he can use. He might then say:

WHAT FIELDS ARE IN THE CITY FILE?

INTELLECT lists the fields and gives characteristics of those fields:

FIELDS IN THE FILE CITY

FIELD NAME	SEARCHABLE	SORTABLE	FORMAT	LENGTH
NAME	FAST	YES	ALPHABETIC	30
STATE	FAST	YES	ALPHABETIC	15
POPULATION	SLOW	NO	NUMERIC	7
.	.	.	.	.
.	.	.	.	.
.	.	.	.	.

The word FAST in the SEARCHABLE column means that the field has a secondary index (search index), so a search on that field can be performed relatively fast. If we enter a request that requires a search on a SLOW field, INTELLECT will do it but it gives us a warning:

User: WHAT ARE THE NAMES OF CUSTOMERS WHOSE ADDRESS IS 1123 MADISON AVENUE?

INTELLECT: YOUR REQUEST REQUIRES SLOW SEARCHING. THE NUMBER OF RECORDS TO BE SEARCHED IS 11,751. HIT THE ENTER KEY TO CONTINUE PROCESSING, OR ENTER A NEW REQUEST.

QUERY TRAPPING With a user-friendly query system, it is easy for the inexperienced user to enter queries that require excessive searching or sorting or ones that produce too many lines in the response. A query *trap* limit can be set such that if the request exceeds this limit, INTELLECT warns the user:

User: WHAT IS THE AVERAGE SALARY FOR THE COMPANY?

INTELLECT: PRINT THE AVERAGE SALARY FOR ALL EMPLOYEES.
THE NUMBER OF RECORDS TO RETRIEVE IS 5,728.
YOUR REQUEST IS RELATIVELY EXPENSIVE TO ANSWER.
HIT THE ENTER KEY TO CONTINUE PROCESSING, OR ENTER A NEW REQUEST.

LEXICON The user may employ a variety of words that have the same meaning. To be able to respond to them, INTELLECT must have these words in its *lexicon*. The lexicon stores the user vocabulary and maps it to its grammar interpreter and to the data in the data base.

A data base employs a data dictionary, which maps from a single *logical view* of the data to the physical representation of the data. The systems analyst is familiar with the names of records and data items that are in the logical view, but these are often not the names the user commonly employs. The lexicon translates the user's words into the words in the *logical view* of the data base.

The following are some samples of lexicon definitions:

```
FIELD STATE, ST, DECODE = YES, SORT_BY = DECODE;
VALUE MAINE, ME;
VALUE NEW HAMPSHIRE, NH;
VALUE VERMONT, VT;
VALUE NEW ENGLAND, (ME, NH, VT, MA, RI, CT);
```

The formal data-base name for *state* is ST; a user's name for it can be STATE. Values of ST in the data base are ME, NH, and VT; users' names for these are MAINE, NEW HAMPSHIRE, VERMONT. The user's name NEW ENGLAND can refer to any or all of ME, NH, VT, MA, RI, and CT.

```
VALUE 370, 'IBM 370', FIELD = CPU MODEL, RELATION =
BEGINNING WITH
```

This says that 370 is a possible value of the CPU MODEL field. So is any character string beginning with 'IBM 370'.

```
PSEUDOFIELD PROFIT MARGIN, 100 * (INCOME − EXPENSES)/INCOME
```

This shows that the user term PROFIT MARGIN is mapped to an arithmetic expression of the data-base field INCOME and EXPENSES.

SEARCH TERM BACHELOR, SINGLE AND MALE;

This shows that BACHELOR is a user name for a field that has SINGLE in the MARITAL STATUS field and MALE in the SEX field. (The words SINGLE and MALE have already been defined to INTELLECT.)

Once a number of words are defined in the lexicon, INTELLECT will respond to many ways of putting those words together, based on its knowledge of English grammar.

When INTELLECT is installed, a system administrator builds the initial lexicon. This lexicon has many words added to it as users employ the system. INTELLECT logs the user inputs and provides the administrator with a list of all words input by users that it could not yet understand. Another facility enables the users themselves to add words to the lexicon. The quality of the lexicon the administrator builds is critical to the success or failure of an INTELLECT installation. To build a good lexicon requires considerable work.

ROOT WORDS AND APPLICATION WORDS

The lexicon contains general English words and application-specific words. General English words are common English words and phrases that do not relate to a specific application. Many of these are provided with the software. They include words such as GIVE ME, PRINT, LESS THAN, THEIR, STATISTICS, WHEN, HOW MANY, ARE THERE ANY, ALL, COUNT. RAMIS ENGLISH software includes several thousand general English words. Future products ought to include almost the entire English vocabulary. The IBM spelling-correcting typewriter, for example, has a dictionary of 50,000 words.

Application-specific words relate to the files used in the particular installation. They include record names, field names, field values, and user synonyms for these.

As discussed earlier, most business professionals think about data in a way different from the way data are represented in a computer, and they do not think in computer-like syntax. There is a conceptual mapping problem to translate from the user's world to the computer world. The human-language query products attempt to bridge this gap.

As shown in Fig. 10.1, the data-base management system maps between the logical view of data and the data as they are physically stored. This gives data independence to the application programmer, who then does not have to care about exactly how the data are stored physically. A data dictionary shows how the mapping takes place, item for item, between the logical view and the physical storage.

INTELLECT plays a similar role using its lexicon. It maps between the

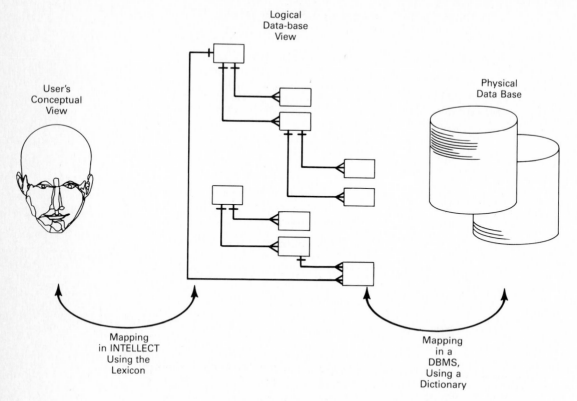

Figure 10.1 INTELLECT's lexicon defines the mapping between the user's conceptual view of information and the logical data-base view. A data-base management system, with its dictionary, maps between the logical data-base view and the data as physically stored.

English with which the user expresses his view of what he wants and the logical data-base view and query-language syntax. INTELLECT automates the conceptual mapping.

AMBIGUITIES

In casual English, many ambiguities arise. When a suitable lexicon is built, INTELLECT is good at dealing with ambiguities. For example, we can enter

LIST ALL NEW YORK EMPLOYEES WHO LIVE IN HOUSES

and it will say

YOUR REQUEST IS AMBIGUOUS TO ME. DO YOU WANT:
1. CITY = NEW YORK
2. STATE = NEW YORK

> PLEASE ENTER THE NUMBER OF THE INTERPRETATION
> YOU INTENDED.

However, if one word of this request is different, thus:

> LIST ALL NEW YORK EMPLOYEES WHO LIVE IN BUFFALO

it does not find an ambiguity because its lexicon tells it that Buffalo is a city, therefore New York could not be a city. To be sure, it gives its interpretation to the user:

> PRINT THE NAME OF ALL EMPLOYEES WITH
> STATE = NEW YORK AND CITY = BUFFALO

Consider the following clause:

> All customers with more than $5000 in their account who have an average monthly balance exceeding $500 or who have been customers for more than five years.

There are two possible meanings to this:

1. All customers (with more than $5000 in their account AND an average monthly balance exceeding $500) OR who have been customers for more than five years.
2. All customers with more than $5000 in their account AND (an average monthly balance exceeding $500 OR who have been customers for more than five years).

The parentheses gives the clause more structure and removes the ambiguity. In general, when a sentence contains *and* and *or* together, there may be ambiguity that can be clarified with parentheses.

If the INTELLECT user says IF A AND B OR C, INTELLECT responds:

> YOUR REQUEST IS AMBIGUOUS TO ME. DO YOU WANT:
> 1. A AND (B OR C)
> 2. (A AND B) OR C
> PLEASE ENTER THE NUMBER OF THE
> INTERPRETATION YOU INTENDED.

There is another problem in the clause about customer balances: "average monthly balance." We need to know over how many months the average is taken. If there is not a field in the file giving "average monthly balance," INTELLECT will calculate an average for all months in the file and tell the user what it has done.

MULTIPLE SENTENCES

RAMIS ENGLISH allows the user to enter multiple sentences:

```
LET REVENUE = UNIT × LISTPRICE.
SHOW ME TOTAL REVENUES FOR TERMINALS.
SORT ON PRODUCT NUMBER AND INCLUDE THE NAME.
NAME MEANS PRODUCT NAME.
```

DISPLAYING A FORMAL QUERY-LANGUAGE EQUIVALENT

A useful way of allowing a user to check his query and at the same time become familiar with a formal query language is to display the English query translated into the formal equivalent. RAMIS ENGLISH can do this, translating the ENGLISH query into the RAMIS II equivalent. Figure 10.2 illustrates this.

It should be noted that the English versions of the queries in Fig. 10.2 are shorter than the RAMIS II versions. One might ask, then, why bother to learn RAMIS II? The answer is that RAMIS II facilitates the entry of more complex requests and programs.

DISADVANTAGES OF USING ENGLISH

The examples at the start of this chapter, comparing INTELLECT with a typical 4GL, illustrate the advantages of using English. It encourages untrained users to start to use computers. It encourages upper-management use of computers. It reduces the time taken learning unnatural syntax and commands and lessens the frustration, bewilderment, and anger caused by repeated blunt rejections by the software of users' attempted inputs.

However, English also has some serious disadvantages. These are listed in Box 10.1.

English is not a good language for expressing complex logic or precise structures. English gives little help in understanding structures. More structured languages, such as QUERY-BY-EXAMPLE, Sperry's MAPPER, or LOTUS 1-2-3, help a user to understand and navigate through more structured data. A structure can offer a sense of order as well as provide road maps through what might otherwise seem an unfathomable morass of data. Languages such as FOCUS, RAMIS, and SAS help in the building of applications using more complex logic.

Once they can employ their own language, some users are encouraged to ask questions the machine cannot answer. This problem is referred to as *semantic overshoot*. In practice, they soon get over asking pointless or funny questions.

Enter your request:
.how many customers have a units entry of at least 15 for terminals.

Equivalent RAMIS II REPORTER request:
TABLE
FILE SALESDATA   FOLD PAGE
COUNT ENTRIES NO PRINT
BY CUSTOMER NO PRINT
IF UNITS GE 15
IF PRODTYPE EQ TERMINALS
END

The answer is 4.

Enter your request:
.list them. Include product and units entries.

Referring to the previous request.
Paraphrase of request:

LIST ALL PRODUCT ENTRIES AND UNITS ENTRIES AND CUSTOMER
ENTRIES IF THE UNITS IS GREATER THAN OR EQUAL TO 15 IF
THE PRODTYPE EQUALS TERMINALS.

Is this acceptable?
Please enter "YES" or "NO":
.yes
Equivalent RAMIS II REPORTER request:
TABLE
FILE SALESDATA   FOLD PAGE
PRINT PRODUCT AND UNITS AND CUSTOMER
IF UNITS GE 15
IF PRODTYPE EQ TERMINALS
END

PAGE   1

PRODUCT	UNITS	CUSTOMER
VIDEO TERMINAL	20	REGAL MFG
VIDEO TERMINAL	15	ANDERSON CONTROLS
VIDEO TERMINAL	15	INFORMATION, INC.
PRINTING TERMINAL	17	ABN
VIDEO TERMINAL	30	ABN

Enter your request:
.fin

RAMIS II English ended.

Figure 10.2   Using English with RAMIS II, the English queries can be translated into the format RAMIS II query language. This can help the user to become familiar with the RAMIS II query language.

BOX 10.1   Advantages and disadvantages of using human-language input to computers

Advantages of using natural human language

- It encourages untrained users to start.
- It encourages upper-management use of computers.
- It reduces the time taken learning complex syntax.
- It lessens the frustration, bewilderment, and anger caused by BAD COMMAND responses.
- It is likely to extend greatly the usage of computers.

Disadvantages of using natural human language	Appropriate response to the disadvantage
<ul><li>It lacks precision</li><li>It is not good for expressing precise and complex logic.</li><li>It is not good for expressing neat structures.</li><li>It encourages semantic overshoot.</li></ul>	<ul><li>It should be combined with other dialogue constructs that aid in the representation of precise logic and structures.</li></ul>
<ul><li>It takes substantial time to key in sentences.</li></ul>	<ul><li>Sentences and words can be abbreviated.</li><li>Speech input as well as typed input will be used.</li></ul>
<ul><li>Ambiguities are possible.</li></ul>	<ul><li>The computer should detect and resolve ambiguities.</li></ul>
<ul><li>Substantial processing is needed.</li></ul>	<ul><li>The processing should be on personal computer workstations. Processing is dropping rapidly in cost.</li></ul>

COST   Substantial processing is necessary to handle the complex interpretation of English grammar and the lexicon mapping. Also, the software itself is complex. For these reasons, the use of natural English has been expensive. However, if INTELLECT or a similar product is sold on personal computers in a large quantity, the cost is likely to become as low as tools such as LOTUS 1-2-3. The personal computer has sufficient power to process English input. A personal computer workstation, networked to mainframe data-base systems, would facilitate user access to information without consuming mainframe processing cycles in interpreting the English input. The user of the personal computer could add to his own lexicon.

VERBOSITY

English is rather long-winded. It takes more time to type English sentences than coded commands. Regular users of INTELLECT become familiar with techniques for abbreviating their inputs. Instead of saying GIVE ME THE NAMES OF ALL OUR CUSTOMERS IN MASSACHUSETTS they say LIST MA CUSTOMERS, or LIST MA CUST if CUST has been defined to the lexicon as an abbreviation for CUSTOMER.

Users can define their own abbreviations.

VOICE INPUT

A potentially very powerful development is to link speech input to software like INTELLECT. This is being done experimentally at the time of writing. Some personal computers already employ speech input. The user has to "train" his personal computer to understand his voice by reading a vocabulary of words to it. This vocabulary could be his INTELLECT lexicon. A combination of speech input and typed input may be used if the computer does not understand all the lexicon words.

As speech input of natural English improves, it may pay to mass-produce specialized devices for speech input rather than use more expensive personal computers.

OVERCOMING THE DISADVANTAGES

The long-term importance of English input to computers is so great that ways of overcoming the negative effects need to be sought. Some of these are listed in Box 10.1.

Having said that, English is only likely to be successful for giving complex instructions to computers if it is supplemented with other techniques. The intriguing question of how to use human language for more complex operations is discussed in the next chapter.

REFERENCES

1. INTELLECT manuals are obtainable from Artificial Intelligence Corporation, 100 Fifth Avenue, Waltham, MA 02254.

2. INTELLECT is also sold by Cullinet, using the IDMS data-base management system and dictionary, under the name ON-LINE ENGLISH. Available from Cullinet Corporation, 20 William Street, Wellesley, MA 02181.

11 CAN WE USE HUMAN LANGUAGE FOR MORE COMPLEX OPERATIONS?

INTRODUCTION Although natural English can be made to work for most data-base queries and simple report and graphics generation, the fact nevertheless remains that English is often very vague and sometimes downright misleading to a computer. We should ask to what extent it is practical to use English for instructions more complex than simple queries.

In Stanley Kubrick's movie *2001: A Space Odyssey,* the computer controlling a space vehicle communicates with the astronauts by human-voice dialogue. A typical specimen of the dialogue in the film follows [1].

Computer: We have a problem.

Astronaut: What is it?

Computer: I am having difficulty maintaining contact with the earth. The trouble is in the AE-35 unit. My fault prediction center reports that it may fail within 72 hours.

Astronaut: We will take care of it. Let's see the optical alignment.

Computer: Here it is, Dave. It's still OK at the moment. (A screen display is given.)

Astronaut: Do you know where the trouble is?

Computer: It's intermittent and I can't localize it. But it appears to be in the AE-35 unit.

Astronaut: What procedure do you suggest?

Computer: The best thing would be to replace the unit with a spare so that we can check it over.

Astronaut: OK. Let us have the hard copy.

A printout is produced. It seems that even in Kubrick's *2001,* old-fashioned printed material is sometimes the most convenient form of record.

Each of the human inputs in the dialogue would be interpretable, in a typed form, by software like INTELLECT or RAMIS ENGLISH. This suggests, perhaps, the great future value of such software. Nevertheless, much of what we need to say to computers consists of far more intricate instructions. Some authorities have stated categorically that English is too sloppy to be a good language for communicating instructions to computers [2, 3].

The language we speak is very disorderly. Its words are ambiguous; its syntax, confused. Many sentences are imperfect expressions of thought because the language is only partially rational. Mechanized parsing is difficult because many words can be verbs at one time and nouns at another, and language is full of irregularities and exceptions. Recognizing the meaning of sentences sometimes requires a wealth of prior knowledge (as does recognizing faces), and this is very difficult to program in today's serial machines.

To the computer, certain simple words are ambiguous because they can assume different shades of meaning. For example, consider the word *nothing*. If A is better than B and B is better than C, a computer could be expected to conclude that A is better than C. However, if we say, "Nothing is better than a good square meal, but a sandwich is better than nothing," the machine concludes that a sandwich is better than a good square meal [4]. The answer to the question "Can anyone walk over Niagara Falls on a tightrope?" is yes, but it does not follow from this that anyone can walk over Niagara Falls on a tightrope. Intricate rules are necessary for a computer to interpret this type of ambiguity correctly.

In response to the advertising claim "Nothing acts faster than Anacin," a computer might reply, "Nothing is also cheaper."

English abounds in ambiguities such as "You wouldn't recognize Mary now. She's grown another foot." A notice in a government office once read, "During the present fuel shortage please take advantage of your secretary between the hours of 12 and 2."

I. D. Hill describes his son's reading that a certain airplane was used for liaison duties. The youngster looked up *liaison* in the dictionary and found it defined as "an illicit sexual adventure" [2].

In the Anglican communion service, the priest offers a chalice of wine and says, "Drink ye all of this." He would be surprised if a communicant drank it all, not knowing that the word *all* referred to the communicants rather than the wine.

It is perfectly grammatical to say, "I feel like going to bed with Jane Fonda again" if it's not the first time you have felt like doing that.

We are used to living with instructions that are too imprecise for a computer. We interpret them by using common sense, which a computer does not have. I. D. Hill points out that the following instructions on a shampoo bottle have bugs in the looping [2]:

For best results, wet hair with warm water. Gently work in the first application. Rinse thoroughly and repeat.

Repeat from where? A computer might decide to repeat the whole instruction, but we do not want to keep wetting hair with warm water after rinsing thoroughly. Suppose that we repeat starting at the second sentence. But that says "first application," so we cannot logically repeat it. The only thing left to repeat is the third sentence. We keep rinsing thoroughly, but when do we stop? We are in a closed loop. A computer would keep rinsing thoroughly until its circuits failed.

I. D. Hill has a solution to this problem. He points out that the language of programming is more precise than English. He suggests that it would be clearer if the shampoo bottle said:

```
BEGIN
WET HAIR WITH WARM WATER;
FOR J: = 1, 2 DO
BEGIN
GENTLY WORK IN APPLICATION (J);
RINSE THOROUGHLY
END
END
```

He says that in his future Utopia, we will not talk to computers as we do to people; instead, we shall be able to write instructions for people in programming languages. A suitable view, perhaps, for *The Computer Bulletin* but hardly for Procter & Gamble.

The problem with trying to make ordinary people use Hill's instructions is that we run straight into an alien and unforgiving syntax. (Are his semicolons correct, for example?)

Assuming that computer users would not find simple graphics an alien syntax, we could write the instruction as follows:

```
┌─ BEGIN

   WET HAIR WITH WARM WATER

   ┌═ REPEAT 3 TIMES

   │  GENTLY WORK IN SHAMPOO

   │  RINSE THOROUGHLY
   └
└
```

Lawyers and drafters of government regulations have attempted to achieve a high level of precision using English. In some cases they have not achieved much success:

> "For the purposes of the pool betting duty, any payment which entitles a person to make a bet by the way of pool betting shall, if he makes the bet, be treated as stake money on the bet, and this subsection shall apply to any payment entitling a person to take part in a transaction which is, on his part, only not a bet made by way of pool betting by reason of his not in fact making any stake as if the transaction were such a bet, and the transaction shall accordingly be treated as a bet for the purpose of pool betting duty."
>
> As Lord Brabazon remarked, "Whoever drafted that must have had something in his mind—God knows what." [2]

Recent experiments at building knowledge-based systems to codify the law have revealed the imprecisions in some legal drafting. An attempt to computer-codify the British immigration laws showed that in some cases it is entirely unclear whether an individual is entitled to British citizenship or not.

Lawyers achieve what precision they do at the expense of lengthy language, which is often misinterpreted because it is tedious:

> The service fee shall be computed by adding the revenue accruing from sales of tapes on a monthly basis to the monthly rental revenue for tapes and multiplying by twelve percent except in the case where the revenue accruing from the sales of tapes exceeds $US 5000 in any one calendar month in which case the service fee shall be computed by adding the revenue accruing from sales of tapes on a monthly basis multiplied by fifteen percent to the monthly rental revenue for tapes multiplied by twelve percent; notwithstanding the above in the circumstance that the revenue accruing from sales of tapes exceeds $US 8000 in any one calendar month the service fee shall be computed by adding the revenue accruing from the sales of tapes on a monthly basis multiplied by eighteen percent to the monthly rental revenue for tapes multiplied by twelve percent.

Using an action diagram and English that INTELLECT can interpret, this becomes:

```
┌── IF MONTHLY SALES REVENUE > 8000
│       FEE = ·18 x MONTHLY SALES REVENUE
│           + ·12 x MONTHLY RENTAL REVENUE
├── ELSE IF MONTHLY SALES REVENUE > 5000
│       FEE = ·15 x MONTHLY SALES REVENUE
│           + ·12 x MONTHLY RENTAL REVENUE
├── ELSE
│       FEE = ·12 x MONTHLY SALES REVENUE
│           + ·12 x MONTHLY RENTAL REVENUE
└──
```

This is much clearer for human beings to understand, and it can be converted automatically to program code. It could be abbreviated further by using algebraic notation.

The INTELLECT version is simple, and the lawyer's wording is precise. Many computing situations are much more complex, with numerous nested conditions and repetitions, and the wording is less precise. There is a greater need for clarity of structure.

COMBINING ENGLISH WITH OTHER MECHANISMS

In such cases it seems that English input like INTELLECT could be extremely useful if combined with other techniques that are much better for expressing structure or complexity. An intriguing question then arises. Of the various constructs in fourth-generation languages, which would be valuable when combined with natural English?

Our purpose in using natural English is to avoid an alien syntax and mnemonics, so we want to select constructs that are easy to remember and use.

Arithmetic is familiar, and the parentheses used in arithmetic can be used elsewhere. Arithmetic statements should be like school arithmetic, not some alien form of arithmetic. In APL, for example, the items in an arithmetic expression are processed in pairs starting from the right; thus $6 + 7 \times 2$ gives 20 but $7 \times 2 + 6$ gives 56. This is extremely confusing to the uninitiated and would cause many people to make errors.

Tabular structures are easy to understand and manipulate on a screen, as with QUERY-BY-EXAMPLE and the spreadsheet tools such as LOTUS 1-2-3.

It is easy to use dialogues in which the computer asks for information or gives the user fill-in-the-blanks panels or pop-on menus over which he can slide a cursor.

If the user is to give the computer complex instructions as in programming, the structure of the program can be represented visually with easy-to-remember graphics. People have no difficulty remembering the brackets of action diagrams and using them to show repetition, conditions, case structures, and nested routines.

An action diagram editor tool linked to INTELLECT-like input of English instructions would enable us to communicate complex instructions to a computer without an alien syntax. This could be enhanced with a screen design aid, report formatter, and graphics chart formatter.

Figure 11.1 shows a program created with action diagram brackets and phrases that software like INTELLECT could interpret using its lexicon and data dictionary. The user would write one such statement at a time, and the software would respond, echoing the statement so that the user would know that it had been interpreted correctly.

Figure 11.2 is created with an action diagram editor [5]. Everything in black on the diagram is displayed by the editor. Everything in red is typed by

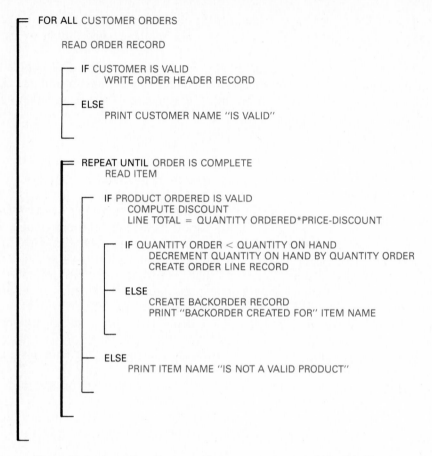

```
┌═ FOR ALL CUSTOMER ORDERS
│
│      READ ORDER RECORD
│
│          ┌─ IF CUSTOMER IS VALID
│          │      WRITE ORDER HEADER RECORD
│          │
│          ├─ ELSE
│          │      PRINT CUSTOMER NAME "IS VALID"
│          └
│
│
│      ┌═ REPEAT UNTIL ORDER IS COMPLETE
│      │      READ ITEM
│      │
│      │          ┌─ IF PRODUCT ORDERED IS VALID
│      │          │      COMPUTE DISCOUNT
│      │          │      LINE TOTAL = QUANTITY ORDERED*PRICE-DISCOUNT
│      │          │
│      │          │          ┌─ IF QUANTITY ORDER < QUANTITY ON HAND
│      │          │          │      DECREMENT QUANTITY ON HAND BY QUANTITY ORDER
│      │          │          │      CREATE ORDER LINE RECORD
│      │          │          │
│      │          │          ├─ ELSE
│      │          │          │      CREATE BACKORDER RECORD
│      │          │          │      PRINT "BACKORDER CREATED FOR" ITEM NAME
│      │          │          └
│      │          │
│      │          ├─ ELSE
│      │          │      PRINT ITEM NAME "IS NOT A VALID PRODUCT"
│      │          └
│      └
└
```

Figure 11.1   An action diagram with statements in natural English like the statements that are input to INTELLECT or RAMIS ENGLISH. The software would respond to each input in turn. With this technique, complexly structured programs could be built.

the user. The black items are selected by the user from simple menus like those of LOTUS 1-2-3. The red words and phrases are, again, similar to those that INTELLECT or RAMIS ENGLISH can interpret.

Figure 11.2 illustrates how a complex procedure could be created without the user having to remember any nonhuman syntax, mnemonics, or computer vocabulary. Both the action diagram editor and the INTELLECT interpreter run, today, on personal computers. At the time of writing, they have not been interconnected. With RAMIS ENGLISH, each line of input could be converted to a RAMIS II statement, as in Fig. 10.2. The user would then, in effect, be building a RAMIS II program using human syntax and words.

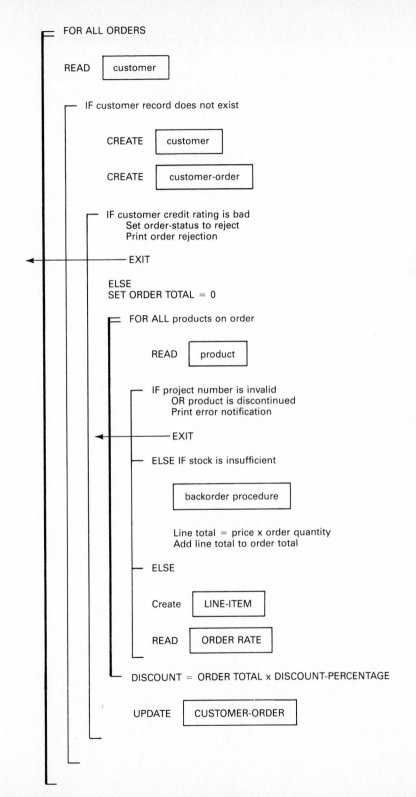

FOR ALL ORDERS

READ [customer]

IF customer record does not exist

  CREATE [customer]

  CREATE [customer-order]

IF customer credit rating is bad
    Set order-status to reject
    Print order rejection
— EXIT

ELSE
SET ORDER TOTAL = 0

  FOR ALL products on order

    READ [product]

    IF project number is invalid
        OR product is discontinued
        Print error notification
    — EXIT

    ELSE IF stock is insufficient

      [backorder procedure]

      Line total = price x order quantity
      Add line total to order total

    ELSE

      Create [LINE-ITEM]

      READ [ORDER RATE]

  DISCOUNT = ORDER TOTAL x DISCOUNT-PERCENTAGE

  UPDATE [CUSTOMER-ORDER]

Figure 11.2

It is to be hoped that software like RAMIS ENGLISH and INTELLECT will be linked to a diversity of 4GL tools, graphics facilities, operating systems, and software mechanisms.

REFERENCES

1. A. C. Clarke, *2001: A Space Odyssey,* New York: Signet Books, 1968.

2. I. D. Hill, "Wouldn't It Be Nice If We Could Write Computer Programs in Ordinary English—Or Would It?" *The Computer Bulletin,* 16, no. 6 (June 1972).

3. B. Shneiderman, *Software Psychology,* Cambridge, MA: Winthrop Publishers, Inc., 1980.

4. C. Longuet-Higgins and S. D. Isond, *The Monkey's Paw,* Conference of Man-Computer Interaction organized by the I.E.E.E., September 1970.

5. Figure 11.2 was created on an IBM PC with Action Diagrammer from Database Design, Inc., Ann Arbor, MI.

12 COMPARISONS OF 4GL CODE

INTRODUCTION The objective of 4GLs is to make it as easy and quick as possible to tell a computer what we want it to do. This chapter compares the effectiveness of several 4GLs in achieving this on a fairly simple operation. The end of the chapter discusses what is required for more complex operations.

GIVING ENGINEERS A SALARY RAISE EMPLOYEE and EMPLOYEE-PROJECT records exist as follows:

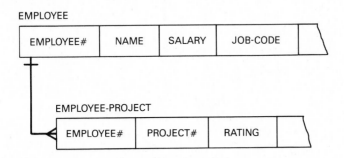

For each EMPLOYEE record there are one or more EMPLOYEE-PROJECT records, containing, among other things, a RATING field showing how well the employee performed on that particular project.

The time has come to give the engineers salary raises. JOBCODE for ENGINEER is 3. If the average RATING on the projects an engineer is working on is greater than 6, we want to give the engineer a salary raise of $1000. Using an action diagram, we can express this in the following manner.

We can tackle this operation *procedurally* or *nonprocedurally*. It is simple enough for fully *nonprocedural* code to work well. Operations of greater complexity need procedural code.

Let us first examine procedural approaches. Using an action diagram, we can express what we want to do as follows:

```
FOR ALL EMPLOYEE RECORDS

    READ EMPLOYEE

        IF JOBCODE = 3

            FOR ALL EMPLOYEE-PROJECT RECORDS
                READ EMPLOYEE-PROJECT

            CALCULATE AVERAGE VALUE OF RATING

                IF AVERAGE RATING > 6

                ADD 1000 TO SALARY

                UPDATE EMPLOYEE
```

MANTIS

Using MANTIS, the code is fairly similar to the action diagram:

```
FILE EMPLOYEE (EMPLOYEE, PASSWORD)
FILE EMPLOYEE-PROJECT (EMPLOYEE, PASSWORD)
GET EMPLOYEE
WHILE EMPLOYEE<> "END"
    IF JOBCODE = 3
    COUNT = 0
    SUM = 0
    GET EMPLOYEE-PROJECT (EMPLOYEE#)
        WHILE EMPLOYEE-PROJECT <> "END"
        COUNT = COUNT + 1
        SUM = SUM + RATING
        GET EMPLOYEE-PROJECT
        END
    AVE-RATING = SUM/COUNT
    IF AVE-RATING > 6
    SALARY = SALARY + 1000
    UPDATE EMPLOYEE
    END
    END
GET EMPLOYEE
END
```

IDEAL

IDEAL is somewhat more concise than MANTIS. It allows us to use selective read statements such as FOR EACH EMPLOYEE WHERE JOBCODE = 3. It also has a COUNT function that we can use in computing an average:

```
FOR EACH EMPLOYEE WHERE JOBCODE = 3
    SET X = 0
    FOR EACH EMPLOYEE-PROJECT
        WHERE EMPLOYEE-PROJECT.EMPLOYEE# = EMPLOYEE.EMPLOYEE#
        ADD RATING TO X
    ENDFOR
    AVE-RATING = X/ $COUNT
    IF AVE-RATING > 6
        ADD 1000 TO SALARY
    ENDIF
```

Neither IDEAL nor MANTIS contains an *average* function in its procedural code, so we had to calculate the average.

NATURAL

NATURAL does have an average function. The code in NATURAL is as follows:

```
FIND EMPLOYEE WITH JOBCODE = 3
    FIND EMPLOYEE-PROJECT WHERE EMPLOYEE# = EMPLOYEE#
    AT END OF DATA MOVE AVER (RATING) TO AV(N2)
    LOOP
    IF AV > 6 DO
    ADD 1000 TO SALARY
    UPDATE SAME RECORD
    END TRANSACTION
    DO END
    LOOP
END
```

This is brief and neat except for the strange bracket terminations commented on earlier. NATURAL would be greatly improved in its clarity by having IDEAL-like bracket terminations.

RAMIS II

RAMIS II permits relational-like operations on the data. Files can be projected and joined to create a much smaller file that contains only engineers who are eligible for the $1000 salary raise:

```
┌─ RELATE
│   PROJECT EMPLOYEE BY EMPLOYEE# IF JOBCODE IS 3
│   PROJECT EMPLOYEE-PROJECT BY EMPLOYEE# IF AVERAGE RATING GT 6
│   SAVE THE INTERSECTION
└─ END
```

This RAMIS file can now be used to update the EMPLOYEE file:

```
┌─ REVISE
│   READ RAMSAVE
│   UPDATE SALARY
│   SALARY = SALARY + 1000
│   FILE EMPLOYEE
└─ END
```

SQL

Where RAMIS and FOCUS create a working file and then, separately, carry out operations on that file, other query-and-update languages express the operations to be performed directly with the data description.

SQL gives purely nonprocedural statements of what is needed:

```
UPDATE EMPLOYEE
SET SALARY = SALARY + 1000
WHERE JOBCODE = 3
AND 6 (SELECT AVE (RATING) FROM EMPLOYEE_PROJECT
WHERE EMPLOYEE.EMP# = EMPLOYEE_PROJECT.EMP#)
```

This is concise, but the use of clauses in parentheses can be somewhat confusing on more complex examples. Some other query-and-update languages are easy to use.

QBE

QUERY-BY-EXAMPLE allows a user to update salary by entering an example such as *500* + 1000 into the SALARY column of a table. This says: "If SALARY is 500, change it to 500 + 1000."

The whole operation can be expressed by filling in a screen representation of the records as follows:

EMPLOYEE	EMPLOYEE#	NAME	SALARY	JOB-CODE	
U.	_10		_500 + 1000	3	

EMPLOYEE-PROJECT	EMPLOYEE#	PROJECT#	RATING	
	_10		AVG > 6	

The typing of *10,* an example of an EMPLOYEE #, into both record images shows that they both refer to the same employee. That employee has a JOBCODE of 3 and an average RATING greater than 6. All employees who fit this example have their salary changed from 500, for example, to 500 + 1000.

AN INTELLECT-LIKE APPROACH

Given a system for interpreting human English like INTELLECT (Chapter 10), the operation could be expressed still more concisely and obviously:

```
FOR ALL ENGINEERS
IF AVERAGE RATING ON PROJECTS > 6
ADD 1000 TO SALARY
```

You might ask why anything more difficult than this is needed. At the time of writing, INTELLECT does not allow its users to *update* data. Perhaps the reason is that it would be too easy for them to make unauthorized or inappropriate changes or to enter operations that are not quite correct. Clearly, tight security and authorization procedures are needed when we make it easy to change data. To help check that the operation will do what was intended, the code may be translated into a more formal representation before execution. RAMIS ENGLISH can do this, as illustrated in Fig. 10.2.

SIMPLE VERSUS COMPLEX APPLICATIONS

In the foregoing succession of examples, the formulation of the operation becomes progressively easier. There is no doubt that the earlier examples used constructs that could be simplified and that a higher level of automation could make the formulation of the task easier. This is shown

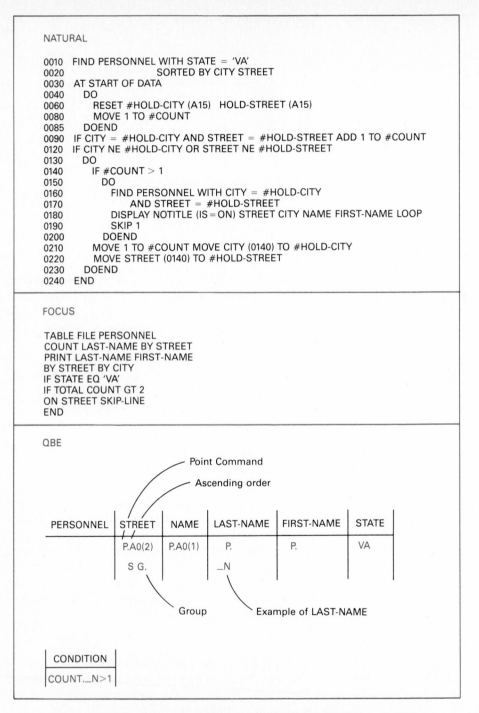

```
NATURAL

0010  FIND PERSONNEL WITH STATE = 'VA'
0020                SORTED BY CITY STREET
0030  AT START OF DATA
0040    DO
0060      RESET #HOLD-CITY (A15)  HOLD-STREET (A15)
0080      MOVE 1 TO #COUNT
0085    DOEND
0090  IF CITY = #HOLD-CITY AND STREET = #HOLD-STREET ADD 1 TO #COUNT
0120  IF CITY NE #HOLD-CITY OR STREET NE #HOLD-STREET
0130    DO
0140      IF #COUNT > 1
0150        DO
0160          FIND PERSONNEL WITH CITY = #HOLD-CITY
0170              AND STREET = #HOLD-STREET
0180          DISPLAY NOTITLE (IS=ON) STREET CITY NAME FIRST-NAME LOOP
0190          SKIP 1
0200        DOEND
0210      MOVE 1 TO #COUNT MOVE CITY (0140) TO #HOLD-CITY
0220      MOVE STREET (0140) TO #HOLD-STREET
0230    DOEND
0240  END
```

```
FOCUS

TABLE FILE PERSONNEL
COUNT LAST-NAME BY STREET
PRINT LAST-NAME FIRST-NAME
BY STREET BY CITY
IF STATE EQ 'VA'
IF TOTAL COUNT GT 2
ON STREET SKIP-LINE
END
```

QBE

Point Command

Ascending order

PERSONNEL	STREET	NAME	LAST-NAME	FIRST-NAME	STATE
	P.A0(2)	P.A0(1)	P.	P.	VA
	S G.		_N		

Group   Example of LAST-NAME

CONDITION
COUNT._N>1

Figure 12.1 A simple task performed in NATURAL, FOCUS, and QBE.
The task is to produce a report showing the streets on which two or more of
a corporation's personnel live. The report is to be ordered by street within
city. (The NATURAL version is courtesy Software AG.) (*Note:* The most
recent version of NATURAL is more powerful and better structured.)

again in Fig. 12.1. The QBE version is simpler than those in procedural languages.

At the same time, it is important to state that the simple-to-use constructs are often limited in their power. Figure 12.2 reiterates what was illustrated in Fig. 1.2—that nonprocedural languages are appropriate for simple operations but that they cannot be used for complex operations unless they are combined with other techniques. We need simple solutions to simple problems. The tasks illustrated in this chapter are fairly simple.

The challenge of the 4GL world is to find quick and easy-to-use techniques that can be applied to complex applications as well as simple ones. The form of syntax has a major effect on this, but the key is to couple a good syntax to two other techniques:

1. The use of on-line graphics

2. Leading the designer through a sequence of steps.

These techniques are discussed in the following two chapters.

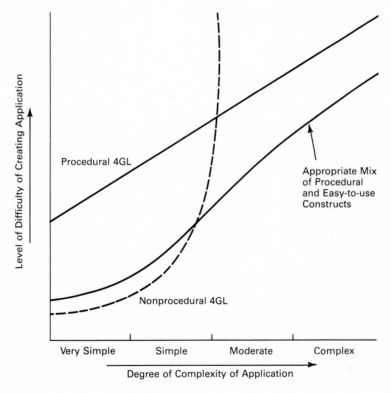

Figure 12.2 Nonprocedural languages are fast for simple operations. For complex operations, a mixture of language constructs is needed.

DIVIDE AND CONQUER

The building of complex systems can be made easier by dividing it into tasks, each of which, by itself, is relatively simple. There are different types of tasks, and different forms of screen interaction are appropriate for these different types. The screen interaction of a good report generator, for example, is quite different from that for expressing nested loops. A mistake in some of the early 4GLs is that they tried to use the same syntax for different types of tasks. If you use the same syntax for report generation and expressing nested loops, you either make report generation unnecessarily difficult or you make the expression of nested loops unclean and clumsy.

Even in a simple query-and-report language, it is desirable that the process of finding the requisite data be separate from the process of formatting and dressing up reports. The generation of graphics charts may again be separate:

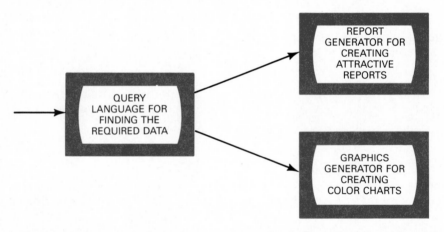

The user often goes through several iterations when finding the data he needs and summarizing them. He may (or may not) move this data to the report generator or graphics generator and go through several iterations to create attractive reports or charts. Combining all three facilities into one syntax can make that syntax more complicated and difficult to learn. The graphics or report facility should use a different type of screen interaction from that of the query language.

Part of the reason the NATURAL code in Fig. 12.1 is more complex is that the designer wanted to do everything with the same syntax rather than dividing the problem and handling different types of tasks in different easy-to-use ways.

Although it is desirable to have a multiplicity of tools, these tools should, where possible, use keys, punctuation, menus, and so on, in a compatible way so that having learned one tool, it is easy to learn the rest.

THE TOOLS REQUIRED

The following types of tools are needed when building a data processing system. Each should be designed with whatever techniques makes it as easy to use as possible.

Data-Base Definition

A data base needs to be designed and structured appropriately. There exist various data-base design or data modeling tools that are independent of any application language or 4GL. An application designer may display a subset of an overall data base or data model. The subset may be manipulated with relational-like operations, such as PROJECT, SELECT, SORT, or JOIN, to produce an application "view" of the data.

Graphic representation of the data structures on a screen is desirable.

Data-Base Operations

Query and update operations need to be expressed. This may involve *joins* and *projects* of the data.

SQL and QBE are effective in expressing simple data-base operations. These can be made easy to use correctly with a graphic technique such as QBE. QBE itself could be made easier to use by beginners.

Procedure Descriptions

Some vendors use as a sales argument that their language is completely "nonprocedural" rather than like structured programming. However, it is difficult to build complex systems with nested conditions and loops without careful structuring. It is necessary to be able to express CONDITION structures, CASE structures, LOOP structures, FOR structures, and so on. These are often nested to several levels. For clean structured design, the ESCAPE construct may be used, but GO TO should not be used.

Graphic representation of these structures greatly clarifies the program. Action diagrams are probably the best technique for this [2]. With an action diagram editor, the user need not enter any control words; they are placed by the software on the brackets he selects.

Screen Design

A screen design aid is needed to design the screens the user will see. The design should be able to "paint" the user's screen designs interactively, possibly with a menu for showing highlighting, data-entry fields, lines and boxes, color, and so forth.

Dialogue Design

Dialogue design is an extension of screen design. The tool may provide certain categories of dialogue, especially:

- Menu dialogue
- Data-entry dialogue
- Dialogue for formatting and manipulating reports
- Dialogue for generating and manipulating business graphics

Report Generation

Reports may be designed interactively at a screen. The designer may be given a list of choices in the formatting, subsetting, sorting, subtotaling, and so on, as with the IDEAL report generator illustrated in Chapter 5.

Rules Tools

Certain types of complex logic or rules may be expressed separately from the main body of the program. They may be expressed in a way that makes them easy to change. This facilitates program maintenance.

Certain types of logic can be expressed with the formulation of rules used in expert systems; for example:

```
IF ACCOUNT being posted is in SALES LEDGER
AND FLAG is marked ACTIVE
AND STATUS is not C or D
AND BALANCE is in debit
AND BALANCE has been negative for 18 days
AND BALANCE < 350
THEN set FLAG to CREDIT_STOPPED
```

If in each of these areas a form of syntax or graphics that is easy and quick to use and powerful in its expressiveness is used, 4GLs will have the capability to build complex data processing systems fast and make them easy to maintain. At the time of writing, every 4GL examined needs major improvements to make it easier and quicker to use, yet more powerful.

REFERENCES

1. *NATURAL Reference Manual* (NAT-120-030), from Software AG, 11800 Sunrise Valley Drive, Reston, VA 22091.

2. J. Martin and P. McClure, *Action Diagrams: Clearly Structured Program Design*, Englewood Cliffs, NJ: Prentice-Hall, Inc., 1985.

13 USE OF GRAPHICS

AVOIDANCE OF UNNATURAL SYNTAX
We have illustrated various ways in which instructions can be given to a computer without unnatural syntax and mnemonics that require the user to train and practice extensively. These include:

- Human-language input
- User responding to menus (possibly with a mouse or finger pointing, possibly with cursor bars that move with decisecond response times)
- User selecting items from lists
- User filling in pop-on instruction panels

Another powerful tool is the use of graphics. People tend to remember the meaning of well-designed graphics, whereas they often forget mnemonics and syntax. Most people can read a map without help. A graphics chart can, like a map, have an explanatory key associated with it. By using graphics, complex logic and complex structures can be represented clearly.

A type of 4GL mechanism that is very appealing is the use of a graphics editor for system design such that programs can be generated directly from the graphics. The graphics may be used in conjunction with a screen design aid, a report generator, a data model and dictionary, and a subroutine library.

A·variety of types of diagrams are appropriate for system design. These are discussed in other works [1, 2].

NEED FOR MORE RIGOROUS DIAGRAMS
For diagrams to form a basis for code generation, they need to be more rigorous than most diagrams that systems analysts have drawn in the past. In the past, analysts' and programmers' diagrams have been drawn with plastic templates. They have usually represented aspects of systems

design but have not been intended to be precise enough to be a basis for code generation. To generate code from them, they need to be more complete. When we examine them with the eye of a computer, wanting to automate as much of programming as possible, they are often remarkably sloppy.

New types of diagrams and improvements to old types have been created to act as a basis for computer-aided design (CAD) for systems analysts, sometimes called CASA (computer-aided systems analysis).

More traditional diagramming techniques have *serious* deficiencies. Flowcharts are falling out of use because they do not give a structured view of a program. Some of the early structured diagramming techniques need replacing because they fail to represent some important constructs. We need more rigorous methods for creating better specifications. Vast improvements are needed and are clearly possible in the specification process. These improvements bring new diagramming methods.

One of the problems with computing is that it is so easy to make a mess. Very tidy thinking about the complex logic is needed, or a rat's nest results. Today's structured techniques are an improvement over earlier techniques. However, we can still make a mess with them. Most specifications for complex systems are full of ambiguities, inconsistencies, and omissions. More precise, mathematically based techniques are evolving so that we can use the computer to help create specifications without these problems. As better, more automated techniques evolve, they need appropriate diagramming methods.

COMPUTER-AIDED THINKING

Philosophers have often stated that what we are capable of thinking depends on the language we use for thinking. Appropriate constructs in 4GLs help users and designers to think clearly about what a computer should be doing. The diagrams we draw of complex processes are a particularly valuable form of language. Incorporating good diagramming techniques into 4GLs helps users to visualize and invent relatively complex applications.

The style or form of a diagram is important. A poor choice of diagramming technique can inhibit a user's thinking. A good choice can enhance his thinking and improve the quality of his work.

A computer can help a designer to create good diagrams in a variety of ways:

- It can guide him with pop-on menus and instruction panels. It can make suggestions and generally provide help.

- It can make diagrams easy to edit and change. When the analyst moves a block, it can automatically reposition the links that connect to that block.

- It can provide a variety of error and integrity checks.

- It can automatically convert one type of diagram into another. Various diagrams representing different ways of visualizing systems logic can be converted *automatically* into action diagrams and thence into code. A designer can window between one representation and another, observing the effect of making changes. The computer can check the design in various ways and prompt the designer to make it correct. If the methodology is designed appropriately, the computer can make very elaborate checks that are much more comprehensive than those a human would be likely to apply. This is necessary in the design of large, complex systems.

- It can link the design to a central data dictionary, data model, encyclopedia, or library of program and subroutine designs.

- It can provide precise intercommunication among separate designers.

- It can act as an expert system applying rules to the design and expert guidance to the designers.

Good use of a sophisticated design tool provides computer-aided thinking. The objective should be to enhance the creativity of the designer while performing for him as many routine tasks as possible.

THE DOCUMENTATION IS THE DIAGRAMS

If code is generated from diagrams, the diagrams become the specifications and documentation for the system. Explanatory comments may be associated with certain blocks on the diagrams, but this separate text is not needed for generating the system.

When systems are modified, diagrams are an essential aid to maintenance. They make it possible for a new team to understand how the programs work. If the code is generated from the diagrams, changes are made by changing the diagram and regenerating the code. In this way the documentation automatically reflects the changes and does not become obsolete, as so many systems do.

Maintenance programmers mistrust most external documentation because they know that in practice it is seldom updated. Even the external documentation for a newly released system is unlikely to describe a program accurately. Documentation can be trusted to be accurate in two cases. The first is when information about a program is *automatically generated from the code* (e.g., cross-reference listings, automatically generated structure charts, flowcharts). Keeping all the program documentation within or generated from the source code will make it more accessible and more accurate. The second is when the documentation is in the form of computerized diagrams or representation, and the program is generated automatically from these. In one of these two ways (preferably the latter), the code and the diagrams are automatically linked, and the diagrams *are* the documentation used for maintenance.

It is valuable to make computable diagrams of the specification. The right type of diagram is concise, precise, and clear and does not allow the sloppiness and woolly thinking that are common in textual specifications.

PRECISION
Mathematics is the preeminent language of precision. However, it would be difficult to describe a large road map in mathematics. If we succeeded in doing so, the road map would still be more useful than the mathematics to most people. Data processing is complex and needs road maps. We need to be able to follow the lines, examine the junctions, and read the words on the diagrams.

Some diagrams, however, have a mathematical basis. With mathematics, we may state axioms that the diagrams must obey. A workstation may beep at a designer and display an explanation whenever he violates one of the axioms. The mathematically based structure that emerges may be cross-checked in various ways and may be the basis of automatic code generation.

Architects, surveyors, and designers of machine parts have *formal* techniques for diagramming that they *must* follow. Systems analysis and program design have even greater need for clear diagrams because these activities are more complex and the work of different people must interlock in intricate ways. There tends, however, to be less formality in programming as yet, perhaps because it is a young discipline full of brilliant people who want to make up their own rules.

One of the reasons building and maintaining software systems is so expensive and error-prone is the difficulty that we have in clearly communicating our ideas to one another. Whether we are reading a functional specification, a program design, or a program listing, we often experience difficulty understanding precisely what its author is telling us. Whenever we must rely on our interpretation of the meaning, the chance of a misunderstanding that could lead to program errors is very great.

The larger the team, the greater the need for precision in diagramming. It is difficult or impossible for members of a large team to understand, in detail, the work of the others. Instead, each team member should be familiar with an overview of the system and see where his component fits into it. He should be able to develop his component with as little ongoing interchange with the rest of the team as possible. He has clear, precisely defined and diagrammed interfaces with the work of the others. When one programmer changes his design, it should not affect the designs of the other programmers unless this is unavoidable. The interfaces between the work of different programmers need to be unchanging. Achieving this requires high-precision techniques for designing the overall structure of the system.

TYPES OF DIAGRAMS
A variety of types of diagrams are appropriate as parts of 4GLs:

Action Diagrams

In Chapter 7 we discussed action diagrams for designing and generating procedural code structures. A complex structure can be built by designing the action diagrams on a screen and automatically fitting the language control words to the diagram. Chapter 11 discussed the potential power of combining human-language processing with action diagrams.

Decision Trees and Tables

For ease of maintenance it is desirable that the expression of complex decisions or rules be separate from overall program code. A useful tool for expressing the logic of complex decisions or rules is a decision tree or table [1].

Figure 13.1 shows an example of a decision tree for computing ORDER.DISCOUNT. Sometimes a decision table is used for showing information like that in Fig. 13.1. A decision tree or table can be converted *automatically* into an action diagram. This may become a subroutine of a larger action diagram. Figure 13.2 shows an action diagram that is equivalent to the decision tree of Fig. 13.1.

Decomposition Diagrams

Many analysts draw diagrams showing how a process or activity is decomposed into lower-level processes or activities. This is equivalent to an action diagram. Action diagrams usually show more detail, such as repetition, conditions, and case structures.

HOS Charts

HOS charts are a form of decomposition diagram designed to provide a high level of verification. Bug-free code can be generated from them. They will be discussed shortly.

Data-Structure Diagrams

Data-structure diagrams represent the associations among data items and records [3]. They are the basis of data analysis and data modeling. Correct representation of data structures is important to avoid certain types of subtle error in high-level data-base operations. This is discussed in Chapter 18.

Data Navigation Diagrams

Data navigation diagrams show, in detail, the use of data-base operations. They can be converted automatically into action diagrams [1]. These are illustrated in Chapter 14.

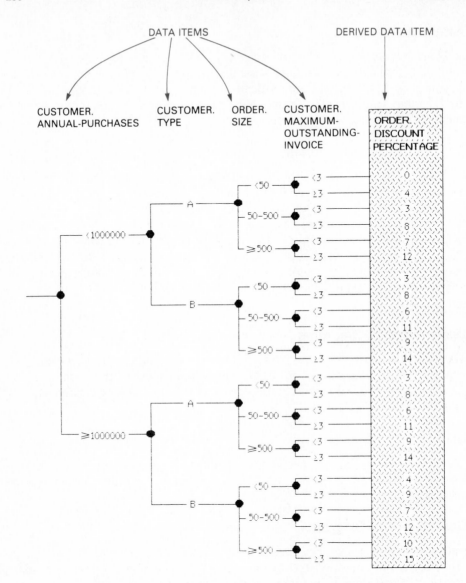

Figure 13.1 Decision tree for computing ORDER.DISCOUNT.

Dependency Diagrams

Dependency diagrams show how one activity is dependent on another. Activities may be interdependent because data have to flow from one activity to another [1]. A *data-flow diagram* is a type of dependency diagram. Dependency diagrams are drawn with more rigor than most data-flow diagrams and can be converted automatically into action diagrams [1].

```
  ┌─── IF CUSTOMER.ANNUAL-PURCHASES ≤ 1000000
  │   ┌─── IF CUSTOMER.TYPE = A
  │   │   ┌─── IF ORDER.SIZE < 50
  │   │   │   ┌── IF CUSTOMER.MAXIMUM-OUTSTANDING-INVOICE = ≤3
  │   │   │   │   ORDER.DISCOUNT = 0
  │   │   │   ├── ELSE
  │   │   │   │   ORDER.DISCOUNT = 4
  │   │   │   └── ENDIF
  │   │   ├── ELSEIF ORDER.SIZE > 50 AND < 500
  │   │   │   ┌── IF CUSTOMER.MAXIMUM-OUTSTANDING-INVOICE = ≤3
  │   │   │   │   ORDER.DISCOUNT = 3
  │   │   │   ├── ELSE
  │   │   │   │   ORDER.DISCOUNT = 8
  │   │   │   └── ENDIF
  │   │   ├── ELSEIF ORDER.SIZE > 500
  │   │   │   ┌── IF CUSTOMER.MAXIMUM-OUTSTANDING-INVOICE = ≤3
  │   │   │   │   ORDER.DISCOUNT = 7
  │   │   │   ├── ELSE
  │   │   │   │   ORDER.DISCOUNT = 12
  │   │   └── └── ENDIF
  │   │       ENDIF
  │   ├── ELSEIF CUSTOMER.TYPE = 8
  │   │   ┌── IF ORDER.SIZE < 50
  │   │   │   ┌── IF CUSTOMER.MAXIMUM-OUTSTANDING-INVOICE = ≤3
  │   │   │   │   ORDER.DISCOUNT = 3
  │   │   │   ├── ELSE
  │   │   │   │   ORDER.DISCOUNT = 8
  │   │   │   └── ENDIF
  │   │   ├── ELSEIF ORDER.SIZE > 50 AND < 500
  │   │   │   ┌── IF CUSTOMER.MAXIMUM-OUTSTANDING-INVOICE = ≤3
  │   │   │   │   ORDER.DISCOUNT = 6
  │   │   │   ├── ELSE
  │   │   │   │   ORDER.DISCOUNT = 11
  │   │   │   └── ENDIF
  │   │   ├── ELSEIF ORDER.SIZE > 500
  │   │   │   ┌── IF CUSTOMER.MAXIMUM-OUTSTANDING-INVOICE = ≤3
  │   │   │   │   ORDER.DISCOUNT = 9
  │   │   │   ├── ELSE
  │   │   │   │   ORDER.DISCOUNT = 14
  │   │   │   └── ENDIF
  │   │   └── ENDIF
  │   └── ENDIF
  ├── ELSE
  │   ┌── IF CUSTOMER.TYPE = A
  │   │   ┌── IF ORDER.SIZE < 50
  │   │   │   ┌── IF CUSTOMER.MAXIMUM-OUTSTANDING-INVOICE = ≤3
  │   │   │   │   ORDER.DISCOUNT = 3
  │   │   │   ├── ELSE
  │   │   │   │   ORDER.DISCOUNT = 8
  │   │   │   └── ENDIF
  │   │   ├── ELSEIF ORDER.SIZE > 50 AND < 500
  │   │   │   ┌── IF CUSTOMER.MAXIMUM-OUTSTANDING INVOICE = ≤3
  │   │   │   │   ORDER.DISCOUNT = 6
  │   │   │   ├── ELSE
  │   │   │   │   ORDER.DISCOUNT = 11
  │   │   │   └── ENDIF
  │   │   ├── ELSEIF ORDER.SIZE > 500
  │   │   │   ┌── IF CUSTOMER.MAXIMUM-OUTSTANDING-INVOICE = ≤3
  │   │   │   │   ORDER.DISCOUNT = 9
  │   │   │   ├── ELSE
  │   │   │   │   ORDER.DISCOUNT = 14
  │   │   │   └── ENDIF
  │   │   └── ENDIF
```

Figure 13.2 Action diagram equivalent to the decision tree of Fig. 13.1.

(Continued)

```
├── ELSEIF CUSTOMER.TYPE = B
│   ┌── IF ORDER.SIZE < 50
│   │   ┌── IF CUSTOMER.MAXIMUM-OUTSTANDING-INVOICE = ≤3
│   │   │   ORDER.DISCOUNT = 4
│   │   ├── ELSE
│   │   │   ORDER.DISCOUNT = 9
│   │   └── ENDIF
│   ├── ELSEIF ORDER.SIZE > 50 AND < 500
│   │   ┌── IF CUSTOMER.MAXIMUM-OUTSTANDING-INVOICE = ≤3
│   │   │   ORDER.DISCOUNT = 7
│   │   ├── ELSE
│   │   │   ORDER.DISCOUNT = 12
│   │   └── ENDIF
│   ├── ELSEIF ORDER.SIZE > 500
│   │   ┌── IF CUSTOMER.MAXIMUM-OUTSTANDING INVOICE = ≤3
│   │   │   ORDER.DISCOUNT = 10
│   │   ├── ELSE
│   │   │   ORDER.DISCOUNT = 15
│   │   └── ENDIF
│   └── ENDIF
└── ENDIF
    ENDIF
```

Figure 13.2   (Continued)

A GRAPHIC SPECIFICATION LANGUAGE

A particularly interesting graphics language is that of HOS (Higher Order Software, Inc.), USE.IT [4]. With this language, an activity (function, process, or procedure) is drawn on the screen as a box. The input data types to the box are written to its right and the output data types to its left:

```
                    ┌───────────┐
                    │  PREPARE  │
PEKING DUCK         │   MEAL    │         INGREDIENTS
                    └───────────┘

                    ┌───────────┐        WOOD 1,
          CHAIR     │   MAKE    │        WOOD 2,
                    │   CHAIR   │        SCREWS
                    └───────────┘
```

The reason the inputs are on the right and the outputs on the left is so as to be similar to mathematical notation:

$$y = F(x)$$

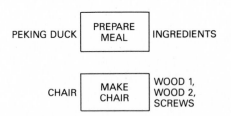

$$y = \text{MAX} \ (a, \ b, \ c)$$

$$y \ \boxed{\text{MAX} \begin{array}{l} a \\ b \\ c \end{array}}$$

The function represented by the box can be decomposed into lower-level functions. The inputs and outputs of the lower-level functions are written by those boxes also:

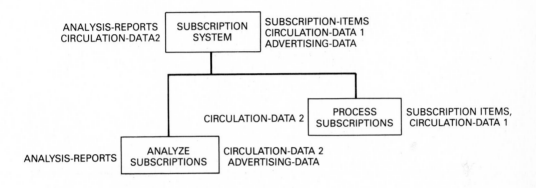

Each of the lower-level functions can be further decomposed. For example, PROCESS SUBSCRIPTIONS can be decomposed as follows:

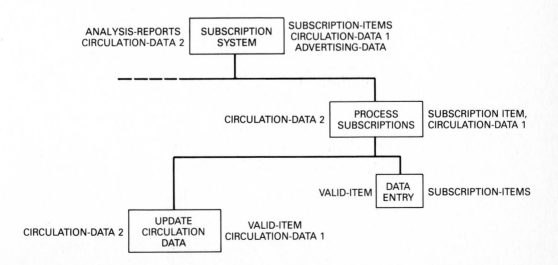

UPDATE CIRCULATION DATA can be further decomposed:

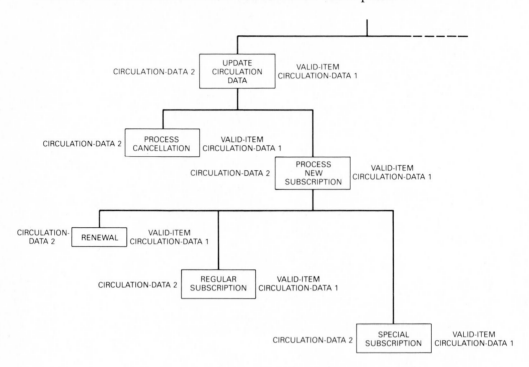

This process of decomposition continues in the HOS technique until blocks are reached for which executable code can be generated.

Decomposition of high-level functions into more detailed functions is a process used by many systems analysts; however, most allow a function to be decomposed in any way that seems convenient. HOS is different. With HOS, only specific types of decomposition are permitted. Each branch of diagrams drawn on the screen would be labeled to show the type of decomposition. This can be seen in Fig. 13.3. Each decomposition is labeled (CC for CONCUR, CJ for COJOIN, CI for COINCLUDE, J for JOIN, and so on).

The data types in HOS are defined with mathematical axioms that specify their behavior precisely. Each type of decomposition is also defined with mathematical axioms that describe precisely the pattern of blocks in the decomposition and how the data types may be passed among the blocks. If the decomposition and the use of data obey the mathematical rules, the internal processes of the design are provably correct. The HOS technique thus allows the generation of highly complex specifications that are internally consistent and bug-free. These graphic specifications are used to generate code.

Code may be generated in three ways from the blocks at the lowest levels of the HOS chart. First, the block may be a *primitive* operation for which provably correct code can be generated by the HOS software. Second, the block may refer to a *subroutine or function* in the library of the system, which itself has been designed with the HOS technique. Third, the block may refer to *external code,* for example, a call to a data-base management system or operating system, or application code created elsewhere.

An indication appears under each leaf node (a node that is not further decomposed), saying which type that node is. In Fig. 13.3, several of the nodes have the letter P under them, indicating that they are *primitive* operations for which provably correct code can be generated. Some of the nodes have OP under them, for example:

This indicates that a process called GET_INTERMEDIATE_RESULTS has already been created with the HOS technique. Its definition is in the HOS library. It uses the inputs and outputs shown. It can be linked into the control map of Fig. 13.3 in such a way that the overall combination is internally consistent and bug-free.

The system analyst using the HOS tool can be entirely unaware of its mathematical foundations or the details of the mathematically based checking that is being performed by the computer as he creates his design. When one person, or a large team, creates a design with many hundreds of nodes, an enormous amount of cross-checking is necessary to ensure that the design is consistent, unambiguous, and complete. Making such a design correct would be beyond the ability of most humans without a lengthy period of trial-and-error testing. A computer can perform the cross-checking meticulously and quickly. The HOS methodology is designed to harness the power of the computer to create error-free systems.

SIMPLIFYING THE DESIGN OF COMPLEX SYSTEMS

While many high-productivity languages are aimed at relatively simple systems (simple methods for simple systems), HOS is intended for creating highly complex systems with complex logic where a large amount of cross-checking is needed to make the system correct.

We are interested in the question "How can we make the technique of building complex systems as easy to use as possible?" Designing with graphics

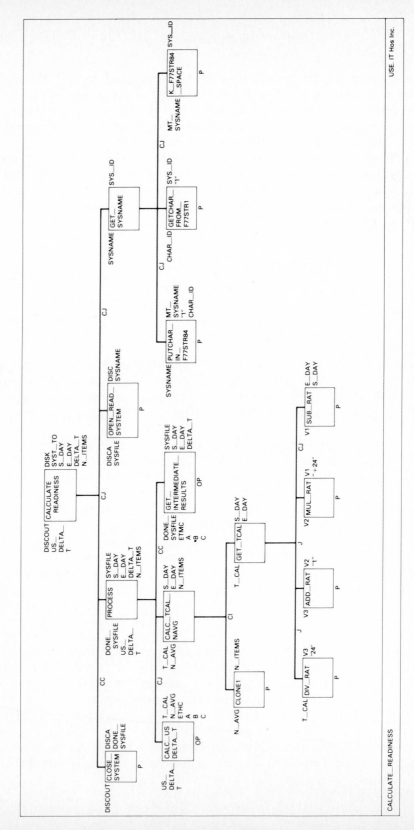

Figure 13.3 Typical example of a chart with *n*-ary branches printed by the HOS software.

helps very much. Using a technique that enables a computer to check the design meticulously as we create it is a great step forward.

In HOS, it can be somewhat tedious to work out exactly which control structures are needed as a complex operation is decomposed. The software helps with this. The designer names the functions and sketches their decomposition into lower-level functions; he keys the data types used against the blocks, and then the software works out in detail the COJOINs, COINCLUDEs, and so on. The designer checks and may modify the result.

The more help the software can give the designer in filling out tedious details and making tedious choices, the better. This creative partnership of person and machine can speed up the creation of rigorous and complex designs.

It is important to incorporate powerful mechanisms such as screen pointers, report generators, dialogue generators, data models, relational operators such as SEARCH and JOIN, decision trees and tables, and means of expressing rules. Arithmetic or algebraic expressions should be expressed in a normal, familiar format.

The user can be given guidance in which, when necessary, the software leads him step by step through what has to be done. The software may put pop-on instruction panels on the screen when necessary, perhaps requesting the user to make selections from the panel or fill in its blanks.

The screen usage should enable the user to avoid unnecessary keying. For example, in the illustration of the subscription system, CIRCULATION_DATA 1 appears many times. There should be a simple means of duplicating it and moving it to the places where it is needed.

Communicating in natural English, as described in Chapters 10 and 11, is appealing. The use of a lexicon may simplify the entry of data types. English sentences may cause segments of the design to appear; for example, segments of HOS control maps.

DO YOU WANT ME TO TRY TO CORRECT THE ERROR?

We would like a computer to try to detect any errors we make while we are designing the system at a screen. Error-detection is a part of many 4GLs. The more the methodology is designed to facilitate error correction, the better. However, we would like more than this. Whenever possible, we would like the computer *to attempt to correct the error*.

For example, if the data types do not cross-check in an HOS decomposition, a computer should be able to adjust them so that they do cross-check. We should be able to say, "Make them cross-check." We then need to observe what the computer does in case the result is not really what we want. The computer should highlight or color the changes it makes and ask us to approve them.

In general, when the computer gives us an error message, it should say, "DO YOU WANT ME TO TRY TO CORRECT THE ERROR?" whenever there is a way of correcting it that is likely to work.

When attempting to correct an error, the computer should look for the minimum change that would solve the problem. Usually a single error can be corrected by changing a single word or command. When correcting an HOS decomposition, for example, there are several possibilities:

1. A data type is spelled incorrectly. The software can check for this by examining a list or library of data types entered so far.

2. An incorrect control structure (type of decomposition) is used. The software could see whether another valid control structure would fit the data types specified.

3. The data types do not obey the axioms of the control structure. The software could adjust them so that they do obey.

Where alternate possibilities exist, the software should give the designer a menu so that he can tell the software which one to use.

Far too much software today bluntly says INVALID COMMAND or some other terse error message when it could say INVALID COMMAND. SHALL I TRY THE FOLLOWING COMMAND: . . .?

The methodologies associated with 4GLs should be designed to give the software the maximum capability in helping to correct errors the user makes.

BATTLE WITH COMPLEXITY

Much of the future of computing is a battle with complexity. To push the frontiers forward, we have to learn how to build more complex systems. We cannot do this without harnessing the power of the computer itself.

The battle with complexity became more urgent in the world of hardware than in the world of software. Designers of the most complex chips and wafers could not succeed without highly sophisticated computer graphics tools. The 3-inch-square ceramic modules that hold a hundred or more chips in IBM mainframes contain over a mile of wiring.

Whereas designers of hardware logic have taken their computer-aided tools very seriously, most analysts and programmers have not. Analysts and programmers often regard themselves as artists needing pencil-and-paper tools. We tolerate errors in their work to a much greater extent than we would in the work of hardware designers.

The use of graphics for computer-aided design is a powerful tool with which to improve the ability of analysts to build better systems. It is desirable that computerized graphics become a major component of future 4GLs.

REFERENCES

1. J. Martin and C. McClure, *Diagramming Techniques for Analysts and Programmers,* Englewood Cliffs, NJ: Prentice-Hall, Inc., 1985.

2. J. Martin, *Recommended Diagramming Standards for Computing,* Carnforth, Lancs., England: Savant Research Institute, 1984.

3. J. Martin, *Managing the Data Base Environment,* Englewood Cliffs, NJ: Prentice-Hall, Inc., 1983.

4. USE.IT manuals are available from Higher Order Software, Inc., Cambridge, MA.

14 LEADING THE DESIGNER THROUGH A SEQUENCE OF STEPS

ADVANTAGES OF A PLANNED SEQUENCE

Some tools for application generation lead the designer through a sequence of steps. This can be very helpful for systems analysts or end users when they first start to use a tool. As they become more experienced, they may use their own initiative in varying the sequence.

Proceeding through the design process in a planned sequence has several advantages:

- The menus or instruction panels can be concise and relatively simple.
- The designer, knowing what to expect, moves through them very quickly.
- The instruction panels can ensure that the designer has considered aspects of the design that might otherwise be forgotten. This can be an important advantage. Too often the effects of failures, invalid keys, security requirements, and the like, are not thought about.
- A well-thought-out methodology can be developed. Many systems analysts make a mess, and leading them through a well-structured methodology can help to produce clean design.
- The resulting system can be made easy to modify.

THE MENUS OF APPLICATION FACTORY

APPLICATION FACTORY, from Cortex [1], directs the work of the application designer with three levels, followed by an instruction panel of menus. The first menu the designer sees is as follows:

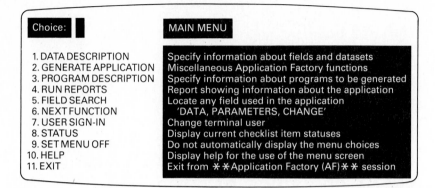

For most of the items on this menu, when the designer selects the item, he will see a second-level menu. For example, if he selects item 1, DATA DESCRIPTION, he will see:

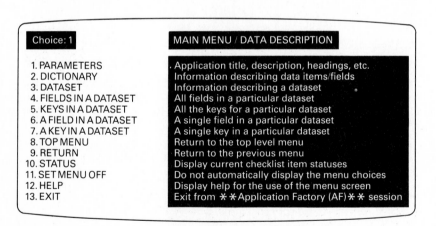

If the designer selects item 1 from this menu also, he will see:

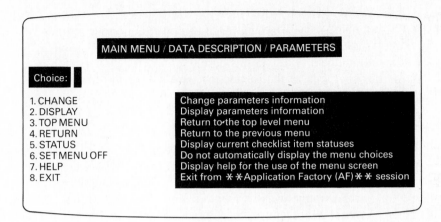

If, once again, he selects item 1, he receives an instruction panel that enables him to change application parameters:

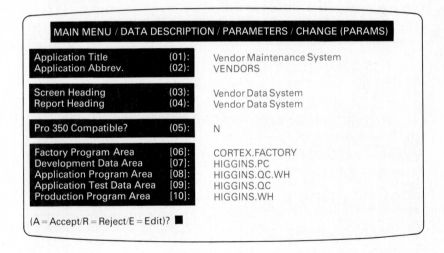

He fills in information about the application as shown in red here. Some of the information (in black) has already been filled in.

The designer builds his application by using several instruction panels like this, linked, where needed, to a procedural language. The title at the top of each instruction panel shows menu items via which it is reached. In the example just shown, the title is MAIN MENU/DATA DESCRIPTION/PARAMETERS/ CHANGE (PARAMS). The user can reach each instruction panel directly if he wants, without going through the menus, by keying its code (which is the sequence of menu numbers, 1.1.1 in this case).

As the designer fills in the instruction panels, this information resides in APPLICATION FACTORY's data dictionary.

Next Function

The designer may return at any time to the MAIN MENU. One of the items on the MAIN MENU is NEXT FUNCTION. NEXT FUNCTION suggests what the designer should do next and is thus intended to lead him through the set of steps he should follow. The value of NEXT FUNCTION is shown (in reverse video) by the NEXT FUNCTION menu line. In the MAIN MENU, it is 'DATA, PARAMETERS, CHANGE.' If the user selects NEXT FUNCTION, he will receive the instruction panel it refers to without going through the second and third levels of the menu. A beginner with APPLICATION FACTORY would normally select NEXT FUNCTION to proceed through its instruction panels in the sequence it recommends. This sequence normally involves:

1. Describing parameters of the application, as above.
2. Defining fields to be used if they are not already in the dictionary. The following is a panel for describing fields:

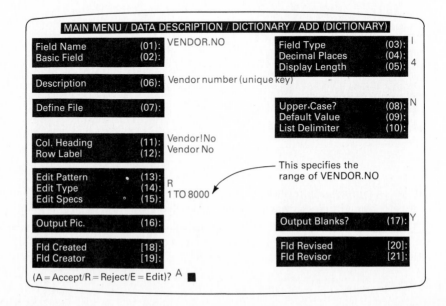

3. Describing a data set:

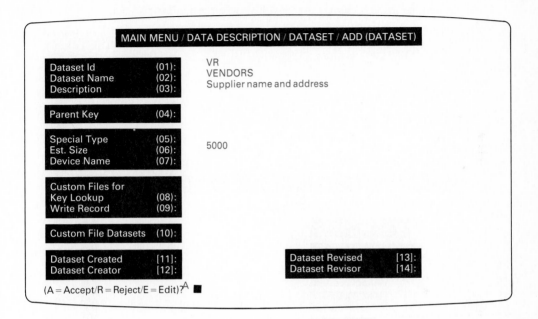

MAIN MENU / DATA DESCRIPTION / DATASET / ADD (DATASET)

Dataset Id	(01):	VR
Dataset Name	(02):	VENDORS
Description	(03):	Supplier name and address

Parent Key	(04):

Special Type	(05):	
Est. Size	(06):	5000
Device Name	(07):	

Custom Files for	
Key Lookup	(08):
Write Record	(09):

Custom File Datasets   (10):

Dataset Created	[11]:	Dataset Revised	[13]:
Dataset Creator	[12]:	Dataset Revisor	[14]:

(A = Accept/R = Reject/E = Edit)?A ■

4. Showing what fields are in a data set:

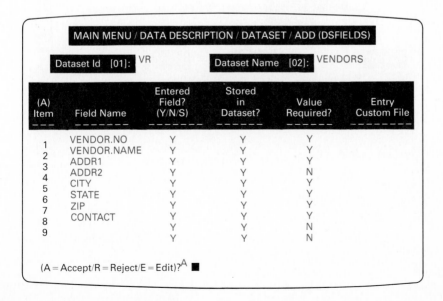

MAIN MENU / DATA DESCRIPTION / DATASET / ADD (DSFIELDS)

Dataset Id [01]: VR   Dataset Name [02]: VENDORS

(A) Item	Field Name	Entered Field? (Y/N/S)	Stored in Dataset?	Value Required?	Entry Custom File
1	VENDOR.NO	Y	Y	Y	
2	VENDOR.NAME	Y	Y	Y	
3	ADDR1	Y	Y	Y	
4	ADDR2	Y	Y	N	
5	CITY	Y	Y	Y	
6	STATE	Y	Y	Y	
7	ZIP	Y	Y	Y	
8	CONTACT	Y	Y	N	
9		Y	Y	N	

(A = Accept/R = Reject/E = Edit)?A ■

5. Indicating which fields are keys of the data set.

6. Describing a program (that is, giving its name and parameters).

7. Describing the menu screens a user employs when using that program.

8. Describing other screens. Here, for example, is an instruction panel in use for creating a user data-entry screen:

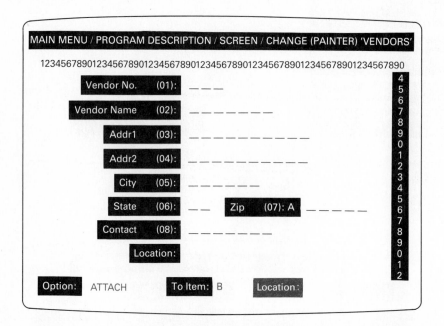

9. Describing the job stream.

10. Describing report formats.

11. Describing reports. The following is one of several instruction panels in use for describing a report:

MAIN MENU / PROGRAM DESCRIPTION / REPORT PARAMETERS / CHANGE (SORTFLDS)

Report Name [01]: PVSUMRPT   Format Name [02]: PVSUMMARY

(A) Item	Sort Field Name	Sort Field Alias	Sort Field Id	Sort Order (A/D)	Sum-mary Brk?	Count Detail Items?	Additional Summary Title Field
1	VENDOR.NAME	VENDOR.NAME	VR	A	N	N	
2	VENDOR.NO	VENDOR.NO	PH	A	Y	Y	
3	PO.NUMBER	PO.NUMBER	PH	A	Y	Y	
4	EXTENDED.PRICE	EXTENDED.PRICE	PL	D	N	N	
				A			
				A			
				A			
				A			
				A			
				A			

(A = Accept/R = Reject/E = Edit)? A ■

12. Describing procedures by means of the procedural language that is part of APPLI-CATION FACTORY.

INSTRUCTION PANELS WITH GRAPHICS TOOLS

With graphics tools, which, as discussed in Chapter 13, can be of great help in designing *complex* systems, instruction panels aid in building the design. A tool may lead the designer through the design with a sequence of instruction panels but allow him to deviate from the sequence to make changes.

Let us illustrate this with the design of a data-base application for an order acceptance system.

A data model exists, showing the data administrator's normalized structures for many types of records. From this overall model, the application designer extracts a subset of record types he will use.

He indicates that he is designing a procedure called ORDER ACCEPTANCE, using this subset of data. The software gives the designer the following instruction panel:

PROCEDURE: ORDER-ACCEPTANCE

Indicate the actions that may be taken on entities of each type during an execution of ORDER-ACCEPTANCE:

	CREATE	READ	UPDATE	DELETE	OTHER	NONE
ACCOUNTS RECEIVABLE	☐	☐	☐	☐	☐	■
BACKORDER	☐	☐	☐	☐	☐	■
CUSTOMER	☐	☐	☐	☐	☐	■
CUSTOMER-ORDER	☐	☐	☐	☐	☐	■
INVOICE	☐	☐	☐	☐	☐	■
INVOICE-LINE-ITEM	☐	☐	☐	☐	☐	■
ORDER-LINE	☐	☐	☐	☐	☐	■
ORDER-RATE	☐	☐	☐	☐	☐	■
PRODUCT	☐	☐	☐	☐	☐	■
PURCHASE-LINE-ITEM	☐	☐	☐	☐	☐	■
QUOTATION	☐	☐	☐	☐	☐	■

CANCEL [ ]   PROCEED [ ]

The designer points, using a mouse, perhaps, to the entity types he intends to create, read, update, or delete:

PROCEDURE: ORDER-ACCEPTANCE

Indicate the actions that may be taken on entities of each type during an execution of ORDER-ACCEPTANCE:

	CREATE	READ	UPDATE	DELETE	OTHER	NONE
ACCOUNTS RECEIVABLE	☐	☐	☐	☐	☐	■
BACKORDER	■	☐	☐	☐	☐	☐
CUSTOMER	☐	■	☐	☐	☐	☐
CUSTOMER-ORDER	■	☐	■	☐	☐	☐
INVOICE	☐	☐	☐	☐	☐	■
INVOICE-LINE-ITEM	☐	☐	☐	☐	☐	■
ORDER-LINE	☐	☐	☐	☐	☐	■
ORDER-RATE	☐	☐	■	☐	☐	☐
PRODUCT	☐	■	☐	☐	☐	☐
PURCHASE-LINE-ITEM	☐	☐	☐	☐	☐	■
QUOTATION	☐	☐	☐	☐	☐	■

CANCEL [ ]   PROCEED ■

He tells the software to proceed, and it displays a submodel of the data-entity types in question with a word written above each showing the data-base action or actions that will occur, as shown in Fig. 14.1. On Fig. 14.1 is an instruction panel asking the analyst to point to each entity type in the sequence in which the entities will be involved in the procedure.

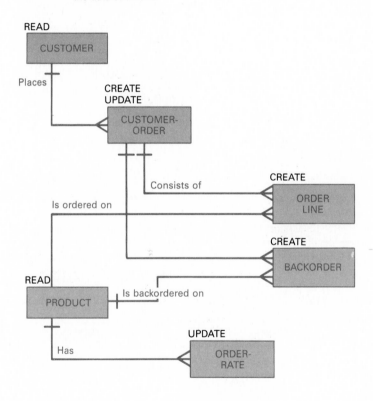

Figure 14.1

The software numbers the data-base actions on the diagram and then proceeds to ask questions about them, starting with the first:

PROCEDURE: ORDER-ACCEPTANCE
ACCESS NO. 1: Read: CUSTOMER

CUSTOMER is read: Once: ☐   Many times: ☐

                               Always: ☐   Sometimes: ☐

Access is by   key CUSTOMER: ☐   Other: ☐

CANCEL ☐   PROCEED ☐

The designer responds by pointing to the boxes:

PROCEDURE: ORDER-ACCEPTANCE
ACCESS NO. 1: Read: CUSTOMER

CUSTOMER is read: Once: ☐   Many times: ■

                               Always: ■   Sometimes: ☐

Access is by   key CUSTOMER: ■   Other: ☐

CANCEL ☐   PROCEED ■

The software now draws the first access of a data navigation diagram on top of the data-model diagram. This is shown in Fig. 14.2. (Discussion of data navigation diagrams can be found elsewhere [2].)

As the analyst goes through the steps of application design, there are certain questions he should ask at each stage. This can be made into a formal procedure. If he is using a computerized tool for carrying out the design steps, the machine should make him address the relevant design questions at each stage. This leads to better-quality design with well-thought-out controls and should go as far as possible toward automatically generating the next stage of the design until executable code is reached.

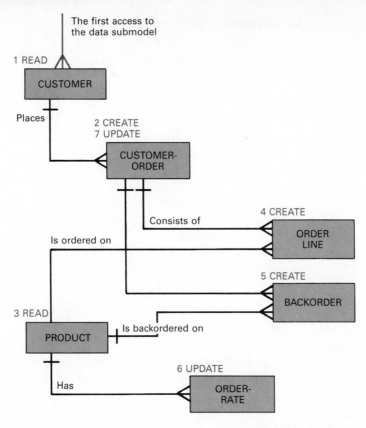

Figure 14.2   The first access to the data submodel (shown in black).

Concerning access 1, the software now asks for the following information:

PROCEDURE: ORDER-ACCEPTANCE

ACCESS NO. 1: READ-CUSTOMER

What happens if no CUSTOMER record is found?

● An exception process is triggered: ☐

The exception process is called: ☐_____

The exception process is:

An interrupt to ACCEPT-ORDER: ☐

Does not return to ACCEPT-ORDER: ☐

● ACCEPT-ORDER is terminated:

The message provided to the user is as follows:

☐_____

CANCEL ☐_____   PROCEED ☐_____

When it has enough information for code generation, the software now proceeds to ask about the second access. The analyst indicates that this is conditional. It occurs "sometimes." So the software asks what condition or conditions control this access:

PROCEDURE: ORDER-ACCEPTANCE

ACCESS NO. 2: Create: CUSTOMER-ORDER

What condition(s) allow me to proceed from reading a CUSTOMER record to creating a CUSTOMER-ORDER record?

CANCEL [   ]   PROCEED [   ]

The designer writes two conditions in the condition box: "IF CUSTOMER # IS VALID" and "IF CREDIT_RATING > 3". The software then continues its drawing of the data navigation diagram, showing the condition on the second access, as shown in Fig. 14.3.

The software continues to ask questions, stepping through each of the accesses. It builds the data navigation diagram on the screen. It collects enough information to be able to convert the data navigation diagram into an action diagram. Figure 14.4 shows all six accesses.

Where it encounters an UPDATE of an entity type, it asks the designer which data items will be changed:

PROCEDURE: ORDER-ACCEPTANCE

ACCESS NO. 6: Update: ORDER-RATE

Which data-items will be changed in ORDER-RATE?

PRODUCT# ☐

WEEK# ☐

FORECAST-USAGE ☐

ACTUAL-USAGE ■

Are any other data-items needed in ORDER-RATE?   Yes: ☐   No: ■

CANCEL [   ]   PROCEED ■■■■

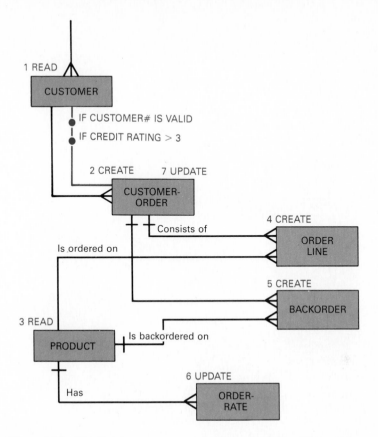

Figure 14.3 The first two accesses on the data navigation diagram (shown in black).

It requests a formula or procedure for updating the data item that is to be changed:

PROCEDURE: ORDER-ACCEPTANCE
ACCESS NO. 6: Update: ORDER-RATE
Enter the formula or procedure for computing ACTUAL-USAGE:
CANCEL ☐   PROCEED ☐

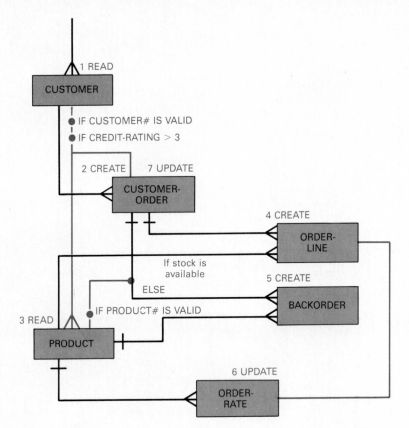

Figure 14.4 The complete navigation diagram for the ORDER ACCEP-TANCE procedure.

Data navigation diagrams can be converted *automatically* to action diagrams. Figure 14.5 shows the action diagram that results from the data navigation discussed above and shown in Fig. 14.4.

The analyst now checks the diagrams of Figs. 14.4 and 14.5 to ensure that they represent the procedure he wants. He then can add, or ask the computer to add, the 4GL control words to the action diagram. The computer may have already produced an action diagram with the words of a particular language.

The analyst may adjust either the navigation diagram or the resulting action diagram. To the action diagram he will add details of the calculations to be performed, the exception actions taken, and so on.

Figure 14.6 shows executable code for the ORDER ACCEPTANCE procedure written in the 4GL IDEAL.

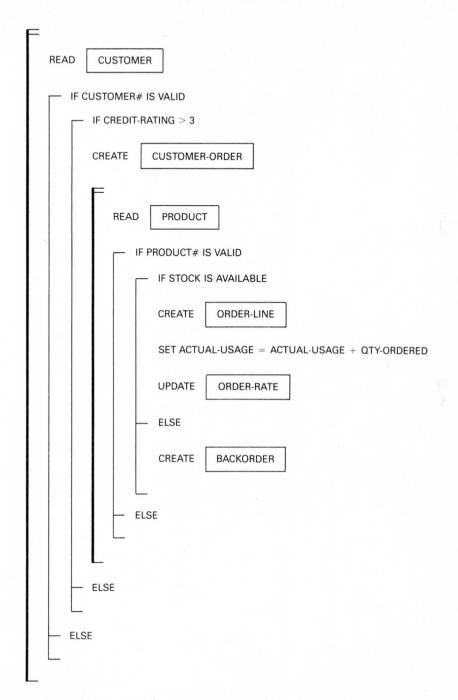

Figure 14.5 Action diagram derived automatically from the data navigation diagram of Fig. 14.4.

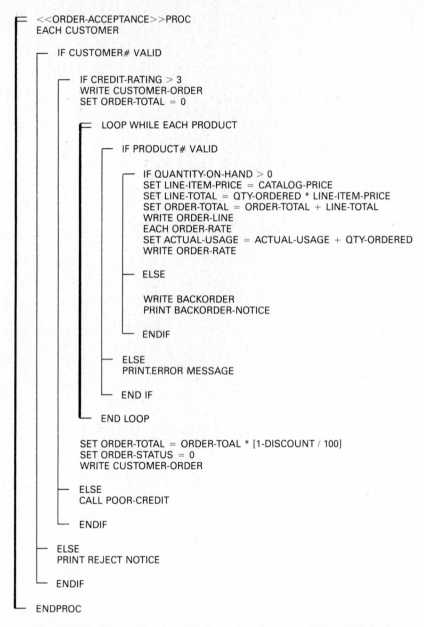

```
<<ORDER-ACCEPTANCE>>PROC
EACH CUSTOMER

    IF CUSTOMER# VALID

        IF CREDIT-RATING > 3
        WRITE CUSTOMER-ORDER
        SET ORDER-TOTAL = 0

            LOOP WHILE EACH PRODUCT

                IF PRODUCT# VALID

                    IF QUANTITY-ON-HAND > 0
                    SET LINE-ITEM-PRICE = CATALOG-PRICE
                    SET LINE-TOTAL = QTY-ORDERED * LINE-ITEM-PRICE
                    SET ORDER-TOTAL = ORDER-TOTAL + LINE-TOTAL
                    WRITE ORDER-LINE
                    EACH ORDER-RATE
                    SET ACTUAL-USAGE = ACTUAL-USAGE + QTY-ORDERED
                    WRITE ORDER-RATE

                    ELSE

                    WRITE BACKORDER
                    PRINT BACKORDER-NOTICE

                    ENDIF

                ELSE
                PRINT.ERROR MESSAGE

                END IF

            END LOOP

        SET ORDER-TOTAL = ORDER-TOAL * [1-DISCOUNT / 100]
        SET ORDER-STATUS = 0
        WRITE CUSTOMER-ORDER

        ELSE
        CALL POOR-CREDIT

        ENDIF

    ELSE
    PRINT REJECT NOTICE

    ENDIF

ENDPROC
```

Figure 14.6 Executable code for the action diagram of Fig. 14.5 in the fourth-generation language IDEAL.

DOCUMENTATION Fourth-generation tools should minimize the work needed to create documentation. When a systems analyst builds his design with instruction panels as illustrated, the information collected by the system *is* the documentation required for maintenance. It should be kept by the computer in such a way that changes can be made quickly and easily.

REFERENCES

1. APPLICATION FACTORY manuals are available for Cortex Corporation, 55 William Street, Wellesley, MA 02181.

2. J. Martin and C. McClure, *Diagramming Techniques for Analysts and Programmers,* Englewood Cliffs, NJ: Prentice-Hall, Inc., 1985.

15 DECISION-SUPPORT LANGUAGES

DSS LANGUAGES   Decision-support languages are an important category of 4GL. They help their users analyze data, answer what-if questions, create financial or other models, and generally extract the truth from complex data. They are sometimes called DSS (decision-support system) languages.

Decision-support languages range from simple two-dimensional spreadsheet tools, such as LOTUS 1-2-3 and SUPERCALC, to tools that can be used to manipulate data of several dimensions, to tools that incorporate elaborate analysis techniques.

Good-decision-support languages are much more comprehensive than query-and-report languages like SQL, QBE, ADRS, and DATATRIEVE. They provide more capability to analyze data than application-building languages such as FOCUS and RAMIS. They are not designed for routine repetitive computing and so do not compete with packages such as ADF, DMS, and ADS/ON-LINE.

The simplest decision-support tools—the two-dimensional spreadsheet packages—are now familiar to many people who have used them on personal computers. At the opposite end of the range are highly sophisticated and expensive tools such as EXPRESS [1], which incorporate many of the techniques of operations research. In the middle of this range is SYSTEM W [2], a powerful tool for analyzing data of multiple dimensions. It is sufficiently easy to use and understand that accountants, financial controllers, marketing planners, and other decision makers use it.

In the past, financial modeling systems or languages have often been complex and difficult to use, requiring a skilled mathematician, an accountant with programming experience, and a very large computer system. Products such as SYSTEM W and EXPRESS now bring sophisticated financial modeling techniques into the range of a much broader spectrum of end users.

MULTIDIMENSIONAL DATA

DSS languages such as EXPRESS and SYSTEM W represent data in a multidimensional fashion. They provide, in effect, a multidimensional matrix of data that we are able to examine two dimensions at a time.

For example, suppose that certain variables are mapped against time. The sales revenue of each project an organization sells, for example, might be mapped against months. To help with market planning, we might like to project past sales into the future in different ways, with different what-if propositions. This gives a three-dimensional array of data, as illustrated in Fig. 15.1.

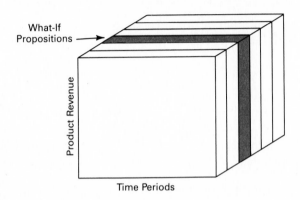

Figure 15.1   Three-dimensional array.

Most DSS languages allow us to explore one two-dimensional slice through the data at a time, as indicated by the shaded slice in Fig. 15.1. We might perform calculations, obtain statistics, or plot charts from this slice. We might do anything that we can do with two-dimensional spreadsheet software, such as LOTUS 1-2-3.

On the other hand, we might want to examine a slice relating to one time period, going through several what-if propositions, as shown in Fig. 15.2.

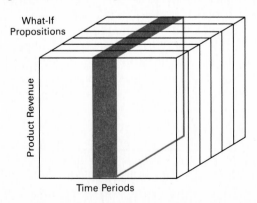

Figure 15.2   Examining one time period.

Product revenue is only one variable that is of interest about products. We might also want to see units sold, price, average order size, average cost of sales, average profit, type of product, age, and so on. We might want these variables mapped against time periods, as shown in Fig. 15.3.

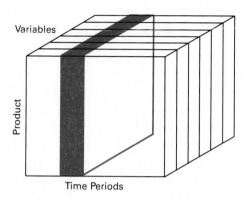

Variables

Product

Time Periods

Figure 15.3   Mapping variables against time periods.

We may not be content with average order size, average cost of sale, and average profit on sale. We might want these broken down by type of product and by customer. We might then like to see a histogram of these variables. Now we need more than three dimensions in our representation of data.

It is difficult to draw diagrams with more than three dimensions (even if the reader wears special glasses!). To view multidimensional data easily, we need a computer. Imagine the shaded slice in Fig. 15.3 moving from one time period to another at the press of a key: click, click, click. A computer enables us to deal with data in multiple dimensions easily.

SYSTEM W supports the analysis of data of up to nine dimensions. Each two-dimensional slice through these data is called a *viewpoint*. The data of a viewpoint can be analyzed or plotted as with a good spreadsheet tool.

For each slice through multidimensional data, different types of reports may be useful. A decision-support system needs a flexible report generator and business graphics generator with which to display the information. A variety of calculations may be done using the data.

EXPRESS allows its users to state what slice through the data they want to see by using LIMIT statements. This is illustrated in Fig. 15.4.

In the top illustration of Fig. 15.4, the user says LIMIT PRODUCT TO PENICILLIN. This gives a two-dimensional slice through the data. The user then says DISPLAY SALES, and a sales report is displayed.

The product manager can look at the sales totals for that product.
—> LIMIT PRODUCT TO PENICILLIN
—> DISPLAY SALES

PRODUCT PENICILLIN SALES
DOLLAR SALES

MONTH	WEST	EAST	SOUTH	CENTRAL	TOTAL
JAN81	980,957	1,004,613	515,221	467,683	2,968,474
FEB81	539,558	579,040	419,527	446,851	1,984,976
MAR81	527,900	639,302	339,811	401,464	1,908,477
APR81	478,699	498,513	351,408	369,857	1,698,477
MAY81	510,750	573,416	334,904	273,907	1,692,977
JUN81	517,737	501,260	283,531	243,446	1,545,974
JUL81	484,558	529,114	249,100	227,206	1,489,978
AUG81	435,095	585,827	189,950	226,606	1,437,478
SEP81	647,541	590,895	267,950	288,589	1,794,975
OCT81	652,618	692,888	319,242	279,805	1,944,545
NOV81	540,578	595,727	357,235	333,405	1,826,945
DEC81	997,931	968,584	429,208	475,781	2,871,504
	7,313,914	7,759,179	4,057,087	4,034,600	23,164,780

The New York district manager can look at sales data for the whole year for each customer in the district.
—> LIMIT YEAR TO 1981
—> LIMIT CUSTOMER TO DISTRICT NEWYORK
—> DISPLAY SALES

NEW YORK DISTRICT SALES
DOLLAR SALES

CUSTOMER	VITA-PLUS	COUGH-OFF	KEN-TRANQ	PENICILLIN	TOTAL
DAVID	21,950	54,297	608,485	922,520	1,607,252
ACE	18,988	100,825	131,642	331,601	583,056
WILSON	64,423	230,586	832,903	1,079,243	2,207,155
LELISTER	119,967	5,197	112,740	86,493	324,397
MAJOR	23,001	20,949	5,281	1,684	50,915
CLASS	113,595	319,333	245,663	579,442	1,258,033
GLUSCO	5,195	22,972	84,422	59,334	171,923
	367,119	754,159	2,021,136	3,060,317	6,202,731

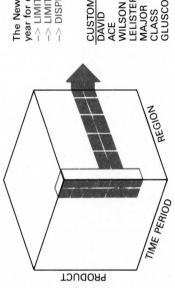

The over-the-counter division manager can product a monthly report showing the national performance data for each product in that division, plus performance a year ago and the variance.

```
-> LIMIT MONTH TO CURRENT.MONTH
-> LIMIT PRODUCT TO DIVISION OTC
-> DISPLAY SALES LAG(SALES,12,MONTH) VARIANCE
```

OTC DIVISION

PRODUCT	SALES CURRENT MONTH	SALES YEAR AGO	SALES VARIANCE
VITAPLUS	101,330	77,972	23,358
COUGHOFF	1,413,494	1,305,945	107,549
	1,514,824	1,383,917	130,907

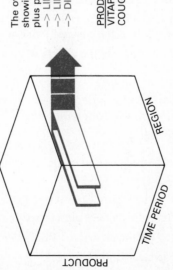

Figure 15.4 LIMIT statements in EXPRESS are used to display slices through multidimensional data. (Courtesy of Management Decision Systems, Inc. [1].)

In the second illustration, the user employs two limit statements:

LIMIT YEAR TO 1981
LIMIT CUSTOMER TO DISTRICT NEWYORK

In the third illustration, the user displays two slices so that he can compare this month's sales with those of a year ago.

The data can be aggregated in various ways. In the third illustration of Fig. 15.4, the user says LIMIT PRODUCT TO DIVISION OTC. The products of this division are then displayed.

A diversity of computations need to be done to aid in decision making. Sometimes fairly elaborate nested conditions are needed to express the rules that govern the calculations.

Many of the calculations that help in decision making need standard types of analysis that can be preprogrammed, such as regression analysis, different types of forecasting, sensitivity analysis, and a variety of statistical functions. The user needs help in employing standard types of computation.

A decision-support language, then, needs the following:

- A data base that facilitates access to multidimensional data
- A flexible report generator with which the user can create reports showing different slices through the data
- A graphics generator that can create charts showing different views of the data
- A language for performing calculations on the data, sometimes with complex nested conditions
- A set of statistical and operations research tools
- A set of tools for various types of financial analysis and forecasting
- The ability to change data or change assumptions and rerun calculations or analyses to explore the effect of the changes (what-if exploration)
- The ability to build models to store the effects of alternate strategies

STAGES IN DSS USE

The user of a decision-support system typically goes through the following stages in building and using a model:

1. The problem is analyzed to determine what types of results would be useful. The requisite variables and calculations are determined.
2. The data arrays, as in Figs. 15.1 through 15.4, are designed and built.
3. Calculations and rules for computing values are entered into the system.
4. The model is filled with data, often data derived from other files or data bases.
5. Reports and graphics are generated from the model.

6. It is determined what analytical or operations research tools can be applied usefully to the data.

7. The results are reviewed with interested executives and staff, and the model is refined to meet their needs.

Often much refining takes place. Major DSS models tend to grow and change with time as people learn how to make more valuable use of the tools.

BUILDING A MODEL IN SYSTEM W

A SYSTEM W model can consist of *periods* and *variables*. To build a model, the user first specifies the periods. They can be expressed in any desired time units: days, weeks, months, years, or any other unit of time. In SYSTEM W, there are two types of periods, *history* and *forecast,* each of which can have up to 250 entries.

A *history period* contains actual data values in elapsed time periods. To build this part of the model, the user issues the SPECIFY HISTORY command:

W >
specify history 12

This statement defines 12 history periods that can be used in the model.

A *forecast period* contains data values for the future. The SPECIFY FORECAST command is used to create forecast periods. For example:

W >
specify forecast 10

This statement defines ten forecast periods that can be used in the model.

Period names are automatically assigned by SYSTEM W as the model is built. History periods begin with H1, H2, H3, up to a maximum of H250. Forecast periods begin with P1, P2, P3, up to a maximum of P250.

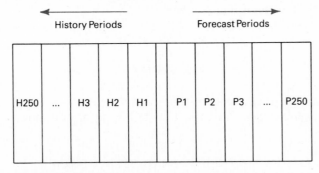

Figure 15.5 Illustration of the history and forecast periods of SYSTEM W.

Figure 15.5 illustrates the conventions that are used by SYSTEM W in creating history and forecast period names. Figure 15.6 shows period descriptions that are associated with the periods.

H1	P1	P2	P3
Last Year	This Year	1985	1986

Figure 15.6   Period descriptions.

To enter the data shown in Fig. 15.6, the user would use the following sequence of commands:

```
W>
specify period headings
INPUT:
h1 'LAST' 'YEAR'
p1 'THIS' 'YEAR'
p2 '1985'
p3 '1986'
//*
```

Defining Variables

Variables are used to contain data values that change with the passage of time. The user can assign names to the variables and can optionally associate a description with a variable to clarify or explain further how the variables are used. SYSTEM W allows two types of variable, *input variables* and *calculated variables*.

Input variables contain values that are entered directly into the model. The following are examples of input variables:

- UNITS_SOLD
- PRICE
- QUANTITY

Calculated variables contain values that are calculated using constants and values contained in other variables. The following are examples of calculated variables:

- REVENUE = UNITS_SOLD * PRICE
- ROYALTY = 10% * REVENUE

The user defines input variables as follows:

```
W>
specify variables
INPUT:
u.sold, 'UNITS SOLD'
price
revenue
inventory
prod.amt, 'PRODUCTION AMOUNT'
//*
```

SYSTEM W Rules

Variable rules enable users to define the calculations that are to be performed in computing the values of calculated variables. The following are examples of variable rules:

$$\text{REVENUE} = \text{UNITS} * \text{PRICE}$$
$$\text{PROFIT} = \text{SALES} - \text{EXPENSES}$$

The user defines these variable rules to SYSTEM W with the following sequence of commands:

```
W>
specify rules
INPUT:
revenue = units * price
profit = sales - expenses
```

The user enters each rule separately and ends each rule with an exclamation mark.

Period rules enable users to define calculations for the forecast periods in the model. An example might be to add together sets of periods quarterly or for year end. The following is an example of the user entering period rules:

```
W>
specify period rules
INPUT:
p10 = p2 + p4 + p6 + p8!
p4 = p5 - p7!
p1 = p2 + p3 - p6 + p8!
```

Rules are often conditional. The user can express conditional rules with a WHEN block:

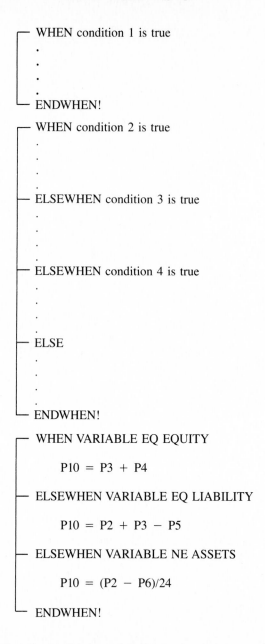

WHEN blocks often need to be nested to express complex sets of rules. Figure 15.7 illustrates the calculation of taxes on income in a financial model. In practice, tax calculations can be much more complex than in Fig. 15.7. Action diagrams as in Fig. 15.7 help to clarify the logic of compound nested rules. Statements such as the WHEN blocks shown enable the model to be built.

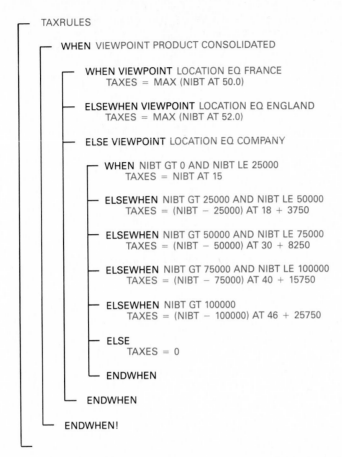

Figure 15.7 A complex rule in SYSTEM W, used to calculate taxes (NIBT is net income before taxes; NIBT AT 15 means 15 percent of NIBT). The exclamation mark indicates the end of the rule.

The model will then be filled with data, either by entering the data directly or, more often, by extracting them from existing files or data bases. The commands and facilities that enable data to be extracted from production data bases are particularly important.

When the model contains data, the user will examine different slices through the data and needs a good-quality report generator and graphics generator.

ANALYTICAL TOOLS   Decision-support systems vary greatly in the analytical tools they provide. Some have little other than the ability to take averages and totals. Others provide a rich and complex set of forecasting, time-series, correlation, and other tools. Many of the tools of operational research are built into decision-support software.

Box 15.1 shows the tools provided by EXPRESS software. This is much more comprehensive than many such products.

PAST AND
FUTURE

Many decision-support models relate to time periods, as in Figs. 15.1 through 15.4. It is often desirable to use forecasting techniques to extend sales, profits, or other variables into the future. Figure 15.8 illustrates this. The future forecasts may be used to generate tentative financials, examine cash flows, plan equipment purchases, plan recruiting, and so on.

BOX 15.1   Tools provided in the EXPRESS decision-support system for analyzing data [1].

Exploratory Data Analysis

- Mean
- Median
- Standard deviation
- Variance
- Other standard statistical functions
- Scatter plots
- Stem-and-leaf plots
- Box plots
- Normal probability plots

Time-Series Analysis and Forecasting

- Moving averages
- Moving totals
- Exponential smoothing
- Linear extrapolation
- Compound growth extrapolation

BOX 15.1 *(Continued)*

- Linear and compound growth triangles
- Trend curve fitting (including linear exponentials, power functions, multiple hyperbolic functions, and S-curves)
- X-11 deseasonalization and forecasting techniques (monthly and quarterly)
- Autocorrelation correction
- Polynomial distributed lags
- Multiple linear regression
- ARIMA (Box-Jenkins analysis)
- ACCUFOR
- Forecast accuracy measurement testing (actual versus forecast)

Causal Models and Survey Analysis (Cross-sectional Analysis)

- Autocorrelation correction
- Polynomial distributed lags
- Multiple linear regression
- Two-stage least squares
- Leapwise regression (which tests and determines best of all possible models)
- Crosstabs
- Correlation matrices
- Cluster analysis
- Factor analysis
- MONANOVA
- Automatic interaction detector (AID)

Advanced Analytical Tools

- Linear programming
- Critical path analysis
- Risk analysis
- Monte Carlo simulation

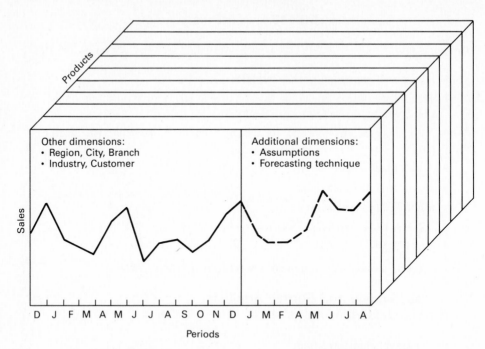

Figure 15.8 Figures from the past can be extended into the future with a variety of forecasting techniques. Future forecasts are then used to examine cash flows and help in making decisions such as capacity planning and labor planning.

There is a diversity of techniques with which to examine past figures, adjust them for seasonal variations and other variations, combine them with growth targets or tentative assumptions about the future, and produce forecasts. Often the intuition of a skilled decision maker responds better to graphic representation of trends and forecasts than to tables of figures.

Some forecasting tools produce figures showing the percentage confidence of the forecast. This information, like the forecast itself, is often best displayed graphically. Figure 15.9 shows a line for actual and forecast sales data. The red line superimposed on this is a smoothed trend line. A band showing 90 percent confidence levels in the forecast surrounds the forecast itself.

The user of this system may have different techniques available to him for creating the forecast, may display different confidence bands, and may keep a file of different forecasts relating to different assumptions.

Financial executives map the forecasts made into tentative cash-flow analyses, profit and loss statements, and other forms of financial analysis. Figure 15.10 shows a cash-flow forecast for a new division.

Figure 15.11 shows the effects on profit and loss of the forecasts made at three different times. This chart shows that the corporation is assuming greater

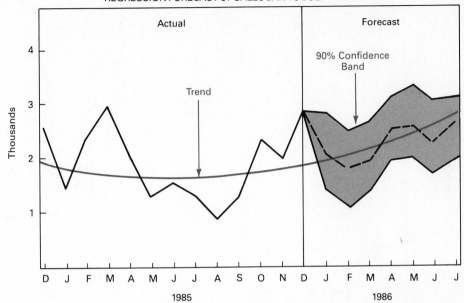

Figure 15.9 Past and future. The forecast line is surrounded by a confidence band, which can be set to different confidence levels. The red curve is a smoothed trend line.

financial risks than originally anticipated, with greater short-term losses and greater eventual profits. The time taken to break in profitability is about the same as originally forecast.

EFFECTIVE USE OF GRAPHICS

Figures 15.9 through 15.13 and Fig. 15.15 show effective uses of graphics. Almost all of the tools in Box 15.1 can be made easier to use and to understand with good graphics.

Appropriate computer graphics can be a major aid to thinking creatively. They help to extract meaning from a complex morass of data and can help to explore the effects of different decisions and actions. A challenge of decision-support systems is to find the types of diagrams that will be most effective in helping to make decisions.

All of the standard reports of accountants can be represented graphically. Figure 15.12 shows a graphics representation of a balance sheet. This helps to see, at a glance, the ratios between different items on the balance sheet. It helps to visualize the effect of proposed changes (the red part of Fig. 15.12). Similarly, one year's balance sheet can be compared with another graphically.

ACTUAL AND FORECAST CASH POSITION, AI DIVISION

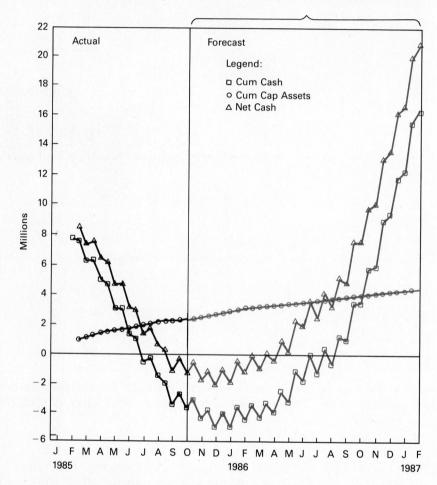

Figure 15.10   Cash-flow forecast for a new division.

It is often useful to put two curves or bar charts onto one diagram. The sales of a product over time can be compared with the sales of a similar product. The sales of a product can be compared with the average sales to see whether it is rising or falling more than the average and to help separate the effects of product excellence from cyclical changes or general market movements.

Often a product that is really unprofitable is manufactured year after year because its detailed performance is hidden in aggregates. Sometimes a product looks good because it has high unit sales but is, in fact, making insufficient profit. A good DSS should isolate the poor performers from the good ones.

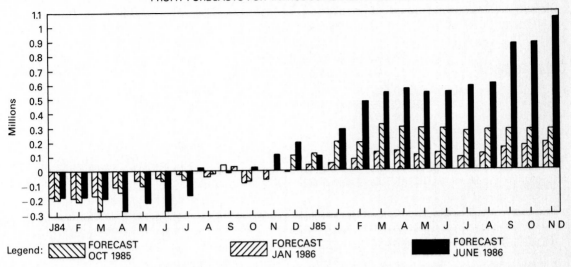

Figure 15.11 Plot showing how forecasts made at different times vary in their profit predictions.

Figure 15.13 shows a scatter diagram relating the sales of a pharmaceutical product to outbreaks of influenza. The marketing analyst may generate a similar diagram for other factors, attempting to find out what affects sales. In particular, he will be interested in the effects of advertising campaigns and mailings. He will want to isolate a variety of factors to attempt to find the most effective ways to spend the promotion budget. Should advertising be intensified quickly during outbreaks of flu, for example?

Figure 15.14 shows a market analyst doing a regression analysis with EX-PRESS to analyze the effects of flu incidence and promotion ratio on the sales of a pharmaceutical.

Figure 15.15 shows graphics used to explore the effects of establishing better air pollution controls on gasoline-powered vehicles. Carbon monoxide emissions, during high traffic densities, can stress persons with cardiovascular conditions because carbon monoxide combines with oxygen-carrying hemoglobin in the blood, forming carboxyhemoglobin. This lessens the oxygen transport to the heart muscles. The black lines in Fig. 15.15 show the number of carbon monoxide–related angina attacks in the city of Denver. The top diagram is a historical diagram for 1975; the bottom diagram is a what-if forecast for 1985 [3]. Many such diagrams were produced to study the effects of alternate pollution control measures.

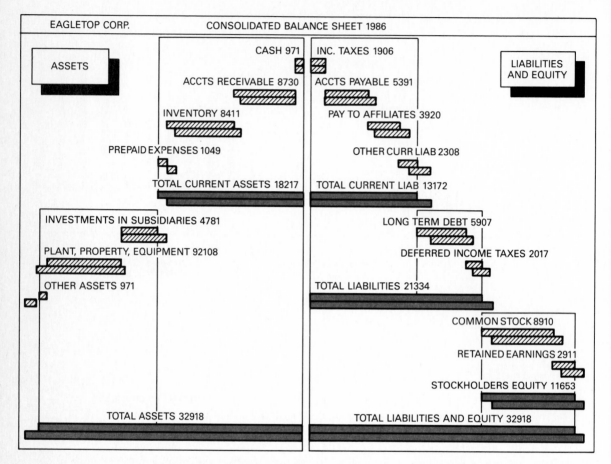

Figure 15.12 Balance sheet shown graphically. The red indicates a possible variation in the balance sheet resulting from a what-if computation.

HELP TO USERS

Given a useful set of decision-support tools, it is important that a DSS language give users as much help as possible in employing them. Most persons who *should* use the tools have no training in operations research or computer science. They are accountants, market analysts, executives, and corporate staff. They need guidance from the software. The better the quality of this guidance, the greater the value likely to be obtained from the product.

The following shows EXPRESS prompting a user in the fitting of a curve to a series of data:

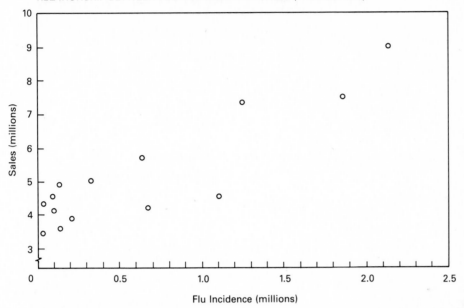

⟶ PLOT SCATTER FLU-INC SALES

RELATIONSHIP BETWEEN FLU-INCIDENCE AND SALES (PRODUCT 248)

Figure 15.13 Scatter plot correlating the incidence of flu with the sales of a given pharmaceutical.

⟶ TRENDFIT
TIME SERIES TO BE ANALYZED: > ACTUALS
DESEASONALIZE BEFORE FITTING TREND? > NO
FOR WHICH MONTH(S). > JAN76 TO DEC80
FOR WHICH DIVISION(S): > CHEMICAL
FOR WHICH LINEITEM(S): > NETSALES
FOR WHICH CURVES?
1-UN,2-EXP,3-PWR,4-HYP1,5-HYP2,6-HYP3 > 1 2 3

(TSRGMIN) BEST-FITTING CURVE: LINEAR

(TSRGRSQ) COEFFICIENT OF DETERMINATION
(TSC1)   COEFFICIENT 1
(TSC2)   COEFFICIENT 2

TSTYPE	TSRGRSQ	TSC1	TSC2
LINEAR	.909165	5,782.18	72.13123
EXPONENTIAL	.898473	5,922.45	.0093221
PWR FUNCTION	.823134	4,568.72	.1729885

```
->REGRESS
```

TITLE FOR REGRESSION: >PROMOTION ANALYSIS
DEPENDENT VARIABLE: >UNIT.SALES
INDEPENDENT VARIABLE(S): >FLO.INCIDENCE, PROMOTION.RATIO
FOR WHICH MONTH(S): >APR79 TO AUG81
                           PROMOTION ANALYSIS
A. REGRESSION EQUATION
UNIT.SALES = 229 + .13*FLU.INCIDENCE + 32.3*PROMOTION.RATIO
B. BASIC INFORMATION ABOUT THE REGRESSION
NUMBER OF OBSERVATIONS: 29
NUMBER OF REGRESSORS (EXPLANATORY FACTORS): 2
DEPENDENT VARIABLE: UNIT.SALES
C. IMPORTANT FACTORS AND GOODNESS OF FIT
THE STATISTICAL SIGNIFICANCE OF THE OVERALL REGRESSION IS 99.9+
REGRESSION EXPLAINS 85.5
EXPLANATORY FACTORS (REGRESSORS) WERE:
    **FLU.INCIDENCE—POSITIVE EFFECT; SIGNIFICANCE LEVEL 99.9+%
    **INTERCEPT—POSITIVE EFFECT; SIGNIFICANCE LEVEL 99.9+%
    **PROMOTION.RATIO—POSITIVE EFFECT; SIGNIFICANCE LEVEL 99.9 %
        **MEANS SIGNIFICANT AT THE 99
        *MEANS SIGNIFICANT AT THE 95
    THE SIGNIFICANCE LEVELS ARE ALL CALCULATED USING A TWO-TAILED TEST.
D. DIAGNOSTIC MEASURES
1 DATA POINTS HAD RESIDUALS WHICH EXCEEDED THE THRESHHOLD OF 2
STANDARD DEVIATIONS. THESE WERE: SCALED REGRESSION RESIDUALS

             MONTH   RG.SCLRES
             DEC80   2.1024429
```

*Figure 15.14*  Regression analysis done using EXPRESS. The user wants to analyze the effects of flu incidence and promotion ratio on the sales of a pharmaceutical.

The software can instantly produce graphics showing the trend fit and its extrapolation into the future. The user may need immediate help in understanding some of the items in the dialogue, and this help should be available on the screen for all tools.

In the example, the user had to enter the word TRENDFIT. It would be better, in a fast-response environment, to give the user a menu of techniques he can use. The menu may appear at the top or bottom of a screen, the items on it being quickly selectable with a mouse, with arrow keys, or by entering letters.
```

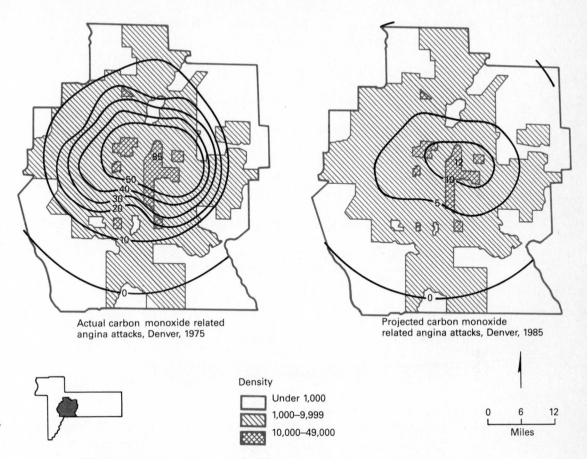

Figure 15.15   What-if study of the effects of reducing auto emissions of carbon monoxide in Denver.

When the menu cursor is moved to any item, a sentence appears giving a simple explanation of that item; for example:

ARIMA, CLUSTER, FORECAST, REGRESSION, SENSITIVITY , TRENDFIT, WHAT IF?
SENSITIVITY ANALYSIS ALLOWS YOU TO CHANGE CERTAIN ITEMS AND SEE THE EFFECTS OF THIS.

On a PC workstation, the sentences change in deciseconds as the menu cursor is slid along the menu. The user may read the sentence before selecting an item. If the user selects the item by pressing the mouse button or ENTER key, a more detailed menu may appear:

ARIMA, CLUSTER, FORECAST, REGRESSION, SENSITIVITY, ⬚TRENDFIT⬚ ,
WHAT IF
COMPUTES THE BEST-FITTING CURVE FOR A SET OF VALUES.

The user presses the mouse button, then moves the cursor to POWER on the following second-level menu:

LINEAR, EXPONENTIAL, ⬚POWER⬚ , HYP1, HYP2, HYP3, MULTIPLE, HELP
COMPUTES THE BEST-FITTING POWER FUNCTION CURVE.

The user moves the cursor to MULTIPLE:

LINEAR, EXPONENTIAL, POWER, HYP1, HYP2, HYP3, ⬚MULTIPLE⬚ , HELP
SELECTS THE BEST FIT OF SEVERAL CHOSEN CURVE TYPES.

The user presses the mouse button:

LINEAR, EXPONENTIAL, POWER, HYP1, HYP2, HYP3, ALL

CLICK THE MOUSE BUTTON ON THE ABOVE ITEMS OF YOUR CHOICE.

The user selects several of the above.

This type of menu system encourages the user to explore. He does not need to learn and memorize a software syntax. When beginning, users tend to slide the menu cursor to each menu item in turn and read its explanatory sentence. They can find out what the software does, asking for a more detailed explanation when they want it, by clicking on the HELP menu item.

AVOIDANCE OF AN ALIEN SYNTAX

More than any other type of 4GL, decision-support languages ought to be used by high-level executives who are too busy to learn and remember a programming-like syntax. More than other 4GLs, decision-support languages ought to be human-factored so that they are extremely easy to use without an alien syntax.

Having said that, I have found the human factoring of many of the major decision-support systems to be rather poor. The excellent analytical tools and decision-support data bases that exist today would probably have much greater usefulness if they did not present a syntax barrier to the most important decision makers. Advertisements for DSS products often extol the extreme ease of use of their ''English-like'' language when in fact their syntax provides a serious barrier to use by overworked executives and analysts.

**PERSONAL
COMPUTERS**

It is very appealing to use personal computers for decision-support work because of their decisecond response times and fast graphics. The relatively long response times of mainframe terminals greatly impede the dialogue mechanisms that can be used, as discussed earlier. So it is appealing to employ personal computers with decisecond response times and better human factoring to work with data stored on the mainframe. The main decision-support data base may be on a mainframe; portions of the data are down-loaded to personal computers for manipulation (Fig. 15.16). The users may sometimes create or revise models on a personal computer and return these to the mainframe.

Many users keep their own decision-support data on a PC, often in the form of spreadsheet files. Many other powerful analytical tools are becoming available on the PC, and some of the mainframe DSS systems allow a PC to extract data for use with PC tools.

The central DSS data bases need to be repositories of data that many

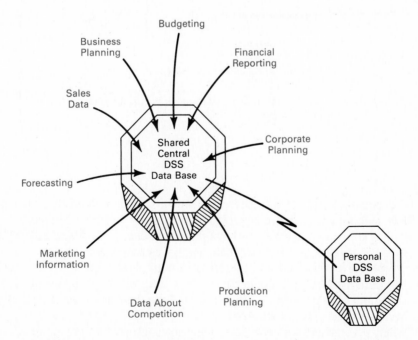

Figure 15.16   It is often very valuable for users to extract a portion of a DSS data base for manipulation in their own personal computer.

decision-makers share and that may be updated continually. Software that facil-itates distributed use of data while preserving the integrity and security of the data is needed.

WIDE SPECTRUM
OF DSS PRODUCTS
There is a wide spectrum of decision-support soft-ware, ranging from simple products to highly com-plex products. A wide diversity of techniques can help in making decisions. Some of the simple software packages, such as the stand-alone spreadsheet tools, are extremely useful, but when users are familiar with them, it becomes desirable that they be able to extend their capability.

Figure 15.17 illustrates the range of functionality in DSS software. The capability to use spreadsheet tools can be extended in many ways—to the use of graphics, to analyzing slices through multidimensional data, to doing com-putations with 4GL languages, to analyzing data with operations research tools.

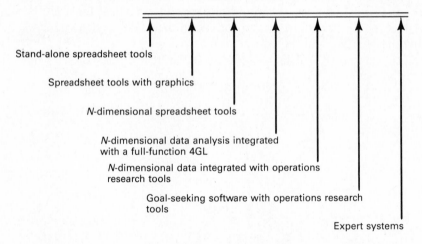

Figure 15.17 There is a wide spectrum of functionality in decision-support software.

The personal computer is becoming steadily more powerful, and most of the tools mentioned in this chapter can operate on personal computers. It is attractive to knowledge workers to have their own decision-making environment of a personal computer. However, many decisions need data that are on a main-frame, centrally maintained and available to many end users. It is desirable to make the micro-mainframe connection as *transparent* as possible, so that the user can employ his personal computer *either* with data stored on its Winchester *or* with data stored on a mainframe.

When several users access data, integrity controls that are more complex than for single-user access are needed. A great deal of decision-support data needs to be shared (and sometimes updated) by many users.

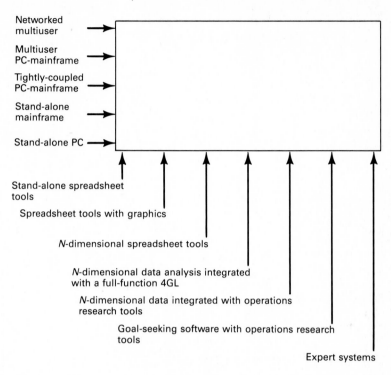

Figure 15.18 One dimension added to Fig. 15.17 showing the types of delivery mechanisms.

Figure 15.18 adds a new dimension to Fig. 15.17, showing environments for DSS ranging from personal computers to networked environments where the user can access several multiuser systems.

Figure 15.19 adds a third dimension relating to data. The data may be single-user data, shared central data, or fully distributed data. They may be kept in the form of files, a decision-support data base, an intelligent data base, or a knowledge base.

The industry needs to evolve from stand-alone products of limited functionality to products that integrate most of what is in Fig. 15.19 (see Fig. 15.20).

DECISION-SUPPORT DATA BASE

The access requirements of a decision-support data base are very different from those of a data base for routine computing. Data bases for routine computing are designed to be efficient with high-volume access

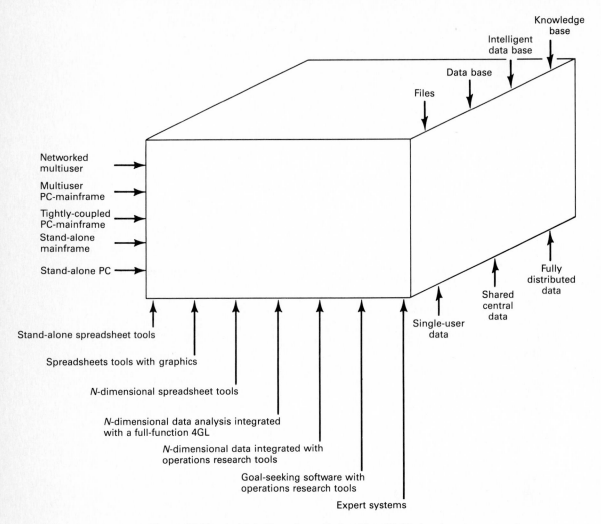

Figure 15.19   A third dimension added to Fig. 15.18 showing the types of data facilities.

and updating. Decision-support data bases are needed to handle multidimensional data efficiently and permit fully flexible relational operations such as searching, projecting, and joining relations.

A variety of mechanisms can be used to facilitate searching and joining of data—secondary indices, inverted files, ring structures, inverted list bit maps, and others. All such mechanisms tend to increase the complexity of updating the data. When the data are changed, the secondary indices, ring bit maps, or

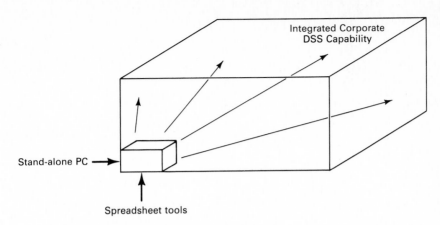

Figure 15.20 It is desirable to extend DSS facilities in a corporation from stand-alone tools to an integrated DSS environment.

whatever, have to be changed. These mechanisms degrade the performance of heavy-duty updating.

The data structures needed to support multidimensional data are different from those that support routine data processing. Data structures for routine data processing have a key such as PRODUCT # and a collection of attributes associated with the key:

PRODUCT#	NAME	DESCRIPTION	SOURCE	RELEASE DATE	PRICE	UNITS SOLD	REVENUE

A record often has child (offspring) records associated with it:

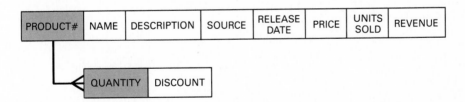

The data are designed with normalization techniques so that the attributes are each associated with a key that fully identifies them.

One of the attributes of the PRODUCT record is revenue. A decision-support data base is likely to be concerned with where the revenue comes from. It can regard revenue as a variable with multiple subscripts:

$$REVENUE_{PRODUCT,\ MONTH,\ REGION}$$

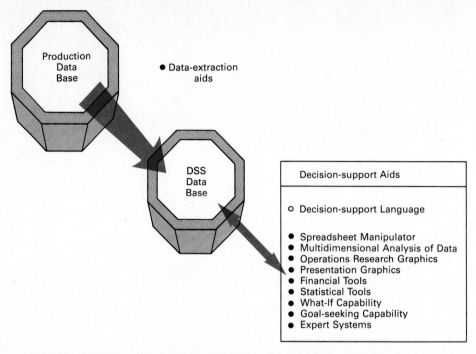

Figure 15.21 Decision-support tools often work on data structured especially for spreadsheet or multidimensional analysis. These data may be extracted from a production data base and restructured.

Three subscripts give a three-dimensional array of data:

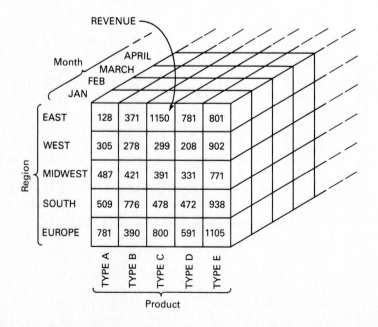

In the production data base, REVENUE was an attribute of PRODUCT. Here PRODUCT is a subscript of REVENUE.

There are often more than three dimensions. The revenues may be broken down further by type of sale, for example (mail order, direct, advertising, retail), or by type of customer, type of advertising, and so on.

The marketing staff might want to explore the effect of different discount structures or explore how different pricing structures would have affected revenues, on the basis of price-elasticity curves:

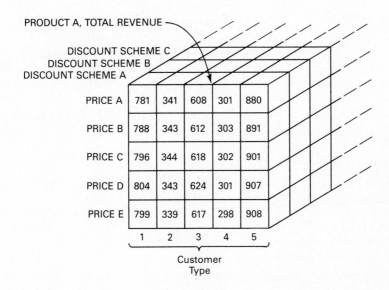

The figures for what-if revenue in this data base are derived from the figures for actual revenue in the previous data base. One decision-support array often needs to derive data from another decision-support array.

The efficient decision-support systems, such as EXPRESS, use data structures quite different from those in data bases such as IMS or IDMS, which support production data processing. EXPRESS uses structures designed to store variables with multiple subscripts, quite different from a relational data base. Some decision-support systems use relational data bases, but the relations would be different from those stored for routine computing. Structures that are efficient for decision support with multidimensional data are inefficient for heavy-duty computing.

Because of this, data are often extracted from a corporation's production data bases into a disjoint data structure that is designed for decision support (Fig. 15.21). This separate DSS data base may be on the same computer as the production data base or on a separate computer.

INTELLIGENT DATA BASE	In an intelligent data base, as discussed in Chapter 6, certain specified logic operations and calculations are applied to the data automatically. These calculations may apply range checks; they may look for trigger values; most commonly, when data in one cell are changed, they automatically compute changes to data in other cells, as with spreadsheet tools such as LOTUS 1-2-3. This can be a valuable facility with multidimensional data as well as with two-dimensional spreadsheets.

KNOWLEDGE BASE	A *knowledge base* stores rules, or assertions, along with data. These rules, or assertions, can be processed with inference-processing software in order to answer questions, arrive at conclusions, or produce other assertions, which are stored in the knowledge base. Knowledge bases are a component of *expert systems*.

Expert systems can be very effective in a decision-support environment. They consist of the following components:

1. *A knowledge base* contains facts and rules.
2. *Inference-processing software.* (One day special hardware will be used for inference processing.) Inference processors operate on rules or assertions to arrive at conclusions. Two main techniques are used: *forward chaining,* in which rules or assertions are processed to arrive at conclusions, and *backward chaining,* in which the inference processing works backward from a proposed conclusion, diagnosis, or goal in order to find what might make it true.
3. *A human interface* for enabling users to communicate with the expert system in an easy fashion.
4. *Links to other systems* (possibly), in order to extract data from data bases or acquire knowledge from other knowledge bases.

REFERENCES

1. EXPRESS, from Management Decision Systems, Inc., 200 Fifth Avenue, Waltham, MA 02254.

2. SYSTEM W, from Comshare, Inc., P.O. Box 1588, 3001 South State Street, Ann Arbor, MI.

3. E. Teicholz and B. J. L. Berry, *Computer Graphics and Environmental Planning,* Englewood Cliffs, NJ: Prentice-Hall, Inc., 1983.

16 PROTOTYPING LANGUAGES

PROTOTYPES VERSUS THE REAL THING

4GLs are used both for creating prototypes and for creating the final application. Prototypes are extremely valuable in data processing. It is desirable to do thorough reality testing before going very far with expensive projects.

With most complex engineering, a prototype is created before the final product is built. This is done to test the principles, ensure that the system works, and obtain design feedback that permits the design to be adjusted before the big money is spent. A chemical plant is built in laboratory form before the plant is finally designed. The hull shape of a boat is tested. A new airplane is simulated in a variety of ways before it is built.

Complex data processing systems need prototyping more than most engineering systems because there is much to learn from experimental operation, and many changes are likely to be made. Prototypes help to solve the problems of systems that do not work in the way the end users really need, and this greatly reduces the modifications that are eventually requested.

In a sense, the system created by the traditional DP life cycle is a prototype. It is not *meant* to be a prototype and is not regarded as such, but it has all the imperfections of a prototype. These imperfections are expensive to correct, so they often remain in the system, leading eventually to costly maintenance.

The reason DP prototypes were not generally used until the 1980s was that the cost of programming a prototype was about as high as the cost of programming the live working system. Fourth-generation languages enable prototypes to be created relatively cheaply.

A systems analyst working with an end user can create and demonstrate dialogues for data-base queries, report generation, and manipulation of screen information. The analyst discusses an end user's needs with him and then creates a specimen dialogue on a terminal. This might take him an hour or a week, depending on the complexity and the language that is being used. Initially, he ignores questions of transaction loads and machine performance. Creating prototypes for user management, especially top management, is very important in allowing them to see and use what they will be provided with when a system is operational. They always make changes.

The end user is shown the dialogue and is quickly trained to use it. Usually he has some suggestions for changes he would like, and the analyst makes these. The user may add subtotals or extra columns. He may want to perform certain calculations. The analyst may show him the different types of charts that could be created—scatter plots, bar charts, charts with regression lines, linear versus log scales, and so on. The user remembers a different type of customer, or some union rule that was forgotten, or other factors that only the user would be likely to know.

Often major misunderstandings surface or ambiguities and inconsistencies are uncovered. Different users have different interpretations of the same data. Omissions are found. Users think of other features they would like added. The users may find parts of the system difficult to use or confusing, and screen clarification or on-line help facilities can be improved.

Operating a system for a few weeks *always* changes users' perceptions of what they really want. Prototyping allows this to occur early in the development cycle, not after implementation, when change is expensive.

As the analyst and user continue their discussion of what is needed, the running prototype is now a focus of the debate; this helps to ensure that they are both talking about the same thing. The screens are printed, and the end user takes them home to think about them. The analyst works further, improving the screen interaction, adding new features, and improving the displays.

Finally the user is satisfied and excited and says, ''When can I get it?'' In some cases he can have it very quickly. The data base exists, and the prototype can become the final application. In other cases he cannot have it yet because design work is needed to achieve machine efficiency, security, auditability, telecommunications networking, or data-base creation.

In the latter case the prototype becomes, in effect, the requirements document for application programming.

WHY CONVERT?   If the prototype can become the final system, why convert it to a system developed with a traditional language?

There are powerful reasons *not* to convert it to COBOL or another third-generation language. As soon as it is rewritten in COBOL, it is expensive to maintain, whereas if it remains in the prototyping language, modifications are easy to make.

The most common argument *for* conversion is machine performance. Machine performance is a major concern only for heavy-duty applications. In a typical DP installation, 50 percent of the applications consume a total of 2 percent of the machine cycles. Their machine costs are much less than their maintenance costs in COBOL. Furthermore, some application generators that are appropriate for prototyping are designed to give good machine performance— sometimes better than COBOL applications, where their building blocks are tightly coded in machine language.

DP staffers who feel the urge to convert prototypes to COBOL should calculate the costs of conversion plus, say, five years' maintenance, and compare these costs with the machine savings and costs of maintenance in the prototyping languages. There is another more subtle cost of having the application in third-generation languages: They inhibit change, and the inability to change the system may result in lost business opportunities or inefficiencies.

Other important reasons for rebuilding the prototype are to achieve better security, integrity controls, protection from crashes, reliability, and auditability. The ability to have larger data bases, more terminals, a better network, or higher transaction volumes may be other reasons.

When the DP group members initially select the prototyping technique, they should have in mind the desirability of making the prototype into the final system.

THREE TYPES OF APPLICATION DEVELOPMENT

There are thus three types of application development:

1. Traditional development with a traditional life cycle. This has the problems discussed earlier of slow development, lengthy backlog, expensive maintenance, and mismatch with user requirements.

2. Use of a 4GL as a prototyping tool. The end user interacts with the prototype and the analyst modifies it until it is a suitable model for application programming in a third-generation language. Sometimes many versions of the prototype are created. The prototyping tool alleviates as much of the need for separate requirements documentation as possible. Modules of code may be created by the prototyping tool to alleviate the need for programming *all* of the application.

3. Use of a 4GL to develop the entire application. The prototype becomes the application. No separate use is made of professional programmers. An end user and DP analyst may work together to create the applications.

The third of these development approaches can be used for most, but not all, commercial data processing. For many data processing applications, there need be little concern with machine efficiency because they do not run frequently. Only a small proportion are high-volume applications.

For heavy-duty applications, high machine efficiency is needed. This can be achieved in one of three ways:

1. First, we have stressed that some fourth-generation languages are designed to achieve high machine efficiency. A specialist who knows all the tricks with an application generator can sometimes achieve much more efficient results than the average analyst. The analyst may create a heavy-duty application in DMS or ADF and then hand it over to a DMS or ADF ''acrobat'' for optimization.

2. Certain routines may be ''time eaters.'' These can be isolated and programmed in a more efficient language if the generator has suitable EXITS.

3. The entire application may be reprogrammed for efficiency. Instead of written requirements documentation, the generator version is used to guide the programming team. Sometimes the generator creates only part of what is needed, so a hybrid of generator input/output and written specifications is needed.

Box 16.1 lists typical characteristics of these three approaches to application development. In many large corporations, all three types of development are likely to coexist. A good DP executive will organize his operation so that they *can* coexist. In some corporations the DP department uses only the traditional development life cycle, and the end users bypass the DP department, using the new languages to create their own applications more quickly and satisfactorily.

The mature DP executive should welcome, not fight, end users' creating their own applications. He should regard it as his job to provide them with the software tools, networks, and consultant systems analysts they need. Particularly important, he should link their activities to the data modeling and data systems created by information engineering [1].

PARTIAL SYSTEM PROTOTYPING

Some prototyping efforts create a pilot version of a complete application. Some tackle only one facet of an application. *Partial* system prototyping has proved particularly valuable on some systems. Often DP managers have not considered this approach because they assume that a complete system prototype is needed. Partial system prototyping can be easier, and there may be less excuse for not using it. Partial prototypes are of a variety of forms:

Dialogue Prototype

The prototype simulates the intended terminal interaction. This is probably the most common form of partial prototyping. It allows the end users to see what they will be receiving, play with it, suggest omissions, improve the ease of comprehension, generally react to the dialogue, and finally sign off on its development. Various software products can be used as dialogue simulators.

BOX 16.1   Three types of application development

	Conventional Application Development (as in Figs. 3.4 and 3.5)	Information Engineering and Fourth-Generation Languages	
		Use of a Prototyping Aid Followed by Programming	Application Development Without Professional Programmers
Requirements Analysis	A time-consuming, formal operation, often delayed by long application backlog	The user's imagination is stimulated. He may work at a screen with an analyst to develop requirements.	The user's imagination is stimulated. He may develop his own requirements or work with an analyst.
System Specification Document	Lengthy document, boring, often inadequate	Produced by prototyping aid; precise and tested	Disappears
User Sign-off	User is often not sure of what he is signing off. He cannot perceive all the subtleties.	User sees the results and may modify them many times before signing off.	No formal sign-off; adjustment and modification are an ongoing process.
Data	Often designed separately for each application	Planned with information analysis and data modeling	Planned with information analysis and data modeling; made available in data systems
Coding and Testing	Slow, expensive, often delayed because of backlog	The prototype is converted to more efficient code; relatively quick and error-free.	Quick, inexpensive; disappears to a large extent
Documentation	Tedious, time-consuming	May be partly automated. Interactive training and HELP responses may be created on-line.	Largely automatic; interactive training and HELP responses are created on-line.
Maintenance	Slow, expensive, often late	Less slow, less expensive, less late; fewer modification are needed to the final system.	A continuing process, with user and analyst making adjustments

The design of the terminal dialogue greatly affects the usability and users' perception of the system. Many systems have been partial failures because of poor terminal dialogues. Amazingly, many systems analysts and programmers are not trained in what constitutes a psychologically effective dialogue. They often create dialogues that are muddled, not clean, and confusing to some of the users. It helps to build a prototype dialogue that can be tested, criticized, and improved before final implementation.

Data Entry

One group of users may perform data entry. The data entry subsystem may be prototyped and adjusted independently and may be linked to an existing system. Data-entry prototyping may be done to check the speed and accuracy of the data entry. Validity and integrity checks may be tested.

Some systems have been split into a *front end* and a *back office*. The front end is interactive. The back office consists of multiple batch-updating runs. The front end may be prototyped independently using software such as MAPPER, FOCUS, RAMIS, or NOMAD. The back office may remain in the form of COBOL programs.

Reporting System

The reports provided to users may be tried out on them before full system implementation. They may be either batch or on-line. Often many adjustments are made in the reporting subsystem. Report generators, such as RPG, NOMAD, or ADRS, may be used.

Data System

A prototype data base may be implemented with a small number of records. Users and analysts interact with it, generating reports or displaying information that might be useful to them. This interaction often results in requests for different types of data, new fields, or different ways of organizing the data.

With some prototyping tools, users or analysts have the ability to build their own files, manipulate them, and display information from them. Such tools are used to explore how the users will employ information and what should be in the data base.

Calculations and Logic

Sometimes the logic of an application or the calculations are complex. Actuaries, engineers, investment analysts, or other such users may use a language such as APL to build examples of the computations they need. These may then be incorporated into larger systems, perhaps linked to other applications, to data bases, or to many terminals. The users may employ their APL prototypes to check the accuracy of the results.

Application Package

An application package may be tried out with a small group of users to determine whether it is satisfactory. The need for various modifications may become clear. These are tried out before the package is linked to other applications or put into volume use.

Concept

Sometimes the concept of an application is in question. It needs testing and refining before too much money is spent on building the system. The test may be done with a quick-to-implement data management system. Standard data-entry screens and standard report formats may be used so that the concepts may be tested and refined without too much work. Later, application-specific reports or screens may be built.

DIFFERENT HARDWARE

Sometimes prototyping is done on different hardware from that of the final system. This may be because the final hardware is not yet available. It may be because it is much easier to experiment on a small minicomputer than on the final complex system. Prototyping aids that are easily adaptable to the final hardware need to be selected.

REAL DATA

With some prototyping, the analyst creates small files of made-up data to illustrate what the system will do. In other cases, made-up data are not good enough. The users need to update real data or explore complex data bases in order to experience what the proposed system will do for them.

If real data are required, the users may be given prototypes connected to a live data system or may be given data that have been extracted from a live data system. The latter is generally safer and more flexible.

If the users do not update the data, they may be given report generators or other facilities that use data in a live data base but cannot modify the data. Often, however, the users want to manipulate or update the data. They should then be given extracted data to do this with and be locked out of the live data.

In some prototyping efforts, the users ask for information of various types. The analyst must find out where such data exist, capture them, and reconstruct them in the data management system of the prototyping tool. Sometimes they exist on batch files, sometimes in corporate data bases; sometimes they can be obtained from external sources.

When real data are used, the prototype sometimes grows into a system that the users do not want to give up; it becomes a real working system.

THROWAWAY PILOTS

When prototyping becomes very easy, the development organization or end-user groups themselves may create pilot systems and try them out to see whether other end users like them. In some organizations, a third or so of the pilots created fall into disuse, whereas some are perceived as being very valuable.

By use of throwaway pilots, system designers can discover the requirements and refinements that end users will actually employ. It is a trial-and-error process: Build a pilot, observe it in use, evaluate, revise it where necessary, or replace it with a different version. Do not worry if some of the pilots are abandoned.

THE DEVELOPMENT PROCESS WITH PROTOTYPING

Prototyping, illustrated in Fig. 16.1, creates a different cycle of DP development from the traditional one. Because prototypes vary widely in their character and use, there are widely different versions of this life cycle.

The first step in Fig. 16.1 is the broad determination of what the end users need. Often the users make a request. An analyst studies it, determines what data it requires, and determines how it might be prototyped. For small systems this can be informal, without any written specifications. For large systems it might involve detailed written descriptions of what data are needed, data-flow diagrams, or action diagrams showing how a data base will be used.

In the second step, a working prototype is created. It is important that this be done *quickly*. The prototype may use the standard default options of a non-procedural facility or data management system in order to demonstrate something to the users quickly. It may initially demonstrate only the major functions and not yet include peripheral details, auditors' requirements, and so on.

The third step may progress from an initial demonstration to a small group of users to a more thorough and refined test with many users. Some changes requested by users can be made immediately at the screen. Other requests are noted for later modifications. With some prototyping tools, end users with terminals in multiple locations may employ the prototype and may record their requests or comments at the terminal.

Sometimes the initial prototypes may be inappropriate; they are scrapped, and different ones are created. When the prototype reaches an acceptable state, multiple users may be trained to use it and to experiment with it.

To demonstrate the prototype's usefulness to management, managers may be asked to bring sample questions that they would like the system to be able to answer. The analysts who created the prototype will either demonstrate this ability or expand the system if possible to meet the requirements.

If in step 5 a conversion to different software takes place, the original version should be kept. The original version may be needed for future enhancement maintenance, feeding back to step 3, as shown in Fig. 16.1.

PROTOTYPING SOFTWARE

The 4GLs used for prototyping are usually the same as those used for application development. The systems analyst building prototypes may, himself, be a customer of the information center that supports users of these languages.

The most important characteristic of the prototyping software is that it should permit prototyping to be performed *quickly*. Prototyping requires a *quick and inexpensive* means of testing a trial balloon. The second most important characteristic is that users, or analysts working with them, should be able to make adjustments quickly and easily.

These two characteristics are also at the top of the requirements list for fourth-generation languages designed to minimize the personnel needed for application creation and maintenance. Is there any difference in the requirements for a prototyping language and a development language?

Yes. The development language may be designed to give good machine performance, whereas this is not a concern in the prototyping language. The development language may give one fixed type of screen format; the prototyper may want more flexibility in designing and experimenting with different screen layouts. The development language may employ a traditional data-base management system; the prototyping language may employ an easy-to-implement data management system.

In spite of these differences, there is a good reason to make the prototyping language the same as the development language: The prototype may evolve into the final system. This has major advantages. First, it saves much development time. Second, it gives continuity between the prototype and the final system as the users become familiar with the final system. Third, it makes it possible to modify the final system in the same way as modifying the prototype.

RESISTANCE

Prototyping seems so vital to the development process, and has in practice saved so much money in maintenance, that it is amazing that so many systems are still developed without prototypes. The reason seems to be reluctance on the part of DP managers to change their methods and lack of education about the tools now available.

In my view, there is *no* data processing system that should *not* be prototyped or built with a 4GL, either partially or completely. There have been too

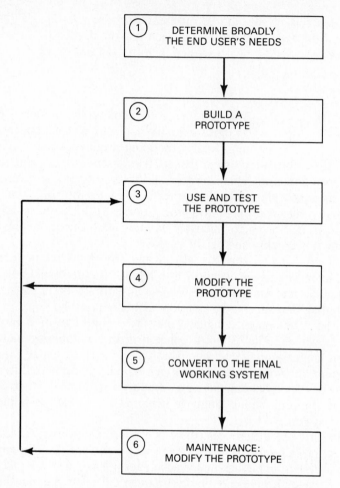

Figure 16.1 Development life cycle with prototyping.

many catastrophes, too many unhappy end users, and too much maintenance expense for anyone to assume that it is safe to go into a lengthy, expensive, third-generation development without the up-front reality testing that prototypes provide. When the end users work with prototypes for a few weeks, they almost always improve the resulting system.

REFERENCE

1. J. Martin and C. Finkelstein, *Information Engineering* (Savant Technical Report No. 22), Carnforth, Lancs., England: Savant Institute, 1981.

17 SPECIFICATION LANGUAGES

INTRODUCTION   Imagine a monastery far away in the mountains where the monks write COBOL programs all day. Unfortunately, the monks do not have a computer, so their programs are never run or tested. They write thousands upon thousands of lines of code but never find out how many bugs their programs contain. They live in happy ignorance of how bad their coding really is.

In this blissful environment we would all no doubt kid ourselves that we do a great job of writing all that code, and we would never need to be disillusioned. The computer destroys this Shangri-La. It runs the code we write and brutally reveals its errors.

Whereas programmers cannot get away with the errors they make, traditional systems analysts can and do. They write voluminous specifications that, like the monks' code, are not fed into a computer for checking. They are, of course, checked manually, like the monks' code, but that catches only a few of the problems.

In traditional methods for creating computer applications, specifications are written in English aided by hand-drawn diagrams such as flowcharts and data-flow diagrams. For large systems the specifications become vast, sometimes occupying several volumes. As I have indicated, there are severe problems with specifications:

- They are often so long and boring that key managers do not read them. They read the summary.

- They lack precision. They cannot be converted into computer code without many assumptions and interpretations.

- They are often ambiguous, inconsistent, and incomplete.

- They are often misinterpreted by both sides. Often readers *think* they understand them but in fact do not.

- Sometimes much trivia and "motherhood" is added to the document. Both sides understand this. It increases the comfort level but has zero value.

- The specification documents are not designed for successive refinement as the problems become better understood. They are intended to be a complete document that users sign.

Various attempts were made in the 1970s to create computer languages for expressing specifications in order to impose discipline on what was a horrifyingly sloppy process. Most of the early specification languages were not precise enough for it to be possible to generate code automatically from the specification. If a specification has this precision, we say that it is *computable*.

Computable specification languages are the subject of this chapter. They will ultimately become the basis of most *prespecified* computing (as opposed to ad hoc uses of computers). The users or analysts will create a formal specification that can be steadily refined until code can be generated from it. Inconsistencies, ambiguities, and omissions that make the specifications noncomputable will be flushed out. The analyst, like the programmer before him, will be confronted with the ruthless discipline of the machine.

Specification languages that enforce computability in specifications are already in use. At the time of writing, most analysts do not employ them. Some analysts would prefer the more casual life of the monastery.

COMPUTER-AIDED SPECIFICATION DESIGN

Specification languages that generate code are a form of 4GL. The word *language* might be misleading. The specification may be a drawing or succession of drawings, just as the specification for an engineering mechanism is a succession of drawings. The engineer's drawings are very precise and are drawn with formal rules. They are, in effect, a language with which specifications are stated.

Today's computers have powerful graphics capability. We can create and manipulate drawings on a screen. We do not need to create a work of art or a drawing with the elegance of, say, Victorian architects' drawings of cathedrals. We need clear diagrams of the logic of computer applications that can be refined and automatically checked for accuracy and consistency so that program code can be generated from them.

As users change their minds or the details of the requirements become better understood, the design can be adjusted and the programs regenerated. Ideally, the specification language should be sufficiently easy to understand that users can employ it or at least study the specifications and be involved in valuable discussions about them with the analysts.

A report generator, such as that illustrated from the IDEAL language in Chapter 5, is a form of specification language. With an easy-to-use tool, the user specifies the information he wants on the report. This specification is then fed into software that generates the required code. A report specification is very simple. We need to find computable means of specifying more interesting applications.

A good report generator makes extensive use of defaults. It makes its own assumptions about what format of report would be most valuable to the user. Similarly, with more complex specifications, the software should make intelligent assumptions wherever it can in an attempt to minimize the work of the analyst and maximize the quality of the result. The analyst should be given a means to override the defaults where desirable.

COMPLEX SPECIFICATIONS

A report generator is an almost trivial example of creating specifications; at the opposite extreme, the language USE.IT has been employed for creating specifications for military and aerospace systems of high complexity. Here a computer language is needed with the capability to check the accuracy of the interfaces and use of data types. The design tool reveals ambiguities, inconsistencies, and omissions because it has to create *computable* specifications. The human mind simply cannot spot the ambiguities, inconsistencies, and incompleteness in highly complex specifications. And a team of human minds is worse because it creates pieces that do not mesh exactly.

The exercise of taking manually created specifications and converting them into a USE.IT design reveals the sheer horror of the mess we make in manual design of complex systems.

TWO TYPES OF LANGUAGES

In the early days of the computer industry, computer languages were thought of only as programming languages. Initially they were close in syntax to the instruction set of the machine. Human language is very different from machine language, so attempts were made to humanize the programming languages by employing English words.

The standardization of languages like COBOL, FORTRAN, and ADA presented programmers with what in effect were virtual computers hiding the physical details of actual computers that differed from machine to machine. The programming language, however, remained a statement of how to execute a set of operations in terms of computer resources.

Understanding the requirements of a complex system and writing specifications for it need a very different type of language. In the early days (and often still today), requirements and specifications were expressed in English. Human language, however, is ambiguous and imprecise. Specifications written in English were usually incomplete and almost always open to misinterpretation. The effort to make them more thorough led to documents more voluminous than

Victorian novels and far more boring. It became clear that many of the problems with systems were not the fault of the programmers but of the specifiers.

Because of this, a variety of techniques grew up for designing and specifying systems. A new type of language began to emerge: specification languages. These languages had little or no resemblance to programming languages. They took a variety of forms. Sometimes a formal language was used, sometimes a diagramming technique. They included SADT (Structured Analysis and Design Technique) [1], SREM (Software Requirements Engineering Methodology) [2], data-flow diagramming techniques [3], HIPO (Hierarchical Input Process Output) [4], PSL/PSA (Problem Statement Language/Problem Statement Analyzer) [5], and IDEF (ICAM Definition Method) [6].

These were all generalized languages intended to specify any type of program. There are also specialized languages, narrow in scope, most of which are not referred to as "specification" languages. These include report-definition languages, data-base query-and-update languages, languages that could generate certain patterns of commercial DP application, and languages for special functions such as financial analysis, circuit design, and coordinate geometry. Specification languages fit into a spectrum of 4GLs.

COMPUTABLE SPECIFICATIONS

The computer industry thus acquired two breeds of languages, one for requirements analysis, problem description, and system specification and one for programming.

It was generally considered to be desirable that the specification languages be independent of machine resources or programming because the specifications were a fundamental statement about requirements and these requirements could be met with a variety of types of hardware and software. Furthermore, the hardware and software would change while the requirements remained the same.

Programming languages had to be computable. This guaranteed rigor and sufficiency in these languages. Most of the *specification* languages and techniques that grew up were not rigorous and did not enforce logical consistency. They were not computable.

It was generally assumed that the output of the specification language was meant to be used by a programmer, who then coded the programs in a different language. This led to the problems associated with conventional programming. I believe that this assumption is wrong for the future of computing. The specification language should be processable so that program code can be generated *automatically,* as with today's report generators and application generators. This means that the specification language requires more rigor than early specification techniques. The specification should contain enough detail and be precise enough to be converted into program code automatically.

Although programming languages have the desirable property of computability, they are not suitable for stating system specifications because of their semantics. What is needed is a specification language that *is* computable, with semantics appropriate for high-level conceptualization of systems. The property of computability will then permit resources to be allocated and programs created automatically (without the errors programmers make).

AUTOMATION OF DESIGN

Many specification techniques were designed to be used by hand. It is only when computers are used that rigorous methods are practical. Humans make too many errors and find rigorous techniques too tedious to use rapidly and thoroughly by hand. Creating design techniques to be run with computerized tools enormously expands the scope of what is practicable. Today the hardware for running computerized tools is inexpensive, so future techniques should be designed to employ computers.

Design will never be completely automated. Human inventiveness and creativity are its most important aspect. Humans will always want to argue at a blackboard and draw sketches on paper, so the technique should provide ways to make simple drawings of concepts.

Figure 17.1 shows the essentials of computerized system design. There

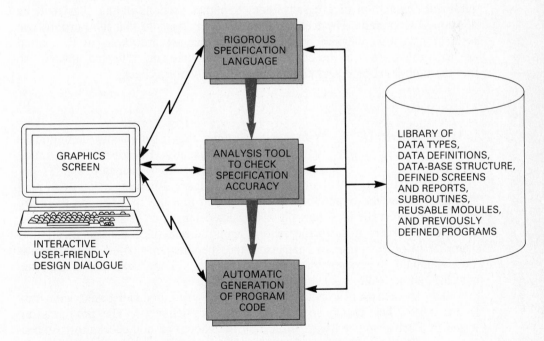

Figure 17.1 Specification languages should be user-friendly and rigorous, have tools for on-line accuracy checking, employ a library for the building of complex systems, and be capable of generating code automatically.

should be a specification language that is rigorous but has an interactive, user-friendly dialogue. Most people think and design with pictures, so an interactive graphics facility is desirable. The design so created should be capable of being analyzed to check its accuracy and consistency. The design and its analysis should be based on *mathematics,* which *enforces correct logic* where possible. The analyzer should check that the mathematical rules have been obeyed so that the logic structure is guaranteed to be correct.

Once it has been checked, the software should generate program code. Some tools generate code in conventional programming languages. This provides programs that are *portable* among different machines (insofar as the languages are portable). It is, however, more efficient to generate machine code and avoid the additional step of compilation, which can degrade code efficiency.

A rigorous specification cannot be created in one shot. There will be much successive refinement. Each step in this refinement needs to be rigorous. A specification process designed for automation is likely to produce a succession of formal representations of the system that can steadily be broken down into more detail. Different individuals are likely to be involved at different levels of detail. It helps if all use the same type of chart.

At the highest level, the chart has a few blocks, which represent the broad requirements of the system. At the lowest level, the chart has enough detail for automatic generation of program code. Separate portions of the chart will be developed separately. The technique must be designed so that the portions can be linked without interface problems. When changes are made, as they often are, at a lower level in the chart, these are automatically reflected upwards so that the high-level representations of the system can be checked.

INTEGRATION OF DEFINITION LEVELS

With many systems the requirements definition is written in one way, usually in English; the specification is created with a different technique; and the implementation is yet again different—a programming language. When the requirements are translated into the specification there are errors, and when the specification is translated into code there are errors. It is difficult and costly to keep the requirements current once the specification is begun or to reflect program changes in the specifications. When the programs are maintained, the documentation or higher-level systems descriptions are often not changed accordingly. They become out-of-date.

The specification is usually verified on a self-contained basis, with only occasional ad hoc checks to the requirements documents. The programs are tested in a self-contained way, with only occasional ad hoc checks to the specifications. The evolution through the development phases is usually not formally traceable.

The solution to this is to have *one language* as formal input to a computerized design tool with which requirements, specifications, and details can be expressed. The requirements statements are decomposed into greater detail and become the specifications. The specifications are decomposed until sufficient detail is reached that code can be generated automatically. Changes made at a lower level are automatically reflected upward. There is then structural integrity among the requirements, specifications, and detail. In fact these words cease to have sharp demarcations. A high-level description is decomposed into successively more detailed descriptions.

The documentation does not slip out of date when successive maintenance changes are made because these changes require regeneration of program code from the specification language. The entire structure, top to bottom, reflects the change. Subsequent maintainers will then have a clear and detailed description from which to work.

A COMMON COMMUNICATION VEHICLE

A major reason for problems with systems is inadequate communication between users and developers or between requirements definers and programmers. The most successful requirement-definition projects are those where the implementers and users work on and understand the requirements together. The implementers understand better what the users need. The users understand better the constraints of implementation. Each group can trigger creativity in the other so that the combination produces something better than either group alone. A few exciting projects catch fire when there is excellent understanding between the instigators and implementers.

A good specification language should build a bridge of understanding among the users, requirements planners, specifiers, and implementers. A common language should be usable by all of them. The high-level view of the users or requirements planners should be decomposable into the detail needed by the implementers. The high-level planners or specifiers should be able to choose the level of detail they want in specifying the system. Changes made at lower levels should reflect into this higher-level specification to preserve integrity of the levels.

A language that provides this communication bridge accelerates the understanding of the user requirements by the implementers and enables the user or planner to understand his requirements better. Particularly important, it reveals misunderstanding among the users, planners, and implementers.

A developer may be better able to evaluate cost trade-off possibilities if he and the users employ a common way of looking at system specifications. This may save much money. Early feedback from the developer to the users is always beneficial.

INTEGRATED TOP-DOWN AND BOTTOM-UP DESIGN

The development methodology should facilitate both top-down and bottom-up design and should integrate them. There is a perennial argument about which is best. In practice, almost all complex systems design uses both. Pure top-down design is impractical. Pure bottom-up design would be a mess. Bottom-up design if uncontrolled, leads to interface problems. In writing a book, I use a mixture of top-down and bottom-up design. I have to start with a table of contents. But writing the details always causes me to change the table of contents. It is the same in systems design, and a tool is needed that allows the changes and inventions that occur when modules are being worked out in detail to be reflected naturally in the higher-level specifications.

A change made in one lower-level module may affect others, and it is desirable that this ripple effect be immediately traceable. The designer needs to be able to add requirements from the top or the bottom. In designing systems with the techniques described in this book, detailed work at a lower level frequently causes data-type references to be changed at a higher level. This continual adjustment can occur easily and should be largely automatic.

Often detailed design is done on one part of a system before another. The language should permit this to occur naturally and not cause later interface problems. On some systems, one component is developed to completion while specifiers are still debating the concepts of another. Detailed design in one area should not be held up waiting for complete top-down specification of the layers above. It is normal to write one or more chapters of a book before the table of contents is complete. The top level is not *really* complete until the lower levels are done and the necessary iterations have taken place.

MATHEMATICALLY RIGOROUS LANGUAGES

To achieve the rigor that is necessary, the best specification languages will be mathematically based. Chapter 13 includes a description of USE.IT, which is one such language in use today. With USE.IT, everything specified relates to data types, functions, and control structures that are based on mathematical axioms. This permits the building of constructs that are provably correct. As separate modules are interlinked, this is done with provably correct interfaces.

Everything in the system is built from mathematically based primitives. The primitives are interlinked in provably correct fashions. Everything that uses them and obeys the rules is then provably correct. The mathematically based interfacing rules distinguish this library concept from a conventional subroutine or program library. Increasingly large constructs can be built from what is in the library and then stored in the library with the knowledge that they are correct. As the library builds, the developers will have less work to do, and there will also be less to verify because it is known that everything in the library is bug-free.

The mathematical rules would be far too tedious and difficult to enforce by hand, so such a method depends on having a fully automated tool.

USER FRIENDLINESS

Particularly important is the user friendliness of the specification language. It may be mathematically based to enforce provably correct logic and interfaces between modules, but the mathematics should be completely hidden because most managers and analysts are terrified of mathematics. The telephone system is exceedingly complex and designed with mathematics, but most of its users know nothing about Erlang equations.

It is likely that different dialects of a specification language will be needed, as well as different forms of representation. All of these should be built from the same fundamental set of primitives.

If separate systems are defined from the same primitives, technical arguments can be resolved by breaking them down to the primitives to see whether there is real disagreement. With most requirements documents and specifications, there are no means of analyzing them into common primitives.

Once the underlying structures of primitives exists, higher-level constructs should make the specification language as powerful and as user-friendly as possible.

PROPERTIES NEEDED

Box 17.1 lists the properties desirable in a specification language. Box 17.2 lists the properties desirable in a specification.

SPECTRUM OF SPECIFICATION LANGUAGES

The properties of being user-friendly and being rigorous often seem in conflict. Mathematical languages are not user-friendly; user-friendly languages are generally not rigorous. We can rank them on a chart like that in Fig. 17.2. Readability, or user friendliness, is on the vertical scale. Traditional axiomatic languages are on the right but at the bottom; they are difficult or impossible for ordinary analysts or users to read.

Traditional English specifications are at the extreme left of Fig. 17.2. They may be (fairly) readable but are entirely nonrigorous. Sometimes software is employed for formatting, editing, and storing specifications. This makes them easier to access, change, and manipulate but does not make them more rigorous.

BOX 17.1 Desirable properties of a specification language

- It should provide a way to think about systems that improves conceptual clarity.

- It should be easy to learn and use. At its higher levels, it should be usable by non-DP personnel.

- It should be computable (that is, it should be possible to generate program code from it automatically).

- It should be designed for maximum automation of systems analysis, design, and programming.

- It should be rigorous and mathematically based so that its designs are provably correct.

- Its mathematical basis should be hidden from the average user because most users are terrified of mathematics.

- It should be versatile enough to remove the need for all manual use of programming languages. (Manual programming immediately violates the requirement of provable correctness.)

- It should extend from the highest-level conceptualization of systems down to the creation of enough detail for program generation. In other words, one language should suffice for creation of the entire system. The more detailed versions of a specification should be a natural extension of the more general ones. The high-level specifier should be able to decide into how much detail he wants to go before handing over to the implementer.

- It should be a common communication medium among managers, designers, implementers, verifiers, maintainers, and documenters.

- It should use graphic techniques that are easy to draw and remember.

- It should employ a user-friendly computerized graphics tool for building, changing, and inspecting the design. The language should be formal input to automated design.

- It should employ testing tools that assist in verification and permit simulation of missing modules so that partially complete designs can be tested.

- It should employ an integrated top-down or bottom-up design approach. Most complex systems come into existence through a combination of top-down and bottom-up design. The technique should allow certain elements of a system to be specified in detail while others, possibly parents or ancestors in the hierarchy, are not yet defined.

- It should indicate when a specification is complete (so that code can be generated from it).

BOX 17.1 *(Continued)*

- It should employ a hierarchy that descends into steadily increasing levels of detail. It should guarantee that each decomposition is logically valid and that each lower level completely replaces the one above it.

- Modifications made lower in the hierarchy should be quickly—perhaps automatically—reflected in the higher levels.

- It should employ an evolving library of subroutines, programs, and all the constructs the language employs. The primitive constructs will be in the library, so everything added to the library will be defined in terms of what is already there. The library becomes, in effect, an extendable requirement-definition language. Everything in such a library employs the common primitives and has been verified by the software.

- It should link automatically to data-base tools, including a dictionary and a directory that stores conceptual data-base models.

- It should guarantee interface consistency when subroutines or callable programs are used or when separate systems intercommunicate. Mathematical techniques should guarantee logical interface consistency as well as data consistency.

- The specification should be easy to change. It should be able to accommodate the unexpected. It should be easily changeable by persons who did not create it.

- All elements of a system should be traceable. All accesses and changes to data should be traceable throughout the system. This process should ensure that the inputs to each operation could come only from the correct source.

- The language may permit multiple dialects or multiple types of nonprocedural representation. These should all translate to a common set of control structures and a common set of rules for verifying correctness.

- A common set of primitives to which the proofs of correctness apply should be used. All nonprimitive structures and semantics should then translate to the primitives. The common primitives provide definitive communication between users employing different semantics or dialects.

- Default options may be used where they simplify specification—for example, with the formatting of screens or reports.

- The language should be independent of hardware or other resources that are likely to change. It should be translatable into different resource environments.

BOX 17.2 Desirable properties of a specification [7]

- A proper specification should be free from errors.
- It should have conceptual clarity.
- It should be easy to understand by managers, analysts, or programmers.
- It should be presentable in varying degrees of detail.
- It should be easy to create.
- It should be computable (that is, it should have enough precision that program code can be generated from it automatically).
- It should be formal input to a program code generator.
- It should be easy to change.
- It should be complete.
- It should be traceable when changes are introduced.
- It should be independent of hardware.
- It should employ a data dictionary.
- It should employ a data model based on formal data analysis.
- It should employ a program module library with automatic verification of interface correctness.
- It should employ computerized tools that make it easy to manipulate and change.

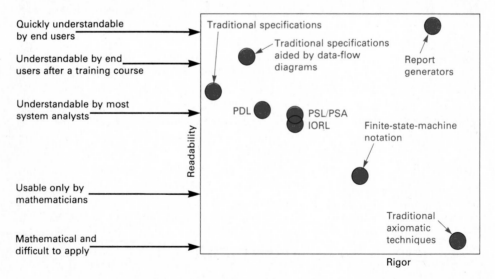

Figure 17.2 Spectrum of specification languages [11]. (Analysts can argue about the exact positioning of the languages on the chart.)

Some text specification formatters have additional capabilities. They detect key-words and format specification phrases and generate tables of contents and indexes. The program design language PDL [8] is an example. This improves the specification readability with clauses such as

```
IF  CUSTOMER_CREDIT_CODE < 3
THEN  ORDER  IS  REJECTED
```

It helps designers to find and cross-reference items in the specifications. It does no consistency or ambiguity checking, so there is little increase in rigor.

Another text approach advocates the use of a limited, well-defined, fairly nonambiguous subset of English [9]. This lessens the scope for misinterpretations and gives slightly more precision to the specifications. Software tools can help search for ambiguities and inconsistencies in such specifications [10].

Clear diagramming techniques in general help analysts to conceptualize systems and clarify complex flows and interrelationships. Diagrams that are too symbolic, however, are not necessarily understood by end users. Most analysts find their diagramming techniques very useful and assume that users find them useful too. In practice, many users are bewildered by the diagrams, thinking that they are more technical than they really are. Users sometimes complain that they understand the written specifications but not the diagrams.

Data-flow diagrams provide a small step toward formality, and most end users can be taught to read them without difficulty. The diagrams are an improvement over unstructured text but are still far from rigorous. They do not offer the desired property that program code could be generated from them automatically. Much more detail is needed. Much more is needed to enforce consistency and completeness.

PSL with its associated PSA (Problem Statement Language and Problem Statement Analyzer) [5] is one of the best-known specification languages. It divides system functions into subfunctions, precisely specifying the inputs and outputs of each. The analyzers perform consistency checking between functions. For example, no function is allowed to use a data item not generated by another function. PSL is farther to the right in Fig. 17.2, but it is still far from completely rigorous or capable of automatic program generation. Beside it in Fig. 17.2 is another language for functional decomposition and input/output specification: IORL (Input/Output Requirements Language) [12]. Although these do some useful specification checking, they cannot check detailed logic or specify the order and timing constraints needed in real-time systems.

A more rigorous approach is the use of *finite-state machine notation*. This permits complex logic to be described in terms of entities that have discrete *states*. The analyst determines what types of stimulus cause a state to change. The state of an entity is a function of the previous state and the inputs received. The output is a function of the inputs and the state when those inputs are received. State diagrams are drawn to represent the possible states and the stimuli that change them. Associated with the diagrams is a table showing all possible states and stimuli to make sure that all combinations have been thought about.

Finite-state machine notation has been used extensively in defining complex protocols for computer networks [13] and communications switching systems. The CCITT standards committee for international telephony and networking has a language for protocol specification based on this approach, SDL (Specification and Description Language) [14]. Other, more generalized specification languages—for example, RSL (Requirements Statements Language) [2]—use this approach.

Finite-state machine notation is farther to the right in Fig. 17.2. It is a major step in the direction of rigorous logic specification, but not sufficiently so for automatic program generation. Some manufacturers' network software designed with finite-state machine notation has exhibited mysterious and infuriating misbehavior. Finite-state machine notation is extremely difficult for most end users to understand, so it is lower on Fig. 17.2. It is not normally used in general data processing or in most scientific computing, and in general it has a limited class of applications. It is possible to build software that translates finite-state machine representation into English-like constructs to aid in user checking [15].

NARROWLY FOCUSED LANGUAGES

Computable specification languages are found in narrowly focused areas. Probably the most commonly used example is report generators.

Broadening the scope somewhat, we have nonprocedural languages for querying, updating, and sometimes manipulating data bases. These are linked to graphics languages and decision-support aids. Very different types of specification or problem statement languages exist for certain specific applications—for example, coordinate geometry, CAD/CAM, architects' drawings, and the building of telephone switching systems [16].

We need to add another dimension to Fig. 17.2 to indicate the *generality* of the language or the degree to which it can handle a comprehensive range of applications. This is done in Fig. 17.3. Given this way of looking at specification languages, it is clear that the computer industry needs to progress in the direction of the arrow in Fig. 17.4.

USE.IT is a completely general specification language that can be applied to any type of system. It is mathematically based, so it completely checks the internal consistency of specifications and generates provably bug-free code. It eliminates interface errors when separately developed modules are linked together, so the combined construct is internally consistent and bug-free. This enables increasingly large and powerful modules to be built and stored in its library. USE.IT is designed for DP professionals and makes a huge difference in achieving rigorous specifications for complex systems. Once one has seen

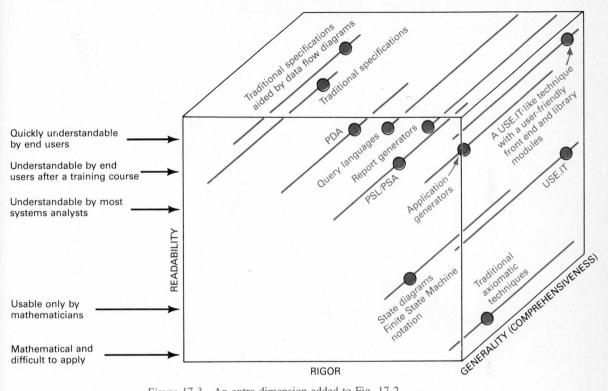

Figure 17.3 An extra dimension added to Fig. 17.2.

complex systems built with USE.IT, it is horrifying to contemplate the mess that exists in most manual specifications.

To build software without this computer-enforced rigor will one day seem like building a bridge without stressing calculations.

RIGOR COMBINED WITH USER FRIENDLINESS

USE.IT is not high on the vertical scale of Fig. 17.3. But it is clear that the mathematically based rigor like USE.IT can be built into user-friendly means of creating specifications. USE.IT could have a report generator, an encyclopedia, and a variety of user-friendly tools. Its basic method of decomposing functions into smaller modules until code can be generated could be made highly user-friendly. Figure 17.3 shows a point at the top right back corner where a user-friendly but rigorous specification language ought to be.

A major challenge to the computer industry today, then, is to create with graphics tools specification languages that are rigorous, powerful, and user-friendly and automatically generate program code.

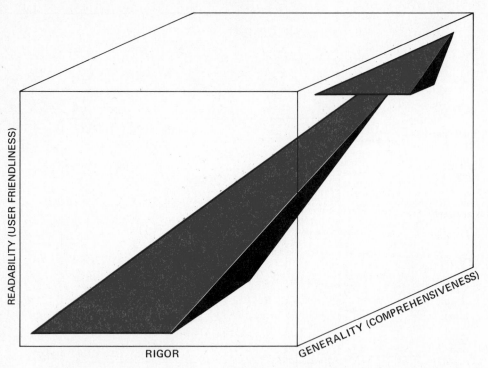

Figure 17.4   The computer industry needs to progress in the direction of the arrow. It is now clear that there are techniques that can take us to the head of this arrow. This portends a complete revolution in software and application building.

REFERENCES

1. D. Ross, "Structured Analysis (SA): A Language for Communicating Ideas," *IEEE Transactions on Software Engineering* SE-3(1), 16–34 (1977).

2. M. Alford, "A Requirements Engineering Methodology for Real-Time Processing Requirements," *IEEE Transactions on Software Engineering* SE-3(1), 1977.

3. Tom De Marco, *Structured Analysis and System Specification,* New York: Yourdon Press, 1979.

4. *HIPO: A Design Aid and Documentation Technique,* White Plains, NY: IBM.

5. D. Teichroew and E. A. Hershey III, "PSL/PSA: A Computer-Aided Tech-

nique for Structured Documentation and Analysis of Information Processing Systems," *IEEE Transactions on Software Engineering* SE-3(1), 1977.

6. *Architect's Manual: ICAM Definition Method (IDEF)* (Version 0, 1978; Version 1, 1978), Waltham, MA: Sof. Tech. Inc.

7. M. Hamilton and S. Zeldin, *Integrated Software Development System/ Higher Order Software Conceptual Description* (Research and Development Technical Report ECOM-76-0329F), Fort Monmouth, NJ: U.S. Army Electronics Command, 1976.

8. S. H. Caine and E. K. Gordon, "PDL: A Tool for Software Design," *AFIPS Conference Proceedings,* 44, 1975.

9. B. E. Casey and B. J. Taylor, *Writing Requirements in English: A Natural Alternative,* IEEE Workshop on Software Engineering Standards, San Francisco, August 1981.

10. R. Balzer et al., "Informality in Program Specifications," *IEEE Transactions on Software Engineering* SE-4(2), 1978.

11. Diagram adapted from one by Alan M. Davis in "The Design of a Family of Application-Oriented Requirements Languages," *Computer,* May 1982.

12. C. R. Everhart, "A Unified Approach to Software System Engineering," *Proceedings of Compsac 80,* IEEE Computer Society, Los Alamitos, CA, October 1980.

13. J. Martin, *Architectures for Distributed Processing* (Savant Technical Report No. 6), Carnforth, Lancs., England: Savant Institute, 1979, chap. 2.

14. CCITT, *SDL User Guidelines,* Study Group X1, Working Paper 3–1, 3–4.

15. A. M. Davies, "Automating the Requirements Phase: Benefits to Later Phases of the Software Life-Cycle," *Proceedings of Compsac 80,* IEEE Computer Society, Los Alamitos, CA, October 1980.

16. The COSS-RL language designed for the definition of central office switching systems at GTE Laboratories, Waltham, MA.

18 SEMANTIC DISINTEGRITY IN RELATIONAL OPERATIONS

INTRODUCTION   Part of the power of some 4GLs comes from their ability to do automatic navigation in a data base. With or without the user's realizing it, they employ relational algebra operations such as *joins* and *projects*. These are employed in query languages and report generators and are a part of some more comprehensive languages.

Unfortunately, it is possible to obtain invalid results with such operations unless certain controls are applied. Users can express a query that appears to be correct but in fact lacks semantic integrity. The users can obtain seemingly correct answers that are in fact wrong.

Consider IBM's language SQL (Structured Query Language), for example. Suppose that a user wanted to see a list of all suppliers who supply department 291. Two data-base records are available, as follows:

DEPARTMENT

DEPARTMENT#	PART

SUPPLIER

SUPPLIER#	SUPPLIER-NAME	PART

The user can enter a query:

```
SELECT SUPPLIER-NAME
    FROM SUPPLIER, DEPARTMENT
        WHERE SUPPLIER.PART = DEPARTMENT.PART
        AND DEPARTMENT# = 291
```

This says, "Select SUPPLIER-NAME from the combination of the SUPPLIER and DEPARTMENT tables where PART in the SUPPLIER table is identical to PART in the DEPARTMENT table and DEPARTMENT# is 291."

The same query could be handled with the screen language QBE (QUERY-BY-EXAMPLE):

DEPARTMENT	DEPARTMENT#	PART	
	291	_x	

SUPPLIER	SUPPLIER#	SUPPLIER-NAME	PART
		P.	_x

Here the user has equated PART in the SUPPLIER table with PART in the DEPARTMENT table by putting an x, with an underline, in both of them. He then indicates DEPARTMENT# by putting 291 in the DEPARTMENT# column and puts P. in the SUPPLIER-NAME column to request that this be printed.

A more automatic facility might make its own assumption about how to *join* the DEPARTMENT and SUPPLIER tables because they have only one data-item type in common. The user might then say something like this:

        LIST SUPPLIER-NAME DEPARTMENT# = 291

All of these are incorrect. Why?

They are examples of semantic disintegrity in query languages. Just because Parker Bros. supplies grappling irons and grappling irons are used by department 291, that does not mean that Parker Bros. supplies department 291. This department might use somebody else's grappling irons.

We can prevent semantic disintegrity, or at least warn the user about it, if we apply certain rules. Clearly these rules ought to be an integral part of 4GLs. However, the rules depend on a detailed knowledge of the functional dependencies among the data items that are employed. Without a thorough data model, semantic disintegrity in relational operations cannot be prevented automatically. Many such languages do not prevent it today, and their users occasionally blunder into wrong results.

RELATIONAL OPERATIONS

The above queries *join* two tables. JOIN is an example of a compound relational operation. Many query languages employ relational operations and sometimes employ a relational data base.

Semantic disintegrity can sometimes occur with the relational operations JOIN and PROJECT. The equivalent of these operations is sometimes employed by languages for nonrelational data bases also.

A relational operation manipulates two-dimensional tables of data. These tables are sometimes called *relations* and sometimes *files*. Let us use the word *relation*. Every record (also called *tuple*) in the relation contains the same set of data-item types.

PROJECT

With the PROJECT operator, the user selects certain columns of a relation and specifies in what order he wants them. Figure 18.1 shows two projections of the relation called ENGINEER.

On the right in Fig. 18.1, the user has created a result called DEPT. He wants two data-item types in the result, DEPT# and LOCATION. He writes:

$$DEPT = \pi \text{ ENGINEER (DEPT\#, LOCATION)}$$

The symbol π is used as the PROJECT operator. There is a smaller number of rows in the result that in the original because redundant rows are not required in the result.

On the left in Fig. 18.1, the user has created a projection called EMP with the statement

$$EMP = \pi \text{ ENGINEER (EMPLOYEE-NAME, EMPLOYEE\#, LOCATION, SALARY)}$$

JOIN

When two relations share a common data-item type, they might be joined. The projection operation splits relations, selecting certain columns. The join operation puts together columns from different relations.

The symbol used as the join operator is $*$. The statement EMPLOYEE = EMP $*$ DEPT does the opposite of the operation shown in Fig. 18.1 and forms the relation EMPLOYEE from the relations EMP and DEPT.

A user may wish to form from two or more separate relations a relation that does not use all the attributes of the source relations. For example, in joining EMP and DEPT, he may wish to create a relation that gives only the employees' names and locations. This can be done with the statement

$$EMPLOC = EMP * DEPT \text{ (EMPLOYEE-NAME, LOCATION)}$$

Figure 18.2 shows several join operations on two relations. The relations in this illustration have the domain B in common. Figure 18.3 shows a join on three relations.

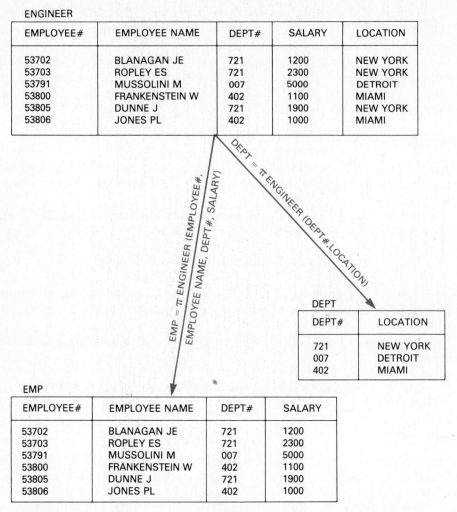

ENGINEER

EMPLOYEE#	EMPLOYEE NAME	DEPT#	SALARY	LOCATION
53702	BLANAGAN JE	721	1200	NEW YORK
53703	ROPLEY ES	721	2300	NEW YORK
53791	MUSSOLINI M	007	5000	DETROIT
53800	FRANKENSTEIN W	402	1100	MIAMI
53805	DUNNE J	721	1900	NEW YORK
53806	JONES PL	402	1000	MIAMI

DEPT

DEPT#	LOCATION
721	NEW YORK
007	DETROIT
402	MIAMI

EMP

EMPLOYEE#	EMPLOYEE NAME	DEPT#	SALARY
53702	BLANAGAN JE	721	1200
53703	ROPLEY ES	721	2300
53791	MUSSOLINI M	007	5000
53800	FRANKENSTEIN W	402	1100
53805	DUNNE J	721	1900
53806	JONES PL	402	1000

Figure 18.1   Illustration of two projections. The relation ENGINEER is split into two relations.

When relations are joined on a given data-item type, only tuples that share the same value of that data item appear in the result. Consequently, the resulting relation may contain fewer tuples than either of the original relations. This is seen in Fig. 18.2. The reduction effect may be used to isolate certain tuples in response to queries. A relation with only one domain, and possibly only one data item, may be joined to other relations to extract a restricted set of the tuples. In Fig. 18.2 for example, the relation R_3 contains only one data item, E, and only one value of that data item, T. When it is joined with R_2 it produces

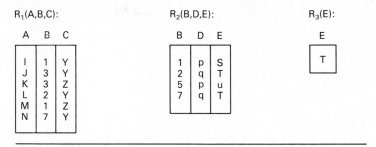

Joins on the above relations:

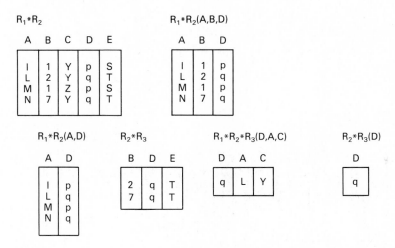

Figure 18.2   Examples of natural joins.

an answer to the query "What tuples in R_2 have a value of data item E equal to T?"

The join we have described, joining on the basis of equal data-item values in shared domains and not duplicating the shared domain in the result, is called a *natural join*. Other types of joins are possible, including ones that search a domain for values *not equal to, greater than,* or *less than* those in a given domain.

R_1 and R_2 in Fig. 18.2 could be joined because they had one data-item type in common, B. If they had no data-item type in common, they could not be joined. If they had two data-item types in common, they could be joined on one, on the other, or on both.

The example with which we started this chapter was a join. The DEPART-MENT and SUPPLIER tables are joined using the data-item type called PART.

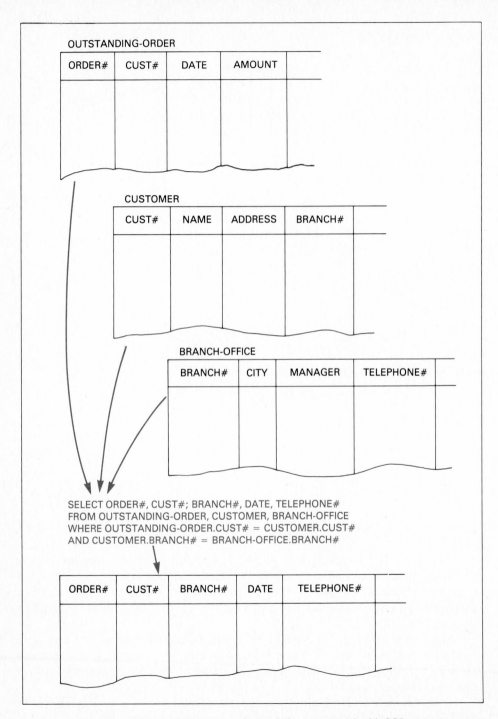

Figure 18.3 A join between three relations expressed with SQL.

This is expressed in SQL with the clause

WHERE SUPPLIER.PART = DEPARTMENT.PART

It was expressed in QBE by putting the same value (x) in the PART column of both the SUPPLIER and DEPARTMENT relations.

DATA MODELS

A major reason this SUPPLIER and DEPARTMENT join is invalid is that it uses incorrectly modeled data. A data model shows how the data items are associated. The association between two data items may be one to one, one to many, or many to many. To represent these, we draw a one-to-one association and a one-to-many association as follows:

One-to-one association:

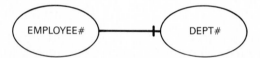

The line with the "1" bar means that one value of EMPLOYEE# has one and only one value of DEPT# associated with it.

One-to-many association:

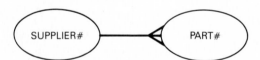

The crow's foot means that one value of SUPPLIER# has zero, one, or many values of PART# associated with it.

Many-to-many association:

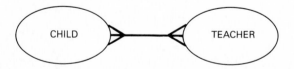

A many-to-many association is a combination of one-to-many associations in each direction.

The data item EMPLOYEE# might be associated with several data items, as follows:

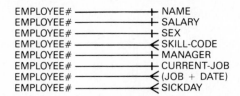

On the basis of such associations, data items are grouped into logical records, and these are grouped into logical data bases from which multiple views of data can be derived.

The overall logical representation of data and the associations among them are called a *data model*.

INVALID RELATIONAL OPERATIONS

Now let us see how relational operations can be invalid.

An Invalid Project

Consider the projection in Fig. 18.1 that creates the relation DEPT(DEPT#, LOCATION) from the ENGINEER relation. If the association between DEPT# and LOCATION is a one-to-one association, the projection is valid. We have the following associations:

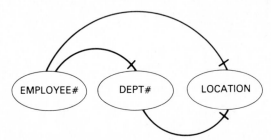

However, it may not be valid if the association between DEPT# and LOCATION is a one-to-many association (i.e., a department can have more than one location):

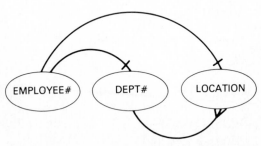

Department 721 in Fig. 18.1 might have an office in Detroit as well as New York for all we know, but the Detroit office may have no engineers.

An Invalid Join

A similar argument applies to *join* operations. Suppose that two relations were joined as follows:

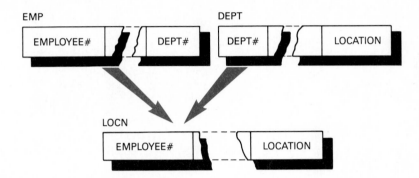

This join is valid if there is a one-to-one association between DEPT# and LO-CATION. It is not valid if there is a one-to-many association between DEPT# and LOCATION, because although a department can have more than one location, an employee works in only one location. Thus:

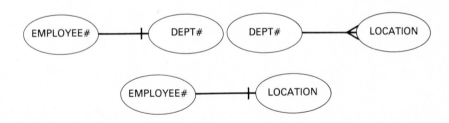

NAVIGATION PATHS

We can understand what a query or relational operation is doing by drawing a navigation path. To perform the join in question, we start with EM-PLOYEE# and find the associated DEPT#. For that DEPT# we find the associated LOCATION. We can draw this navigation path as follows:

Here we have only one-to-one paths, so there is no problem. If, however, there were a one-to-many path from DEPT# to LOCATION, we would draw:

This is invalid because there is *one* LOCATION, not many, for an employee.

Similarly, for the query "List all suppliers who supply department 291" we have this navigation path:

This lacks integrity because we cannot be sure which SUPPLIER# to associate with a given PART (or that any SUPPLIER# is associated with that PART for that DEPARTMENT#).

We have the possibility of semantic disintegrity if the navigation path has a one-to-many link that is not the first link; for example:

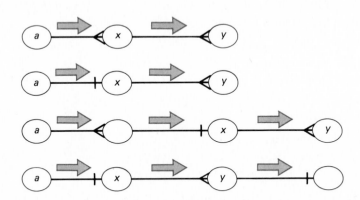

Many values of *y* are associated with *x,* but they might not all be associated with *a.*

We do not necessarily know whether such a navigation path *will* be valid or not. Figure 18.4 shows two queries employing a join. Their data and navigation paths are similar in structure. Both use fully normalized data. The one-to-many path makes the bottom one invalid, but not the top one. Because the software cannot tell for sure, it should warn the user that the results might be invalid.

A VALID JOIN:

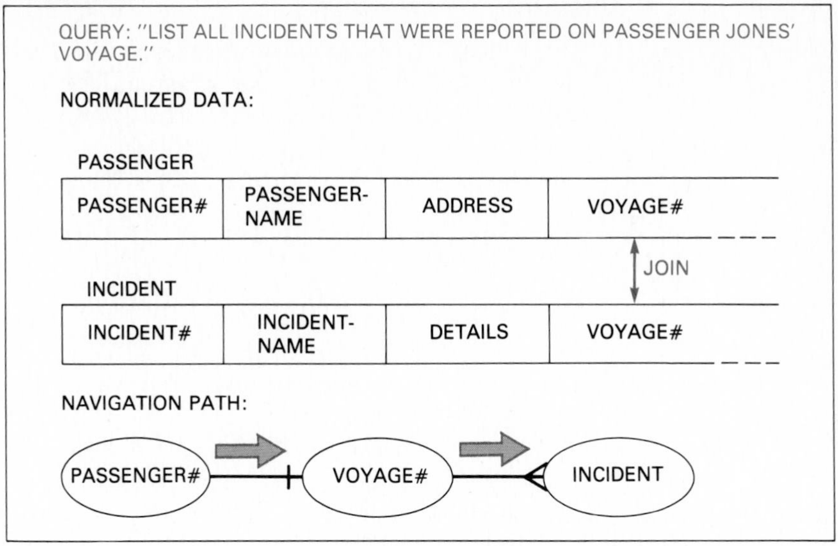

QUERY: "LIST ALL INCIDENTS THAT WERE REPORTED ON PASSENGER JONES' VOYAGE."

NORMALIZED DATA:

PASSENGER

PASSENGER#	PASSENGER-NAME	ADDRESS	VOYAGE#

| | | | ↕ JOIN |

INCIDENT

INCIDENT#	INCIDENT-NAME	DETAILS	VOYAGE#

NAVIGATION PATH:

PASSENGER# ⟶ VOYAGE# ⟶ INCIDENT

AN INVALID JOIN:

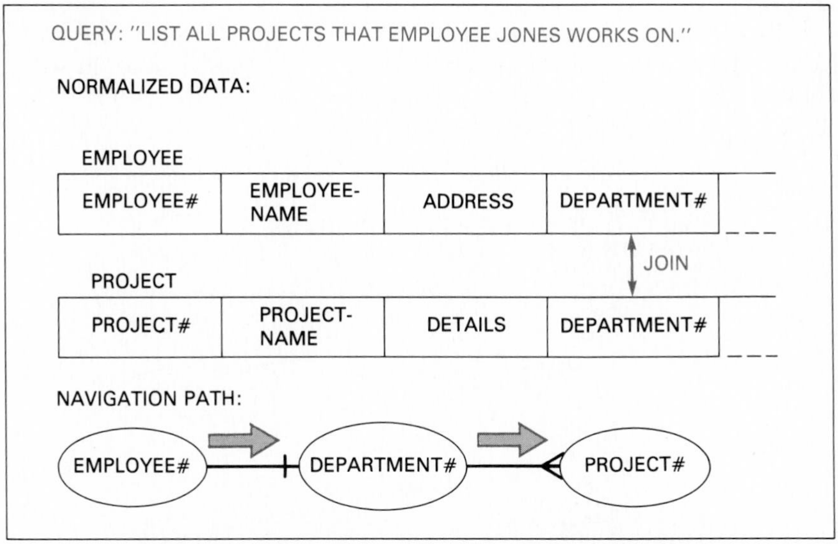

QUERY: "LIST ALL PROJECTS THAT EMPLOYEE JONES WORKS ON."

NORMALIZED DATA:

EMPLOYEE

EMPLOYEE#	EMPLOYEE-NAME	ADDRESS	DEPARTMENT#

| | | | ↕ JOIN |

PROJECT

PROJECT#	PROJECT-NAME	DETAILS	DEPARTMENT#

NAVIGATION PATH:

EMPLOYEE# ⟶ DEPARTMENT# ⟶ PROJECT#

The top join is valid because every incident on passenger JONES' voyage is needed.

The bottom join is *not* valid because employee JONES does not work on *every* project in his department.

The software does not know for certain whether the one-to-many link in the navigation path will cause trouble, so it should warn the user.

Figure 18.4   Using a join with two queries that have similar data structures.

INCORRECTLY MODELED DATA

We cannot control semantic disintegrity in data that are modeled incorrectly. For example, the records used in the DEPARTMENT-SUPPLIER example are imprecise and incorrect:

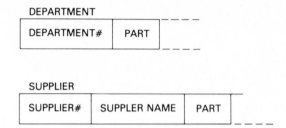

DEPARTMENT

DEPARTMENT#	PART

SUPPLIER

SUPPLIER#	SUPPLER NAME	PART

Each part needs to have a unique identifier PART#. A grappling iron supplied by Parker Bros. must have a different PART# from a grappling iron supplied by Jones, Inc. If we want to say merely "grappling iron," we use a data-item PART-TYPE.

A department has many part numbers, and a part number has many departments. We therefore use intersection data in the model with the key DEPARTMENT# + PART#. This key identifies such items as QUANTITY-SOLD. The model, then, includes the following:

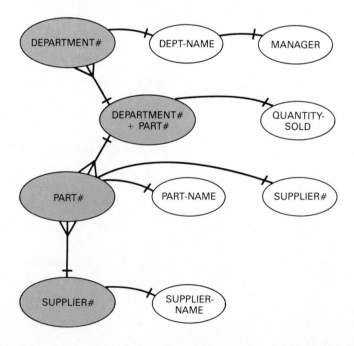

We draw these as relations as follows:

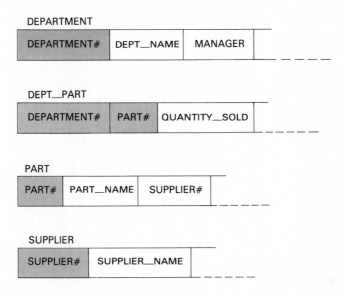

DEPARTMENT

DEPARTMENT#	DEPT_NAME	MANAGER

DEPT_PART

DEPARTMENT#	PART#	QUANTITY_SOLD

PART

PART#	PART_NAME	SUPPLIER#

SUPPLIER

SUPPLIER#	SUPPLIER_NAME

Now we can reformulate the query:

```
SELECT SUPPLIER-NAME
FROM SUPPLIER, PART, DEPT-PART
WHERE DEPT-PART.PART# = PART.PART#
AND PART.SUPPLIER# = SUPPLIER.SUPPLIER#
AND DEPARTMENT# = 291
```

The navigation path is

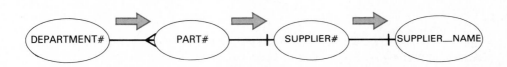

In this navigation path there is no ambiguous linking to a one-to-many path.

Suppose an accountant is concerned that accounts receivable are becoming too high. He wants to phone any branch office manager who has a six-month-old debt outstanding from a customer. The following record structures exist:

OUTSTANDING ORDER

ORDER#	CUST#	DATE	AMOUNT

CUSTOMER

CUST#	NAME	ADDRESS	BRANCH#

BRANCH OFFICE

BRANCH#	CITY	MANAGER	TELEPHONE#

The accountant enters the following query:

```
SELECT CITY, MANAGER, TELEPHONE#
FROM ORDER#, CUST#, BRANCH#
WHERE OUTSTANDING ORDER.CUST# = CUSTOMER.CUST#
AND CUSTOMER.BRANCH# = BRANCH-OFFICE.BRANCH#
AND DATE < 5.12
```

This, in effect, joins the three records. We have the following navigation path:

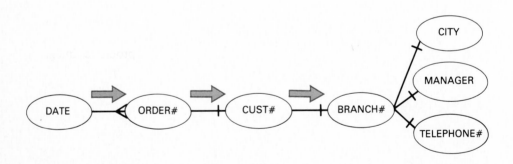

This is valid because we do not have any one-to-many links after the first. The correct normalization of the data protects us.

Suppose, however, that there was a mistake in the data modeling. A few customers are served by more than one branch office. We have

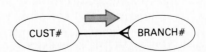

The query then has disintegrity. The accountant might phone the wrong branch manager.

PREVENTION OF SEMANTIC DISINTEGRITY

To ensure integrity in relational operations, it is essential that the data be completely and correctly modeled. The following rules will prevent semantic disintegrity:

A relation may be projected if

1. The relation is in third normal form [1, 2] *and*
2. The resulting relation contains the same key or an equivalent candidate key.

Relations A and B may be joined on data-item types A.x and B.y if

1. The relations A and B are in third normal form *and*
2. A.x is an attribute of A (including a key attribute) *and* B.y is a key or candidate key of B.

MORAL

The message of this chapter is simple and clear. Automatic data-base navigation is a powerful and valuable facility in 4GLs. Relational languages are here to stay and can be made very easy to use. However, if they are used without appropriate integrity checks, they can lead to false results.

It is desirable that 4GL dialogues or interpreters check for the possibility of semantic disintegrity and warn users when their operations might incur this problem. Rules such as the ones given should be used to detect potentially invalid operations. However, such rules work only if the data are correctly modeled (that is, if the records are in third normal form). We have commented before that the powerful 4GLs link into a dictionary or encyclopedia. This resource needs to contain a representation of the data model.

Usually a data administrator is responsible for the data dictionary and data model [1]. That responsibility may be expanded to central control of a system encyclopedia.

Unfortunately, at the time of writing, many of today's data-base products do not attempt to detect semantic disintegrity in join and project operations. This does not mean that the products are not valuable; they are. It does mean that care should be taken with data modeling, and users should be encouraged to check the results they obtain heuristically.

REFERENCES

1. Data associations, models, and third normal form are explained in J. Martin, *Managing the Data Base Environment,* Englewood Cliffs, NJ: Prentice-Hall, Inc., 1983.

2. Third normal form was originally described in E. F. Codd's classic paper ''Further Normalization of the Data Base Relational Model'' in *Data Base Systems* (Courant Computer Science Symposia 6), edited by R. Rustin, Englewood Cliffs, NJ: Prentice-Hall, Inc., 1972.

19 AN IDEAL DEVELOPMENT FACILITY FOR COMMERCIAL DP

INTRODUCTION   Many fourth-generation languages are now on the market. They employ a surprising diversity of techniques, syntaxes, and semantic structures. None of them is perfect. Each one, though shrouded in the spectacular praise of its promotional writers, has deficiencies. With some it is worth correcting the defects and improving the functionality because they are having a huge effect on DP productivity. Others are hardly worth the effort. Some will turn belly up and float slowly to the top of the tank.

Given the experience with this software so far, we can describe what would now appear to be an ideal development facility for today's state of the art *in commercial data processing*. This chapter lists some of its desirable properties.

USES OF DATA   The heart of the facility is a data-base management system, much more flexible than the data-base management systems of the 1970s, which are now regarded as traditional.

The user has an extremely user-friendly language with which he can create a data base. He can state the fields he wants in the records. The system will ask him to fill in details so that a logical data-base description is created.

The user can either create his own personal data-base structure, independently of other users, or can employ a data-base structure that is derived from the corporate data model and dictionary, which are maintained by the data administrator. He will be encouraged (or instructed) to employ the official data representations wherever possible.

The user can employ three categories of data base:

1. *A personal data base created independently of the corporate data bases.* The user may regard this as his own personal electronic filing system. Although this category is independent, the user will often employ data representations from the corporate dictionary. The system will make it easy for him to do this (on-line).

2. *A data base extracted from the corporate data bases.* This will contain data that have been updated by other systems. The user will employ them for his own information and possibly manipulate the data, doing calculations with them and developing answers to what-if questions. The data may be extracted periodically. The user will not be able to modify the corporate data bases from which the extract is taken.

3. *Shared corporate data bases.* The user has access to corporate data bases that are updated by other systems. This form of access is carefully controlled for reasons of security, accuracy of data, and machine performance. Security controls may prevent the user from making any change to the data. In some cases the user will enter data with accuracy and integrity controls that have the approval of the data administrator.

BASIC FACILITIES

Creation of a Data Base

The system will make it easy for the user to create or derive a data-base structure (schema). The data-base creation facility will employ certain tools. A data dictionary is essential. The dictionary should represent a corporate data model maintained by the data-base administrator. Tools are needed for analyzing user views of data and synthesizing these into a fully normalized data model. The system may enforce usage of the data model to ensure that all systems built employ compatible data. Subsets of the data model will be extracted by users for building specific systems. The data-model representation will help to speed up the system building.

Figure 19.1 illustrates the data-base creation facilities.

Creation of a Data-Entry Dialogue

The user can select the fields for which new values are to be entered. The system will request details of integrity checks that are to be applied to any data that are entered. These include range and data-type checks, checks for permissible values, and checks involving cross-references to other data. The system will then create a well-human-factored data-entry dialogue that other users may employ.

Creation of a Data-Update Dialogue

The user can select fields in the data base that may be updated. The system will request details of integrity checks, as for data entry, and will then create a well-human-factored data-update dialogue that other users may employ. This will use the same input panel design as the data-entry dialogue.

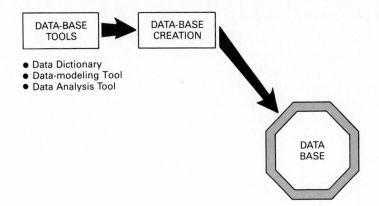

Figure 19.1   Tools for building a data base.

Detailed psychological studies have shown that good human factoring and screen layout have a strong effect on the error rate in data-entry and data-update dialogues. The ultimate cost of errors in data entry and updates is much higher than is usually realized. Most systems analysts and programmers are not acquainted with the research results that show how to minimize errors in data entry and updates. A well-designed generator of such dialogues is likely to provide better screen layouts and interaction than those designed by most analysts and programmers.

Figure 19.2 illustrates the data input and update tools.

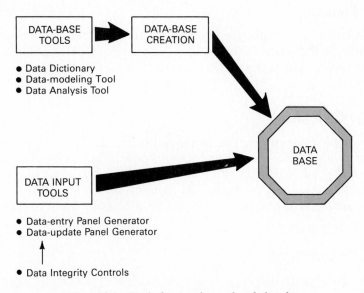

Figure 19.2   Tools for entering and updating data.

Query-and-Update Language

The system provides a very user-friendly means of quering the data base, either for simple queries that display a single record or for complex queries that cause data to be projected, joined, or searched, with various conditions applying. The query language incorporates data-update facilities. These make it possible to update many records with one command. Security and integrity controls regulate the use of such facilities. Complex queries and updates may be cataloged and referred to by name so that they do not have to be reentered every time they are used.

Report Generator

A means is provided for generating and formatting reports. A simple, powerful, screen-oriented facility should make it possible to build complex reports very quickly. The report generator is a natural extension of the query language. The report formats specified may be cataloged, referred to by name, and easily modified.

Graphics Generator

A means is provided for generating graphics charts of data and for manipulating these charts. The user can adjust the formats, color, shading, and labeling of the charts to create well-designed presentations. The chart formats can be cataloged, referred to by name, and easily modified.

Screen Painter

A simple means is provided for generating screens for person-machine interaction. The screen painter facility should be able to create highlighting, color blocks, reverse video, fields for user entry of data, fields to display variables, and so on.

Dialogue Generator

A means is provided to generate menu dialogues, command-and-response dialogues, and other types of user-machine dialogue. This facility may be an extension of the screen painter, or it may allow the quick building of specific dialogues such as menu dialogues. In some cases, the form of dialogues for using the applications are the same as the form of dialogues for building applications.

Arithmetic and Logic

The user can express arithmetic and mathematical operations to be performed on the data. Such operations often create new variables that the user can store in his data base and use in query, report, or graphics generation. Logic expressions can be used so that tests or conditions can be applied.

Rules Tools

It is desirable that rules that are likely to change not be tangled into program logic. A separate facility should make it easy to express complex rules in a nonprocedural way. This may be done with decision trees and tables or with language constructs for expressing rules. Such rules tools may automatically generate action diagram modules.

Production systems can be built quickly with the foregoing set of facilities (Fig. 19.3). Decision-support systems need different types of tools from production systems.

Procedural Code and Action Diagrams

All of these facilities, shown in Fig. 19.4, are nonprocedural and can be made extremely easy to use. To create more complex applications, procedural control

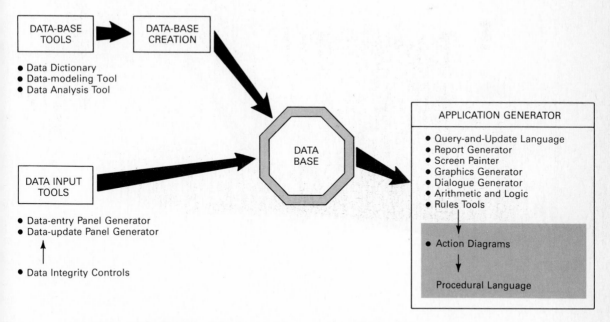

Figure 19.3   The procedural-language component can be made easy to use by means of an action diagram tool. Graphics editors can be used for expressing complex rules and procedural constructs. This can remove much of the difficulty of conventional programming.

structures with which loops, case structures, and nested routines can be built are needed. The procedural language should be, as far as possible, compatible in syntax with the nonprocedural language.

The control structures should enforce clean structuring and ensure that difficult-to-maintain spaghetti code cannot exist.

The control structures should be built with action diagram graphics and an action diagram editor. The control words of the language should be automatically attached to the action diagrams. Comprehensive checking should be used by the action diagram editor.

DECISION-SUPPORT SYSTEMS

A data-base structure that is efficient for heavy-duty production systems is often inefficient for decision-support systems, and vice versa. The user of a decision-support system takes actions that require fast searching, joining, and other compound relational operations. He needs to work with multidimensional data and to examine quickly slices through different dimensions. The indices and other mechanisms that facilitate these operations have to be updated when the data are changed or new data are added. They thus degrade the performance of production runs that change the data.

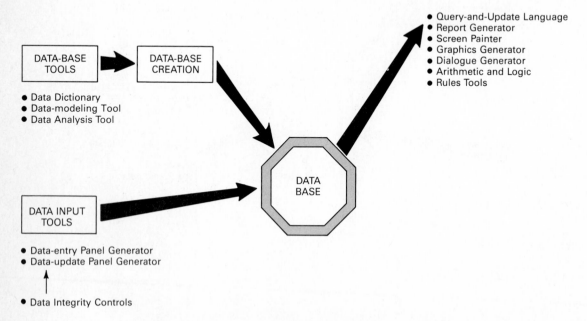

Figure 19.4 Everything on this diagram can be a nonprocedural language with a full-screen editor and can be made extremely user-friendly.

Efficient and elegant decision-support data-base structures exist, but they are usually separate from data-base structures for high-volume production computing.

Data-extraction aids are needed for extracting data from a production data base into a decision-support data base. The decision-support data base may be on the same mainframe or may be in a separate computer. Increasingly, it is likely to be on powerful personal computers (Fig. 19.5).

Figure 19.6 shows some of the facilities needed in a decision-support system.

Spreadsheet Manipulation

The system provides spreadsheet facilities (like LOTUS 1-2-3), which enable the user to create and manipulate tables of values. Spreadsheet applications may be created in which users are prompted to fill in certain values before calculations (sometimes complex computations) are performed. The user can express calculations and logic for calculating the values of items in the spreadsheet.

Multidimensional Analysis

Data of many dimensions can be analyzed. Any two-dimensional slice through multidimensional data can be displayed. Slices through multidimensional data can be manipulated as with the spreadsheet tools. Multidimensional analysis should thus be an extension of spreadsheet manipulation, such as with LOTUS spreadsheets, using the same syntax and techniques.

Presentation Graphics

Elegant graphics for management presentation can be created from the spreadsheets of multidimensional data. The graphics can be labeled, manipulated, and

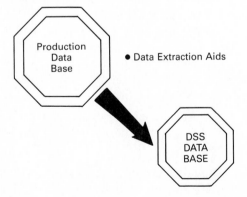

Figure 19.5   A decision-support data base often needs to be structured differently from a data base for production data processing.

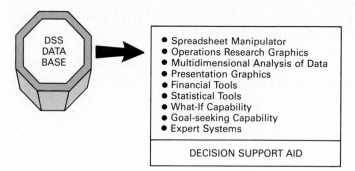

Figure 19.6 Decision-support tools employing a data base specially structured for decision support.

combined to reveal facts as clearly as possible. The user may be provided with
a rich set of capabilities to edit, label, annotate, and color such charts.

Operations Research Graphics

Most of the techniques of operations research can be made easy to understand
and use with appropriate computer-manipulated graphics. Different techniques
are useful in different types of decision making: regression analysis, multiple-
regression analysis, time-series analysis, Box-Jenkins analysis, linear programming, nonlinear programming, cause-effect models, querying, simulation, forecasting techniques, and so on. An appropriate set of such techniques may be
built.

Financial Tools

Sophisticated financial tools that facilitate financial calculations much more revealing than those of standard accounting practice are available. Such tools can
reveal the financial sensitivity of alternate courses of action. Persons without a
high level of financial sophistication may be guided by the software through the
most effective use of such computations.

Statistical Tools

A set of techniques for statistical analysis of data may be provided.

What-if Capability

Decision-support tools should enable their users to ask and explore what-if questions. What if sales are 20 percent lower than forecast? What if the prime rate

rises 2 points? For such purposes, separate data files may be kept showing changed values of variables. Different what-if scenarios may be kept as different dimensions of a multidimensional data base.

Goal-Seeking Techniques

The ability to explore alternate courses may be linked to goal-seeking techniques. A required outcome is stated, and the software computes the optimum way of achieving this outcome or enables alternate ways to be explored.

Expert Systems

Expert systems permit computer representation of rules that an expert uses when carrying out complex tasks. These rules are often nonquantitative. They may be associated with probabilities. The formal representation of such rules can enable an expert to do his job better and can give less trained persons a high level of expertise. Expert systems can guide naive users through complex decision making. A user can challenge the software to show how it arrives at certain conclusions by using the rules available to it.

Expert systems will become an increasingly important form of decision-support tools.

COMMONALITY OF DSS TOOLS AND APPLICATION-GENERATION TOOLS

Figures 19.3 and 19.6 make the tools for the generation of routine applications and the tools for decision support appear separate, and such is often the case. However, the decision-support user needs some, or all, of the tools in Fig. 19.3. He needs to query and update the DSS data base. He needs to generate reports. He may need to express complex rules, use action diagrams, and employ procedural code.

Figure 19.7 shows this integration. The box showing tools for decision-support aid links around to the tools required for conventional application development.

INTELLIGENT DATA BASE

Data bases of the past have been dumb data bases. They merely store the values of data that are entered. We can contrast a *dumb* data base with an *intelligent* data base (just as we can compare dumb and intelligent terminals). An intelligent data base may take certain types of action when specified types of data item are entered or updated:

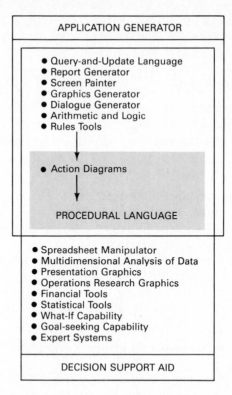

Figure 19.7   The decision-support aid needs some of the same tools required by the generator of routine applications.

Automatically Derived Data

The data base may contain data items that can be derived from other data items by employing an arithmetical or logical expression. When a data item in the input of the expression is entered or changed, the derived data item will be automatically created or changed accordingly.

Spreadsheet tools perform automatic derivation of data. When the user changes one cell, many other cells may change on the basis of formulas that relate to those cells. We might describe a spreadsheet file as an "intelligent" file. To apply a similar technique to large data bases would have a severe machine-performance implication. It is, however, desirable to apply it to certain decision-support bases.

Data-Base Triggers

Triggers can be expressed such that when a specified data value falls into a specified range, an action is taken. This action may be to notify a user, possibly with an "urgent" message-sending facility. The action may be the execution of a named procedure. The value to which a trigger applies will often be that of a *derived* data item.

Most data bases have been *passive* repositories of data. A data base with triggers is sometimes referred to as an *active* data base. Instead of always being given data, it sometimes *gives out* data.

Integrity Controls

The data base may check the values of data items that are entered to ensure that they are valid values.

Audit Controls

The data base may create audit records showing who read, created, updated, or deleted data items. It may create an audit trail data base that auditors can search and interrogate.

Figure 19.8 shows intelligent data base-facilities.

A dumb data base is *passive*. Operations against the data are specifically requested each time they occur by a user or by a program associated with a specific transaction. The dumb data base does not initiate any actions of its own. All logic is associated with the transactions and applications, and none with the data base itself.

An intelligent data base has logic associated with specific data that is invoked independently of the application or transaction that causes the change. An intelligent data base can thus be an *active* facility.

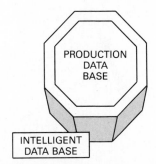

- Automatically Derived Data
- Data-base Triggers
- Integrity Controls
- Audit Controls

Figure 19.8   An intelligent data base takes certain actions dependent on the values of the data, which are independent of any one application.

OFFICE AUTOMATION TOOLS

Office automation tools may be linked into the other facilities. The facility may provide a word processing tool (which is needed for creating specifications and documentation), general electronic filing facilities, communications, and mailbox facilities.

A user should be able to send messages to other users. Each user has a "mailbox." The messages sent may be reports, charts, spreadsheets, or programs created with the generators, as well as other messages. Specified messages may be designated "urgent," and the system may take action to enforce these on the recipient's attention.

PACKAGES

A variety of application packages may be linked into the data bases and generators. Fourth-generation tools greatly increase the flexibility and usefulness of application packages. Figure 19.9 shows application packages and office automation tools.

INTEGRATION

The tools described are shown together in Fig. 19.10. These tools needed to be integrated. They should have a common syntax and style of operation so that a user who has learned one can easily extend his capability to learn others.

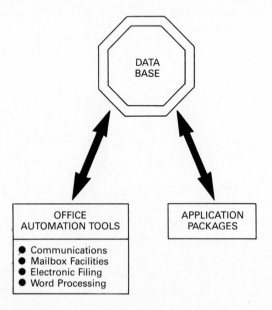

Figure 19.9 Office automation tools and packaged applications may be integrated with the fourth-generation language and information center tools.

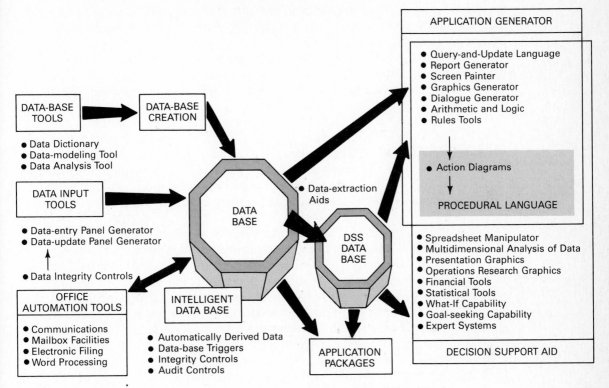

Figure 19.10 The various tools needed to be integrated and linked to data-base facilities.

USER FRIENDLINESS

Most of the facilities described so far use nonprocedural dialogues. Nonprocedural dialogues can be designed to be highly user-friendly. Procedural coding can be made easy to use by a good action diagram editor. The success of the development facility depends to a large extent on the ease of use of its dialogues.

The dialogues for the facility described would be two-dimensional; the computer creates displays, and the user reacts to them by moving different types of cursors around a screen, entering data or commands into it, and possibly pointing to it with a finger or a mouse. Two-dimensional dialogues give the capability to create much more user-friendly interfaces. Color can greatly help with such dialogues, though excellent monochrome dialogues can be created employing reverse video and flashing characters. For some applications, a large monochrome screen is better than a smaller, lower-resolution color one of the same price.

There should be the maximum use of default options, with the user having the capability to override the automatic default selections. The objective of default options is both to make applications easy to build and to minimize the amount of work required.

Report and graphics generation can be made easy by permitting the user to key in a brief, simple statement of what he wants without giving full details of how it should be formatted. The software makes its own decisions about formatting.

SUBSECOND RESPONSES

The dialogue for different functions should have a compatible syntax. It should take maximum advantage of the subsecond response times available with local area networks and/or the decisecond response time of the personal computer.

The user may have several workspaces available to him in such a way that he can switch almost instantly from one to another on the screen. A knowledge worker often has many different pieces of paper on his desk at one time. He switches his attention from one to another. A person doing complex work, such as a system designer or a textbook writer, may have a big desk with many different types of document. When a workstation replaces his desk activity, he needs to switch, at high speed, between computer images. He may need a split screen to have more than one image in front of him at one time. He may need to scroll rapidly over large virtual diagrams or spreadsheets or flick a window from one part of a large listing or image to another part.

SUBSETTING

A comprehensive development language can become complex, with a bewildering array of features and a thick manual. To make it easy for beginners, it should be designed for subsetting. Raw beginners may be exposed to only a data-base query language, a report generator, or a facility for doing arithmetic on data like an extension of a pocket calculator. When they become completely familiar with such a subset, they are exposed to a planned follow-on subset. When they are completely familiar with this, the next level is revealed to them, and so on.

Subsetting of this type is very important for wide acceptance of a language. There have been innumerable cases of languages being rejected by people who could benefit greatly from them because they appeared too complex at the start.

HUMAN USAGE AIDS

Even though the syntax of the system can be made very user-friendly, the users will often need help and training. The system should provide this to them on-line. They should be able to invoke a HELP function at any time. Using menus, the system asks them what type of help they require and provides it.

Computer-based instruction in how to use the system should be built into it. This should be user-friendly and self-contained. (Computer-based instruction varies substantially in quality). The user, after taking a short training course, should be able to expand his own knowledge of how to use the system.

When a user creates an application that is to be employed by other users, he should create on-line HELP and documentation for them. The system should have features that make this easy to do.

SPECIFICATION TOOLS

The application designer needs ways of sketching an application before he builds it (except when it is so simple that no sketch is needed). The generator should incorporate user-friendly graphics tools that are easy to learn, allow the sketches to be edited on the screen, and convert directly into code.

Simple queries or report generation need no sketch; procedures with loops or nested routines do. The form of sketching such procedures, which is the easiest for end users, is an *action diagram*. Action diagrams were designed to convert automatically into the code of fourth-generation languages and to be as user-friendly as possible.

GRAPHICS FOR DESIGN

Graphics tools provide a powerful and appealing way to build applications. They can enable a designer to visualize complex logic and flow. Complex systems can be decomposed into successively more detailed diagrams.

The types of diagrams used need to be rigorous and to be capable of representing the required set of structures. They should give the designer as much help as possible in automating the design work and in making it free of errors. Most of the diagramming techniques emerged in the 1980s [1].

The developer often needs to see diagrams of the data model that is used. Subsets of an overall data model are extracted for use on a particular project [2]. Diagrams superimposed on this data submodel can then indicate the sequence of usage of the data.

Diagrams representing data flow, dependencies, data navigation, decision trees, state transitions, and decomposition can all be converted *automatically* into action diagrams with program code, if they are drawn with suitable rigor [1]. The diagram editor should enforce this rigor, guiding the developer through the decisions that are needed.

Whatever form of diagramming is adapted, the development facility should provide a tool for sketching and editing diagrams on the screen and then converting them into code. The diagrams should relate to the constructs of high-productivity languages. The facility should link directly to the data administrator's tools.

Personal computers, especially those with screen resolutions of 600 by 400 pixels or more, are ideal tools for creating and editing the diagrams needed for system design.

Figure 19.11 shows Fig. 19.10 surrounded by a layer that represents the facilities needed for good human factoring and graphics design.

DATA BASE   The generator should employ a *relational* data-base management system that is dynamically changeable, such as IBM's DB2. The tool should permit the definition of *logical user views* that are derived from the larger data structure. The user can refer to and employ these logical views. The user can view the data in either a relational or hierarchical form.

To be fully useful, a data-base management system requires many properties, such as security controls, concurrency controls, access optimization, failure protection, checkpoint/restart, and auditing features [2]. The generator should have all of these. It is much more than just a set of language interpreters and compilers. It needs a complex infrastructure that provides the requisite system foundations.

The user can quickly create a data structure, or schema, that he wants to use, and with this, data-entry panels can be generated for the input of any specific data.

In existing products, a good example of a system for data-base creation and generation of data-entry facilities is FOCUS (using FILETALK), from Information Builders, Inc. An example of a data-base query-and-update language that is particularly well human-factored is IBM's QUERY-BY-EXAMPLE. A good example of an easy-to-use report generator is that in ADR's IDEAL language. An example of powerful business graphics is TELL-A-GRAF, from ISSCO. A good example of a product that leads the designer step by step through the design process is Cortex's APPLICATION FACTORY.

The system should provide on-line data administration aids. It should have a data dictionary and a means of representing the data model used, showing the associations among data items.

In most commercial application design, data analysis should be done before procedures are designed [2]. The facility should have a tool for this built into it.

SEMANTIC   The ability to perform relational joins and projects is
DISINTEGRITY   an essential aspect of relational data bases. When
users employ some relational languages, they may trigger join or project operations without knowing it. Unfortunately, these can

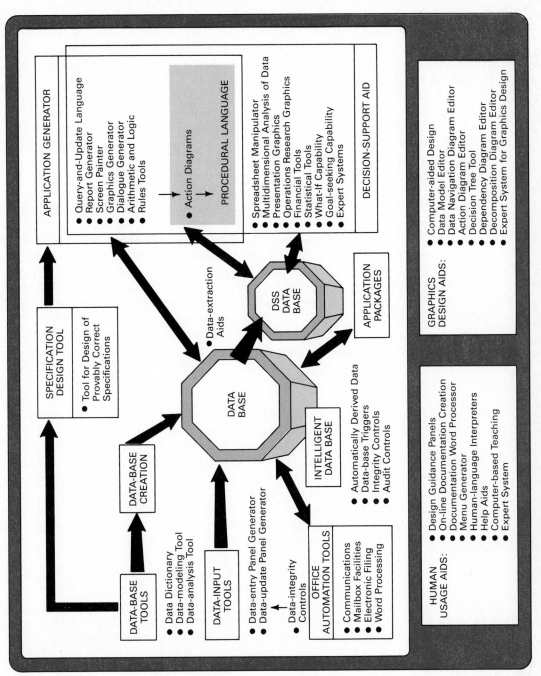

Figure 19.11 The ideal fourth-generation facility should contain these tools, fully integrated.

give invalid results under certain circumstances. Protection from the danger of *semantic disintegrity* should be automatic (see Chapter 18). This depends on the data relations' being correctly modeled. All functional dependencies must be correctly represented (this topic is covered elsewhere [2]). Semantic disintegrity warnings can then be generated. For this reason the development facility *should include a tool for data analysis.*

The user may encounter two situations: First, the data are fully modeled, in which case semantic disintegrity warnings can be issued for potentially incorrect usage of the data; second, the data are *not* fully modeled, in which case a general caution may be given to users who *join* and *project* data, much like the Surgeon General's warning on cigarette packages.

SYSTEM CONTROLS   A variety of other system controls is needed, many of which are more obvious than the semantic disintegrity trap. Mechanisms are needed to permit several users to employ the system at the same time. This requires concurrency controls to prevent invalid updating of the data. There must be means of recovering from failures and system crashes to ensure that data are not damaged or lost. When failures occur, operations must be backed out to a point at which they may be safely restarted. Appropriate restart points or checkpoints are needed. Security controls are needed. Tools are needed for the auditors to ensure that they can investigate system usage appropriately. Audit trails may be created automatically.

CODE GENERATION AND CHECKING   The development facility needs an interpreter to convert the syntax, which is designed for humans, into executable code. The interpreter produces code while the user is at the terminal so that it can then be executed and tested. As with a human interpreter of foreign languages, this interpretation allows immediate interaction between the user and the system.

The development facility should also have a compiler that produces optimized code. A compiler may operate in a batch fashion and may go through several stages to produce optimized code and allocate machine resources in an efficient fashion.

If the code will be run many times or will produce large throughputs, a compiler is needed to achieve machine efficiency. If the code is used for personal decision making, an interpreter is needed to achieve direct interaction between the decision maker and the computer, and optimized code is generally not needed. The same development facility should be usable for both decision-support computing and for production runs, so both an interpreter and compiler are needed.

Some interpreters and compilers generate a third-generation language such as COBOL, FORTRAN, or PASCAL. This, then, has to go through another interpreter or compiler to produce machine code. This is generally undesirable except to achieve portability. It is more efficient to produce machine code *directly*.

The intermediate code is sometimes thought to help developers who are familiar with COBOL, FORTRAN, or PASCAL. In practice, it does not help them. The COBOL is strange and hard to read and should *never* be modified by the developers because this introduces bugs and severe maintenance difficulties.

PORTABLE CODE   The only good argument for generating code in a third-generation language is to achieve portability: programs that can be run on different vendors' machines. Unfortunately, most third-generation languages are not completely portable to different types of machines. For example, DEC's FORTRAN does not run on IBM without modification.

One exception to this is ADA. ADA source code specifications should be exactly the same for all machines. Compiling to ADA should give truly portable code. This is highly desirable for some applications. It is desirable for a software company that wishes to sell its programs to customers with all types of computers. Sometimes the language C is generated to achieve portability in UNIX-based systems.

COMPREHENSIVE   There are many ways in which the user's input may
VALIDATION   be checked. All possible syntax and semantic checks should be made before the executable code is generated. When these checks detect inconsistencies, errors, or omissions, the system should give the developer a full and complete explanation that is easy to understand.

The techniques of HOS, with their language USE.IT, for making specifications and code generation provably consistent and internally correct, represent a breakthrough of major importance in software evolution. It is desirable to apply such a technique wherever possible and to link it to user-friendly tools.

The ability to prove specifications and code internally consistent represents a change from ad hoc methods to true engineering in software. It is particularly important for specifications with complex logic and for systems in which modules created by different developers must work together. In the latter case, the interface between modules must be verifiable.

PROVABLY   For systems with complex specifications, tools are
CORRECT   needed for designing the specifications. A diversity
SPECIFICATIONS   of graphics tools can help in specification design. When using good specification languages, with

graphics, a designer tends to make fewer errors than with manual specification techniques.

Most specifications for complex systems have been full of errors, omissions, and inconsistencies, as discussed in Chapter 17. HOS software enables specifications to be built from provably correct constructs so that a complex specification can be internally consistent and correct. The designer using HOS is forced to resolve ambiguities and design a specification without internal omissions.

It is desirable that the tools for creating provable specifications link into the other tools in Fig. 19.11. Bug-free code should be generated directly from bug-free specifications.

The specification design tool is included in Fig. 19.11, at the top right.

LIBRARY

A library of functions, data types, screen panels, subroutines, and previously developed applications is needed. Some development organizations need a ''software factory'' environment that permits applications to be created quickly from previously built modules.

As time goes by, higher-level library modules come into existence. It is desirable that the linkage to these be provably correct.

INFRASTRUCTURE

Fourth-generation languages, or application generators, require a substantial infrastructure to support them. The cost of creating the infrastructure is often greater than the cost of the language dialogues and their interpreters and compilers. A good development facility requires that this infrastructure be excellent and that the languages be as user-friendly as possible.

The infrastructure requires a good data-base management system that is as flexible as possible. It should provide numerous *logical user views* of the same data, differing at the field level. The data base needs to handle several users at the same time without integrity or deadlock problems. The accessing of data needs to be optimized to give good machine performance. The system needs security, recovery features, checkpointing, and protection from crashes. The auditors need facilities for investigating how the system was used.

MULTISYSTEM INFRASTRUCTURE

Often the system in question will need to access other systems—for example, to use data that reside in other systems. The interconnection of systems will become more common as data networks become more widespread and distributed systems and small computers continue to proliferate.

The left-hand side of Fig. 19.12 shows the infrastructure needed for mul-

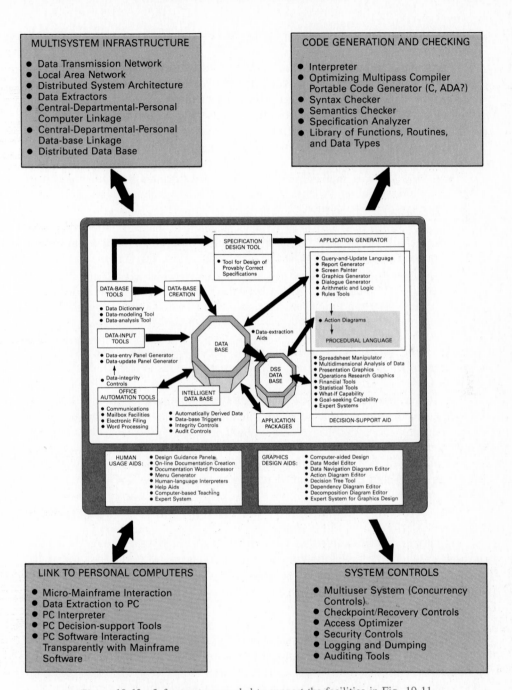

MULTISYSTEM INFRASTRUCTURE

- Data Transmission Network
- Local Area Network
- Distributed System Architecture
- Data Extractors
- Central-Departmental-Personal Computer Linkage
- Central-Departmental-Personal Data-base Linkage
- Distributed Data Base

CODE GENERATION AND CHECKING

- Interpreter
- Optimizing Multipass Compiler Portable Code Generator (C, ADA?)
- Syntax Checker
- Semantics Checker
- Specification Analyzer
- Library of Functions, Routines, and Data Types

SPECIFICATION DESIGN TOOL

- Tool for Design of Provably Correct Specifications

APPLICATION GENERATOR

- Query-and-Update Language
- Report Generator
- Screen Painter
- Graphics Generator
- Dialogue Generator
- Arithmetic and Logic
- Rules Tools

- Action Diagrams

PROCEDURAL LANGUAGE

DATA-BASE TOOLS

- Data Dictionary
- Data-modeling Tool
- Data-analysis Tool

DATA-BASE CREATION

DATA-INPUT TOOLS

- Data-entry Panel Generator
- Data-update Panel Generator

- Data-integrity Controls

DATA BASE

Data-extraction Aids

DSS DATA BASE

- Spreadsheet Manipulator
- Multidimensional Analysis of Data
- Presentation Graphics
- Operations Research Graphics
- Financial Tools
- Statistical Tools
- What-If Capability
- Goal-seeking Capability
- Expert Systems

DECISION-SUPPORT AID

OFFICE AUTOMATION TOOLS

- Communications
- Mailbox Facilities
- Electronic Filing
- Word Processing

INTELLIGENT DATA BASE

- Automatically Derived Data
- Data-base Triggers
- Integrity Controls
- Audit Controls

APPLICATION PACKAGES

HUMAN USAGE AIDS

- Design Guidance Panels
- On-line Documentation Creation
- Documentation Word Processor
- Menu Generator
- Human-language Interpreters
- Help Aids
- Computer-based Teaching
- Expert System

GRAPHICS DESIGN AIDS:

- Computer-aided Design
- Data Model Editor
- Data Navigation Diagram Editor
- Action Diagram Editor
- Decision Tree Tool
- Dependency Diagram Editor
- Decomposition Diagram Editor
- Expert System for Graphics Design

LINK TO PERSONAL COMPUTERS

- Micro-Mainframe Interaction
- Data Extraction to PC
- PC Interpreter
- PC Decision-support Tools
- PC Software Interacting Transparently with Mainframe Software

SYSTEM CONTROLS

- Multiuser System (Concurrency Controls)
- Checkpoint/Recovery Controls
- Access Optimizer
- Security Controls
- Logging and Dumping
- Auditing Tools

Figure 19.12   Infrastructure needed to support the facilities in Fig. 19.11.

373

tisystem linkage. The development facility may stand alone, or it may be linked to other systems.

Particularly important in some systems is a *data extractor* with which data can be extracted from other (often older) data-base systems for use in the new system. The data will be transmitted and restructured in the data base of the development facility. The extraction may be periodic, real-time, or ad hoc. Periodic extraction is appropriate for many information systems.

Three types of data storage facilities are needed in an organization:

- *Central facilities* on mainframes, with data bases that are shared by many parts of the organization. A large organization will have many such mainframe data bases in different locations.

- *Departmental facilities,* often on minicomputers or multiuser microcomputers. These will be designed for the filing, decision making, and processing that is unique to a particular department.

- *Personal facilities,* often on personal computers, which contain the files, data bases, and spreadsheets of one individual. The personal facilities will often extract data from the departmental or control facilities and occasionally may send data to the higher-level facilities (with appropriate controls).

All three types of computers, but especially personal computers, will sometimes need access to external data bases. Figure 19.13 illustrates these linkages.

As far as possible, the software that the user employs should make the user unaware of where the data reside. The software should handle the micro-mainframe link in a fully transparent fashion. Handling *fully* distributed data in a transparent fashion is, however, very complex to accomplish.

A variety of system controls is needed, and these controls are more complex in a distributed environment. The bottom right of Fig. 19.12 refers to the system controls.

The top right of Fig. 19.12 lists facilities for code generation and checking.

Figure 19.12 illustrates that much more than merely a language is needed as high-productivity development facilities pervade a corporation. All of the products available at the time of writing are less integrated than Fig. 19.12, and often stand-alone products are elegant and simple to use.

ENCYCLOPEDIA

The term *encyclopedia* is used to refer to a data base containing information about systems. It includes the information in a data model and data dictionary but also contains information about strategic planning of data, where data are used, what applications exist and who uses them, goals and critical success factors relating to information planning, information sources, library control, designs for screens, reports, dia-

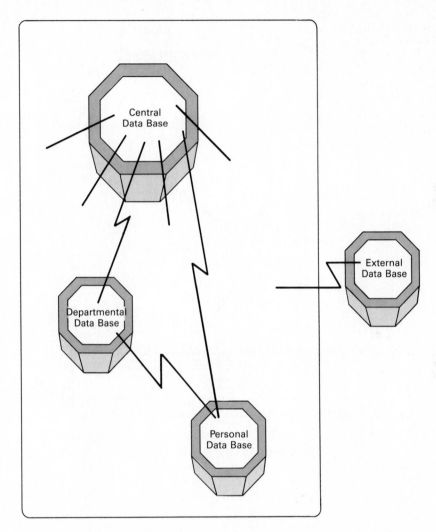

Figure 19.13 Central corporate data bases contain data that are shared by many systems. They are linked to departmental data bases, with which departmental applications are built. Personal computer data bases may contain extracts from either of these. Appropriate transparent linkages between these types of data bases are needed. Data may also be derived from external data bases.

logues, and system logic. The information represented by computerized diagrams is encoded in the encyclopedia, and the diagrams should be generatable from the encyclopedia. Some high-productivity design facilities of the future will link to such an encyclopedia (Fig. 19.14). The term *encyclopedia-driven development aids* is used.

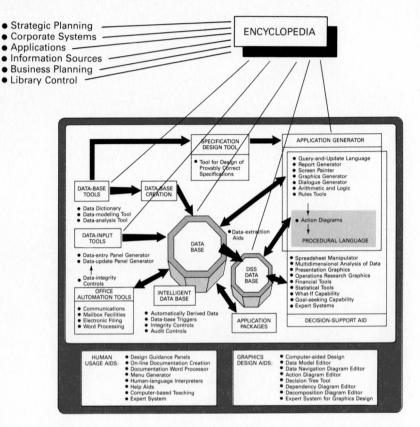

Figure 19.14   An encyclopedia is a data base for managing data processing resources. It contains strategic data planning information, details of existing applications, corporate systems, details of entities and relationships, and information to aid in the building of application. It is one of the *central database facilities* in Fig. 19.13. Subsets of the encyclopedia may be down-loaded to smaller machines.

The type of information in a corporate DP encyclopedia is likely to differ from one corporation to another. Different methods of strategic planning are in use, and there are different approaches to the balance between central control and individual application building.

THEORETICAL PRINCIPLES

Most 4GLs have been created so far by craftsman-programmers with no interest in the theory of languages, whereas most computer scientists who specialize in languages or proofs of program correctness have taken no interest in 4GLs. We need the fusion of sound theoretical principles, superb human factoring, and the pragmatism of 4GL writers determined to make it simpler to build computer applications.

REFERENCES

1. J. Martin and C. McClure, *Diagramming Techniques for Systems Analysts and Programmers,* Englewood Cliffs, NJ: Prentice-Hall, Inc., 1985.

2. J. Martin, *Managing the Data Base Environment,* Englewood Cliffs, NJ: Prentice-Hall, Inc., 1983.

20 SELECTION CRITERIA FOR 4GLs

There are several hundred 4GLs on the market. What criteria should a buyer use in choosing one? This chapter gives checklists to use in the selection process.

WHAT APPLICATION ENVIRONMENT? The first and most important set of questions should relate to what the purchaser wants to do with the language. Different 4GLs are designed for different application environments. Here is a list of questions about the application environment:

1. For End Users or DP Professionals?

Is it intended for use by end users, possibly in an information center environment, by DP professionals, or by both?

2. Prespecified or Ad Hoc Computing?

Is it for an environment with meticulous specifications or one where the tool will be used in an ad hoc, dynamically changeable fashion?

3. Batch Systems, On-Line Systems, or Exploratory Computing?

Is it for batch processing, routine terminal-based computing, or exploratory unpredictable computing?

4. Commercial or Scientific Work?

Is it for commercial data processing or for scientific, engineering, or complex-logic computing? Many 4GLs are designed only for commercial DP.

5. Decision-Support Computing?

Will it be used for decision-support computing? If so, what categories of decisions—simple spreadsheet or graphic operations or decisions needing sophisticated algorithms?

6. Heavy-Duty Computing?

Is it needed for heavy-duty computing or low transaction volumes?

7. What Class of Computer?

Is it intended for a personal computer, a minicomputer, a mainframe environment, or a combination of these?

8. What Size Data Base?

Is it intended for a very large data base (more than 10 billion bytes), medium-sized data base, or small data base (less than 10 million bytes)?

9. Existing Data Base or Files?

Will it be used to access an existing data base or files? What type (IMS, VSAM)? Will it access these existing data on-line, or will data be extracted for its use?

10. Complex Specification?

Will it be used for systems with extremely complex specifications (such as large military or aerospace systems)?

11. Prototype or Final Application?

Will it be used to build a prototype or the final application?

12. Access via Computer Network?

Will it be used via an existing computer network? What type? With distributed mainframes? With distributed data bases?

13. Linked to Application Packages?

Will it be used with application packages, to increase their flexibility or to add decision-support capability?

14. Linked to Office Automation?

Will it be linked to the functions of an office automation workstation, including text processing, electronic mail, electronic filing, and office management applications?

FUNCTION CATEGORIES

The broad classes of functions of 4GLs can be categorized as in Chapter 2. Figure 20.1 repeats Fig. 2.1. Any one 4GL may occupy more than one slot in Fig. 20.1. The purchaser can compare 4GLs by a tick or grading in the appropriate boxes. They are changing fast, and new features are being added to them continually.

The term *full-function 4GL* is used to denote a 4GL that can do anything a mature third-generation language can do. Many 4GLs are less than full-function languages. Some can generate reports, handle queries, perhaps update a data base, but cannot do everything that COBOL can do. Some languages that are very limited in their capabilities are sold as being the ultimate 4GL.

	Suitable for End Users	Suitable for Systems Analysts	Suitable for Professional Programmers
Simple-Query Languages			
Complex-Query-and-Update Languages			
Report Generators			
Graphics Languages			
Decision-Support Languages			
Application Generators			
Specification Languages			
Very High Level Programming Languages			
Parameterized Application Packages			
Application Languages			

Figure 20.1 Categorization for comparing fourth-generation languages. Many languages include facilities in more than one category.

Some 4GLs were designed for certain categories and perform these well, but they were then expanded to full functionality with inelegant constructs that are not easy to use or well thought out. The buyer should judge the architectural integrity of the language and the elegance of its syntax.

CAN THE LANGUAGE REPLACE COBOL COMPLETELY

One of the most important concise questions about a 4GL is, "If you adopt the 4GL, could you abandon all future use of COBOL or PL/I?" (except for maintaining old programs). In other words, can the 4GL do everything that COBOL can do?

There are two aspects to this question:

1. Does the language have sufficient functionality to replace COBOL?
2. Does the language give machine performance good enough to replace COBOL?

In answer to the first question, some 4GLs are not intended to replace COBOL, for example, query-and-report languages and decision-support languages. Some application generators work well with certain types of applications and not with other, so they would not replace COBOL for all applications.

Some 4GLs have the functionality to replace COBOL but give poor machine performance with heavy-duty computing. The installation that uses them still needs a machine-efficient language for a small fraction of its applications.

Some 4GLs can, and should, *completely* replace third-generation languages.

COBOL-TO-4GL RATIO

The purpose of buying a 4GL is to create programs with much less work than with a third-generation language. 4GLs vary widely in the degree to which they meet this objective. A buyer might try to establish a COBOL-to-4GL ratio for numbers of lines of code. A program needing 1000 lines of COBOL might be written in 50 lines with 4GL. The COBOL-to-4GL ratio would be 20.

It is nearly impossible to establish a single COBOL-to-4GL ratio for most 4GLs. They exhibit an impressive ratio for certain activities and do much less well with others. Vendors tend to select applications that demonstrate the highest COBOL-to-4GL ratio. A language might have a high ratio for report generation and a low one for complex logic.

The expression "lines of code" is meaningless for many nonprocedural operations, especially those where the user interacts rapidly with a workstation screen. Here the COBOL-to-4GL ratio might relate to the relative time taken to create an application. This makes objective measurement still more difficult because highly trained and skilled 4GL users work much faster than beginners and unskilled users. The industry average for COBOL programmers is about 20 lines of code per day (total project lines of code per total project programmer-days). But many programmers would protest that they code much faster than this.

DEFAULTS

The work of creating some applications is greatly reduced by intelligent use of defaults in 4GLs. The buyer should examine the power of the defaults in the 4GL. Some use defaults powerfully; others miss the opportunity to use defaults where they could. A vendor demonstrating a high COBOL-to-4GL ratio may have selected an application where the defaults work most effectively.

As stated earlier, application-oriented defaults can be powerful, save much work, and help analysts and users to create quality results quickly.

EVOLUTIONARY LEVEL OF SYNTAX

I commented that one can observe several waves of evolution in 4GL development that increase the power of their dialogue:

1. Off-line operation
2. One-dimensional dialogue that can be used with typewriter-like terminals
3. Two-dimensional dialogue that can be used with simple visual display terminals
4. Dialogue oriented to decisecond response times on personal computers, workstations, or local area networks
5. Dialogue employing graphics for design of the system and its logic
6. Tools using expert-system techniques

The buyer might judge into which of these waves the language fits. Some wave 2 and wave 3 fourth-generation languages are mature and powerful. Eventually the later waves ought to predominate over the earlier ones.

USER FRIENDLINESS

Almost every vendor claims that his 4GL is "designed for end users." However, 4GLs vary enormously in the quality of their human factoring. Many in practice are poor for end users. Some are appropriate for systems analysts. Some are more appropriate for professional programmers than for business analysts. It is clearly desirable to select products that are appropriate for end users or business analysts.

The buyer might ask the questions about user friendliness listed in Box 20.1.

BOX 20.1 Checklist of questions about human factors

- Is the language appropriate for end users, systems analysts, or programmers?
- How long is it likely to take a typical end user to start obtaining useful results with it, (one hour, half a day, two days, a week, two weeks)?
- Is it designed so that a user can install and learn it on his own?
- Does it give fully self-explanatory error messages that make it clear to the user what he must do differently?
- Is the syntax easy to learn?
- Is the syntax easy to remember?
- Does it force the user to remember mnemonics? (For well-human-factored dialogues, the correct response is *no*.)
- Does it force the user to remember formats or fixed sequences? (The answer to this is also no.)
- Does it use defaults extensively and well? Can the user easily override the defaults?
- Does it have simple, obvious-to-use sign-on procedures?
- Is it tolerant of typographical entry mistakes?
- Is it procedural, nonprocedural, or both?
- If procedural, does it enforce or encourage structured code?
- Is the language syntax good for maintenance? (With some languages it is easy to understand another person's code; with others it is difficult).
- Is it self-teaching, with computer-aided instruction or effective responses to HELP requests on all its functions? Can the user ask for HELP at any instant—for example, by pressing the ? key.
- Can it operate at different levels of verbosity in its dialogue?
- Can it store and catalog user procedures?
- Can the user switch instantly from one operation and work space to another?
- Does it have clear, good documentation, on-line as well as in a manual?
- How are the quality, richness, and appearance of the charts, screens, reports, and graphics it generates?
- Does it have a split-screen capability to review data, procedures, reports, error messages, and the like from different areas?

STRUCTURE

Was the language designed with a good understanding of structured techniques? This is very important in the building of complex systems. Some 4GLs encourage their users to create spaghetti code, which caused severe maintenance problems with third-genera-

BOX 20.2 Does the 4GL use good structured techniques?

An ideal 4GL should have all the features in this table. Three languages are evaluated with the checklist. (Note that the evaluation may become out-of-date as new features are added to these languages.)		IDEAL (from ADR)	NATURAL (from Software AG)	MANTIS (from Cincom)
Avoidance of GO TOs		√	√	
REFORM (named subroutine)		√	√	√
Single-execution brackets	DO	√	√	√
	IF	√	√	√
	IF-ELSE	√		√
	CASE	√		√
Repetition brackets	DO WHILE	√		√
	DO UNTIL	√	√	√
	FOR (relating to variables)	√		√
	FOR (relating to files or data bases)	√	√	√
ESCAPE (one bracket)		√	√	
ESCAPE (more than one bracket)		√		
Clear END statements for all brackets		√		√
LOOP-INITIALIZATION and LOOP-TERMINATION brackets			√	
Loop-controlled variables			√	

tion languages. Box 20.2 repeats a checklist for examining how well a language handles structured techniques.

In general, it is desirable to avoid GO TO instructions, and this is easy to do with the best-structured 4GLs.

SPECIFICATION AND DESIGN

Some 4GLs are merely programming languages. Others help in the design of systems. With some, the specification is partially or completely created with the 4GL itself. Languages that help in specification and design have a greater effect on the development life cycle than 4GLs that are merely programming languages.

TOOLS

The 4GL may have a set of tools that can each be judged in quality. The tools needed are:

- Data-base creation facility
- Data dictionary, data model, and/or encyclopedia
- Query language
- Report generator
- Graphics generator
- Procedural language (which may be aided by graphics)
- Screen pointer
- Dialogue creator
- Tools for expressing rules
- Tool for generating documentation
- Tools for system design and specification (which may be graphically oriented)
- Tool for guiding the designer
- Computer-based training

HANDS-ON COMPARISON

Although checklists such as those in the boxes of this chapter are useful, there are many subtleties in human factoring and in the diverse techniques of 4GLs in building applications. The buyer of 4GLs needs an expert (often home-grown) who compares the languages by putting them to use. He should select half a dozen applications with different characteristics and develop them with the software in question. This reveals all sorts of deficiencies and good characteristics, some of which often surprise the person making the comparison. The languages are very different. Something that one does well, another sometimes does surprisingly badly.

CHECKLISTS   Boxes 20.3 through 20.5 list properties to look for in query languages, report generators, and graphics facilities. Some 4GLs are packaged with, or coexist with, other user tools. This is valuable for the information center environment or the use of workstations in general by end users. Box 20.6 lists some of the other tools that may link to a 4GL. In some cases the 4GL itself is an adjunct to comprehensive application packages.

BOX 20.3 Checklist for selection of report generators

- Does the report generator make the maximum use of defaults?
- Can the default choices be easily overridden by the user?
- Can reports be printed on special stationery or preprinted forms?
- Can sensitive reports be password-protected for good security?
- Can a report be displayed on a screen and its contents reviewed before printing?
- Can the report generator produce:

  Subtotals?
  Control totals?
  Table handling?
  Accumulators (e.g., 12-month totals)?

- Does it have special formatting for complex reports (e.g., a financial planning option)?
- Can it produce reports from data items defined by assignment, arithmetic calculation, or conditional statements, just as if they were physically in the file?
- Can the selection of data test for:

  Equal, not equal?
  Greater than, greater than or equal, less than, less than or equal?
  Contains, omits?
  Includes, excludes?

- Can it produce several vertical and horizontal sorts?
- Can it sort in either ascending or descending sequences?
- Does it edit report items for:

  Zero suppression?
  Commas?
  Floating dollar sign?
  Parentheses for negative number?

(Continued)

BOX 20.3 *(Continued)*

- Does it print attractive, automatically formatted reports that include:

  Column titles?
  Column spacing?
  Row spacing?
  Good page breakdown?

- Does it use a data dictionary that will *automatically* supply column headings?

- Can the user supply:

  Column titles?
  Report headings?
  Footnotes?

- Can it provide substitution of variable data into headings and footnotes?

- Can it have control of footnote location?

- Can you specify column totals, row totals, multiple subtotals?

- Does it have summarization with:

  Percent?
  Minimum, maximum?
  First, last?
  Average standard deviation?

- Can the user control:

  Page breaks?
  Line spacing?
  Column spacing?
  Column repositioning?
  Report width?
  Pagination?
  Other report parameters with a simple menu-selection screen?

- Can report data be held for subsequent processing?

- Can report data be used to create a new file?

- Can report data be spun off for processing by other program products?

- Can a report include data items selected for a previous report?

- Can several reports be produced with one data-base pass?

- Can a user at a screen work with several reports at the same time?

- Can the report-generator syntax be used with an *extractor* for extracting data from existing data bases or files?

BOX 20.4 Checklist for selection of a query language

- Does the query language use screen interaction effectively for ease of use?
- Can a naive user learn to obtain useful results with it in one hour?
- Does it link to a good report formatter (see Box 20.3)?
- Does it link to an intelligent spreadsheet facility?
- Does it link to a powerful graphics generator?
- Can the search for data be based on:

  Any field (no need to prespecify fields to be used for selection)?
  A portion of a field (mask)?
  Character strings?
  Computed values?
  Phonetic equivalents?
  Inclusion or exclusion from a set of specified values?

- Can the selection of data be based on specified ranges?
- Is there the ability to specify a list of test values with one group name?
- Is there selection of text by scanning for a string or pattern of characters?
- Is there decoding via table lookup?
- Does the query language have the following:

  Complete arithmetic and logic functions (including IF-THEN-ELSE logic)?
  Conditional and unconditional branching?
  Editing of integer to/from alphanumeric?
  Concatenation of data strings?
  Decode/encode capability?
  Date conversion and computations?
  Table lookup conversions?
  Ability to reference a prior record?
  Capability to change sequence of computations based on values of data items?
  Mathematical functions:

    Log, square root?
    Absolute value?
    Integer part?
    Maximum, minimum?

- Is there an automatic count of number of occurrences of specified data items? Can the user check this count before initiating a scan of the files (to avoid excessively expensive searches)?
- Can the user adjust the query by viewing data on-line before printing or committing to expensive searches?
- What data bases or files can the software be used with?
- Can the software be used with distributed data?
- Can it be used with a good computer network architecture?

BOX 20.5 Checklist of questions about graphics

- What types of graphics are supported?

    Character graphics using a conventional character set?
    Alphamosaic graphics (like the videotex character set)?
    Vector graphics (i.e., composed of lines on the screen)?
    Alphageometric graphics (like the TELIDON viewdata system)?
    Raster graphics (composed of dots)?

- Can it show three-dimensional arrays graphically?

- Can it show N-dimensional arrays where $N > 3$, using colors, shapes, or other means?

- Does it use color? How many separate colors?

- Can the graphics generator be linked to:

    Query language?
    Report generator?
    Text processor?
    Intelligent spreadsheet facilities?
    Statistics aids?
    Financial support package?
    System design tools?
    Other forms of decision-support tools?
    Other forms of computer-aided design?

- Does the graphics generator use intelligent defaults?

- What quality of images does it create? Does it put labels on variables, possibly from a data dictionary?

- Does it select chart types itself when asked to display variables?

- Does it scale the chart itself?

- Can the user manipulate the chart:

    By positioning labels?
    By selecting colors?
    By selecting shading and crosshatching?
    By deleting or adding parts?
    By using large print with computer-generated type fonts?
    By changing scales?

- Can the user store charts in a library?

- Can the user transmit or print charts?

BOX 20.6   Does the 4GL link to other user tools?

Decision Support

- What decision-support tools are provided?

    Ability to do what-if calculations?
    Intelligent spreadsheets?
    Three-dimensional (or multidimensional) intelligent spreadsheets?
    Graphics charting and manipulation?
    Statistical tools?
    Forecasting and trend-analysis tools?
    Operations research tools?
    Cash-flow, rate-of-return analysis?
    General financial analysis?

Word Processing

- Does the system provide word processing capability?
- Does it provide the following word processing features?

    Delete word, texts, lines?
    Automatic carriage return?
    Underscore text, word, titles, lines?
    Highlight text, words, titles, lines?
    Indentation of text?
    Page-length control?
    Justification right or left?
    Automatic title and page numbering?
    Repaging?
    Search and replace?
    Variable line spacing?
    Centering of titles?
    Forms design?
    Creation of graphics?
    Single-sheet feed capability for printing one page at a time?
    Insertion of text?

Financial

- Does the system offer these financial tools?

    Financial modeling and analysis package?
    Handling of multiple currencies?
    Financial graphics?

(Continued)

BOX 20.6 *(Continued)*

Office Automation

- Does the 4GL provide the following office automation features?

    Electronic mail?
    Mailbox?
    Calendar management?
    Status updates?
    Budget planning?
    Resource scheduling?
    Monthly reporting?
    Job tracking?
    Electronic filing cabinet?
    Information retrieval tools?
    Integrated text and graphics?
    Integrated text and speech?
    Telephone management?

Particularly important is the data-base environment. Questions should be asked about what data-base management systems the 4GL can work with and whether it can be on-line. It may *extract* data from existing files or data bases. Questions should be asked about the extractor.

Sometimes the 4GL has its own data base. Questions should be asked about the quality and properties of the data base. Box 20.7 lists these.

Box 20.8 lists a collection of further questions about other aspects of 4GL selection.

BOX 20.7   Checklist of questions about the data base

- Does the 4GL use its own DBMS?
- Can it operate with other DBMSs or files that the user employs?
- Is it DBMS-independent?

    Assuming that the 4GL has its own data base, the following questions apply:

BOX 20.7 *(Continued)*

Flexibility

- Is the data base relational?
- Is it capable of automatic navigation? Can it perform joins, projects, and other relational operations?
- Is it efficient in executing a search?
- Is it efficient in executing a join?
- Can new secondary indices (or other search mechanisms) be added for any field?
- Can they be added dynamically (while other users are using the data base)?
- Can new fields be added to the existing data base dynamically (while other users are using the data base)?
- Does the DBMS allow alternative keys—the efficient retrieval of records by more than one identifier?
- Does alternative-key usage incur high overhead? Can the DBMS handle variable-length records and variable-length data items?
- Can the system handle text data?
- Can the system handle large records, used for voice or noncoded information?
- Is the 4GL independent of data structuring?
- Is there a maximum number of fields that can be defined in a file or a data base?
- What is the maximum number of files?
- Are the files of unlimited size in terms of number of records?
- Are there automatic procedures for creating and initializing a new data base?
- If multiple data bases are available, can they be concatenated for reporting?
- Does it have automatic maintenance of all data-base pointers? Or is a separate utility required to resolve or maintain network pointers?
- Can file space be reserved in advance or acquired as needed?
- Is there automatic reuse of deleted space?
- Can the data segments at each level of the file be stored, sorted, or be in unsorted sequence?

(Continued)

BOX 20.7 *(Continued)*

- Does it have concurrent access to the data base for users updating different logical files?

Requirements Relating to Other Software and Hardware

- Does the DBMS operate on the computers or minicomputers that are likely to be employed?
- Does the DBMS work with the latest releases of the chosen operating system(s)?
- Does the DBMS work with the chosen terminal's teleprocessing monitor or network architecture?
- Does the DBMS support the storage devices that are likely to be employed, including hierarchies of storage devices, large solid-state cache memories, and so on?

Efficiency

- Is it multithread (that is, can it process more than one transaction simultaneously), or are transactions processed serially?
- Are input and output operations overlapped?
- How much extra storage space is needed for pointers, secondary indices, directories, inverted files, and so on?
- What are the normal storage-load factors (user data stored per total storage space)?
- Does it use data compression and compaction?
- How much main memory is used in different circumstances?
- What is the region size? (Excessive region-size requirements degrade operating system performance.)
- What is the working-set size (average number of active pages used)? (Excessive working-set size increases paging overhead.)
- Does it support a back-end processor or hardware search, join, or indexing mechanisms?
- Does it support automatic data storage between different levels of storage media?
- Is it designed to use a large solid-state buffer or cache memory effectively?

BOX 20.7 *(Continued)*

- Does it precompile, optimize, and store access modules for use with high-level query or relational operations?
- If automatic navigation is used, how does it optimize this?
- Does access degrade over time due to data inserts, area splits, chain length growing, and so on?

Monitoring

- What facilities exist for monitoring the performance of the data base?
- What facilities exist for monitoring and reporting on the use of the data base?
- Can the DBMS handle variable-length records or variable-length data items?
- Can data be searched efficiently on any data item?
- Can the system handle text data?
- Can data be searched or accessed by alphabetic identifiers with phonetic synonyms (e.g., Smith - Smythe)?

Security and Privacy

- Does the DBMS have record-level, or data-item-level, security protection?
- Are the security controls powerful and unlikely to be bypassed?
- Can sensitive data be enciphered?
- Does the DBMS give a hierarchy of locks for different types of personnel?
- Are there good facilities for a security officer?
- Can audit trails be made automatically?
- Are the internal auditors satisfied with the system's auditing facilities?

Restart and Recovery

- Is there automatic protection of data when a transaction aborts?
- Is there a clear *point of commitment* in transaction processing and the ability to *back out fully and automatically* if an abort occurs prior to the commitment?

(Continued)

BOX 20.7 *(Continued)*

- Are there automatic system restarts after a crash or power failure with complete protection of data?
- What is the mean time to recovery following a crash?
- Are there means of recovery after a media failure or bad data written on the media, based on archives and activity logs?
- What is the mean time to recovery following a media failure? How automatic is the recovery?
- Can restart be performed at a task level, or does the entire system have to be restarted?
- What is the frequency of transaction aborts, system crashes, and media failures on a typical system? Do the recovery times provide high enough system availability?
- Can the system be on the air 24 hours per day?
- Are there good system controls to prevent operator errors from causing failures, particularly unrecoverable failures?
- Can the system give nonstop operation when a storage unit fails by duplicating critical data on a separate storage unit and providing automatic recovery after the failure?
- Are data-base restart and recovery procedures integrated with those of the teleprocessing system?

Integrity

- Can the system use automatic range checks and accuracy controls?
- Are there tight concurrency controls to prevent errors from occurring when more than one transaction is concurrently updating the same data?

Performance

- For specified transaction applications, how many transactions per second can the DBMS handle?
- How long do specified batch runs take?
- For specified applications, what are the mean and standard deviation response times?
- How do the performance figures vary as the data bases become large?
- Are there limits on the size of data bases that can be handled?

BOX 20.7 *(Continued)*

- How fast can searching operations be carried out?
- How badly does the addition of secondary indices or other search mechanisms degrade the performance of updating operations?
- How does the addition of many terminals affect performance?
- How do performance figures vary when complex data structures are used?

Portability

- Can application systems using the data base be moved:

  To another computer using the same architecture?
  To another computer using a different architecture?
  To a peripheral distributed computer?

- If the choice of DBMS would tend to lock the user into that DBMS or that vendor, is the lock-in acceptable? Is it likely to be fully supported in the future? Will it provide the growth that may be needed? Will the DBMS and vendor be at the leading edge of technology evolution, including evolution that migrates data-base features to hardware for greater efficiency?

BOX 20.8   Other 4GL selection criteria

Performance

- Is the language system designed to give good machine performance? (Some have compilers or interpreters designed for high machine efficiency; some give poor machine efficiency, but this may not matter if the transactions volume is low.)
- How does its performance compare with programs written in third-generation languages?
- Does it use an optimizing compiler?
- Does it use a high-speed interpreter?
- Are both optimizer and interpreter available?

(Continued)

BOX 20.8 *(Continued)*

- If applications created with the system show poor performance, can these be tuned or enhanced to give better performance?
- Are the tuning tools effective?
- Is the system designed for fast response times?
- Is it designed to search or join data at high speed?
- Does it automatically optimize data-base accesses, especially complex relational ones?

Chargeback

- Is there a built-in chargeback mechanism for charging users?
- Are the charges clear?
- Can a user enter different billing codes?
- Can a user obtain estimates of charges before executing an operation?
- Does the software give the user advanced warning when he might incur high charges?

Link to Third-Generation Programs

- Does the language have an escape feature (that is, can it call modules written with conventional programming)?
- Can the nonprocedural language be used in conventional programs (as can SQL and DATATRIEVE)?

Data Dictionary

- Does it employ a dictionary?

    Is it an active or a passive dictionary?
    Is it linked to a major DBMS dictionary?
    Can it use aliases?
    Does it store or generate column headings or report and chart labels?

- Does the data, dictionary have security features?
- Can the data dictionary be "customized" with user remarks or user terminology?
- Can data fields be referenced by field name or synonym?

BOX 20.8 *(Continued)*

- Does the data dictionary provide:

    Cross-reference usage tables?
    File description?

Library

- Can it store cataloged procedures? Can these be parameterized?
- Can it catalog routine reports?
- Can it catalog routine screen formats or dialogues?
- Can procedures and formats be easily stored, displayed, and modified?
- Can variable data be entered into procedures by:

    Prompting user?
    Specification at run time?
    Concatenation?
    System substitution?
    Calculation from other variables?
    Name or position?
    Branching?
    Logical comparison?
    Editing?

Integrity Controls

- Does it have good protection from system crashes?
- Does it automatically detect the possibility of semantic disintegrity—for example, in a relational join—and warn the user?
- If so, does it suggest to the user what alternative forms of query or statement would be appropriate?
- Are complex queries echoed back to the user, differently worded, for verification?
- Does it have extensive error-detection facilities and diagnostics?
- Can the explanation of how to respond to diagnostic message be obtained on-line?
- Can transactions be edited for:

    Proper format?
    Range check?

(Continued)

BOX 20.8 *(Continued)*

Complete match of all keys?
Table lookup?

- Can transactions be edited, validated, and matched to the data base without being applied to the data base?

Testing Aids

- Is it easy to debug? Does it have good testing tools?
- Does it give clear, self-explanatory error messages?
- Can the user specify how many records to process for report in order to control costs during testing?

Documentation

- Does it have good, clear documentation?
- Are there pocket reference cards?
- Does it have an easy-to-follow installer's guide?
- Are a sample data base and a complete range of procedures supplied with the system to permit verification of proper installation?

Security

- Can passwords be used to protect programs as well as data, reports, and the like?
- Are unauthorized attempts to enter the system immediately highlighted?
- Can you sound an alarm or buzzer on a terminal equipped with one?
- Does it have good security?
- Is security based on:
    Scrambled passwords?
    Data-base passwords?
    File passwords?
    Record passwords?
    Data-item access control?
    Command type?

BOX 20.8 *(Continued)*

Auditability

- Does it have good auditing features?

    Automation audit trails?
    Accuracy controls?
    Logs of usage?

- Does it have transaction logging for:

    All transactions?
    Specified transactions?
    All or specified types of rejected transactions?
    All valid transactions?

- Is audit-trail information provided after processing of each file of transactions?

System Characteristics

- Does it operate on personal computers?
- Can it operate on a personal computer linked to a mainframe data base?
- Are there any memory constraints? Will the system work in ½ megabyte or less?
- Can a user direct reports to terminal, printer, disk, tape, or cards?
- Are there automatic interfaces to external files and data bases?
- Can data be automatically extracted from an existing data base or file system and rebuilt for this system?
- Can data be moved from this system to a separate file or data-base system?
- Can numerous "views" of the data be defined?
- Can access to a data base or file be performed automatically by the system, or is it necessary to "program" the access or use an access method such as VSAM?
- Does the system require specialized telecommunications access methods, such as CICS or VTAM?
- Does the system cater to all types of data (hexadecimal, binary, packed decimal, zoned decimal, etc.)?

(Continued)

BOX 20.8 *(Continued)*

Training

- Is it self-teaching with computer-aided instruction or effective responses to HELP requests on all its functions?
- Does the vendor offer many different types of training?
- Are on-site courses available?
- What is the professional quality of the training materials and staff?
- Does the training consist of conveniently located and regularly scheduled training courses?
- Does the vendor have a "teach the teachers" course for client personnel?

Pricing

- Is the 4GL system available for a trial period?
- Does the vendor have different types of plans?
  Leasing ?
  Rental ?
  Purchase ?
- Are there any other costs, such as yearly maintenance fees?
- Is there a minimum rental period of one year for the product?
- Can the 4GL be used at multiple sites, at discount?

Vendor

- Does the organization selling the system give good service and support?
- Is there support for the product worldwide?
- Does the vendor have facilities to correct bugs or problems quickly and easily, such as toll-free telephone "hotline"?
- Does the vendor offer on-site software support? At what extra cost?
- How quickly can a software-support person be at the site to correct a problem?
- Is the vendor committed to future releases, enhancements, and evolution of the product?
- What is the frequency of new releases of the 4GL from the vendor?
- Does the 4GL have a user group? How active is it?
- Can you exchange experiences and new ideas in the user group?
- Are consulting services available? At what cost?
- Assuming a high death rate among 4GLs, is this one likely to be a long-term survivor?
- How many copies are already installed?

21 FUTURE EVOLUTION OF LANGUAGES

INTRODUCTION   Many articles have been written about the future of computer languages. Most have described languages that are extensions of traditional computer languages. The evolution of computer languages may, however, be completely different because of the following:

1. Application developers will use personal computers. In the future these machines will be much more powerful than they are today. A single user will have a machine the power of a 1970s mainframe dedicated to him alone. It will give decisecond responses to most inputs. It will have a megabyte or more of main memory. It may be linked by a local area network (or other network) to a parent mainframe.

2. Because of the power and decisecond response times of this development machine, most application development will employ fast two-way interaction on a screen. In response to user inputs, the machine can take actions that require much computation. Decisecond respond times completely change what are the most appropriate dialogue structures.

3. The use of color graphics will become very sophisticated (partly as a byproduct of the multibillion-dollar market for computer games).

4. The main language emphasis will be on specification languages rather than programming languages. Computable specifications will be built with computer-aided design techniques and automatically converted to program code.

5. The use of sophisticated graphics will be important for the design of specifications. System designers will use a variety of CAD graphics tools. Code will be generated directly from the graphics representations.

6. The documentation of system specification will be the graphics-oriented specifications from which code can be generated.

7. Great emphasis will be placed on human factoring so that user-seductive dialogues encourage users to build their own applications.

8. Nonprocedural techniques will be used wherever possible.

9. Application-creation software will be designed to employ the maximum use of defaults in order to minimize development effort. The application creator will be able to override the default. Intelligent software is needed for selecting the best defaults.

10. Techniques for creating software with provably correct internals will spread. This will be done by avoiding the ad hoc nonprovable constructs of earlier languages.

11. Software will be designed to catch as many of the application creator's errors as possible when he makes them—semantics errors as well as syntax errors. This fast feedback is a powerful teaching tool and is the way to break the law of conservation of human mistakes (Chapter 9).

12. Most applications will employ a data base with a data dictionary on-line to the development languages.

13. Data bases will become intelligent (as opposed to the dumb data bases of today). A major function of logic in the intelligent data base will be to aid the application developer, automate as many functions in the development as possible, and provide the maximum semantic and integrity checking. The developer will be on-line to an intelligent encyclopedia and a library of predefined screen panels, reports, dialogue structures, and preprogrammed routines.

14. Powerful development languages will use both an interpreter for fast prototyping and an optimizing compiler to give good machine performance.

15. Techniques will be used to link modules from development libraries in such a way that the interface is provably correct. This requires axiomatic definition of the data types that are passed across the interface.

16. New languages are forging ahead of the hardware needed for efficient execution. The hardware will be changed to fit the languages, with microcoded routines, front-end dialogue processes, and back-end relational data-base engines using parallelism for executing searches, joins, and projects. Microprocessors operating in parallel for speeding up operations will be used wherever possible. Certain forms of nonprocedural language yield naturally to the use of parallel processors; von Neumann–like languages do not. Machines based on parallel microprocessors can give much power at low cost.

17. Knowledge-based systems with inference-processing engines will become available, including personal computer versions. The Japanese specifications for a fifth generation of computers describes these. Knowledge-based systems require languages for expressing rules and inferences. LISP, LISP-based languages, and the language PROLOG are in use today.

18. Tools for designing expert systems will become sophisticated, and expert systems will aid the developer of more conventional applications. Expert systems will link into graphically oriented computer-aided design (CAD).

19. Knowledge-based systems will be employed for human speech processing and for the analysis of meaning in human language. Human language will be used interactively as one input to some future development systems.

COMPLEX SPECIFICATIONS

One of the biggest problems in computing today is the creation of specifications for complex systems. As we discussed in Chapter 17, manually created specifications are normally full of inconsistencies, ambiguities, and omissions, especially if they are complex enough to have required a team of analysts rather than one person.

We already have software that can be used by analysts to create specifications without internal inconsistencies, ambiguities, and omissions, because each step in the functional decomposition is based on mathematical axioms and ensures correct use of axiomatically defined data types. This software can automatically generate bug-free code to execute the specifications. The existence of such techniques is bound to change the whole future of computing. If you have any doubt about this, take a manually created set of complex specifications and redo them with USE.IT. This process reveals the sheer horror of the mess the manual specification process creates.

Future languages, then, need to be specification languages that create rigorous, computable specifications and generate machine code from them. There will be many forms of specification language, but underlying their operation should be the provable correctness USE.IT demonstrates.

Many forms of specification and human interaction with machines can be translated under the covers into rigorously checked representations from which code is generated.

Given the capability to analyze specifications to ensure that they obey axiomatic rules that ensure consistency and computability, what form should the specifications take? A large number of forms of specification are needed. Different people have different ways of looking at problems and different ways of thinking about and sketching solutions. Different professional disciplines have different languages and different diagramming techniques. The languages and tools of all disciplines need to form the input to computer specifications that can be automatically verified.

The process of creating programs in the past has had one automatic translation:

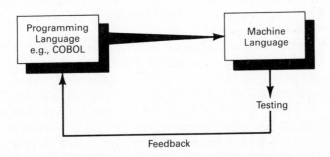

The process of the future may have two stages of automatic translation:

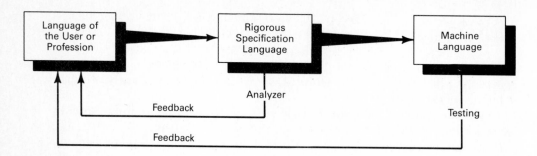

DIAGRAMS

To represent complex logic or specifications we usually draw diagrams. A variety of diagramming techniques have evolved, some good, others less so.

Some diagramming techniques are designed to be user-friendly and as easy to understand as possible. Some are designed to be rigorous. Some are designed to be directly convertible into code. These three objectives are not necessarily incompatible if the diagram is drawn on a screen and the user interacts with it. A user-friendly means of sketching system functions that can be steadily broken into more detail is required. The computer should guide the person creating the diagram and provide powerful screen drawing and editing aids. The diagram is decomposed until a level of detail is reached from which code can be generated. Computer languages in this way may become highly graphic. Formal diagramming may replace coding.

A logical data-base structure is usually diagrammed. An application designer may interact with the data-base diagrams, editing out user views and planning data navigation or automatic navigation. The diagrams of procedures, as they evolve, should be formally linked to the data-base structure.

Rigorous specification checking can be applied to the diagrams in such a way as to give the maximum help to the designer, flashing blocks, lines, or data types that do not pass the analyzer tests and displaying messages to give help in correcting the errors.

The systems analyst of the future will employ a variety of diagramming techniques. Different forms of diagrams will be appropriate to different ways of thinking about systems. Because the analyst will be using computer-aided design, his diagrams must be more formal and rigorous than the rather sloppy diagrams of the past, drawn with plastic templates. It is desirable that the graphics language used allow greater precision than in the past and that a common family of graphic symbols and icons apply to a diversity of diagramming tools. The diagrams should facilitate the automatic generation of executable code [1].

NATURAL INTERACTION

During their early decades, computers were unfriendly, esoteric machines hidden away from users. At first they were in engineering or mathematical laboratories, later in machine rooms guarded by a DP priesthood. This changed when users acquired their own personal computers and computer games became a billion-dollar industry.

At first a little of the mumbo jumbo of the priesthood found its way into personal computers. To leave an application and return to MS.DOS, you had to press CTRL, ALT, and DEL *simultaneously*. Typing in the mysterious character sequence for loading a new piece of software could result in bewildering problems. But steadily it became understood that the mass public needed to use computers directly and that that was a vast market. Computers had to adapt to the language of the masses because the masses would not learn JCL or ADA.

The operating systems of Apple's Lisa and Macintosh computers are a major advance over operating systems such as MS.DOS and UNIX, in terms of being easy to use. The user is not forced to remember strange strings of characters; does not have to press CTRL, ALT, and DEL simultaneously; and does not sit in front of the screen angered and frustrated by messages saying BAD COMMAND. Instead, he points at pictorial icons, can open clearly labeled folders by clicking a mouse cursor on them, and then can select their contents.

Further improvements are needed. It is desirable that computers be able to respond to human language. They need enough intelligence to be able to sort out the possible ambiguities. For example, it is difficult for a machine to know that when a notice on an escalator says DOGS MUST BE CARRIED, it does not mean that people are not allowed on the escalator unless they carry a dog. A robot using the escalator might, like the INTELLECT software, say:

```
YOUR INSTRUCTION IS AMBIGUOUS. DO YOU MEAN:
1. NO ADMITTANCE UNLESS I CARRY A DOG.
2. IF I HAVE A DOG I MUST CARRY IT.
PLEASE ENTER THE NUMBER OF THE INTERPRETATION YOU
DESIRE.
```

The robot would become an insufferable nuisance if it responded like that every time it confronted a human ambiguity. Some accommodation has to be reached.

The accommodation might be that the robot knows about escalators. It knows about the application areas that it is intended to work with. The software must have the ability to understand and manipulate knowledge. This is the idea behind the Japanese drive to build fifth-generation computers.

Technology is dropping in cost to a level where all people in society ought to employ computers. There are many social problems and opportunities that would benefit from this. However, present-day computers are too difficult to use for many of the socially valuable functions. The fifth generation must find solutions to this problem. Pictures, speech, and human language should be employed to provide natural interaction between the machine and its users. Means of representing and processing knowledge in computers is necessary so that the computer can appear intelligent and provide expertise far beyond the capability of the human brain for certain highly specialized areas.

KNOWLEDGE-BASE TECHNOLOGY

In the early 1980s the artificial intelligence community began to create some financially attractive applications. These employed ''knowledge-base'' technology. A data base contains data; a *knowledge base* contains both data and rules or assertions about those data. The rules are represented symbolically in a computer-processable form. The computer organizes and stores the rules or assertions and can process them to make inferences. Here are some examples of assertions:

COW is an ANIMAL.
COW produces MILK.

PATHOGENS associated with GASTROINTESTINAL TRACT are EN-TEROCOCCUS, CLOSTRIDIUM-GANGRENE, BACTEROIDES, KLE-BISELLA, PSEUDOMONAS, E. COLI, ENTEROBACTER. PROTEUS.

Complex rules are stored in a knowledge base, such as:

```
IF THE ACTION PRIOR TO THE PROBLEM WAS REAMING
AND THE TEMPERATURE WAS OVER 42° C
AND THE ROCK WAS INTERBEDDED
AND THE DRILL SPEED WAS BELOW 180 RPM
AND THERE WAS NO FLUID IN THE UPCUTTINGS
AND THE BIT WAS TYPE 478 OR 479
THEN THERE IS SUGGESTIVE EVIDENCE (0.4 PROBABILITY) THAT
    THE BHK NEEDS LUBRICATION
```

A knowledge-base system stores such assertions and rules and can combine them to deduce other assertions. For example:

```
FOR ORGANISM 1: (The MORPHOLOGY of the ORGANISM is
COCCUS) is FALSE.
```

The deductions are the result of syllogistic inferences carried out on the assertions. A syllogistic inference is one that is supported by two assertions. One assertion contains a term that is the *subject* of the conclusion; the other assertion contains a term that is the *predicate* of the conclusion. Both assertions contain a term that is excluded from the conclusion. A typical form might contain the two assertions ''All A is B'' and ''All B is C'' and produce the conclusion ''All A is C.''

Just as a data-base system can contain a vast amount of data, so a knowledge-base system can contain far more facts and rules than a human expert, such as a doctor, could possibly store in his head. It can process inferences that employ these facts and rules extremely rapidly.

Perhaps the most common mass-produced use of knowledge-base technology will be the interpretation of human language. The INTELLECT software employs this technique. It uses a knowledge base containing human vocabulary and grammatical rules. The rules are more numerous than might be imagined because there are so many ambiguities in the way we use our vocabulary and grammar.

EXPERT SYSTEMS　　Some types of knowledge-base systems are referred to as *expert systems*. They codify the knowledge of a specific domain of expertise. This computerized expert may then be used by another expert in the field to supplement his own knowledge, or it may be used by persons not expert in that area to provide them with expertise. An example of the former would be a doctor. He is himself an expert, but medicine is so complex that he needs the help of a ''specialist'' to supplement his knowledge in given areas.

One of the most famous medical expert systems is MYCIN, a system for diagnosing a certain class of infectious diseases [2]. The diagnostic success rate achieved by this system is better than that of almost all doctors except those who specialize in this branch of therapy. A general practitioner needs knowledge of many hundreds of branches of medicine like this and cannot possibly be an expert in more than a few. The doctor of the future may carry a case with a screen in the lid for access to medical expert systems.

When using an expert system, the human expert can ask the computer questions about its deductions:

Doctor:　Did you use rule 163 to find out anything about organism 1?

Computer:　RULE 163 WAS TRIED IN THE CONTEXT OF ORGANISM 1, BUT IT FAILED BECAUSE IT IS NOT TRUE THAT THE PATIENT HAS HAD A GENITOURINARY TRACT MANIPULATIVE PROCEDURE (CLAUSE 3).

A target of the Japanese fifth-generation project is to produce a knowledge-base machine by 1990 that can access up to a 100 million data items (each of which might require 1000 bytes of storage) and a vast number of rules. Initially the knowledge-base machine will employ a separate inference machine for processing the assertions. Later the inference machine will be fused with the knowledge-base machine. The inference machine will be able to process 100 million to 1 billion logical inferences per second. To a large extent the inferences can be processed in parallel. A highly parallel architecture capitalizing on the costs of future microcomputers will therefore be used. The control mechanisms and software for this are highly innovative and complex.

In addition to large fifth-generation mainframes, *personal computers* will be produced employing knowledge bases and inference-processing computers. These will be produced sooner, and much valuable feedback is expected from their many potential users. There will be a mass market for expert systems on personal computers.

EXPERT SYSTEMS FOR SYSTEMS EXPERTS

Someone who particularly needs help from expert systems is the person who builds computer applications and systems. The job of the systems analyst is becoming more complex. We want him to build more interesting systems and to do so much faster by using automated tools—the automation of automation. Systems engineers have to work with more elaborate configurations—distributed computing, distributed data, complex networks, configurations with very small and very large computers, the need for high reliability and availability. In the future a much richer family of software modules and tools in a library will be available. The analyst will need guidance in what is available and how to use it.

The physical design of data-base systems, so that they give good machine performance, is complex. Many designers do a poor job of optimization. There are few designers who are able to do an excellent job of designing an IMS system. This task can, however, be reduced to algorithms and rules—far fewer rules than those in a medical diagnosis system. There ought to be rule-based software for tasks such as data-base optimization and network design and optimization. Expert systems should give guidance in the use of complex software.

Particularly important, knowledge-base inference processing can be used to improve greatly the user friendliness of computers. It can be used in several ways:

- Human-language processing so that users can communicate with the machine in English (or Japanese)
- Assistance in operating the machine
- Assistance in operating complex software
- Assistance in locating data, knowledge, and software (which may be in the machine's library or elsewhere accessible by networks)
- Diagnosis of faults, problems, and operator mistakes
- Assistance in creating specifications from which programs can be generated automatically
- Assistance in creating graphics designs from which programs are generated.

It is repeatedly stressed in the goals and budgeting of research for the fifth generation that the human interface must make the systems easy to use *by the mass public,* not just by trained professionals.

COMPUTER-AIDED THINKING

Much guidance is needed in the specification of systems. Today there is usually an urge to start programming before the specifications are clear. It is desirable that specifications be precise enough to generate the programs automatically.

To create precise specifications for complex systems, the designer needs much help. Software can provide him with techniques that clarify his thinking. It can lead him, a step at a time, through design processes. Computerized graphics can provide a framework for clear thinking.

Interactive graphics and expert-system technology are a powerful combination. Together they can provide computerized help in conceptualizing and designing complex systems. Computer-aided thinking can take many forms. It starts, as indicated in Fig. 6.9, with sketches that are not yet computable. The designer successively refines the initial ideas with prompting and guidance from the software until segments of the design are precise enough for code generation. The segments of code generated are inspected and refined, and the designer builds other segments until a complete design is achieved.

The code initially generated is intended for aid in prototyping and testing. When this is satisfactory, refinement of the code and system design may take place to achieve good performance, now under the guidance of a different expert system, which applies rules oriented to system optimization.

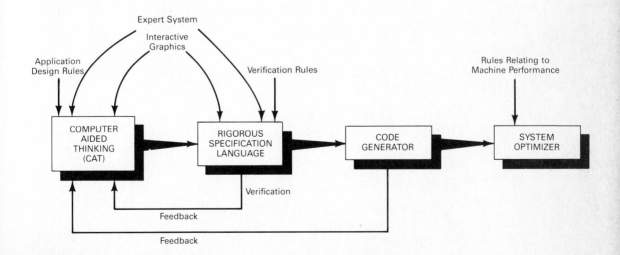

The combination of powerful, interactive design graphics with human language processing and expert-system technology should make possible the building of highly elaborate computer applications without the need to know a command language or any alien syntax.

SOFTWARE CHIPS A major factor affecting productivity of system building is the extent to which previously coded modules can be employed. In the future large libraries of standard modules will be used which can be linked into applications. The precoded modules are likely to become highly elaborate where useful. One research project uses the name *software chips* for these. Just as a hardware designer has a family of chips to use, the software designer has available precoded routines.

Mathematical definitions of data types and interfaces may be used to ensure that modules taken from a library link without errors into a partially built system.

The precoded routines may be designed so that they can be modified quickly. They may themselves be created with 4GL techniques or rule-based techniques which facilitate modification.

The building blocks of application design are likely to become fundamentally different from those associated with conventional programming. The constructs used may be selected so that proofs of correctness are applicable to the systems that combine them. Front-end verification will, to a large extent, replace back-end debugging.

RULE-BASED DESIGN Software design based on rules, as with expert systems, has major advantages for maintenance. To change the behavior of a conventional system one has to reprogram part of it, which is difficult and time-consuming. To change the behavior of a rule-based system one merely has to change the rules. The behavior of a rule-based program could thus be changed many times a day if necessary.

Rule-based application building permits very complex applications to be created fairly quickly and permits their behavior to be modified with relative ease.

This is applicable to relatively mundane data processing. For example, a rule might be:

```
IF ACCOUNT being posted is in SALES LEDGER
AND FLAG is marked ACTIVE
AND STATUS is not C or D
```

AND BALANCE is in debit
AND BALANCE has been negative for 18 days
AND BALANCE < 350
THEN set FLAG to CREDIT_STOPPED.

REASONABLENESS IN SOFTWARE

As systems become more intelligent, they will acquire more capability to make reasonable assumptions about what their users want. This "reasonableness" is needed in future language interpreters and dialogues. We need to build a type of computer "common sense." Computer common sense will be very different from human common sense, just as a horse's common sense is different.

The computer may make spectacular computational leaps when a situation appears to warrant them. Just as the manservant Jeeves impressed his employer in the P. G. Wodehouse novels by anticipating his needs, so the computer may anticipate its users' needs. It might understand a corporation's needs when an employee is using it. It may ask for information the user had not thought to enter. If the user is making decisions, it might, of its own accord, produce impressive graphics that help. It might perform its own what-if computations and show the user graphically.

The default options that are appearing in today's report generators and application generators are a simplistic form of computer common sense. You do not have to tell the software how to format a report; it produces a *reasonable* format. It should do its own optimization of files, accesses, distributed data use, and so on. It might automatically ensure security protection. More application-oriented, it might do its own analysis of a balance sheet or investment results. It might anticipate and try to prevent stock outages, electricity grid overloads, or failures of vital parts.

It is common sense for a car driver not to overtake on a blind corner—just in case. It should be computer common sense to back up files—just in case. It is human common sense to buy a jacket and trousers that match. Computer common sense may involve ensuring that there are no inconsistencies or ambiguities in complex specifications, enforcing axiomatic rules in the use of data types, or saying to a doctor: STREPTOCOCCUS IS NOT CONSIDERED A POSSIBILITY FOR ORGANISM 1. RULE 033 COULD BE USED TO DETERMINE THAT THE IDENTITY OF ORGANISM 1 IS STREPTOCOCCUS BUT CLAUSE 2 (THE MORPHOLOGY OF THE ORGANISM IS COCCUS) IS ALREADY KNOWN TO BE FALSE FOR ORGANISM 1.

The future evolution of computer languages, then, should take us into far more rich and complex language usage than in the first three generations. Default options should evolve into computer common sense, and computer common sense will sometimes involve algorithms with much computation and knowledge-base use, far beyond the ability of a slow muddle-headed human. The machine ability to be rigorous and to verify complex specifications should be used to the fullest.

REFERENCES

1. For a full discussion, see J. Martin and C. McClure, *Diagramming Techniques for Analysts and Programmers,* Englewood Cliffs, NJ: Prentice-Hall, Inc., 1985.

2. E. H. Shortliffe, *Computer-based Medical Consultations: MYCIN,* New York: American Elsevier, 1976.

INDEX